The RoutledgeFalmer R
in Multicultural Educati

This invaluable publication brings together some of the best scholarship from both sides of the Atlantic, focusing on central questions that shape the field of Multicultural Education. It offers the reader an insight into key debates and makes important topics, concepts and theories accessible to a broad audience.

The collection is divided into four parts, covering the ideas that are at the core of contemporary Multicultural Education:

- Part I, *Theories*: covers important conceptual territory and discusses key ideas including 'race', multiculturalism, anti-racism and critical race theory.
- Part II, *Identities*: draws together writing that focuses explicitly on the question of identities, examining the meaning of 'race' in different contexts.
- Part III, *Practices*: looks at life inside diverse classrooms and considers how racialised and racist processes operate on a day-to-day level.
- Part IV, *Methods*: addresses key aspects of educational research including the role of the researcher and questions of power.

The editors have assembled a collection of articles of immense scope and pertinence, making this an essential resource book for undergraduates, postgraduates, education practitioners, academics and anyone concerned with race equity and Multicultural Education.

Gloria Ladson-Billings is Professor and H. I. Romnes Fellow in the Department of Curriculum and Instruction at the University of Wisconsin, Madison, USA.

David Gillborn is Professor of Education at the Institute of Education, University of London, England.

Readers in education

The RoutledgeFalmer Reader in Higher Education
Edited by Malcolm Tight

The RoutledgeFalmer Reader in Inclusion
Edited by Keith Topping and Sheelagh Maloney

The RoutledgeFalmer Reader in Language and Literacy
Edited by Teresa Grainger

The RoutledgeFalmer Reader in Multicultural Education
Edited by Gloria Ladson-Billings and David Gillborn

The RoutledgeFalmer Reader in Psychology of Education
Edited by Harry Daniels and Anne Edwards

The RoutledgeFalmer Reader in Science Education
Edited by John Gilbert

The RoutledgeFalmer Reader in Sociology of Education
Edited by Stephen J. Ball

The RoutledgeFalmer Reader in Teaching and Learning
Edited by E. C. Wragg

The RoutledgeFalmer Reader in Multicultural Education

Edited by
**Gloria Ladson-Billings and
David Gillborn**

RoutledgeFalmer
Taylor & Francis Group

LONDON AND NEW YORK

First published 2004
by RoutledgeFalmer
2 Park Square, Milton Park, Abingdon, Oxon, OX14 4RN

Simultaneously published in the USA and Canada
by RoutledgeFalmer
270 Madison Avenue, New York, NY 10016

Reprinted 2005, 2006 (twice)

*RoutledgeFalmer is an imprint of the Taylor and Francis Group,
an informa business*

© 2004 Gloria Ladson-Billings and David Gillborn for selection
and editorial matter

Typeset in Sabon and Futura by
Newgen Imaging Systems (P) Ltd, Chennai, India
Printed and bound in Great Britain by
MPG Books Ltd, Bodmin

British Library Cataloguing in Publication Data
A catalogue record for this book is available from the British
Library

Library of Congress Cataloging in Publication Data
A catalog record for this book has been requested

ISBN 10: 0–415–33662–7 (hbk)
ISBN 10: 0–415–33663–5 (pbk)
ISBN 13: 978–0–415–33662–8 (hbk)
ISBN 13: 978–0–415–33663–5 (pbk)

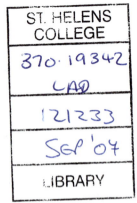

CONTENTS

ACKNOWLEDGEMENTS

Joyce E. King (1991) Dysconscious racism: ideology, identity and the miseducation of teachers, *Journal of Negro Education,* 60(2), 133–46 is reproduced with the permission of *The Journal of Negro Education.*

Lisa D. Delpit (1988) The silenced dialogue: power and pedagogy in educating other people's children, *Harvard Educational Review,* 58(3), 280–98 is reproduced with the permission of *Harvard Education Publishing Group.*

Maud Blair (1998) The myth of neutrality in educational research, from *Researching Racism in Education* by P. Connolly and B. Troyna (eds). Reproduced by permission of Open University Press.

Tony Sewell (1998) Loose canons: exploding the myth of the 'black macho' lad, from *Failing Boys?* by D. Esptein *et al.* (ed.). Reproduced by permission of Open University Press.

Michèle Foster (1994) The power to know one thing is never the power to know all things: methodological notes on two studies of Black American teachers, from *Power and Method: Political Activism and Educational Research* by A. Gitlin (ed.). Reproduced by permission of Routledge/Taylor & Francis Books, Inc.

Michael Omi and Howard Winant (1993) On the theoretical status of the concept of race, from *Race Identity and Representation in Education* by C. McCarthy and W. Crichlow (eds). Reproduced by permission of Routledge/Taylor & Francis Books, Inc.

Christine E. Sleeter (1993) How white teachers construct race, from *Race Identity and Representation in Education* by C. McCarthy and W. Crichlow (eds). Reproduced by permission of Routledge/Taylor & Francis Books, Inc.

All other articles are reproduced with the permission of Taylor & Francis Ltd. http://www.tandf.co.uk

INTRODUCTION

David Gillborn and Gloria Ladson-Billings

. . . two countries divided by a common language.

This quotation, usually attributed to George Bernard Shaw (1856–1950), captures something of the strange relationship between Britain and the United States of America; at once apparently very similar, but at the same time with important differences historically, economically, socially, and culturally. The two nations are, of course, linked by both historical and contemporary political alliances. As the driving forces behind the trans-Atlantic slave trade, Britain and the United States share a past and present forged in racial domination (Gilroy, 1993). This is a vital point of similarity and is crucial to the way that this collection of articles has been constructed with a particular focus in mind.

As critical scholars working against racism in two of the World's most powerful economies, we have been struck by a general lack of collaboration and awareness in our respective nation's approaches to multicultural education. With a few notable exceptions, there are very many leading scholars in the United States who never appear in British textbooks and *vice versa*. This is especially surprising in view of key similarities in the forms of inequity that scar our educational systems and the threats posed by current policy developments. On both sides of the Atlantic periods of reform have further entrenched existing inequities. In the United States, for example, there is growing evidence that White women, because of their large numbers, are the major beneficiaries of affirmative action policies that were designed to improve the position of people of color (US Bureau of the Census, 2000). Similarly, in Britain more than fifteen years of far-reaching educational reforms have been justified by asserting the need to raise "standards for all" but have resulted in a situation where Black children are now further behind their White counterparts than was the case in 1989 (Department for Education and Skills, 2003). Policy-makers are increasingly taking inspiration from reforms enacted elsewhere as "policy borrowing" reaches a global scale (Apple, 1996; Whitty *et al.*, 1998). Although the particular focus of reform may vary in certain locations at different times, increasingly the changes come as a package that includes competition (especially via the creation of educational markets), an assertion of increased choice (in practice only a privileged few enjoy any real choice), devolution (often a joint process whereby the national state assumes greater control while passing on responsibilities to individual districts or schools), managerialism (which views education as a technical exercise), and performativity (i.e. a fetishization of crude statistical data that are taken as indicators of "standards" despite their partial and biased nature) (Ball, 2003, p. 30). In all of this, education policy tends to adopt a color-blind rhetoric that enthusiastically asserts the benefits of change for all children. On the rare occasions that children of color and/or those living in poverty receive any dedicated attention, it is usually through compensatory or marginal programmes, separate to the mainstream, which trade on deficit models that further exacerbate the problems.

These characteristics are true of the British reforms[1] and the *No Child Left Behind* legislation enacted by the George W. Bush administration. At a time when the dangers of ever greater inequity are so pronounced, it is vital that educators dedicated to social justice should learn from each other. With this in mind, we have designed this collection to bring together some of the most important work undertaken by critical educators dedicated to racial equity on either side of the Atlantic.[2] Neither authors' nor editors' royalties are generated by this publication: our aim is simply to get this scholarship into the hands of a greater number of people; from interested lay persons, to undergraduates, would-be teachers, practitioners throughout the system (from Kindergarten to University), and academic writers/ researchers. In order to make this selection accessible to the widest number of people it has been necessary to limit the number of articles we include; this in turn led us to a choice between a focused but selective series of articles or a more wide ranging but possibly incoherent succession of "greatest hits." We chose the former. Consequently there are certain issues that are not addressed here at length, including bilingual education (see Valdés, 2001) and questions of culturally responsive pedagogies (Callender, 1998; Gay, 2000). Nevertheless, despite the limitations of space, we have been able to pull together a selection of scholarship that takes seriously the complex dynamics of racial oppression in education and focuses on the central questions that shape the field in relation to pressing theoretical and conceptual debates; questions of identity; the practices that shape education in context; and the methods by which education may be further researched and critiqued.

The first part, *Theories*, begins by charting some basic conceptual territory. It includes discussions of key ideas that appear throughout the collection, including "race," "multiculturalism," and "anti-racism." It quickly becomes clear that although there is some common ground, notably a complete rejection of "race" as anything except a socially constructed and constantly changing category of exclusion, the field is marked by continuing debate and controversy. One of the most important recent developments has been an attempt to identify a more *critical* approach to the field. This development is highly significant. The struggles to identify and apply critical multiculturalism, critical antiracism, and critical race theory, are each informed by an understanding that past approaches (despite some notable achievements) have largely been appropriated into a mainstream discourse that has robbed them of their radical edge and, if anything, helped to sustain the status quo by signalling an apparent change that has left present inequities intact. Despite their different labels, these approaches are not mutually exclusive. They do not offer easy answers but we are convinced that they raise vital questions and can help on the way to finding solutions.

The second part draws together writing that focuses explicitly on the question of *Identities*. In particular, these chapters examine the meaning of "race" and racial signifiers as they are experienced, challenged, made and re-made through countless social interactions, especially in educational contexts such as schools and colleges. Recent years have seen an explosion of academic work on identity, much of it uncritical and highly descriptive. In contrast, each of the contributions in this part shares two key characteristics. First, each examines how racial and ethnic categories intersect with (and sometimes conflict with) additional identity markers, such as social class, gender, and sexuality. Second, each contribution addresses questions of power. They do not all share the same concept of power, but each is centrally concerned with how identity works for and against certain interests. This is a refreshing and important corrective to some of the worst excesses of postmodernist writing. As Henry Giroux has argued:

> postmodernism has a tendency to democratize the notion of difference in a way that echoes a type of vapid liberal pluralism. There is in this discourse the danger of affirming difference simply as an end in itself without acknowledging how difference is formed, erased, and resuscitated within and despite asymmetrical relations of power. Lost here is any understanding of how difference is forged in both domination and opposition.
>
> (Giroux, 1991, p. 72)

This concern with questions of power and equity is also central to both the remaining parts of the collection. In the third part, *Practices*, the chapters reflect on the nature of life inside multiracial classrooms and consider how racialized and racist processes operate on a day-today level. These chapters are especially challenging for readers who self-identify as "White" and may never have realized how their routine actions and assumptions can be deeply implicated in the racial structuring of power and opportunity. A key aspect of much of this work is to understand the perceptions and experiences of different participants, especially students – whose voices are often silenced or ignored inside schools. Similarly, the contributions in the final part also stress the importance of seeing, thinking, and acting differently; this time through the research act itself.

The chapters that make up the final part, *Methods*, each address different aspects of educational research. Unlike traditional methodological writing, which can tend to lapse into a formulaic "how to" style, these contributions recognize that research (like the rest of education) cannot escape the wider currents that shape racism and inequity in society. Indeed, a critical approach to the field demands that we question previously taken for granted assumptions about what counts as research; who conducts research; and what/who research is for? The chapters here reflect on the authors' own practices, their lived experiences, and confront the centrality of power in all these debates.

Having begun this introduction with reference to language, it is fitting to end with a note of caution on the same topic. Some terms ("race," "racism," "multiculturalism") are the focus of attention in the following chapters and so it would be disingenuous of us, as editors, to offer any simple over-arching definitions. Other terms may appear strange or contradictory to readers who are not familiar with the particularities of British- and American-English. In the United States, for example, *public schools* are those funded and maintained by public authority whereas, in Britain, the term "public school" is reserved for what are actually *private* institutions, run independently of the state and funded largely through the fees paid by parents. More significantly, the words used to describe particular groups of people vary between the different nation-states and within them over time. For example, in the 1980s it was common in Britain for the word "Black" to be used as a general term denoting all minority ethnic groups subject to White racism, regardless of their family origins and self-identifications. This was meant as a political gesture and has now largely passed from usage (see Modood, 1997). "Black" is now most often used in Britain to refer to people with family origins in the Caribbean and/or Africa. In this sense, academic work reflects the label most frequently used by the people themselves. Similarly, the term "Asian" is commonly used on both sides of the Atlantic but, reflecting different historical processes of aggression and migration, in the US the term generally refers to people with family origins in China and South East Asia, whereas in the UK the same term generally relates to people with family heritage in the Indian subcontinent, especially in India, Pakistan, and Bangladesh.

When wishing to refer jointly to several different racialized minorities, in Britain the phrases "ethnic minority" or "minority ethnic" are most common. These have been criticized, however, for echoing popular discourse where "ethnic" can operate as a code for "not-white" and for falling into the trap of imagining that "minority" is equivalent to separate or second-rate (Runnymede Trust, 2000, p. xxiii). In the United States, the term "people of color" is a commonly accepted form of words that serves the same function but is open to similar misuse and misinterpretation. Put simply, the words that are used to frame these debates are part of the debates themselves and reflect the contested nature of the issues that are at stake in this work. These problems are not mere questions of semantics, they are political issues that address questions of meaning and power. Throughout this collection we have retained the terminology used by each author: we believe that this will cause few problems for most readers and hope that everyone (regardless of their national- and self-identifications) takes time to reflect critically on the words and their meanings.

Notes

1   A limited form of devolution has been introduced in Britain, meaning that certain policies (including education) are no longer centrally determined for the whole of the United Kingdom. Nevertheless, the systems in Scotland, Wales, and England share many key features, not least their failure adequately to address racism and race inequity.

2   Of course, important work is also taking place elsewhere and ideally we would have liked to broaden the scope to include colleagues working towards similar ends in other parts of the world, especially in Africa, South America, and Australasia. However, in a collection of this size it would be impossible to do justice to such diversity of scholarship while retaining coherence.

References

Apple, M. W. (1996) *Cultural Politics and Education*. New York: Teachers College Press and Buckingham: Open University Press.

Ball, S. J. (2003) *Class Strategies and the Education Market: The Middle Classes and Social Advantage*. London and New York: RoutledgeFalmer.

Callender, C. (1998) *Education for Empowerment*. Stoke-on-Trent: Trentham.

Department for Education and Skills (2003) *Youth Cohort Study: The Activities and Experiences of 16 Year Olds: England and Wales*. SFR 04/2003. London: Department for Education and Skills.

Gay, G. (2000) *Culturally Responsive Teaching: Theory, Research, and Practice*. New York: Teachers College Press.

Gilroy, P. (1993) *The Black Atlantic: Modernity and Double Consciousness*. London and New York: Verso.

Giroux, H. A. (1991) Postmodernism and the Discourse of Educational Criticism. In S. Aronowitz and H. A. Giroux, *Postmodern Education: Politics, Culture, and Social Criticism*, pp. 57–86. Minneapolis and Oxford: University of Minnesota Press.

Modood, T. (1997) 'Difference', Cultural Racism and Anti-Racism. In P. Werbner and T. Modood (eds), *Debating Cultural Hybridity: Multi-Cultural Identities and the Politics of Anti-Racism*, pp. 154–172. London and New Jersey: Zed Books.

Runnymede Trust (2000) *The Future of Multi-Ethnic Britain: The Parekh Report*. London: Profile Books.

US Bureau of the Census (2000) *Report of the Population*. Internet release at www.census.gov

Valdés, G. (2001) *Learning and Not Learning English: Latino Students in American Schools*. New York: Teachers College Press.

Whitty, G., Power, S. and Halpin, D. (1998) *Devolution and Choice in Education: The School, the State and the Market*. Buckingham and Philadelphia: Open University Press.

PART I

THEORIES
Making sense of race, racism and education

CHAPTER 1

ON THE THEORETICAL STATUS OF THE CONCEPT OF RACE

Michael Omi and Howard Winant

In C. McCarthy and W. Crichlow (eds), *Race Identity and Representation in Education*, New York: Routledge, pp. 3–10, 1993

Introduction

Race used to be a relatively unproblematic concept; only recently have we seriously challenged its theoretical coherence. Today there are deep questions about what we actually mean by the term "race." But before (roughly) the Second World War, before the rise of Nazism, before the end of the great European empires, before the decolonization of Africa, before the urbanization of the US black population and the rise of the modern civil rights movement, race was still largely seen in Europe and North America (and elsewhere as well) as an essence, a natural phenomenon, whose meaning was fixed – constant as a southern star.

In the earlier years of this century only a handful of pioneers, people like W. E. B. DuBois and Franz Boas, conceived of race in a more social and historical way. Other doubters included avant-garde racial theorists emerging from the intellectual ferment of the Harlem Renaissance; black nationalists and pan-Africanists who sought to apply the rhetoric of national self-determination expressed at Versailles to the mother continent, and who returned from the battlefields of France to the wave of antiblack race riots that swept the country in 1919; a few Marxists (whose perspectives had their own limitations); and to some extent the Chicago school of sociology led by Robert Ezra Park. But even these intellectuals and activists made incomplete breaks with essentialist notions of race, whether biological or otherwise deterministic.

That was then; this is now. Today the theory of race has been utterly transformed. The socially constructed status of the concept of race, which we have labeled the *racial formation* process, is widely recognized (Omi and Winant, 1986), so much so that it is now often *conservatives* who argue that race is an illusion. The main task facing racial theory today, in fact, is no longer to problematize a seemingly "natural" or "common sense" concept of race – although that effort has not been entirely completed by any means. Rather our central work is to focus attention on the *continuing significance and changing meaning of race*. It is to argue against the recent discovery of the illusory nature of race; against the supposed contemporary transcendence of race; against the widely reported death of the concept of race; and against the replacement of the category of race by other, supposedly more objective categories like ethnicity, nationality, or class. All these initiatives are mistaken at best, and intellectually dishonest at worst.

In order to substantiate these assertions, we must first ask, what is race? Is it merely an illusion, an ideological construct utilized to manipulate, divide, and deceive? This position has been taken by a number of theorists, and activists as well, including many who have heroically served the cause of racial and social justice in the US. Or is race something real, material, objective? This view too has its adherents, including both racial reactionaries and racial radicals. From our perspective both these approaches miss the boat. The concept of race is neither an ideological construct nor does it reflect an objective condition. In this essay, we first reflect critically on these two opposed viewpoints on the contemporary theory of race. Then we offer an alternative perspective based on the approach of racial formation.

Race as an ideological construct

The assertion that race is an ideological construct – understood in the sense of a "false consciousness" that explains other "material" relationships in distorted fashion – seems to us highly problematic. This is the position taken by the prominent historian Barbara Fields in a recent, well-known article, "Slavery, Race and Ideology in the United States of America" (1990). Although Fields inveighs against various uses of the concept of race, she directs her critical barbs most forcefully against historians who "invoke race as a historical explanation" (p. 101).

According to Fields, the concept of race arose to meet an ideological need: its original effectiveness lay in its ability to reconcile freedom and slavery. The idea of race provided "the means of explaining slavery to people whose terrain was a republic founded on radical doctrines of liberty and natural rights" (p. 114). But, Fields says, to argue that race – once framed as a category in thought, an ideological explanation for certain distinct types of social inequality – "takes on a life of its own" in social relationships, is to transform (or "reify") an illusion into a reality. Such a position could be sustained "only if race is defined as innate and natural prejudice of color."

> Since race is not genetically programmed, racial prejudice cannot be genetically programmed either, but must arise historically. . . . The preferred solution is to suppose that, having arisen historically, race then ceases to be a historical phenomenon and becomes instead an external motor of history; according to the fatuous but widely repeated formula, it "takes on a life of its own." In other words, once historically acquired, race becomes hereditary. The shopworn metaphor thus offers camouflage for a latter-day version of Lamarckism.
>
> (p. 101)

Thus race is either an illusion that does ideological work, or an objective biological fact. Since it is certainly not the latter, it must be the former. No intermediate possibility – for instance the Durkheimian notion of a "social fact" – is considered.

Some of this account – for example, the extended discussion of the origins of North American race-thinking – can be accepted without major objection.[1] Furthermore, Fields effectively demonstrates the absurdity of many commonly held ideas about race. But her position is so extreme that at best it can only account for the origins of race-thinking, and then only in one social context. To examine how race-thinking evolved from these origins, how it responded to changing sociocultural circumstances, is ruled out. Why and how did race-thinking survive after emancipation? Fields cannot answer, because her theoretical approach rules out the very perpetuation of the concept of race. As a relatively orthodox Marxist, Fields could argue that changing "material conditions" continued to give rise to changes in racial "ideology," except that even the limited autonomy this would attach to the concept of race would exceed her standards. Race cannot take on "a life of its own"; it is a pure ideology, an illusion.

Fields simply skips from emancipation to the present, where she disparages opponents of "racism" for unwittingly perpetuating it. In denunciatory terms she concludes by arguing for the concept's abolition:

> Nothing handed down from the past could keep race alive if we did not constantly reinvent and re-ritualize it to fit our own terrain. If race lives on today, it can do so only because we continue to create and re-create it in our social life, continue to verify it, and thus continue to need a social vocabulary that will allow us to make sense, not of what our ancestors did then, but of what we choose to do now.
>
> (p. 118)

Fields is unclear about how "we" should jettison the ideological construct of race, and one can well understand why. By her own logic, racial ideologies cannot be abolished by acts of will. One can only marvel at the ease with which she distinguishes the bad old slavery days of the past from the present, when we anachronistically cling, as if for no reason, to the illusion that race retains any meaning. We foolishly "throw up our hands" and acquiesce in race-thinking, rather than . . . doing what? Denying the racially demarcated divisions in society? Training ourselves to be "color-blind"?[2]

We venture to say that only a historian (however eminent) could have written such an article. Why? Because at the least a sociologist would know W. I. Thomas's famous dictum that if people "define situations as real, they are real in their consequences" (Thomas and Thomas, 1928, p. 572). Nor is Fields alone in claiming that racial ideology persists because people insist on thinking racially. Her position is espoused by many, on both the left and the right of racial debates.[3]

In any case the view that race is a kind of false consciousness is not held only by intellectuals, based on both well-intentioned and ulterior motivations; it also has a common sense character. One hears in casual discussion, or in introductory social science classes, variations on the following statement: "I don't care if a person is black, white, or purple, I treat them exactly the same; a person's just a person to me." Furthermore, some of the integrationist aspirations of racial minority movements, especially the civil rights movement, invoke this sort of idea. Consider the famous phrases from the "I Have a Dream" speech, the line that made Shelby Steele's career: ". . . that someday my four little children will be judged, not by the color of their skin, but by the content of their character."

The core criticisms of this "race as ideology" approach, in our view, are two. First, it fails to recognize that the salience of a social construct can develop over half a millennium or more of diffusion, or should we say enforcement, as a fundamental principle of social organization and identity formation. The longevity of the race concept, and the enormous number of effects race-thinking (and race-acting) have produced, guarantee that race will remain a feature of social reality across the globe, and a fortiori in our own country, despite its lack of intrinsic or scientific merit (in the biological sense). Our second, and related, criticism of this approach is that it fails to recognize that at the level of experience, of everyday life, race is an almost indissoluble part of our identities. Our society is so thoroughly racialized that to be without racial identity is to be in danger of having no identity. To be raceless is akin to being genderless. Indeed, when one cannot identify another's race, a microsociological "crisis of interpretation" results, something perhaps best interpreted in ethnomethodological or perhaps Goffmanian terms. To complain about such a situation may be understandable, but it does not advance understanding.

Race as an objective condition

On the other side of the coin, it is clearly problematic to assign objectivity to the race concept. Such theoretical practice puts us in quite heterogeneous, and sometimes unsavory, company. Of course the biologistic racial theories of the past do this: here we are thinking of the prototypes of fascism such as Gobineau and Chamberlain (see Mosse, 1978), of the eugenicists such as Lothrop Stoddard and Madison Grant, and of the "founding fathers" of scientific racism such as Agassiz, Broca, Terman, and Yerkes (see Chase, 1977; Kevles, 1985). Indeed up to our own time we can find an extensive legacy of this sort of thinking. Stephen Jay Gould makes devastating critiques of such views (1981).

But much liberal and even radical social science, though firmly committed to a social, as opposed to biological, interpretation of race, nevertheless also slips into a kind of objectivism about racial identity and racial meaning. This is because race is treated as an *independent variable* all too frequently. Thus, to select only prominent examples, Daniel Moynihan, William Julius Wilson, Milton Gordon, and many other mainstream thinkers theorize race in terms that downplay its variability and historically contingent character. Even these major thinkers, who explicitly reject biologistic forms of racial theory, fall prey to a kind of creeping objectivism of race. For in their analyses a modal explanatory approach emerges: as sociopolitical circumstances change over historical time, racially defined groups adapt or fail to adapt to these changes, achieving mobility or remaining mired in poverty, etc. In this logic there is no problematization of group identities, of the constantly shifting parameters through which race is understood, group interests are assigned, statuses are ascribed, agency is attained, and roles performed.

Contemporary racial theory, then, is often "objectivistic" about its fundamental category. Although abstractly acknowledged to be a sociohistorical construct, race in practice is often treated as an objective fact: one simply *is* one's race; in the contemporary US, if we discard euphemisms, we have five color-based racial categories: black, white, brown, yellow, and red.

This is problematic, indeed ridiculous, in numerous ways. Nobody really belongs in these boxes; they are patently absurd reductions of human variation. But even accepting the nebulous – "rules" of racial classification – such as "hypodescent" (see Harris, 1964; Davis, 1991) many people don't fit anywhere. Into what categories should we place Arab Americans, for example? Brazilians? South Asians? Such a list could be extended almost indefinitely. Objectivist treatments, lacking a critique of the *constructed* character of racial meanings, also clash with experiential dimensions of the issue. If one doesn't act black, white, etc., that's just deviance from the norm. There is in these approaches an insufficient appreciation of the *performative* aspect of race, as postmodernists might call it.[4]

To summarize the critique of this race-as-objective-condition approach, then, it fails on three counts. First, it cannot grasp the process-oriented and relational character of racial identity and racial meaning. Second, it denies the historicity and social comprehensiveness of the race concept. And third, it cannot account for the way actors, both individual and collective, have to manage incoherent and conflictual racial meanings and identities in everyday life. It has no concept, in short, of what we have labeled racial formation.

Toward a critical theory of the concept of race

The foregoing clearly sets forth the agenda that any adequate theorization of the race concept must fulfill. Such an approach must be constructed so as to steer between the Scylla of "race as illusionary" and the Charybdis of "racial objectivism." Such a critical theory can be consistently developed, we suggest, drawing upon the racial formation approach. Such a theoretical formulation, too, must be explicitly historicist. It must recognize the importance of historical context and contingency in the framing of racial categories and the social construction of racially defined experiences.

What would be the minimum conditions for the development of such a critical, process-oriented theory of race? We suggest that it must meet three requirements:

- it must apply to contemporary political relationships;
- it must apply in an increasingly global context;
- it must apply across historical time.

Let us address each of these points briefly.

Contemporary political relationships

The meaning and salience of race are forever being reconstituted in the present. Today such new relationships emerge chiefly at the point where some counter-hegemonic or postcolonial power is attained. At that point the meanings and the political articulations of race proliferate.

A central example is the appearance of competing racial projects, by which we mean efforts to institutionalize racial meanings and identities in particular social structures, notably those of individual, family, community, and state (see Winant, 1990, 1991). As egalitarian movements contend with racial "backlash" over sustained periods of time, as binary logics of racial antagonism (white/black, ladino/indio, settler/native, etc.) become more complex and decentered, political deployments of the concept of race come to signal qualitatively new types of political domination, as well as new types of opposition.

Consider the US case. It is now possible to perpetuate racial domination without making any explicit reference to race at all. Subtextual or "coded" racial signifiers, or the mere denial of the continuing significance of race, may suffice. Similarly, in terms of opposition, it is now possible to resist racial domination in entirely new ways, particularly by limiting the reach and penetration of the political system into everyday life, by generating new identities, new collectivities, new (imagined) communities that are relatively less permeable to the hegemonic system.[5] Much of the rationale for Islamic currents among blacks in the United States, for the upsurge in black anti-Semitism, and to some extent for the phenomenon of Afrocentrism, can be found here. Thus the old choices, integration vs separatism and assimilation vs nationalism, are no longer the only options.

In the "underdeveloped" world, proliferation of so-called postcolonial phenomena also has significant racial dimensions, as the entire Fanonian tradition (merely to select one important theoretical current) makes clear. Crucial debates have now been occurring for a decade or more on issues such as postcolonial subjectivity and identity, the insufficiency of the simple dualism of "Europe and its others," and the subversive and parodic dimensions of political culture at and beyond the edges of the old imperial boundaries.[6]

The global context of race

The geography of race is becoming more complex. Once more easily seen in terms of imperial reach, in terms of colonization, conquest, and migration, racial space is becoming *globalized* and thus accessible to a new kind of comparative analysis. This only becomes possible now, at a historical moment when the distinction "developed/underdeveloped" has been definitively overcome. Obviously by this we don't mean that now there are no disparities between North and South or rich and poor. We mean that the movement of capital and labor has internationalized all nations, all regions. Today we have reached the point where "the empire strikes back" (see Centre for Contemporary Cultural Studies, 1982), as former (neo)colonial subjects, now redefined as "immigrants," challenge the majoritarian status of the formerly metropolitan group (the whites, the Europeans, the "Americans" or "French," etc.). Meanwhile such phenomena as the rise of "diasporic" models of blackness, the creation of "pan-ethnic"[7] communities of Latinos and Asians (in such countries as the UK or the US), and the breakdown of borders in both Europe and North America all seem to be internationalizing and racializing previously national polities, cultures, and identities. To take just one example, popular culture now internationalizes racial awareness almost instantaneously, as reggae, rap, samba, and various African pop styles leap from continent to continent.

Because of these transformations a global comparison of hegemonic social/political orders based on race becomes possible. We think that in a highly specified form, that is, not as mere reactions to or simple negations of "Western" cultural/theoretical dominance, such notions as diasporic consciousness or racially informed standpoint epistemologies deserve more serious attention as efforts to express the contemporary globalization of racial space (see Harding, 1986; Rabinow, 1986; Mudimbe, 1988). Indeed, recent developments such as the construction of new racial identities or the phenomenon of pan-ethnicity simply cannot be understood without recognizing that the territorial reach of racial hegemony is now global.

The dissolution of the transparent racial identity of the formerly dominant group, that is to say, the increasing racialization of whites in Europe and the US, must also be recognized as proceeding from the increasingly globalized dimensions of race. As previous assumptions erode, white identity loses its transparency and the easy elision with "racelessness" that accompanies racial domination. "Whiteness" becomes a matter of anxiety and concern.

The emergence of racial time

Some final notes are in order in respect to the problem of the epochal nature of racial time. Classical social theory had an enlightenment-based view of time, a perspective that understood the emergence of modernity in terms of the rise of capitalism and the bourgeoisie. This view was by no means limited to Marxism.

Weberian disenchantment and the rise of the Durkheimian division of labor also partake of this temporal substrate. Only rarely does the racial dimension of historical temporality appear in this body of thought, as for example in Marx's excoriation of the brutalities of "primitive accumulation":

> The discovery of gold and silver in America, the extirpation, enslavement, and entombment in mines of the aboriginal population, the beginning of the conquest and looting of the East Indies, the turning of Africa into a warren for the commercial hunting of blackskins, signalized the rosy dawn of the era of capitalist production. These idyllic proceedings are the chief momenta of primitive accumulation. On their heels treads the commercial war of the European nations with the globe for a theater. It begins with the revolt of the Netherlands from Spain, assumes giant dimensions in England's AntiJacobin War, and is still going on in the opium wars with China, etc.
>
> (Marx, 1967, p. 751)

Yet even Marx frequently legitimated such processes as the inevitable and ultimately beneficial birth-pangs of classlessness – enacted by the ceaselessly revolutionary bourgeoisie.

Today such teleological accounts seem hopelessly outmoded. Historical time could well be interpreted in terms of something like a racial *longue durée*. For has there not been an immense historical rupture represented by the rise of Europe, the onset of African enslavement, the *conquista*, and the subjugation of much of Asia? We take the point of much poststructural scholarship on these matters to be quite precisely an effort to explain "Western" or colonial time as a huge project demarcating human "difference," or more globally, as Todorov, say, would argue, of framing partial collective identities in terms of externalized "others" (Todorov, 1985). Just as, for example, the writers of the *Annales* school sought to locate the deep logic of historical time in the means by which material life was produced – diet, shoes, etc. (Braudel, 1981) – so we might usefully think of a racial *longue durée* in which the slow inscription of phenotypical signification took place upon the human body, in and through conquest and enslavement to be sure, but also as an enormous act of expression, of narration.

In short, just as the noise of the "big bang" still resonates through the universe, so the overdetermined construction of world "civilization" as a product of the rise of Europe and the subjugation of the rest of us still defines the race concept. Such speculative notes, to be sure, can be no more than provocations. Nor can we conclude this effort to reframe the agenda of racial theory with a neat summation. There was a long period – centuries – in which race was seen as a natural condition, an essence. This was only recently succeeded, although not entirely superseded, by a way of thinking about race as subordinate to supposedly more concrete, "material" relationships; thus we have become used to thinking about race as an illusion, an excrescence. Perhaps now we are approaching the end of this racial epoch too.

We may, to our dismay, have to give up our familiar way of thinking about race once more. If so, there may also be some occasion for delight. For it may be possible to glimpse yet another view of race, in which the concept operates neither as a signifier of comprehensive identity, nor of fundamental difference, both of which are patently absurd, but rather as a marker of the infinity of variations we humans hold as a common heritage and hope for the future.

Notes

1   Minor objections would have to do with Fields's functionalist view of ideology, and her claim that the race concept only "came into existence" when needed by whites in North American colonies beginning in the late seventeenth century. The concept of race, of course, has a longer history than that (Fields, 1990, p. 101).
2   Fields's admirer David Roediger also criticizes her on this point. "At times she nicely balances the ideological creation of racial attitudes with their manifest and ongoing importance and their (albeit ideological) reality. . . . But elsewhere, race disappears into the 'reality' of class" (see Roedinger, 1991, pp. 7–8).
3   Another important thinker who has at least flirted with the idea of race as illusion is Kwame Anthony Appiah (Appiah, 1985, 1990).
4   "The question of identification is never the affirmation of a pregiven identity, never a self-fulfilling prophecy – it is always the production of an image of identity and the transformation of the subject in assuming that image" (Bhabha, 1990b, p. 188).
5   The work of Paul Gilroy, which focuses on the British racial situation, is particularly revealing in regard to these matters. Gilroy's analysis of the significance of popular music in the African diaspora is indispensable (see Gilroy, 1991).
6   There is a vast literature by now on these matters, whose founding statement is undoubtedly Edward Said's *Orientalism* (Said, 1978); also useful is Bhabha, ed., 1990a.
7   David Lopez and Yen Espiritu define pan-ethnicity as ". . . the development of bridging organizations and solidarities among subgroups of ethnic collectivities that are often seen as homogeneous by outsiders." Such a development, they claim, is a crucial feature of ethnic change – "supplanting both assimilation and ethnic particularism as the direction of change for racial/ethnic minorities." While pan-ethnic formation is facilitated by an ensemble of cultural factors (e.g. common language and religion) and structural factors (e.g. class, generation, and geographical concentration), Lopez and Espiritu conclude that a specific concept of race is fundamental to the construction of pan-ethnicity (Lopez and Espiritu, 1990, p. 198).

References

Appiah, K. A. (1985). The uncompleted argument: DuBois and the illusion of race. In H. L. Gates (ed.), *"Race," Writing, and Difference*. Chicago: Chicago University Press.
—— (1990). Racisms. In D. T. Goldberg (ed.), *Anatomy of Racism*. Minneapolis: Minneapolis University Press.
Bhabha, H. K. (ed.) (1990a). *Nation and Narration*. New York: Routledge.
—— (1990b). Interrogating identity: the postcolonial prerogative. In D. T. Goldberg (ed.), *Anatomy of Racism*. Minneapolis: Minneapolis University Press.
Braudel, F. (1981). *The Structures of Everyday Life: The Limits of the Possible*, vol. 1 of *Civilization and Capitalism, 15th–18th Century* (S. Reynolds, trans.). New York: Harper.
Centre for Contemporary Cultural Studies (1982). *The Empire Strikes Back: Race and Racism in 70s Britain*. London: Hutchinson.
Chase, A. (1977). *The Legacy of Malthus: The Social Costs of the New Scientific Racism*. New York: Knopf.
Davis, F. J. (1991). *Who is Black: One Nation's Definition*. University Park: Pennsylvania State University Press.
Fields, B. (1990). Slavery, race, and ideology in the United States of America. *New Left Review*, 181, 95–118.
Gilroy, P. (1991). *"There Ain't No Black in the Union Jack": The Cultural Politics of Race and Nation*. Chicago: Chicago University Press.
Gould, S. J. (1981). *The Mismeasure of Man*. New York: Norton.
Harding, S. (1986). *The Science Question in Feminism*. Ithaca: Cornell University Press.
Harris, Wilson (1964). *Patterns of Race in the Americas*. New York: Norton.
Kevles, D. J. (1985). *In the Name of Eugenics: Genetics and the Uses of Human Heredity*. New York: Knopf.
Lopez, D. and Espiritu, Y. (1990). Panethnicity in the United States: a theoretical framework. *Ethnic and Racial Studies*, 13, 198–224.

Marx, K. (1967). *Capital*, vol. 1. New York: International Publishers.

Mosse, G. L. (1978). *Toward the Final Solution: A History of European Racism*. New York: Fertig.

Mudimbe, V. Y. (1988). *The Invention of Africa: Gnosis, Philosophy, and the Order of Knowledge*. Bloomington: Indiana University Press.

Omi, M. and Winant, H. (1986). *Racial Formation in the United States: From the 1960s to the 1980s*. New York: Routledge.

Rabinow, P. (1986). Representations are social facts: modernity and post-modernity in anthropology. In J. Clifford and G. E. Marcus (eds), *Writing Culture: The Poetics and Politics of Anthropology*. Berkeley: University of California Press.

Roedinger, D. (1991). *The Wages of Whiteness: Race and the Making of the American Working Class*. London: Verso.

Said, E. (1978). *Orientalism*. New York: Pantheon.

Thomas, W. I. and Thomas, D. S. (1928). *The Child in America: Behavior Problems and Programs*. New York: Knopf.

Todorov, T. (1985). *The Conquest of America: The Question of the Other* (R. Howard, trans.). New York: Harper.

Winant, H. (1990). Postmodern racial politics in the United States: Difference and inequality. *Socialist Review*, 90 (1), 121–47.

—— (1991). Rethinking race in Brazil. *Journal of Latin American Studies*, 24 (1), 173–92.

CHAPTER 2

RACE, KNOWLEDGE CONSTRUCTION, AND EDUCATION IN THE USA

Lessons from history[1]

James A. Banks

Race Ethnicity and Education, 5(1), 7–27, 2002

Studies in the Historical Foundations of Multicultural Education Series (hereafter *Series*) was initiated by the Center for Multicultural Education at the University of Washington in 1992. The purpose of this research project is to uncover the roots of multicultural education, to identify the ways in which it is connected to its historical antecedents, and to gain insights from the past that can inform school reform efforts today related to race and ethnic diversity (Banks, 1996a).

Another aim of the *Series* is to identify the ways in which the knowledge constructed within a society reflects the social, political, and economic contexts in which it is created as well as the subsocieties and personal biographies of historians and social scientists (Banks, 1998). Studies in the *Series* identify important ways in which theory, research, and ideology in multicultural education are both linked to and divergent from past educational reform movements related to race and ethnic diversity (J. A. Banks, 1995, 1996a,b, 1998; C. A. M. Banks, 1996, in progress; Hillis, 1996; Roche, 1996).

This chapter extends the ongoing work of the *Series* by examining the historical and social contexts from 1911 to 2000 to identify ways in which the research and knowledge constructed about race and ethnic groups mirrored and perpetuated these contexts. This historical survey will of necessity be highly abbreviated and condensed. Race relations research on both adults and children will be discussed and related to the social, historical, and political contexts in which it was conducted. In this chapter, I describe research that supports the claims I made in an earlier work in the *Series* project (Banks, 1998).

- The cultural communities in which individuals are socialized are also epistemological communities that have shared beliefs, perspectives, and knowledge.
- Social science and historical research are influenced in complex ways by the life experiences, values, personal biographies and epistemological communities of researchers.
- Knowledge created by social scientists, historians, and public intellectuals reflects and perpetuates their epistemological communities, experiences, goals and interests.

- How individual social scientists interpret their cultural experiences is mediated by the interaction of a complex set of status variables, such as gender, social class, age, political affiliation, religion, and region.

(p. 5)

The rise of nativism in the early 1900s

In the early decades of the last century – 1900–24 – the USA experienced massive immigration from southern, central, and eastern Europe. Europeans were leaving their homelands in massive numbers because of economic dislocations in Europe and the power and promise of the American dream. The American dream and its promises were conveyed across the Atlantic to potential newcomers by letters from European immigrants already in America and by steamship companies. The companies were anxious to profit from the "huddled masses" from Europe described in Emma Lazarus's (1886/1968) poem that is inscribed on the base of the Statue of Liberty.

The "old" European immigrants – who had come largely from northern and western Europe – considered themselves "native Americans" by the turn of century. They became alarmed by the large number of immigrants from southern, eastern, and central Europe who were settling in the USA (Higham, 1972) because, they believed, these immigrants differed from themselves in several important ways. A large percentage of the new immigrants were Catholics, and most spoke languages different from those spoken by the "native Americans." Also, the "old" immigrants believed that the "new" immigrants were easy pawns for city politicians because they exchanged their votes for patronage. Consequently, individuals who spoke for the old immigrants argued that the new immigrants threatened democracy in America. They were also a threat to US democracy because of the possibility of a papal takeover in the USA (Higham). This belief developed because of the large percentage of the new immigrants who were Catholic. A significant percentage were also Jews; some also came from China – and, after 1882, Japan.

The nativists were also alarmed about the new immigrants because they considered the immigrants – such as Jews, Italians and Poles – to be members of races that were separate from and inferior to the descendants of northern and western Europeans (Jacobson, 1998). Madison Grant (1923) argued that the mixing of these inferior races with the northern and western European groups would result in the emergence of a lower type of civilization in the USA. His book had the evocative title, *The Passing of the Great Race*.

The construction of knowledge about race in the early 1900s

As is usually the case during a particular historical period, conflicting and oppositional paradigms were constructed about the southern, central, and eastern European immigrants during the early decades of the twentieth century. One was a *nativist paradigm*, which was given voice and legitimacy by a number of influential books and other publications. Researchers and writers who embraced this paradigm documented ways in which the new immigrants differed from the northern and western Europeans and how they were a threat to American democracy and to the survival of the Anglo-Saxon "race."

Researchers and writers such as Madison Grant (1923) and T. Lothrop Stoddard (1920) documented the ways in which southern, central, and eastern Europeans were genetically inferior to northern and western Europeans by using findings from craniometry, the method and science of measuring skull sizes (Gould, 1996). This research indicated that southern, central, and eastern Europeans had smaller skulls than those of northern and western Europeans and consequently were genetically inferior. Jews and Blacks, both regarded as inferior to northern and western Europeans, were also targets of the nativists. Jews were targets because they were considered a distinct race from Whites in the early 1900s and made up a significant percentage of the new immigrants (Brodkin, 1998; Jacobson, 1998). African-Americans had been in America since 1619 and made up a substantial percentage of the nation's population, especially in the southern states. In 1790, for example, African-Americans made up approximately 19.2 percent of the US population (Bailey, 1961, p. 67).

An oppositional paradigm emerges

A group of social scientists and philosophers within marginalized ethnic communities – primarily Jewish and African-American scholars – created a *transformative paradigm* that challenged nativist theories (Banks, 1993a). They included the anthropologist Franz Boas (1910) and the philosophers Horce Kallen (1924) and Randolph Bourne (1916). Boas (1938/1963) rejected genetic explanations of racial differences and argued that human behavior could best be explained by the interaction of genetic characteristics with the environment. In response to calls for the forced and rapid assimilation of the new immigrants by educators and policy-makers, Kallen and Bourne argued that the new immigrants were entitled to "cultural democracy" in America, which was an extension of the political democracy guaranteed by the Constitution. Kallen and Bourne argued that the new immigrants had the right to maintain important aspects of their ethnic cultures and identities as they became Americans. Gordon (1964), summarizing Kallen's work writes:

> A second theme that highlights Kallen's development of the cultural pluralism position is that his position is entirely in harmony with the traditional ideals of American political and social life, and that, indeed, any attempt to impose Anglo-Saxon conformity constitutes a violation of those ideals.
>
> (p. 145)

Nativism triumphs

The nativistic sentiments directed against the southern, central, and eastern European immigrants gave rise to the influential and inflammatory nativistic Know-Nothing movement (Bennett, 1988), whose aim was to rid the USA of foreign influences. In 1911, the Dillingham Commission – a Congressional Committee created in 1907 to investigate immigration – issued a report that validated and reinforced the views of the nativists. The Commission concluded that the new and the old immigrants were different in significant ways. Historical research today indicates that the two groups of immigrants were more alike than different (Higham, 1972; Bennett, 1988).

The Dillingham Commission, which was appointed by members of Congress who represented and identified with powerful groups in America, created knowledge and findings that reinforced the dominant prejudices, sentiments, and perceptions of mainstream groups in the USA. The Commission, in the words of Manning Marable (1996), did not "speak truth to power." Rather, it reinforced and legitimized mainstream popular knowledge and the groups that exercised the most power in society rather than challenged prevailing conceptions and the people who benefited from them.

The nativists won several major Congressional victories that eventually curtailed the flow of southern, eastern, and central European immigrants to the USA and completely stopped immigration from China. These victories included the Chinese Exclusion Act of 1882 – the first immigration act directed toward a specific nationality group. The Immigration Act of 1917 required immigrants to pass a literacy test in their native language. The era of massive immigration to the USA was ended by the Immigration Act of 1924, which discriminated blatantly against the southern, central, and eastern European immigrants.

The nativists and the assimilationist were victorious in part because most of the immigrants themselves surrendered their ethnic cultures and languages to gain full inclusion into American society. This was a possibility for White European immigrants, but not for people of color such as Native Americans, Mexican-Americans, and African-Americans. Even when people of color became highly culturally assimilated, they were still denied structural inclusion into American society. This is to a large extent still true today, although it is mediated and made more complex by social class factors (Wilson, 1978). In the USA today, in large part because of opportunities that resulted from the civil rights movement of the 1960s and 1970s, there is a significant group of middle-class African-Americans. Although middle-class Blacks are able to enjoy most of the material benefits that middle-class Whites experience, they encounter racism in both their personal and professional lives (Feagin and Sikes, 1994).

Knowledge, power, and transformative knowledge

A significant finding of the *Series* is that individuals and groups on the margins often challenge mainstream and established paradigms that violate human rights and American democratic ideals (Banks, 1996a). Boas, Kallen, and Bourne were immigrant Jews. African-American social scientists such as W. E. B. DuBois (Aptheker, 1983; Lewis, 1995), Carter G. Woodson (1933) and Kelly Miller (1908) also challenged the prevailing theories about race and intelligence during the early decades of the twentieth century. As Okihiro (1994) has perceptively argued, it is "outsiders" and groups and individuals in the margins who frequently keep democratic ideals and practices alive in democratic nation states because they are among the first people to take actions to defend these ideals when they are most seriously challenged.

Social scientists and philosophers such as Boas, Bourne, Kallen, DuBois, Woodson, and Miller created oppositional knowledge – which I call *transformative knowledge* – because of their socialization and experiences within marginalized communities (Banks, 1993a). These communities enable individuals to acquire unique ways to conceptualize the world and an epistemology that differs in significant ways from mainstream assumptions, conceptions, values, and epistemology. Knowledge is in important ways related to power. Groups with the most power within society often construct – perhaps unconsciously – knowledge that maintains their power and protects their interests. Scholars and public intellectuals who are outside the mainstream often construct transformative knowledge that challenges the existing and institutionalized metanarrative (C. A. M. Banks, 1996).

The *Series'* hypotheses about the relationship between knowledge and power are influenced by the work of transformative scholars such as Mannheim (1936),

Clark (1965), Myrdal (1969), Ladner (1973), Code (1991), Harding (1991), and Collins (2000). These scholars have described the ways in which knowledge is not neutral but is highly related to the social, economic, and political contexts in which it is created. Code, the feminist epistemologist, writes, "Knowledge does not transcend, but is rooted in and shaped by, specific interests and social arrangements" (p. 68).

Scholars and researchers less centered in the mainstream tend to have different epistemologies, in part because change and reform, rather than maintenance of the status quo, more frequently serves their social, cultural, political, and economic interests. The epistemological communities in which researchers on the margins are socialized provide them with a unique standpoint or cultural eye that Patricia Hill Collins, the African-American sociologist, calls the "outsider/within" perspective.

Despite the oppositional knowledge created by scholars such as Boas, Bourne, and Kallen, the nativists were destined to win the battle to stop the massive influx of immigrants from southern, eastern, and central Europe, to culturally assimilate the immigrants, and to maintain Anglo-Saxon cultural and political hegemony. The nativists won the battle for several reasons. Although the knowledge and arguments created by scholars such as Boas, Bourne, and Kallen were incisive and cogent, they largely fell on deaf ears. The political and economic power was on the side of the nativists. Knowledge, no matter how thoughtful and logical, usually fades when it goes against powerful political and economic forces. *Knowledge is viewed as most influential when it reinforces the beliefs, ideologies, and assumptions of the people who exercise the most political and economic power within a society.* Neither the knowledge created by nativist scholars nor that created by transformative scholars such as Boas, Kallen, and Bourne was the decisive factor that resulted in the victory of the nativists. Political and economic factors, rather than knowledge, were the most significant factors in their triumph.

The intercultural and intergroup education movements

The intercultural education movement

The assimilationist and pluralist paradigms that emerged within the larger society were mirrored in the nation's schools, colleges, and universities. In the 1930s, an educational movement emerged in the USA to help immigrant students adapt to American life, to maintain aspects of their ethnic heritages and identity, and to become effective citizens of the commonwealth. This movement was called the *intercultural education movement* (Montalto, 1982). New York City, where most of the European immigrants arrived when they came to the USA, became one of the most important sites for the intercultural education movement.

Rachel Davis DuBois, one of the leaders of the intercultural education movement, initiated ethnic assemblies in schools that celebrated the cultures of the immigrants (C. A. M. Banks, 1996). An important aim of the assemblies was to teach immigrant youths ethnic pride and to help mainstream students appreciate the cultures of immigrant youths.

The intergroup education movement

When the Second World War began, most African-Americans lived in the southern states, such as Arkansas, Mississippi, and South Carolina. Blacks were heavily concentrated in the southern states because as captive workers they most frequently worked in cotton and tobacco fields. African-Americans began the Great Migration to northern, middle western, and western cities when the war began (Lemann, 1991). They rushed to cities such as St Louis, Chicago, New York, and Los Angeles. Like the southern, central, and eastern European immigrants, African-American migrants were searching for better economic opportunities and for the elusive American dream. They also left the South in large numbers to escape the institutionalized racism and discrimination that became pernicious and rampant in the decades after the Civil War (Logan, 1954/1997).

When they arrived in northern and western cities, African-Americans discovered that these regions were not promised lands. They experienced discrimination in housing, employment, and in public accommodation. Racial tensions developed and erupted in a series of race riots that destroyed many lives and millions of dollars' worth of property. In 1943, riots occurred in Los Angeles, Detroit, and New York City. The Detroit riot lasted more than thirty hours. When it was over, twenty-five African-Americans and nine Whites had been killed and millions of dollars in property had been destroyed.

The racial riots and incidents in the nation's cities, as well as Nazi anti-Semitism in Europe, provided a new emphasis for intercultural educators. By this time, they frequently referred to themselves as intergroup educators (C. A. M. Banks, in progress). During the 1940s, the intergroup education movement in the nation's schools, colleges, and universities gave birth to a new era of research in race relations and intergroup relations. Like intercultural education, the aims of intergroup education were to minimize ethnic cultures and affiliations, to help students become mainstream Americans and effective citizens, and to teach racial and ethnic tolerance (Taba *et al.*, 1952).

Research during the intergroup education era: 1940–54

The intergroup education period in the USA, from about 1940 to 1954, was one of the nation's most prodigious periods for interracial and intergroup research, theory development, and activities. Although the nation's schools, as well as most of its other institutions – especially in the South – were tightly segregated along racial lines, a group of the nation's social scientists, educators, civil rights organizations, and foundations focused on what Myrdal (1944) called the "American Dilemma." Most of this research, theory development, and activities originated within ethnic communities that were rather separate and apart from mainstream institutions. Jewish American and African-American scholars and civil rights organizations provided much of the leadership in the intergroup and ethnic studies developments during the years that preceded and followed the Second World War.

Three seminal studies marked this period: *An American Dilemma* (Myrdal, 1944), *The Authoritarian Personality* (Adorno *et al.*, 1950), and *The Nature of Prejudice* (Allport, 1954). Each of these studies was designed to provide knowledge and insights that would improve race relations and contribute to the development of theory and research in the social sciences.

An American Dilemma, funded by the Carnegie Corporation of New York, is the most comprehensive single study of race relations in the USA (Myrdal, 1944). Gunnar Myrdal, a Swedish economist, led the research team that gathered the data for this ambitious study and authored the book that resulted from it. One of Myrdal's key findings was that the discrepancy between American democratic ideals and institutionalized racism and discrimination created an "American Dilemma" that had the potential to lead to the reform of race relations in the USA.

He believed that most Americans had internalized American Creed values such as equality and justice, and that a dilemma was created for Americans because of the gap between their ideals and realities. Effective leaders, he argued, could bring about reform in race relations by making this dilemma visible to Americans and appealing to their basic democratic beliefs.

The leaders at the Carnegie Foundation who funded the study, who identified with America's power elite, were surprised and embarrassed by Myrdal's candid criticism of racism and discrimination in the American South. They responded to the study with benign neglect. The major findings of the study challenged the status quo in the South. Although *An American Dilemma* was destined to attain the status of a classic within the American academic community, it received a chilly response in the foundation and corporate worlds (Southern, 1987). One consequence of its publication and reception was a drying up of foundation support for race relations research. Substantial funds for race relations research in the USA would not become available again until the civil rights era of the 1960s and 1970s.

The Authoritarian Personality (Adorno et al., 1950) was another path-breaking research study during the intergroup education period in the USA. Supported and sponsored by the American Jewish Committee as a volume in its *Studies in Prejudice Series*, it was created in the aftermath of Nazi anti-Semitism. It was designed to reveal the personality and social conditions that caused individuals to become anti-Semitic. The first author of the study, Theodor W. Adorno, was a founder of the Frankfurt School in Germany. He was considered Jewish by the Nazi authorities; his father was an assimilated Jew and his mother was a Catholic (Jarvis, 1998; O'Connor, 2000). Adorno immigrated to the USA to escape anti-Semitism in Germany and to find work.

Adorno et al. (1950) concluded that family socialization practices were a major factor that caused individuals to develop authoritarian personalities and consequently to become anti-Semitic. Their research indicated that certain individuals, because of their early childhood experiences, have insecure personalities and need to dominate and to feel superior to other individuals. These individuals, concluded the authors, have an authoritarian personality which is manifested not only in their anti-Semitism but also in their religious and political views. Although Adorno and his colleagues overemphasized personality variables as a cause of prejudice and underestimated structural factors, their theory is an important one. It made substantial contributions to methodology and to theory development in race relations research.

Gordon Allport's (1954) book, *The Nature of Prejudice*, has had a major influence on intergroup education theory and research since its publication. Allport presented his now famous contact hypothesis in this book. He stated that contact between groups will improve intergroup relations if the contact is characterized by these conditions: (1) equal status; (2) cooperation rather than competition; (3) sanctioned by authorities; and (4) characterized by interpersonal interactions in which people become acquainted as individuals.

Most of the research on cooperative learning and interracial contact that has been conducted within the last three decades is based on Allport's (1954) contact hypothesis. This research lends considerable support to the postulate that cooperative interracial contact situations in schools, if the conditions stated by Allport are present in the contact situations, have positive effects on both student interracial behavior and student academic achievement (Slavin, 1979, 2001; Aronson and Gonzalez, 1988).

African-American scholarship during the intergroup education period

The books by Myrdal (1944), Adorno *et al.* (1950), and Allport (1954) received notable attention, discussion, and reviews in mainstream academic publications and discourse. However, the mainstream intellectual and popular communities largely ignored most of the research work and publications by African-American scholars during this period. An exception was *The Souls of Black Folk* by W. E. B. DuBois (1953/1973), which was widely reviewed and sold briskly. DuBois was the most prolific African-American scholar during this period (Lewis, 1995). Although he was a historian and sociologist of first rank, DuBois found it difficult to secure funds to support his research and was unable to obtain a teaching position at a predominantly White university.

Carter G. Woodson, an African-American historian who obtained his doctorate from Harvard, produced a long list of distinguished scholarly works. He also wrote textbooks for students in the elementary and high schools. Woodson's publications, like that of other African-American historians – such as John Hope Franklin and Rayford Logan – were widely used in predominantly Black schools, colleges, and universities. Woodson probably had more influence on the teaching of African-American history in the nation's schools and colleges from the turn of the century until his death in 1950 than any other scholar (Banks, 1996b). With others, he founded the Association for the Study of Negro Life and History in 1912. He established the *Journal of Negro History* in 1916.

A number of other publications and research studies by African-American scholars published during this period also became very influential in predominantly Black colleges and universities, including John Hope Franklin's *From Slavery to Freedom: A History of Black Americans*, first published in 1947, and Rayford Logan's (1954/1997) *The Betrayal of the Negro*, a study of the post-Reconstruction period. Oliver C. Cox's (1948) important study, *Caste, Class and Race: A Study in Social Dynamics*, never became influential in the mainstream academic community. Cox, an African-American sociologist who taught at Lincoln University – a historically Black college – gave a Marxist interpretation of race and class.

Research on children's racial attitudes during the intergroup education period

The pace of research on children's racial attitudes quickened during the intergroup education period and attempts to modify their racial attitudes with experimental interventions began. Scholars within the Jewish and African-American communities did most of this research. Research on children's racial attitudes had begun as early as 1929 with the publication of *Race Attitudes in Children* by Bruno Lasker. Eugene and Ruth Horowitz, and Kenneth and Mamie Clark conducted other early studies of children's racial attitudes in the 1930s (Horowitz and Horowitz, 1938; Clark and Clark, 1939). This early research was designed to describe, and not to modify, children's racial attitudes.

The early research on children's racial attitudes by researchers such as Horowitz and Horowitz (1938), Clark and Clark (1939), and Goodman (1946) indicates that very young children are aware of racial differences, that their racial attitudes mirror those of adults that are institutionalized within mainstream society, and that both African-Americans and White children express a white bias. This early research established a paradigm in race relations research that is still highly influential. It states that the preference that African-American children express for white indicates self-rejection or self-hate. More recent research by Spencer (1982) and Cross (1991) confirms the early findings that both White and Black young children express a white bias. However, they interpret the findings quite differently. Spencer distinguishes *personal identity* and *group identity*. Her research indicates that children can have a high personal self-concept and yet express a bias against their ethnic group. She concludes that the white bias often expressed by young African-American children indicates an accurate understanding of the status of Blacks and Whites in American society rather than a rejection of self.

Intervention studies during the intergroup education years

During the intergroup education period of the 1940s and 1950s, a number of curriculum interventions were conducted by researchers to determine the effects of teaching units, lessons, multicultural materials, role-playing activities, and other kinds of simulated experiences on the racial attitudes of students. Jackson (1944) and Agnes (1947) found that curriculum materials about African-Americans had a positive effect on the racial attitudes of students. Trager and Yarrow (1952) found that a democratic curriculum helped students to develop more positive racial attitudes. They titled their study, *They Learn What They Live*. A variety of curriculum interventions helped students to acquire more positive racial attitudes in a study conducted by Haynes and Conklin (1953). Collectively, these studies indicate that curriculum interventions can help student develop more positive racial attitudes if certain conditions exist in the interventions.

The American civil rights movement

When a group of African-American college students sat down at a lunch counter reserved for Whites in a Woolworth's store in Greensboro, North Carolina on February 1, 1960 and refused to leave until they were served, the civil rights movement had begun (Halberstam, 1998). Race relations in the USA were destined to be transformed. A series of events had given rise to the civil rights movement, including the desegregation of the public universities in the southern and border states, and the desegregation of the armed forces by President Truman with Executive Order 9981 in 1948. The *Brown* vs *Board of Education* Supreme Court decision, which declared *de jure* school segregation unconstitutional in 1954, was also an important procurer of the civil rights movement of the 1960s and 1970s. The movement had a profound influence on most of the nation's institutions – including schools, colleges, and universities – as well as on research and theory in the social sciences and education.

The National Advisory Commission on Civil Disorders (1968) was established by President Johnson to identify the causes of the urban race riots that had raged in many American cities in the late 1960s. Many people had died and millions of dollars' worth of property had been destroyed in this series of riots. The Commission's report set the tone for much of the research, publications and public declarations of this period. The Commission – which issued its report in 1968 – concluded that institutionalized racism was the root cause of the riots and that America was moving toward two societies – one Black and one White. The Commission called upon the nation to act decisively to heal its racial wounds. It wrote:

> This is our basic conclusion: our Nation is moving toward two societies, one black, one white – separate and unequal . . . What white Americans have

never fully understood – but what the Negro can never forget – is that white society is deeply implicated in the ghetto. White institutions created it, white institutions maintain it, and white society condones it.

(vol. 1, p. 1)

This was also the period in which Michael Harrington (1962) published *The Other America*, President Lyndon B. Johnson initiated affirmative action with Executive Order 11246 (in 1971), and the nation began its war on poverty. There was a widespread belief within the nation, which was often voiced by its leaders, that by harnessing its tremendous human resources the USA could eliminate racism and poverty. These ideals were publicly expressed by influential leaders such as John F. Kennedy, Martin Luther King, Jr, and Lyndon B. Johnson. In a message to Congress in 1964 in which he declared a war on poverty in America, President Johnson said:

> The path forward has not been an easy one. But we have never lost sight of our goal – an America in which every citizen shares all the opportunities of his society, in which every man has a chance to advance his welfare to the limit of his capacities. We have come a long way toward this goal. We still have a long way to go.
>
> The distance which remains is the measure of the great unfinished work of our society. To finish that work I have called for a national war on poverty. Our objective: total victory.

(p. 212)

The American civil rights movement, initiated and led by African-Americans, played a major role in the democratization and humanization of American society. As a direct result of action by African-Americans and their supporters in the civil rights movement, Congress passed the Civil Rights Act of 1964. Franklin and Moss (1988) call it "the most far-reaching and comprehensive law in support of racial equality ever enacted by Congress" (p. 449). As a result of the legal, political, and human rights precedent set by the Civil Rights Act of 1964, equal rights were extended to many other groups in American society, including women, people with disabilities, and groups immigrating to the USA. Related legislation that Congress passed after it enacted the Civil Rights Act of 1964 included Title IX of the Elementary and Secondary Education Act in 1972, which made sex bias in education illegal, and Public Law 94–142 in 1975 – The Education for All Handicapped Children Act – which requires free public education and non-discrimination for all students with disabilities.

The Immigration Reform Act of 1965 was also an extension of the ideas embodied by the civil rights movement and the Civil Rights Act of 1964. This act abolished the highly discriminatory national origins quota system and made it possible for immigrants from nations in Asia and Latin America to enter the USA in significant numbers for the first time in US history. The tremendous demographic changes now taking place in American society are a direct result of this act, and consequently the civil rights movement. Because of its passage, massive numbers of immigrants from nations in Asia and Latin America are now entering the USA. The US Census Bureau projects that people of color will make up 47 percent of the US population by 2050. In that year, the US population is projected to be 53 percent White, 25 percent Hispanic, 14 percent African-American, 8 percent Asian-Pacific-American, and 1 percent American Indian and Alaska Native (Franklin, 1998).

Research during the civil rights era

Much of the research and publications during the 1960s and 1970s reflected the social and political ethos of possibility, hope, and the quest for knowledge that would help to eliminate poverty, create equality, and eradicate racism in the USA. People of color – such as African-Americans, Mexican-Americans, and Puerto Rican-Americans – entered predominantly White colleges and universities in significant numbers for the first time in US history as both students and professors. They established ethnic studies programs, conducted research within their communities, and published a score of academic publications that described their histories and cultures from "insider" perspectives (Gutiérrez, 2001; Rodríguez, 2001).

Scholars of color published critiques of much of the previous research that had been done on their histories and cultures by White scholars. They argued that much of this research presented inaccurate and distorted views of their experiences, histories and cultures (Ladner, 1973; Acuña, 1981). They revealed ways in which many White scholars described their histories and cultures from deficit perspectives (Rodríguez, 2001). These scholars developed and published a group of studies that presented their histories and cultures from "insider" perspectives that were more accurate, complex, and compassionate (Acuña, 1981; Gates, 1988; Rodríguez, 1989; Takaki, 1993; Collins, 2000).

Research on children's racial attitudes: 1960 through the 1980s

The hope that the civil rights movement ushered in resulted in federal and foundation funds for research on children's racial attitudes and on ways to intervene to help students to acquire more democratic racial attitudes and values. I will discuss only the intervention research studies in this chapter, although much descriptive research was also published during the 1970s and 1980s (Aboud, 1988; Stephan, 1999). I will use a Weberian-like typology to classify this research into four types of studies: (1) reinforcement studies; (2) perceptual differentiation studies; (3) curriculum intervention studies; and (4) cooperative activities and contact studies (Banks, 1993b). Although these categories overlap, they highlight the important ways in which the four groups of studies differ.

Reinforcement studies.   In the late 1960s, John E. Williams and his colleagues at Wake Forest University conducted a series of studies with pre-school children that were designed to modify their attitudes toward the colors black and-white and to determine whether a reduction of white bias toward animals and objects would generalize to people (Williams and Edwards, 1969). Using reinforcement techniques, the researchers were able to reduce – but not eliminate – white bias in pre-school children. This reduction in bias was generalizable to people. Williams and Morland (1976) summarize this work in their book.

Perceptual studies.   In a series of trenchant and innovative studies, Katz (1973) and Katz and her colleagues (Katz *et al.*, 1975; Katz and Zalk, 1978) were able to help pre-school White and African-American children acquire more positive racial attitudes by teaching them to perceptually differentiate the faces of outgroup members. Katz and Zalk (1978) also investigated the effects of perceptual differentiation, vicarious interracial contact, direct interracial contact, and reinforcement of the color black on the racial attitudes of second- and fifth-grade children.

They found that each of these interventions resulted in a short-term reduction of prejudice.

Curriculum intervention studies. A number of researchers investigated the effects of curriculum interventions such as teaching units and lessons, multiethnic materials, role-playing, and simulation on children's racial attitudes between 1969 and 1980. These investigators included Litcher and Johnson (1969), Weiner and Wright (1973), and Yawkey and Blackwell (1974). In general, these studies indicate that curriculum interventions can modify student racial attitudes if certain conditions exist in the experimental situations. Highly focused interventions of sufficient duration are more likely to modify the racial attitudes of students than those that lack these characteristics. The younger the students are, the more likely that the interventions will be successful. It becomes increasingly more difficult to modify the racial attitudes of students as they grow older.

Cooperative learning and interracial contact studies. During the 1970s and 1980s, a group of investigators accumulated an impressive body of research on the effects of cooperative learning groups and activities on students' racial attitudes, friendship choices, and academic achievement. Most of this research is based on the contact hypothesis of intergroup relations formulated by Allport (1954). Investigators such as Aronson and his colleagues (Aronson and Bridgeman, 1979; Aronson and Gonzalez, 1988), Cohen (Cohen, 1972; Cohen and Roper, 1972), Johnson and Johnson (1981), and Slavin (1979) have conducted much of this research. It strongly supports the postulate that cooperative interracial contact situations in schools, if the conditions stated by Allport exist in the contact situations, have positive effects on both student interracial behavior and student academic achievement.

Very few studies on children's racial attitudes were published during the 1990s (Van Ausdale and Feagin, 2001). Several factors may explain the paucity of studies during this decade. These include the rise of conservatism in the USA during this decade, the shifting of the nation's priorities to other research areas, and the view held by some leaders that the nation had focused enough energy and attention on the problems of minority groups and race. Many Americans also believed that the nation's racial problems had been solved during the civil rights period of the 1960s and 1970s (Schuman *et al.*, 1997).

A ray of hope in race relations research on children developed when the Carnegie Corporation of New York funded sixteen studies that investigated ways to improve race relations among adolescents in the late 1990s (National Research Council and Institute of Medicine, 2000). This group of studies produced important findings and provided essential support for scholars doing race relations research in schools. The National Research Council sponsored a workshop that focused on these studies. However, funding for this project was discontinued when the new leadership at the Carnegie Corporation formulated its priorities for the late 1990s and early 2000s.

The loss of hope and the fading of the dream

By the beginning of the 1980s, hope about the possibility of America eliminating poverty and racism had began to fade, a culture of narcissism was on the rise, and conservative politicians were gaining increasing power in the states and in the federal government. The election of Ronald Reagan – the conservative Republican governor of California – to the presidency in November 1980 epitomized the political mood of the nation. Write Franklin and Moss (1988):

> Ronald Reagan had said during his campaign – and he repeated if after his election – that government handouts made people "government dependent, rather than independent," and he wanted to put a stop to that. In office he pushed through Congress a number of programs in keeping with his views. His first budget as well as subsequent ones reduced the number of people eligible to participate in federal social programs such as food stamps, Medicaid, student loans, unemployment compensation, child nutrition assistance, and Aid to Families with Dependent Children.
>
> (p. 475)

A group of neo-conservative scholars, such as Edward Banfield and Charles Murray – in books and articles – argued that the federal government should reduce help to the poor because it made people dependent. Murray's book, *Losing Ground: American Social Policy 1950–1980*, published in 1984, marked the birth of a new paradigm that attacked the poor and argued for little government intervention. Just as Michael Harrington's 1962 book signaled the beginning of the war on poverty, Murray's book marked the beginning of "the war against the poor," the apt title of Herbert J. Gans's (1995) incisive book. The "war against the poor" experienced a major victory when the Welfare Reform Act of 1996 was enacted by both houses of Congress and signed by President Clinton. This bill drastically reduced welfare benefits and institutionalized the idea that many low-income people were "the undeserving poor" (Katz, 1989).

The coexistence of conservative and progressive political forces in US society

The neo-conservative movement in the USA that began in the post-civil rights years is characterized by attacks on the poor, affirmative action (Edley, 1996), ethnic studies programs (D'Souza, 1991), and bilingual education (Epstein, 1977). However, the period from 1980 to 2000 was marked by contradictions and competing forces in US society. Both progressive and neo-conservative forces competed to shape a new American identity and to influence research, policy, and educational practice.

Two political developments of the 1990s indicate the extent to which both progressive and conservative forces are influencing American society. Proposition 209, which prohibits affirmative action in state government and universities, was passed by the voters in California in November 1996. However, President Clinton, who opposed the initiative, received the electoral votes for the state, which helped him to win re-election. President Clinton's "Mend it, but don't end it" position on affirmative action epitomizes the extent to which both progressive and conservative forces are competing to influence public policy in the USA.

The inability of conservative candidate George W. Bush to win a plurality of the popular votes in the 2000 Presidential election and the remarkable showing of Green Party candidate Ralph Nader in several Western states also indicate the extent to which conservative and progressive forces coexist in the USA. The strong negative reaction by many American citizens to the US Supreme Court making a decision that resulted in Bush becoming the winner of the disputed election of

2000 is another indication of the political divisions and competing political forces in US society.

Neo-conservative and progressive forces and movements are both influencing research, curriculum, and teaching in US society today. Books that attack diversity, such as Arthur M. Schlesinger, Jr's (1991) *The Disuniting of America* and Dinesh D'Souza's (1991) *Illiberal Education*, became best sellers and were widely discussed and influential within the academic and popular communities. *The Bell Curve* by Herrnstein and Murray (1994) – which argues that poor people and African-Americans have less intellectual ability than middle-class Whites – was on the *New York Times* best seller list for a number of weeks. It echoed and gave academic legitimacy to many of the institutionalized beliefs about poor people and African-Americans within American society.

At the same time that books which attacked ethnic studies and multicultural education – and supported inequality – were enjoying a wide public reception, seminal research was being conducted and published in ethnic studies and in multicultural education. The years from 1980 to 2000 were one of the most pro-lific and productive periods in the development of ethnic studies scholarship and curriculum reform in the USA. Seminal and important works published in ethnic studies during this period include *The Signifying Monkey: A Theory of African-American Literary Criticism* by Henry Louis Gates, Jr (1988), *Black Feminist Thought* by Patricia Hill Collins (2000), *A Different Mirror: A History of Multicultural America* by Ronald Takaki (1993), *Black Women in America: An Historical Encyclopedia* by Darlene Clark Hine (1993, 2 volumes), and the *Handbook of Research on Multicultural Education*, edited by James A. Banks and Cherry A. McGee Banks (1995/2001). Each of these titles has enjoyed remarkable sales and warm receptions within the academic community.

The work by multicultural scholars has not been as successful at reaching the popular market as has the work of conservative scholars. There are a few notable exceptions, such as works by African-American public intellectuals like bell hooks, Henry Louis Gates, and Cornell West. West's (1993) *Race Matters* was on the *New York Times* best seller list for many weeks. hooks has written a score of popular books that enjoy wide sales and high visibility among the public. Gates has published several popular books that have been widely disseminated. He also frequently contributes editorials to popular newspapers and magazines such as the *New York Times* and the *New York Times Book Review*. The reception of works by public intellectuals such as West, hooks, and Gates – and the success of the books by conservatives such as Schlesinger and D'Souza – indicate that the American public is as divided in its views as the academic community.

Lessons from history: transformative knowledge and human freedom

The studies that I have examined in this chapter indicate that the knowledge which scholars and public intellectuals create reflects the epistemological communities in which they are socialized, their social, political, economic, and cultural interests, and the times in which they live. This review also indicates that in every historical period, competing paradigms and forms of knowledge coexist: some reinforce the status quo and others challenge it. The groups who exercise the most power within a society heavily influence what knowledge becomes legitimized and widely disseminated.

Scholars and public intellectuals in marginalized communities create knowledge that challenges the status quo and the dominant paradigms and explanations within a society. However, this knowledge is often marginalized within the mainstream academic community and remains largely invisible to the larger public. The knowledge that emanates from marginalized epistemological communities often contests existing political, economic, and educational practices and calls for fundamental change and reform. It often reveals the inconsistency between the democratic ideals within a society and its social arrangements and educational practices.

By revealing and articulating the inconsistency between the democratic ideals within a society and its practices, transformative knowledge becomes a potential source for substantial change. When combined with political and social action that reinforces its major claims, assumptions and tenets, transformative knowledge can become an important factor in social, political, and educational change that promotes human rights and other democratic values.

The ethnic studies and multicultural education movements in the USA – which grew out of and reinforced the civil rights movement of the 1960s and 1970s – have created transformative knowledge that has brought many benefits to American intellectual and scholarly life. It has not only facilitated the process of democratization in the USA, but has deeply influenced mainstream academic knowledge by helping to make it more truthful and more consistent with the realities of American life. It has also helped to liberate American students from many national myths and misconceptions and consequently given them more human freedom – which includes having the capacity to choose, the power to act to attain one's purposes, and the ability to help transform a world lived in common with others (Greene, 1988).

Acknowledgments

I am grateful to Cherry A. McGee Banks for her insightful and encouraging comments on an earlier draft of this chapter. I especially appreciate her keen observations about my discussion of the intercultural and intergroup education movements.

Note

1   This paper was presented when the author received the Jean Dresden Grambs Distinguished Career Research in Social Studies Award at the 81st Annual Conference of the National Council for the Social Studies, November 16–18, 2001, Washington, DC.

References

Aboud, F. (1988) *Children and Prejudice* (Cambridge, MA: Blackwell).

Acuña, R. (1981) *Occupied America: A History of Chicanos*, 2nd edn (New York: Harper and Row).

Adorno, T. W., Frenkel-Brunswik, E., Levinson, D. J., and Sanford, R. N. (1950) *The Authoritarian Personality* (New York: Norton).

Agnes, M. (1947) Influences of reading on the racial attitudes of adolescent girls, *Catholic Educational Review*, 45, pp. 415–20.

Allport, G. W. (1954) *The Nature of Prejudice* (Reading, MA: Addison-Wesley).

Aptheker, H. (ed.) (1983) *The Complete Published Works of W. E. B. DuBois: Writings in Periodicals edited by W. E. B. DuBois, Selections from the Crisis (vol. 1, 1911–1925)* (Millwood, NY: Kraus-Thomson Organization).

Aronson, E. and Bridgeman, D. (1979) Jigsaw groups and the desegregated classroom: in pursuit of common goals, *Personality and Social Psychology Bulletin*, 5, pp. 438–46.

Aronson, E. and Gonzalez, A. (1988) Desegregation, jigsaw, and the Mexican-American experience, in: P. A. Katz and D. A. Taylor (eds) *Eliminating Racism: Profiles in Controversy*, pp. 301–14 (New York: Plenum Press).

Bailey, T. A. (1961) *The American Pageant: A History of the Republic* (Boston, MA: D. C. Heath).

Banks, C. A. M. (1996) The intergroup education movement, in: J. A. Banks (ed.) *Multicultural Education, Transformative Knowledge, and Action*, pp. 251–77 (New York: Teachers College Press).

—— (in progress) *The Intergroup Education Movement: Insights from the Past, Lessons for the Present and Future* (New York: Teachers College Press).

Banks, J. A. (1993a) The canon debate, knowledge construction, and multicultural education, *Educational Researcher*, 22(5), pp. 4–14.

—— (1993b) Multicultural education for young children: racial and ethnic attitudes and their modification, in: B. Spodek (ed.) *Handbook of Research on the Education of Young Children*, pp. 236–50 (New York: Macmillan).

—— (1995) The historical reconstruction of knowledge about race: implications for transformative teaching, *Educational Researcher*, 24(2), pp. 15–25.

—— (1996a) *Multicultural Education, Transformative Knowledge, and Action: Historical and Contemporary Perspectives* (New York: Teachers College Press).

—— (1996b) The African American roots of multicultural education, in: J. A. Banks (ed.) *Multicultural Education, Transformative Knowledge, and Action: Historical and Contemporary Perspectives*, pp. 30–45 (New York: Teachers College Press).

—— (1998) The lives and values of researchers: implications for educating citizens in a multicultural society, *Educational Researcher*, 27(7), pp. 4–17.

Banks, J. A. and Banks, C. A. M. (eds) (1995/2001) *Handbook of Research on Multicultural Education* (San Francisco, CA: Jossey–Bass).

Bennett, D. H. (1988) *The Party of Fear: From Nativist Movements to the New Right in American History* (Chapel Hill, NC: University of North Carolina Press).

Boas, F. (1910) The real racial problem, *Crisis*, 1(2), pp. 2–15.

—— (1938/1963) *The Mind of Primitive Man*, revised edn (New York: The Free Press; original work published 1938).

Bourne, R. S. (1916) Trans-national America, *Atlantic Monthly*, 18 (July), p. 95.

Brodkin, K. (1998) *How the Jews became White Folks and What that Says about Race in America* (New Brunswick, NJ: Rutgers University Press).

Clark, K. B. (1965) *Dark Ghetto: Dilemmas of Social Power* (New York: Harper and Row).

Clark, K. B. and Clark, M. P. (1939) The development of consciousness of self and the emergence of racial identification in Negro preschool children, *Journal of Social Psychology*, 10, pp. 591–9.

Code, L. (1991) *What Can She Know? Feminist Theory and the Construction of Knowledge* (Ithaca, NY: Cornell University Press).

Cohen, E. (1972) Interracial interaction disability, *Human Relations*, 25, pp. 9–24.

Cohen, E. G. and Roper, S. S. (1972) Modification of interracial interaction disability: an application of status characteristic theory, *American Sociological Review*, 37, pp. 643–57.

Collins, P. H. (2000) *Black Feminist Thought: Knowledge, Consciousness, and the Politics of Empowerment*, revised edn (New York: Routledge).

Cox, O. C. (1948) *Caste, Class and Race: A Study in Social Dynamics* (New York: Monthly Review Press).

Cross, W. E. Jr (1991) *Shades of Black: Diversity in African-American Identity* (Philadelphia, PA: Temple University Press).

D'Souza, D. (1991) *Illiberal Education: The Politics of Race and Sex on Campus* (New York: The Free Press).

DuBois, W. E. B. (1953/1973) *The Souls of Black Folk: Essays and Sketches* (Millwood, NY: Kraus–Thompson Organization; original work published 1953).

Edley, C. (1996) *Not all Black and White: Affirmative Action, Race and American Values* (New York: Hill and Wang).

Epstein, N. (1977) *Language, Ethnicity, and the Schools* (Washington, DC: Institute for Educational Leadership, George Washington University).

Feagin, J. R. and Sikes, M. P. (1994) *Living with Racism: the Black Middle-Class Experience* (Boston, MA: Beacon Press).

Franklin, J. H. (1947) *From Slavery to Freedom: A History of Negro Americans* (New York: Knopf).

—— (Chairman) (1998) *One America in the 21st Century: Forging a New Future*. The President's Initiative on Race, The Advisory Board's Report to the President (Washington, DC: US Government Printing Office).

Franklin, J. H. and Moss, A. A. Jr (1988) *From Slavery to Freedom: A History of Negro Americans* (New York: McGraw–Hill).

Gans, H. J. (1995) *The War against the Poor: The Underclass and Antipoverty Policy* (New York: Basic Books).

Gates, H. L. Jr (1988) *The Signifying Monkey: A Theory of African-American Literary Criticism* (New York: Oxford University Press).

Goodman, M. E. (1946) Evidence concerning the genesis of interracial attitudes, *American Anthropologist*, 48, pp. 624–30.

Gordon, M. M. (1964) *Assimilation in American Life* (New York: Oxford University Press).

Gould, S. J. (1996) *The Mismeasure of Man*, revised and expanded edn (New York: Norton).

Grant, M. (1923) *The Passing of the Great Race* (New York: Charles Scribner's).

Greene, M. (1988) *The Dialectic of Freedom* (New York: Teachers College Press).

Gutiérrez, R. A. (2001) Historical and social science research on Mexican Americans, in: J. A. Banks and C. A. M. Banks (eds) *Handbook of Research on Multicultural Education*, pp. 203–22 (San Francisco, CA: Jossey–Bass).

Halberstam, D. (1998) *The Children* (New York: Random House).

Harding, S. (1991) *Whose Knowledge? Whose Science? Thinking from Women's Lives* (Ithaca, NY: Cornell University Press).

Harrington, M. (1962) *The Other America* (New York: Macmillan).

Haynes, M. L. and Conklin, M. E. (1953) Intergroup attitudes and experimental change, *Journal of Experimental Education*, 22, pp. 19–36.

Herrnstein, R. J. and Murray, C. (1994) *The Bell Curve: Intelligence and Class Structure in American Life* (New York: Free Press).

Higham, J. (1972) *Strangers in the Land: Patterns of American Nativism 1860–1925* (New York: Atheneum).

Hillis, M. R. (1996) Research on racial attitudes: historical perspectives, in: J. A. Banks (ed.) *Multicultural Education, Transformative Knowledge, and Action: Historical and Contemporary Perspectives*, pp. 278–93 (New York: Teachers College Press).

Hine, D. C. (ed.) (1993) *Black Women in America: An Historical Encyclopedia*, 2 vols (Brooklyn, NY: Carlson).

Horowitz, E. L. and Horowitz, R. E. (1938) Development of social attitudes in children, *Sociometry*, 1, pp. 301–38.

Jackson, E. P. (1944) Effects of reading upon attitudes toward the Negro race, *Library Quarterly*, 14, pp. 47–54.

Jacobson, M. F. (1998) *Whiteness of a Different Color: European Immigrants and the Alchemy of Race* (Cambridge, MA: Harvard University Press).

Jarvis, S. (1998) *Adorno: A Critical Introduction* (New York: Routledge).

Johnson, L. B. (1964) The war on poverty, in: *The Annals of America*, vol. 18 , pp. 212–16 (Chicago, IL: Encyclopaedia Britannica).

Johnson, D. W. and Johnson, R. T. (1981) Effects of cooperative and individualistic learning experiences on interethnic interaction, *Journal of Educational Psychology*, 73, pp. 444–9.

Kallen, H. (1924) *Culture and Democracy in the United States* (New York: Boni and Liveright).

Katz, M. B. (1989) *The Undeserving Poor: From the War on Poverty to the War on Welfare* (New York: Pantheon).

Katz, P. A. (1973) Perception of racial cues in preschool children: a new look, *Developmental Psychology*, 8, pp. 295–9.

Katz, P. A. and Zalk, S. R. (1978) Modification of children's racial attitudes, *Developmental Psychology*, 14, pp. 447–61.

Katz, P. A., Sohn, M., and Zalk, S. R. (1975) Perceptual concomitants of racial attitudes in urban grade school children, *Developmental Psychology*, 11, pp. 135–44.

Ladner, J. (1973) *The Death of White Sociology* (New York: Vintage).

Lasker, G. (1929) *Race Attitudes in Children* (New York: Henry Holt).

Lazarus, E. (1968) The new colossus, in: *The Annals of America*, vol. 11, p. 108 (Chicago, IL: Encyclopaedia Britannica; original work published 1886).

Lemann, N. (1991) *The Promised Land: The Great Black Migration and How it Changed America* (New York: Alfred A. Knopf).

Lewis, D. L. (ed.) (1995) *W. E. B. DuBois: A Reader* (New York: Henry Holt).

Litcher, J. H. and Johnson, D. W. (1969) Changes in attitudes toward Negroes of White elementary school students after use of multiethnic readers, *Journal of Educational Psychology*, 60, pp. 148–52.

Logan, R. W. (1954/1997) *The Betrayal of the Negro: from Rutherford B. Hayes to Woodrow Wilson* (New York: Da Capo Press; original work published 1954).

Mannheim, K. (1936) *Ideology and Utopia: An Introduction to the Sociology of Knowledge* (New York: Harper).

Marable, M. (1996) *Speaking Truth to Power: Essays on Race, Resistance, and Radicalism* (Boulder, CO: Westview Press).

Miller, K. (1908) *Race Adjustment: Essays on the Negro in America* (New York: Neale).

Montalto, N. V. (1982) *A History of the Intercultural Education Movement 1924–1941* (New York: Garland).

Murray, C. (1984) *Losing Ground: American Social Policy, 1950–1980* (New York: Basic Books).

Myrdal, G. (1944) *An American Dilemma: The Negro Problem and Modern Democracy* (New York: Harper and Row).

—— (1969) *Objectivity in Social Research* (Middletown, CT: Wesleyan University Press).

National Advisory Commission on Civil Disorders (1968) *Report of the National Advisory Commission on Civil Disorders*, 2 vols (Washington, DC: US Government Printing Office).

National Research Council and Institute of Medicine (2000) *Improving Intergroup Relations among Youth: Summary of a Workshop* (Washington, DC: National Academy Press).

O'Connor, B. (ed.) (2000) *The Adorno Reader* (Malden, MA: Blackwell).

Okihiro, G. Y. (1994) *Margins and Mainstreams: Asians in American History and Culture* (Seattle, WA: University of Washington Press).

Roche, A. M. (1996) Carter G. Woodson and the development of transformative scholarship, in: J. A. Banks (ed.) *Multicultural Education, Transformative Knowledge and Action: Historical and Contemporary Perspectives*, pp. 91–114 (New York: Teachers College Press).

Rodríguez, C. E. (1989) *Puerto Ricans Born in the USA* (Boston, MA: Unwin Hyman).

—— (2001) Puerto Ricans in historical and social science research, in: J. A. Banks and C. A. M. Banks (eds) *Handbook of Research on Multicultural Education*, pp. 223–244 (San Francisco, CA: Jossey–Bass).

Schlesinger, A.M. Jr (1991) *The Disuniting of America: Reflections on a Multicultural Society* (Knoxville, TN: Whittle Direct Books).

Schuman, H., Steeh, C., Bobo, L., and Krysan, M. (1997) *Racial Attitudes in America*, revised edn (Cambridge, MA: Harvard University Press).

Slavin, R. E. (1979) Effects of biracial learning teams on cross-racial friendships, *Journal of Educational Psychology*, 71, pp. 381–7.

—— (2001) Cooperative learning and intergroup relations, in: J. A. Banks and C. A. M. Banks (eds) *Handbook of Research on Multicultural Education*, pp. 628–34 (San Francisco, CA: Jossey–Bass).

Southern, D. W. (1987) *Gunnar Myrdal and Black–White Relations: The Use and Abuse of an American Dilemma* (Baton Rouge, LA: Louisiana State University Press).

Spencer, M. B. (1982) Personal and group identity of black children: an alternative synthesis, *Genetic Psychology Monographs*, 106, pp. 59–84.

Stephan, W. (1999) *Reducing Prejudice and Stereotyping in Schools* (New York: Teachers College Press).

Stoddard, T. L. (1920) *The Rising Tide of Color against White World Supremacy* (New York: Charles Scribner's).

Taba, H., Brady, E., and Robinson, J. (1952) *Intergroup Education in Public Schools* (Washington, DC: American Council on Education).

Takaki, R. (1993) *A Different Mirror: A History of Multicultural America* (New York: Little Brown).

Trager, H. G. and Yarrow, M. R. (1952) *They Learn What They Live: Prejudice in Young Children* (New York: Harper).

United States Census Bureau (2000) *Statistical Abstract of the United States: 2000*, 120th edn (Washington, DC: US Government Printing Office).

Van Ausdale, D. V. and Feagin, J. R. (2001) *The First R: How Children Learn Race and Racism* (New York: Rowman and Littlefield).

Weiner, M. J. and Wright, F. E. (1973) Effects of undergoing arbitrary discrimination upon subsequent attitudes toward a minority group, *Journal of Applied Social Psychology*, 3, pp. 94–102.

West, C. (1993) *Race Matters* (Boston, MA: Beacon Press).

Williams, J. E. and Edwards, C. D. (1969) An exploratory study of the modification of color and racial concept attitudes in preschool children, *Child Development*, 40, pp. 737–50.

Williams, J. E. and Morland, J. K. (1976) *Race, Color, and the Young Child* (Chapel Hill, NC: University of North Carolina Press).

Wilson, W. J. (1978) *The Declining Significance of Race: Blacks and Changing American Institutions* (Chicago, IL: University of Chicago Press).

Woodson, C. G. (1933) *The Mis-education of the Negro* (Washington, DC: Associated Publishers).

Yawkey, T. D. and Blackwell, J. (1974) Attitudes of 4 year-old urban Black children toward themselves and Whites based upon multi-ethnic social studies materials and experiences, *Journal of Educational Research*, 67, pp. 373–7.

CHAPTER 3

ANTI-RACISM

From policy to praxis

David Gillborn

In Bob Moon, Sally Brown and Miriam Ben-Peretz (eds) *Routledge International Companion to Education*, London: Routledge, pp. 476–88, 2000

Anti-racism is an ill-defined and changing concept. For some the term denotes any opposition to racism, ranging from organised protest to individual acts of resistance through a refusal to adopt white supremacist assumptions (Aptheker, 1993). For others anti-racism describes a more systematic perspective that provides both a theoretical understanding of the nature of racism and offers general guidance for its opposition through emancipatory practice (Mullard, 1984). The former, broad conception of anti-racism is among the most common understandings internationally, while in Britain the latter more specific usage is dominant. Anti-racism has achieved a degree of public recognition in Britain beyond that attained in most other countries. For this reason I shall begin by using the British case as a vehicle for describing anti-racism in education, especially in relation to the sometimes complementary, sometimes conflicting understandings of *multiculturalism*. I shall broaden the focus later in the piece, particularly with reference to newly emerging discourses of critical anti-racism and praxis.

In Britain, anti-racism was most prominent in social policy debates during the 1980s. Although this period saw a Conservative government re-elected to power at a national level throughout the decade, it was at the local level, especially through the work of local authorities, that anti-racism enjoyed its most influential period. Anti-racism in the 1980s came to denote a wide variety of practices, especially those associated with radical left authorities (such as those in London, Sheffield and Manchester), trade unions and organisations (such as the Anti-Nazi League) which attempted to mobilise young people in opposition to racist organisations like the National Front and later the British National Party (Solomos and Back, 1996). Education emerged as a particularly important arena for anti-racist debate. Although anti-racist policies were adopted in many spheres, it was in education that local policy-makers and practitioners (including teachers' trade unions) achieved some notable changes in policy and practice, although progress was by no means universal or unproblematic.

Attempts to challenge racism in British education have a long and troubled ancestry. Historically, schools and local authorities have been able to take advantage of a system that allowed for an unusually high degree of autonomy, freeing educationists to be among the most consistently active professional groups in the struggle against racism. In the 1980s and 1990s, however, these activities came under severe threat. Education emerged as a key ideological battleground; an arena where each new government initiative was assumed to have a natural consequence requiring further reform of an already shell-shocked system. A succession of reforms, for example, institutionalised a national system of testing linked to a compulsory (and overwhelmingly Eurocentric) curriculum. This added to the divisive effects of an education system that already operated in racialised ways that disadvantaged many minority pupils (Gillborn and Gipps, 1996; Gillborn and Youdell, 2000). In addition to its symbolic importance as a crucial field of social policy, therefore, education is especially significant because it provides a testing ground for many new initiatives and strategies. It highlights both the damage that can be done and the progress that is possible.

Always a target for right-wing critics, during the 1990s anti-racism increasingly came under attack from *left* academics who questioned the notions of identity and politics that underlay certain versions of anti-racist practice. Additionally, attempts to marketise the education system (e.g. by introducing direct competition between schools) and the adoption of a colour-blind rhetoric of 'standards' (that privileged average attainments and ignored race-specific inequalities) further diverted attention away from equal opportunities issues. Despite this hostile environment, anti-racism continues to feature prominently in research and policy debates, particularly at the level of the local state and in community activism. Always a highly controversial aspect of policy and practice, the search for distinctively anti-racist pedagogy and philosophy continues.

Anti-racism and multiculturalism

> For the conservative critics, it [multicultural education] represents an attempt to politicize education in order to pander to minority demands, whereas for some radicals it is the familiar ideological device of perpetuating the reality of racist exploitation of ethnic minorities by pampering their cultural sensitivities.
>
> (Bhikhu Parekh quoted in Modgil *et al.*, 1986, p. 5)

Right-wing critics have attacked even the most limited attempts to introduce multicultural elements into the formal curricula of British schools. John Marks (a member of several influential pressure groups and an official advisor to successive Conservative governments) contributed to a volume entitled *Anti-Racism – An Assault on Education and Value*, arguing that attacks on racism in education (regardless of their 'multicultural' or 'anti-racist' label) shared a common goal of 'the destruction and revolutionary transformation of all the institutions of our democratic society' (Marks, 1986, p. 37). At the other end of the political spectrum, during the 1980s many left-wing education critics devoted their time to a deconstruction of multicultural education, presenting it as a tokenist gesture meant to placate minority students and their communities while preserving intact the traditional curricular core of high status ('official') knowledge (Figueroa, 1995). Barry Troyna, for example, used the phrase '*the three S's*' (saris, samosas and steel bands) to characterise the superficial multiculturalism that paraded exotic images of minority peoples and their 'cultures' while doing nothing to address the realities of racism and unequal power relations in the 'host' society (Troyna, 1984). Godfrey Brandt's (1986) study *The Realization of Anti-Racist Teaching* made a significant contribution to the development of the field at that point, summarising the anti-racist critique of multiculturalism and offering strategies for the development of an anti-racist pedagogy.

In many ways Brandt's work typified the dominant characteristics of 1980s anti-racist education in Britain, including a strident attack on multiculturalism and an emphasis on oppositional forms. Drawing heavily on the work of Chris Mullard (1982, 1984), Brandt argued that 'multicultural education can be seen as the Trojan horse of institutional racism. Within it resides an attempt to renew the structure and processes of racism in education' (Brandt, 1986, p. 117). He argued that whereas multiculturalists typically sought to *respond* to ethnic minorities' experiences, anti-racist teaching should accord minorities an active and central role: 'anti-racism must be dynamic and led by the experience and articulations of the Black community as the ongoing victims of rapidly changing ideology and practice of racism' (ibid., p. 119). Throughout his analysis Brandt was keen to foreground the oppositional nature of anti-racism: 'The aims of anti-racist education must be, by definition, oppositional' (ibid., p. 125). This strand was exemplified in the language that Brandt used, for example, by carefully contrasting the language of multiculturalism and anti-racism. According to Brandt, multiculturalism focused on key terms that shared a rather distant and liberal character, such as monoculturalism/ethnicism, culture, equality, prejudice, misunderstanding and ignorance; its process was characterised as providing information and increasing 'awareness'. In contrast, Brandt presented anti-racism in terms of a hard-edged, more immediate lexicon as concerned with conflict, oppression, exploitation, racism, power, structure and struggle: its process was described as *'dismantle, deconstruct, reconstruct'* (ibid., p. 121, original emphasis). These differences in language are not superficial, they indicated a conscious stance that distanced itself from previous multicultural concerns and adopted an openly political position that emphasised the need actively to identify and resist racism.

The oppositional language of anti-racism has been both a strength and a weakness. On one hand it has highlighted the dynamic and active role that schools and teachers can play in confronting racism; on the other hand, it has also provided ammunition to those cultural restorationists who would characterise any left-liberatory reforms as necessarily lowering academic standards, threatening the majority culture and de-stabilising society (see Ball, 1990; Apple, 1996). Additionally, the issue of language points to one of the most important weaknesses in much 1980s anti-racism; the dominance of rhetoric over practical applications.

In both the United States and Britain, under Reagan and Thatcher respectively, the 1980s witnessed increased centralisation of power, the dominance of market economics and attacks on state intervention in social policy areas such as public health, welfare and education. In Britain it was local authorities, usually controlled by the Labour Party (then in opposition nationally), who defended the need for state intervention and, in some cases, funded high-profile anti-racist campaigns. The Greater London Council (GLC) and the Inner London Education Authority (ILEA) were especially active – both bodies were eventually abolished by a Thatcher government. Despite the hostile national government, therefore, for most of the 1980s anti-racism retained a strong presence in some areas: many education authorities, for example, adopted multicultural and/or anti-racist policy statements. However, the impact of such policies was often negligible. Troyna argued that such policies continued to present 'race' and racism as 'superficial features of society; aberrations, rather than integral to our understanding of the way society functions' (Troyna, 1993, pp. 41–2). In this way, the policies deployed key terms, such as 'pluralism', 'justice' and 'equality', as 'condensation symbols' (after Edelman, 1964). That is, they functioned as textual devices that could generate widespread support (and reassure diverse groups that their interests were taken into account) when in fact their meaning was shifting and imprecise, so that power-holders were not constrained by any meaningful directives with clear practical consequences.

In Britain, therefore, the 1980s marked anti-racism's most prominent policy phase but produced uncertain achievements; although many local education authorities committed themselves to anti-racist positions, this was a field where rhetoric far outweighed practical action. As the decade came to an end, anti-racism was dealt, what many commentators (mistakenly) interpreted, as a wholesale critique from within; at the same time, left academics and cultural critics became increasingly vocal in their attacks on anti-racism: it is to these developments that I turn next.

Left critiques of municipal anti-racism

Most left critiques of anti-racism in Britain take as their focus a brand of high-profile, 'municipal' anti-racism (Gilroy, 1987) practised by certain Labour-controlled local authorities, most notably the GLC. Tariq Modood has been particularly critical of the emphasis on 'colour racism', arguing that this excludes minority groups whose most dearly felt identity concerns culture, not colour (Modood, 1996). Modood has argued against 'racial dualism', a view that splits society into two groups: white and black. Not only does this ignore significant social, economic, religious and political differences (between and within different ethnic groups), it also leads to a narrow definition of what counts as legitimate anti-racist politics:

> Media interest, reflecting the social policy paradigm of the 1980s, has been narrowly circumscribed by racism and anti-racism: ethnic minorities are of interest if and only if they can be portrayed as victims of or threats to white society.
>
> (Modood, 1989, p. 281)

Modood argued that this 'radicals and criminals' perspective played an important role in stifling peaceful protest against *The Satanic Verses* (Rushdie, 1988), thereby fuelling Muslim anger and encouraging 'the unfortunate but true conclusion that they would remain unheeded till something shocking and threatening was done' (Modood, 1989, p. 282). In a succession of critical pieces Modood argued that anti-racists should recognise that 'culture' is not a surface factor that can be dismissed as unimportant – as if minorities who do not see themselves in terms of colour are somehow deluded about where their true interests lie. Municipal anti-racism's constant privileging of 'colour', he argued, meant that it was bound to fail to connect with many minority populations:

> [I]n terms of their own being, Muslims feel most acutely those problems that the anti-racists are blind to; and respond weakly to those challenges that the anti-racists want to meet with most force. . . . We need concepts of race and racism that can critique socio-cultural environments which devalue people because of their physical differences but also because of their membership of a cultural minority and, critically, where the two overlap and create a double disadvantage.
>
> (Modood, 1990, p. 157)

Modood's critique identified several weaknesses in the kinds of emphasis characteristic of the local state's attempt to challenge racism. In particular, the failure to acknowledge ethnic *culture*, as a genuine and vital part of shifting and complex ethnic identities, was revealed as a serious mistake in attempts to encourage wider political mobilisation around anti-racist concerns.

The absence of culture from many anti-racist agendas reflected the bitter disputes between multiculturalists and anti-racists in the late 1970s and 1980s. Modood's critique highlighted one of many negative consequences that arose because of the way the debate became polarised. However, we should not forget the historical reasons for anti-racists' unease about the political and epistemological status of culture. Paul Gilroy, for example, has attacked some anti-racists for accepting too readily 'the absolutist imagery of ethnic categories beloved of the New Right' (Cross, 1990, p. 3). Gilroy (like Modood) has attacked the simplistic assumptions that exposed much 'municipal anti-racism' to ridicule while failing to connect with the lived experiences and struggles of minority groups. At the same time, however, he took a rather different position on the politics of culture within anti-racism; a position that highlights the complexity of identity, 'race' and culture in contemporary society.

Paul Gilroy has been especially critical of the conceptions of 'race' and racism that underlie municipal anti-racism. He attacked the 'coat-of-paint theory of racism' that viewed racism as a blemish 'on the surface of other things' and never called into doubt 'the basic structures and relations of [the] British economy and society' (Gilroy, 1990, p. 74). He argued that such an approach effectively placed racism outside key debates, characterising it as a complicating factor of marginal importance rather than a central defining concern. In contrast, he sought to position racism 'in the mainstream' as 'a volatile presence at the very centre of British politics actively shaping and determining the history not simply of blacks, but of this country as a whole at a crucial stage in its development' (ibid., p. 73). He argued for a wider and more dynamic understanding of 'race' and racism; one that foregrounds the socially constructed nature of 'racial' categories and draws attention to their historically constituted and specific nature – an analysis that strongly echoed some of the most influential and insightful work by prominent cultural theorists in the US (see, e.g. Omi and Winant, 1986). By accepting a fixed and simple notion of culture, therefore, municipal anti-racism had itself come to accept a spurious ideology of 'culturalism and cultural absolutism' (Gilroy, 1990, p. 82) that paralleled the position of the New Right. This development reflected several factors, not least a concern to support campaigns by minority groups and to highlight distinctive cultural identities and activities as a corrective to the deficit pathological models proposed by right-wing politicians and commentators (Apple and Zenck, 1996). By simply *inverting* the right's pathological view of minority culture, however, municipal anti-racism unwittingly repeated and sustained the basic culturalist analyses that presented 'culture' as if it were a fixed, ahistorical 'thing' rather than a constructed, contested and continually changing discourse. For example:

> 'Same-race' adoption and fostering for 'minority ethnics' is presented as an unchallenged and seemingly unchallengeable benefit for all concerned. It is hotly defended with the same fervour that denounces white demands for 'same race' schooling as a repellent manifestation of racism.
>
> (Gilroy, 1990, p. 81)

Paul Gilroy's attack on such policies highlighted their *essentialist* and *reductionist* character: although born of anti-oppressive aims, they actually committed the same errors that typified the racist thinking they sought to oppose. That is, such policies came to argue that there is some innate quality that characterises the true/authentic *essence* of a particular 'racial'/cultural group. This 'sad inability to see beyond the conservation of racial identities to [the] possibility of their transcendence' reinforced assumptions about inherent difference between cultural groups and trivialised 'the rich complexity of black life by reducing it to nothing more than a response to racism' (Gilroy, 1990, pp. 81, 83). Gilroy argued that just as they must adopt a more sophisticated understanding of 'race', so anti-racists had to break with limiting notions of 'culture' as in any way natural, homogeneous or fixed:

> Culture, even the culture which defines the groups we know as races, is never fixed, finished or final. It is fluid, it is actively and continually made and re-made. In our multicultural schools the sound of steel pan may evoke Caribbean ethnicity, tradition and authenticity yet they originate in the oil drums of the Standard Oil Company rather than the mysterious knowledge of ancient African griots.
>
> (Gilroy, 1990, p. 80)

Gilroy argued, therefore, for a conception of culture and 'race' politics that recognised the fluid, dynamic and highly complex character of the new cultural politics of difference (see also West, 1990; Hall, 1992; Goldberg, 1993, 1997). These arguments reflect a shift in social theory often associated with post-modern or post-structuralist approaches (see, e.g. Aronowitz and Giroux, 1991; Thompson, 1992). At times such approaches can seem overly complex and removed from the lived reality of schools, teachers and students (Skeggs, 1991). However, many of the same points have been raised (in a more immediate and school-focused way) in relation to a racist murder, and the conditions that surrounded it, in a Manchester secondary school, called Burnage High. The episode and the subsequent inquiry represent a fault line in British anti-racist politics.

The failure of symbolic anti-racism: learning from Burnage

On Wednesday 17 September 1986, Ahmed Iqbal Ullah (a 13-year-old Bangladeshi student) was murdered in the playground of Burnage High School, Manchester (England). His killer was a white peer at the same school. A subsequent inquiry, led by Ian Macdonald QC, investigated the background to the murder and presented a full report to Manchester City Council. Afraid of possible legal action by people mentioned in the report, the Council refused to publish the inquiry's findings. Following widespread 'leaks' and misreporting in the popular press, the inquiry team itself decided to publish their findings (Macdonald *et al.*, 1989).

> The committee of inquiry, composed of individuals with impressive antiracist credentials – Ian Macdonald, Gus John, Reena Bhavnani, Lily Khan – delivered a strong and, for some, an astonishing condemnation of the antiracist policies apparently vigorously pursued at the school, castigating them as doctrinaire, divisive, ineffectual and counterproductive.
>
> (Rattansi, 1992, p. 13)

The inquiry team were highly critical of the particular form of anti-racism that had been practised in Burnage; what they called *'symbolic, moral and doctrinaire'* anti-racism. It is a form of anti-racism that is essentialist and reductionist in the extreme. Within such a perspective 'race' and racism are assumed always to be dominant factors in the experiences of black and white students, with the former cast as victims, the latter as aggressors. According to symbolic anti-racism:

> since black students are the victims of the immoral and prejudiced behaviour of white students, white students are all to be seen as 'racist', whether they are ferret-eyed fascists or committed anti-racists. Racism is thus placed in some kind of moral vacuum and is totally divorced from the more complex reality of human relations in the classroom, playground or community. In this model of anti-racism there is no room for issues of class, sex, age or size.
>
> (Macdonald *et al.*, 1989, p. 402)

The inquiry report documented the way this approach combined with several other factors (including the style of management and 'macho' disciplinary atmosphere in the school) to increase tension and damage relationships (between school and community; staff and students; students and their peers; teachers and their colleagues). While the report was damning in its criticism of Burnage's 'symbolic' anti-racism, it was absolutely clear about the reality of racism and the need for more sensitive and sophisticated approaches to anti-racism. Although this point was reflected in the first press coverage (in a local paper in Manchester), the national press took a rather different line, representing the report as 'proof' that anti-racism is a damaging extremist political creed. One national paper presented Ahmed as a victim, not of a white racist, but of anti-racism: 'Anti-racist policy led to killing' (*The Daily Telegraph* quoted in Macdonald *et al.*, 1989, p. xx). The distorted press coverage had a significant effect: in education and academia, the 'Burnage report' – though rarely read in detail – was frequently understood as an attack on anti-racism *per se* (see, e.g. Rattansi, 1992). Such an interpretation does the report a major disservice. The inquiry team were careful to reject the press interpretation of events at Burnage and emphasised their continuing support for anti-racist education policies:

> It is because we consider the task of combating racism to be such a critical part of the function of schooling and education that we condemn symbolic, moral and doctrinaire anti-racism. We urge care, rigour and caution in the formulating and implementing of such policies because we consider the struggle against racism and racial injustice to be an essential element in the struggle for social justice which we see as the ultimate goal of education. . . . We repudiate totally any suggestion that the anti-racist education policy of Burnage High School led . . . to the death of Ahmed Ullah . . . [W]e state emphatically that the work of all schools should be informed by a policy that recognises the pernicious and all-pervasive nature of racism in the lives of students, teachers and parents, black and white, and the need to confront it.
>
> (Macdonald *et al.*, 1989, pp. xxiii–xxiv)

In its attack on essentialist and reductionist analyses of 'race' and racism, the Burnage report shared several key features with other left critiques of anti-racist theory and practice. Although the critiques have been generated by a range of writers with diverse agendas, several important lessons can be learnt.

The critical revision of anti-racism

The critical thrust of left academics like Gilroy and Modood in Britain has been echoed internationally by authors who emphasise the complexity and fluidity of 'racial' and ethnic categories (McCarthy, 1990; Rizvi, 1993; Walcott, 1994; Carrim, 1995a,b). In the light of such theoretical advances, it is argued, anti-racism must grow into a more sophisticated and flexible strategy that moves away from the racial dualism of its past – what Bonnett and Carrington (1996) characterise as a model of 'White racism versus Black resistance'. However, much anti-racism continues to be characterised by a preference for rhetoric over practical application. Writing with reference to the Australian case, for example, Rod Allen and Bob Hill have commented on the 'lamentable absence of studies evaluating school-based programs to combat racism' (Allen and Hill, 1995, pp. 772–3). There may be several reasons for this. First, academics have a history of critique that enables them to perceive many shortcomings in practical strategies, but does not dispose them well to identifying things that work. This is particularly the case with sociologists, who have been especially active in developing theoretical approaches to anti-racism. Their disciplinary roots teach sociologists to be aware of the many constraints that shape, limit and frustrate attempts to reform the educational systems of advanced capitalist economies. Given their acute awareness of such limits, it can be difficult for them to move from a 'language of critique' to a 'language of possibility' (McCarthy and Apple, 1988, p. 31). More practically, research on anti-racism at the school level is likely to require careful and lengthy qualitative research that can prove expensive in terms of time and resources. Despite these problems, there is now a small, but growing, range of studies that attempt to identify, describe and (constructively) critique the development of anti-racist practice at the school level – including work from pre-school through to post-compulsory education. In Britain, for example, there are now studies of anti-racist practice in early years education (Siraj-Blatchford, 1994), primary schools (Epstein, 1993; Connolly, 1994), secondary schools (Troyna, 1988; Gillborn, 1995) and beyond (Troyna and Selman, 1991; Neal, 1998). The studies reveal the complex, politically explosive and often painful nature of anti-racist change. They demonstrate the futility of attempts to create an anti-racist 'blueprint' for school change, but point to the micro-political nature of change (Ball, 1987), where conflict may be more or less hidden, but consensus is always fragile and prone to destabilisation by events locally (such as a racist incident in the vicinity of the school), nationally (e.g. a scare story about 'political correctness' in the media) and globally (the Gulf War and Salman Rushdie affair, for example, galvanised Muslim communities in Britain and forced many schools to reappraise previous perspectives and practices: Gillborn, 1995; Parker-Jenkins and Haw, 1998).

Studies of anti-racist school practice show that advances are easier where there is wider institutional support for anti-oppression politics (at a local and/or national government level): nevertheless, even where the national government has never accepted anti-racism as a legitimate policy direction, considerable headway can be made at the school level (see Carrim and Gillborn, 1996). Meaningful school change requires the support of the headteacher/principal and cannot be won without the involvement of wider sections of the school staff, its pupils and feeder communities. Anti-racist changes threaten many deeply held assumptions and, in larger schools, it seems that small 'core' groups of staff may be needed to act as the vanguard for anti-racist developments: researching initiatives elsewhere, organising events, and pushing forward school policy. Making genuine links with local communities is a vital part of successful anti-racist change: such developments can be extremely difficult to engineer but once established, they offer schools an immense resource of support and continually argue the need for schools to deal with the complexities of racialised identities by challenging received stereotypes. Finally, students themselves can play a crucial role in pushing forward school-based, anti-racist change. The democratic participation of *all* students (including whites) strengthens anti-racist change where teachers come to realise the need to see beyond simple 'race' labels, to engage with the cross-cutting realities of gendered, sexualised and class-based inequalities that also act on and through the lives of young people.

Studies of anti-racist developments in school show that a concern with theory and practice need not be mutually exclusive. Although anti-racists' historical preference for rhetoric over practice has not always encouraged school-based developments, it is possible to reflect critically on some of the theoretical assumptions that have informed earlier approaches by focusing on the experiences, failures and advances of anti-racist practitioners. To take a single example, it has often been argued that anti-racism should adopt a theoretical position that defines racism as a whites-only activity, in order to 'acknowledge the asymmetrical power relations between black and white citizens' (Troyna and Hatcher, 1992, p. 16). A frequent observation among post-structuralist critics has been that such a view is essentialist and, paradoxically, refuses to allow minorities the same diversity and complexity of perspective recognised in whites. At a practical level such a position can be difficult to justify to white students without falling into the doctrinaire and morally condemnatory tone of symbolic anti-racism: put simply, white working-class young people rarely feel very powerful; to argue that their skin colour alone identifies them as beneficiaries of centuries of exploitation can destroy the credibility of anti-racism in their eyes. In contrast, it has been noted that some schools have, for reasons of pragmatism, adopted a standpoint that echoes the revisionist critics' point that '*racism and ethnocentrism are not necessarily confined to white groups*' (Rattansi, 1992, p. 36, original emphasis). This is not to say, of course, that racism is equally a problem for all groups: in 'the West' the dominant racist ideologies and the most frequent racists are white. Nevertheless, to deny that white students *can ever* be victims of racist violence is to devalue anti-racism. In schools that have adopted a wider understanding of racism, for example, it is still the case that the vast majority of students using racist harassment procedures are black; however, the acknowledgement that all students can, in principle, use the procedures has served to strengthen wider commitment to the developments and helped support the involvement of all student groups (Gillborn, 1995; Dei, 1996b). Pragmatism is no panacea – it has too often served as an excuse for doing nothing to challenge racism: the point here is that anti-racism (as both theory and practice) can learn from the complex and changing realities faced by students, teachers, parents and other community members. Anti-racism is not a *gift* bestowed by intellectuals and liberals; it is a vital, developing and changing combination of activism and opposition that must continually involve diverse groups and be sensitive to its own limitations in vision and action. The best anti-racism seems likely to reflect a dynamic mix of experience and critical reflection – *praxis*. The need to focus on developments at the school level does not militate against further theoretical developments in this field.

Opposing racism and staying 'critical'

The adjective 'critical' is seemingly one of the most frequently used terms in contemporary social science, running a close second to 'the almost ritualistic ubiquity of "post" words in current culture' (McClintock, 1995, p. 10). In many cases, 'critical' is invoked as a descriptor to signal a break with previous assumptions about an issue or approach while maintaining a sense of uncertainty, avoiding closure about the necessary form of future analyses and/or actions. Critical social research, for example, 'tries to dig beneath the surface. . . . It asks how social systems really work, how ideology or history conceals the processes which oppress and control people' (Harvey, 1990, p. 6). Critical social research may take many forms but is not bound by the limits of conventional positivist assumptions about what counts as 'scientific' rigour, since such assumptions may themselves be implicated in the very processes of oppression that are at issue (Troyna, 1995). Similarly, 'critical multiculturalism' has been proposed – though adherents differ about the precise meaning of the term (cf. Berlant and Warner, 1994; Chicago Cultural Studies Group, 1994; McLaren, 1994, 1995; May, 1994, 1999; Nieto, 1999). It has also been argued that a *critical anti-racism* should learn from past errors (such as the Burnage tragedy) to position a more complex and contextualised understanding of racialised difference at the centre of attempts to oppose racism in the policy and practice of education (Gillborn, 1995; Carrim and Gillborn, 1996; Dei, 1996a; Carrim and Soudien, 1999). The emerging, contested and varied approaches that are sometimes described as 'critical race theory' similarly display a wide variety of perspectives, pedagogy and praxis but often share a determination to identify, name and oppose racism in its many diverse forms: recognising that racism is a deeply ingrained feature of capitalist societies; challenging claims to legal, academic and political neutrality; and pursuing a complex and contextually sensitive understanding of the construction of knowledge/identity boundaries (see Matsuda *et al.*, 1993; Tate, 1997). Whatever nomenclature is adopted, the processes are frequently difficult, always opposed and sometimes pursued at considerable personal cost (see Banks, 1998; Grant, 1999).

To some readers such debates about terminology might seem trivial or obsessive. It has been argued, for example, that the 'unhelpful dichotomisation of multicultural and antiracist education' in Britain (May, 1999, p. vii) diffused anti-oppressive efforts during the height of Thatcherism and still detracts from shared agendas. But as Nazir Carrim and Crain Soudien (1999) have argued, in relation to education in South Africa, there is frequently a qualitative and historically significant difference between interventions informed by multiculturalism and anti-racism. In the UK, South Africa, Canada and Australia, for example (where multiculturalism versus anti-racism debates have attained prominence), the former have frequently been associated with exoticised, superficial approaches more concerned with lifestyles than life chances (Troyna, 1993). To argue that multiculturalism can conceivably be as critical, oppositional and dynamic as anti-racism may be to underestimate the historical and practical dangers in concepts, such as 'culture' and 'multiculturalism', that have too often been framed in unidimensional and fixed ways that are irreconcilable with the decentred and anti-essentialised view of identity, knowledge and power at the heart of critical anti-racist praxis (Dei, 1996b). As Carrim and Soudien have noted:

> A critical antiracism, which incorporates a notion of 'difference' would, therefore, work with complex, non-stereotypical and dynamic senses of identity, and would 'talk to' the actual ways in which people experience their lives,

worlds, and identities ... the use of culturalist language in the schools we report on tends to be assimilationist. . . . These 'bad' multiculturalist practices essentialize cultures, homogenize and stereotype people's identities and do not address the power dimensions of racism. . . . [The] possibility of 'good', critical multicultural practices is indeed conceivable . . . but we do not have evidence of this existing in any of the South African experiences, either historically or in the contemporary situation.

(Carrim and Soudien, 1999, pp. 154–5, 169)

What is perhaps of central importance in these debates is the requirement to remain critical, not only of others, but also of our own attempts to understand and oppose racism. An examination of anti-racist policy and practice demonstrates clearly that there is no blueprint for successful anti-racism – no one 'correct' way. What succeeds at one time, or in one context, may not be appropriate at a later date or in another context. Racism changes: it works differently through different processes, informs and is modified by diverse contemporary modes of representation, and changes with particular institutional contexts. Anti-racism must recognise and adapt to this complexity. In practice this means facing up to the complexities of racism: identifying and combating racism will always be difficult. Racism is often entrenched in commonsense understandings about 'ability', 'aptitude', 'the right attitude', etc. Race is a constant presence in policy and pedagogy – even when it appears absent (Apple, 1999). When legislation adopts a de-racialised discourse, for example, by espousing a desire to help 'all' children regardless of ethnic origin, the consequences of reform have almost invariably been to remake differences that further entrench and extend all too familiar patterns of exclusion and oppression (Gillborn and Youdell, 2000). Although anti-racism has enjoyed more prominent periods, therefore, the need for anti-racist research, analysis and practice is as great as ever. It is to be hoped that anti-racism can win wider acceptance and affect more meaningful change in the future than has been achieved generally in the past.

References

Allen, R. and Hill, B. (1995) 'Multicultural education in Australia: historical development and current status', in James A. Banks and Cherry A. McGee Banks (eds) *Handbook of Research on Multicultural Education*. New York: Macmillan, pp. 763–77.

Apple, M. W. (1996) *Cultural Politics and Education*. Buckingham: Open University Press.

—— (1999) 'The absent presence of race in educational reform', *Race Ethnicity and Education*, 2 (1), 9–16.

Apple, M. W. and Zenck, C. (1996) 'American realities: poverty, economy, and education', in M. W. Apple (ed.) *Cultural Politics and Education*. Buckingham: Open University Press.

Aptheker, Herbert (1993) *Anti-racism in US History: The First Two Hundred Years*. Westport, CT: Praeger.

Aronowitz, S. and Giroux, H. A. (1991) *Postmodern Education: Politics, Culture and Social Criticism*. Oxford: University of Minnesota Press.

Ball, S. J. (1987) *The Micro-Politics of the School: Towards a Theory of School Organisation*. London: Methuen.

—— (1990) *Politics and Policy Making in Education: Explorations in Policy Sociology*. London: Routledge.

Banks, J. A. (1998) 'The lives and values of researchers: implications for educating citizens in a multicultural society', *Educational Researcher*, 27 (7), 4–17.

Berlant, L. and Warner, M. (1994) 'Introduction to "critical multiculturalism" ', in D. T. Goldberg (ed.) *Multiculturalism: A Critical Reader*. Oxford: Blackwell.

Bonnett, A. and Carrington, B. (1996) 'Constructions of anti-racist education in Britain and Canada', *Comparative Education*, 32 (3), 271–88.

Brandt, G. L. (1986) *The Realization of Anti-Racist Teaching*. Lewes: Falmer Press.

Carrim, N. (1995a) 'From "race" to ethnicity: shifts in the educational discourses of South Africa and Britain in the 1990s', *Compare*, 25 (1), 17–33.

—— (1995b) 'Working with and through difference in antiracist pedagogies', *International Studies in Sociology of Education*, 5 (1), 25–39.

Carrim, N. and Gillborn, D. (1996) 'Racialized educational disadvantage, antiracism and difference: countering racism at the school level in South Africa and England'. Paper presented at the annual meeting of the American Educational Research Association, New York, April.

Carrim, N. and Soudien, C. (1999) 'Critical antiracism in South Africa', in S. May (ed.) *Critical Multiculturalism: Rethinking Multicultural and Antiracist Education*. London: Falmer Press.

Chicago Cultural Studies Group (1994) 'Critical multiculturalism', in D. T. Goldberg (ed.) *Multiculturalism: A Critical Reader*. Oxford: Blackwell.

Connolly, P. (1994) 'All lads together?: Racism, masculinity and multicultural/anti-racist strategies in a primary school', *International Studies in Sociology of Education*, 4 (2), 191–211.

Cross, M. (1990) 'Editorial', *New Community*, 17 (1), 1–4.

Dei, G. J. S. (1996a) *Anti-Racism Education in Theory and Practice*. Halifax: Fernwood.

—— (1996b) 'Critical perspectives in antiracism: An introduction', *Canadian Review of Sociology and Anthropology*, 33 (3), 247–67.

Edelman, M. (1964) *The Symbolic Uses of Politics*. Urbana: University of Illinois Press.

Epstein, D. (1993) *Changing Classroom Cultures: Anti-Racism, Politics and Schools*. Stoke-on-Trent: Trentham.

Figueroa, P. (1995) 'Multicultural education in the United Kingdom: Historical development and current status', in J. A. Banks and C. A. M. Banks (eds) *Handbook of Research on Multicultural Education*. New York: Macmillan.

Gillborn, D. (1995) *Racism and Antiracism in Real Schools: Theory. Policy. Practice*. Buckingham: Open University Press.

Gillborn, D. and Gipps, C. (1996) *Recent Research on the Achievements of Ethnic Minority Pupils*. London: HMSO.

Gillborn, D. and Youdell, D. (2000) *Rationing Education*. Buckingham: Open University Press.

Gilroy, P. (1987) *There Ain't No Black in the Union Jack*. London: Hutchinson.

—— (1990) 'The end of anti-racism', *New Community*, 17 (1), 71–83.

Goldberg, D. T. (1993) *Racist Culture: Philosophy and the Politics of Meaning*. Oxford: Blackwell.

—— (1997) *Racial Subjects: Writing on Race and America*. London: Routledge.

Grant, C. A. (ed.) (1999) *Multicultural Research: A Reflective Engagement with Race, Class, Gender and Sexual Orientation*. London: Falmer Press.

Hall, S. (1992) 'New ethnicities', in J. Donald and A. Rattansi (eds) *'Race', Culture and Difference*. London: Sage.

Harvey, L. (1990) *Critical Social Research*. London: Allen & Unwin.

McCarthy, C. (1990) *Race and Curriculum: Social Inequality and the Theories and Politics of Difference in Contemporary Research on Schooling*. Lewes: Falmer, Press.

McCarthy, C. and Apple, M. W. (1988) 'Race, class and gender in American educational research: towards a nonsynchronous parallelist position', in L. Weis (ed.) *Class, Race and Gender in American Education*. Albany: State University of New York Press.

McClintock, A. (1995) *Imperial Leather: Race, Gender and Sexuality in the Colonial Contest*. London and New York: Routledge.

Macdonald, I., Bhavnani, R., Khan, L. and John, G. (1989) *Murder in the Playground: The Report of the Macdonald Inquiry into Racism and Racial Violence in Manchester Schools*. London: Longsight.

McLaren, P. (1994) 'White terror and oppositional agency: towards a critical multiculturalism', in D. T. Goldberg (ed.) *Multiculturalism: A Critical Reader*. Oxford: Blackwell.

—— (1995) *Critical Pedagogy and Predatory Culture*. London and New York: Routledge.

Marks, J. (1986) ' "Anti-racism" – revolution not education', in F. Palmer (ed.) *Anti-Racism – An Assault on Education and Value*. London: Sherwood Press.

Matsuda, M. J., Lawrence, C. R., Delgado, R. and Crenshaw, K. W. (eds) (1993) *Words that Wound: Critical Race Theory, Assaultive Speech, and the First Amendment*. Boulder CO: Westview.

May, S. (1994) *Making Multicultural Education Work*. Clevedon: Multilingual Matters.

—— (ed.) (1999) *Critical Multiculturalism: Rethinking Multicultural and Antiracist Education*. London: Falmer Press.

Modgil, S., Verma, G. K., Mallick, K. and Modgil, C. (eds) (1986) *Multicultural Education: The Interminable Debate*. Lewes: Falmer Press.

Modood, T. (1989) 'Religious anger and minority rights', *Political Quarterly*, July, 280–4.

—— (1990) 'British Asian Muslims and the Rushdie affair', *Political Quarterly*, April, 143–60.

—— (1996) 'The changing context of "race" in Britain', *Patterns of Prejudice*, 30 (1), 3–13.

Mullard, C. (1982) 'Multiracial education in Britain: from assimilation to cultural pluralism', in J. Tierney (ed.) *Race, Migration and Schooling*. London: Holt, Rinehart & Winston.

—— (1984) *Anti-Racist Education: The Three O's*. Cardiff: National Antiracist Movement in Education.

Neal, S. (1998) *The Making of Equal Opportunities Policies in Universities*. Buckingham: Open University Press.

Nieto, S. (1999) 'Critical multicultural education and students' perspectives', in S. May (ed.) *Critical Multiculturalism: Rethinking Multicultural and Antiracist Education*. London: Falmer Press.

Omi, M. and Winant, H. (1986) *Racial Formation in the United States: From the 1960s to the 1980s*. New York: Routledge.

Parker-Jenkins, M. and Haw, K. F. (1998) 'Educational needs of Muslim children in Britain: accommodation or neglect?' in S. Vertovec and A. Rogers (eds) *Muslim European Youth: Reproducing Ethnicity, Religion, Culture*. Aldershot: Ashgate.

Rattansi, A. (1992) 'Changing the subject? Racism, culture and education', in J. Donald and A. Rattansi (eds) *'Race', Culture and Difference*. London: Sage.

Rizvi, F. (1993) 'Race, gender and the cultural assumptions of schooling', in C. Marshall (ed.) *The New Politics of Race and Gender*. London: Falmer Press.

Rushdie, S. (1988) *The Satanic Verses*. London: Viking.

Siraj-Blatchford, I. (1994) *The Early Years: Laying the Foundations for Racial Equality*. Stoke-on-Trent: Trentham.

Skeggs, B. (1991) 'Postmodernism: what is all the fuss about?', *British Journal of Sociology of Education*, 12 (2), 255–67.

Solomos, J. and Back, L. (1996) *Racism and Society*. Basingstoke: Macmillan in association with the British Sociological Association.

Tate, W. F. (1997) 'Critical race theory and education: history, theory, and implications', in M. W. Apple (ed.) *Review of Research in Education*, vol. 22. Washington, DC: American Educational Research Association.

Thompson, K. (1992) 'Social pluralism and post-modernity', in S. Hall, D. Held and T. McGrew (eds) *Modernity and its Futures*. Cambridge: Polity Press.

Troyna, B. (1984) 'Multicultural education: emancipation or containment?', in L. Barton and S. Walker (eds) *Social Crisis and Educational Research*. Beckenham: Croom Helm, pp. 75–92.

—— (1988) 'The career of an antiracist education school policy: some observations on the mismanagement of change', in A. G. Green and S. J. Ball (eds) *Progress and Inequality in Comprehensive Education*. London and New York: Routledge, pp. 158–78.

—— (1993) *Racism and Education: Research Perspectives*. Buckingham: Open University Press.

—— (1995) 'Beyond reasonable doubt? Researching "race" in educational settings', *Oxford Review of Education*, 21 (4), 395–408.

Troyna, B. and Selman, L. (1991) *Implementing Multicultural and Anti-Racist Education in Mainly White Colleges*. London: Further Education Unit.

Troyna, B. and Hatcher, R. (1992) *Racism in Children's Lives: A Study of Mainly White Primary Schools*. London and New York: Routledge.

Walcott, R. (1994) 'The need for a politics of difference', *Orbit*, 21 (2), 4–6.

West, C. (1990) 'The new cultural politics of difference'. Reprinted in S. During (ed.) *The Cultural Studies Reader*. London and New York: Routledge.

CHAPTER 4

JUST WHAT IS CRITICAL RACE THEORY AND WHAT'S IT DOING IN A *NICE* FIELD LIKE EDUCATION?

Gloria Ladson-Billings

International Journal of Qualitative Studies in Education, 11(1), 7–24, 1998

Introduction

Almost five years ago a colleague and I began a collaboration in which we grappled with the legal scholarship known as "critical race theory" (Delgado, cited in Monaghan, 1993). So tentative were we about this line of inquiry that we proceeded with extreme caution. We were both untenured and relatively new to our institution. We were unsure of how this new line of inquiry would be received both within our university and throughout the educational research/scholarly community. Our initial step was to hold a colloquium in our department. We were pleasantly surprised to meet with a room filled with colleagues and graduate students who seemed eager to hear our ideas and help us in these new theoretical and conceptual formulations.

That initial meeting led to many revisions and iterations. We presented versions of the paper and the ideas surrounding it at conferences and professional meetings. Outside the supportive confines of our own institution, we were met with not only the expected intellectual challenges, but also outright hostility. Why were we focusing only on race? What about gender? Why not class? Are you abandoning multicultural perspectives? By the fall of 1995, our much discussed paper was published (Ladson-Billings and Tate, 1995). We have, however, held our collective intellectual breaths for almost a year because, despite the proliferation of critical race legal scholarship, we have seen scant evidence that this work has made any impact on the educational research/scholarly community. Thus, seeing critical race theory (CRT) as a theme in an educational journal represents our first opportunity to "exhale."

> It had been a good day. My talk as a part of the "Distinguished Lecture" Series at a major research university had gone well. The audience was receptive; the questions were challenging, yet respectful. My colleagues were exceptional hosts. I spent the day sharing ideas and exchanging views on various phases of their work and my own. There had even been the not so subtle hint of a job offer. The warm, almost tropical climate of this university stood in stark contrast to the overly long, brutal winters of my own institution. But it also had been a tiring day – all that smiling, listening with rapt interest to

everyone's research, recalling minute details of my own, trying to be witty and simultaneously serious had taken its toll. I could not wait to get back to the hotel to relax for a few hours before dinner.

One of the nice perks that comes with these lecture "gigs" is a decent hotel. This one was no exception. My accommodation was on the hotel's VIP floor – equipped with special elevator access key and private lounge on the top floor overlooking the city. As I stepped off the elevator, I decided to go into the VIP lounge, read the newspaper, and have a drink. I arrived early, just before the happy hour, and no one else was in the lounge. I took a seat on one of the couches and began catching up on the day's news. Shortly after I sat down comfortably with my newspaper, a White man peeked his head into the lounge, looked at me sitting there in my best (and conservative) "dress for success" outfit – high heels and all – and said with a pronounced Southern accent, "What time are y'all gonna be servin'?"

I tell this story both because storytelling is a part of CRT and because this particular story underscores an important point within the critical race theoretical paradigm, that is race [still] matters (West, 1992). Despite the scientific refutation of race as a legitimate biological concept and attempts to marginalize race in much of the public (political) discourse, race continues to be a powerful *social* construct and signifier (Morrison, 1992):

> Race has become metaphorical – a way of referring to and disguising forces, events, classes, and expressions of social decay and economic division far more threatening to the body politic than biological "race" ever was.
>
> Expensively kept, economically unsound, a spurious and useless political asset in election campaigns, racism is as healthy today as it was during the Enlightenment. It seems that it has a utility far beyond economy, beyond the sequestering of classes from one another, and has assumed a metaphorical life so completely embedded in daily discourse that it is perhaps more necessary and more on display than ever before.
>
> (p. 63)

I am intrigued by the many faces and permutations race has assumed in contemporary society. Our understanding of race has moved beyond the bio-genetic categories and notions of phenotype. Our "advanced ideas" about race include the racialization of multiple cultural forms. Sociologist Sharon Lee (1993) suggests that "questions of race have been included in all US population censuses since the first one in 1790" (p. 86). Although racial categories in the US census have fluctuated over time, two categories have remained stable – Black and White. And, while the creation of the category does not reveal what constitutes within it, it does create for us a sense of polar opposites that posits a cultural ranking designed to tell us who is White or, perhaps more pointedly, who is *not* White!

But determining who is and is not White is not merely a project of individual construction and/or biological designation. For example, in early census data, citizens of Mexican descent were considered White, though over time, political, economic, social, and cultural shifts have forced Mexican Americans out of the White category. Conversely, Haney López (1995) pointed out that some groups came to the USA and brought suit in the courts to be declared White. Omi and Winant (1993) argue, however, that the polar notions of race as either an ideological construct or as an objective condition both have shortcomings. That is, thinking of race strictly as an ideological concept denies the reality of a racialized society and its impact on people in their everyday lives. On the other hand, thinking of race solely as an objective condition denies the problematic aspects of race – how to decide who fits into which racial classifications.

Our notions of race (and its use) are so complex that even when it fails to "make sense" we continue to employ and deploy it. I want to argue, then, that our conceptions of race, even in a postmodern and/or postcolonial world, are more embedded and fixed than in a previous age. However, this embeddedness or "fixed-ness" has required new language and constructions of race so that denotations are submerged and hidden in ways that are offensive though without identification. Thus, we develop notions of "conceptual whiteness" and "conceptual blackness" (King, 1995) that both do and do not map neatly on to bio-genetic or cultural allegiances. Conceptual categories like "school achievement," "middle classness," "maleness," "beauty," "intelligence," and "science" become normative categories of whiteness, while categories like "gangs," "welfare recipients," "basketball players," and "the underclass" become the marginalized and de-legitimated categories of blackness.

The creation of these conceptual categories is not designed to reify a binary but rather to suggest how, in a racialized society where whiteness is positioned as normative, *everyone* is ranked and categorized in relation to these points of opposition. These categories fundamentally sculpt the extant terrain of possibilities even when other possibilities exist. And, although there is a fixedness to the notion of these categories, the ways in which they actually operate are fluid and shifting. For example, as an African American female academic, I can be and am sometimes positioned as conceptually White in relation to, perhaps, a Latino, Spanish-speaking gardener. In that instance, my class and social position override my racial identification and for that moment I become "White."

The significance of race need not be overly debated in this chapter. But, as Toni Morrison argues, race is always already present in every social configuring of our lives. Roediger (1991) asserts, "Even in an all-white town, race was never absent" (p. 3). However, more significant/problematic than the omnipresence of race is the notion that "whites reach the conclusion that their whiteness is meaningful" (Roediger, p. 6). It is because of the meaning and value imputed to whiteness that CRT becomes an important intellectual and social tool for deconstruction, reconstruction, and construction: deconstruction of oppressive structures and discourses, reconstruction of human agency, and construction of equitable and socially just relations of power. In this chapter, then, I am attempting to speak to innovative theoretical ways for framing discussions about social justice and democracy and the role of education in reproducing or interrupting current practices.

I hope to provide a brief synopsis of CRT[1] and discuss some of its prominent themes. Then I will discuss its importance to our understanding of the citizen in a democracy, its relationship to education and finally some cautionary implications for further research and study. As is true of all texts, this one is incomplete (O'Neill, 1992). It is incomplete on the part of both the writer and the reader. However, given its incompleteness, I implore readers to grapple with how it might advance the debate on race and education.

What is critical race theory?

Most people in the USA first learned of CRT when Lani Guinier, a University of Pennsylvania Law Professor, became a political casualty of the

Clinton administration. Her legal writings were the focus of much scrutiny in the media. Unschooled and unsophisticated about the nature of legal academic writing, the media vilified Guinier and accused her of advocating "un-American" ideas. The primary focus of the scorn shown toward Guinier was her argument for proportional representation.

Guinier (1991) asserted that in electoral situations where particular racial groups were a clear (and persistent) minority, the only possibility for an equitable chance at social benefits and fair political representation might be for minority votes to count for more than their actual numbers. Guinier first proposed such a strategy as a solution for a postapartheid South Africa. Because Whites are in the obvious minority, the only way for them to participate in the governing of a new South Africa would be to insure them some seats in the newly formed government.

Guinier made a similar argument in favor of African Americans in the USA. She saw this as a legal response to the ongoing lack of representation. Unfortunately, her political opponents attacked her scholarship as an affront to the American tradition of "one person, one vote." The furore over Guinier's work obscured the fact that as an academic, Guinier was expected to write "cutting-edge" scholarship that pushed theoretical boundaries (Guinier, 1994). Her work was not to be literally applied to legal practice. However, in the broad scope of critical race legal studies, Guinier may be seen as relatively moderate and nowhere near the radical the press made her out to be. But, her "exposure" placed CRT and its proponents in the midst of the public discourse.

According to Delgado (1995, p. xiii), "Critical Race Theory sprang up in the mid-1970s with the early work of Derrick Bell (an African American) and Alan Freeman (a white), both of whom were deeply distressed over the slow pace of racial reform in the United States." They argued that the traditional approaches of filing *amicus* briefs, conducting protests and marches, and appealing to the moral sensibilities of decent citizens produced smaller and fewer gains than in previous times. Before long they were being joined by other legal scholars who shared their frustration with traditional civil rights strategies.

CRT is, thus, both an outgrowth of and a separate entity from an earlier legal movement called critical legal studies (CLS). CLS is a leftist legal movement that challenged the traditional legal scholarship that focused on doctrinal and policy analysis (Gordon, 1990) in favor of a form of law that spoke to the specificity of individuals and groups in social and cultural contexts. CLS scholars also challenged the notion that "the civil rights struggle represents a long, steady, march toward social transformation" (Crenshaw, 1988, p. 1334).

According to Crenshaw (1988), "Critical [legal] scholars have attempted to analyze legal ideology and discourse as a social artifact which operates to recreate and legitimate American society" (p. 1350). Scholars in the CLS movement decipher legal doctrine to expose both its internal and external inconsistencies and reveal the ways that "legal ideology has helped create, support, and legitimate America's present class structure" (Crenshaw, p. 1350). The contribution of CLS to legal discourse is in its analysis of legitimating structures in the society. Much of the CLS ideology emanates from the work of Gramsci (1971) and depends on the Gramscian notion of "hegemony" to describe the continued legitimacy of oppressive structures in American society. However, CLS fails to provide pragmatic strategies for material social transformation. Cornel West (1993) asserts that:

> . . . critical legal theorists fundamentally question the dominant liberal paradigms prevalent and pervasive in American culture and society. This

thorough questioning is not primarily a constructive attempt to put forward a conception of a new legal and social order. Rather, it is a pronounced disclosure of inconsistencies, incoherences, silences, and blindness of legal formalists, legal positivists, and legal realists in the liberal tradition. Critical legal studies is more a concerted attack and assault on the legitimacy and authority of pedagogical strategies in law school than a comprehensive announcement of what a credible and realizable new society and legal system would look like.

(p. 196)

CLS scholars critique mainstream legal ideology for its portrayal of US society as a meritocracy but failed to include racism in its critique. Thus, CRT became a logical outgrowth of the discontent of legal scholars of color.

CRT begins with the notion that racism is "normal, not aberrant, in American society" (Delgado, 1995, p. xiv), and, because it is so enmeshed in the fabric of our social order, it appears both normal and natural to people in this culture. Indeed, Bell's major premise in *Faces at the bottom of the well* (1992) is that racism is a permanent fixture of American life. Thus, the strategy becomes one of unmasking and exposing racism in its various permutations.

Second, CRT departs from mainstream legal scholarship by sometimes employing storytelling to "analyze the myths, presuppositions, and received wisdoms that make up the common culture about race and that invariably render blacks and other minorities one-down" (Delgado, 1995, p. xiv). According to Barnes (1990) "Critical race theorists . . . integrate their *experiential knowledge* (emphasis added), drawn from a shared history as 'other' with their ongoing struggles to transform a world deteriorating under the albatross of racial hegemony" (pp. 1864–5). Thus, the experience of oppressions such as racism or sexism has important aspects for developing a CRT analytical standpoint. To the extent that Whites (or in the case of sexism, men) experience forms of racial oppression, they may develop such a standpoint. For example, the historical figure John Brown suffered aspects of racism by aligning himself closely with the cause of African American liberation.[2] Contemporary examples of such identification may occur when White parents adopt transracially. No longer a White family, by virtue of their child(ren), they become racialized others. A final example was played out in the infamous O. J. Simpson trials. The criminal trial jury was repeatedly identified as the "Black" jury despite the presence of one White and one Latino juror. However, the majority White civil case jury was not given a racial designation. When Whites are exempted from racial designations and become "families," "jurors," "students," "teachers," etc. their ability to apply a CRT analytical rubric is limited. One of the most dramatic examples of the shift from non-raced to CRT perspective occurred when Gregory Williams (1995) moved from Virginia where he was a White boy to Muncie, Indiana, where his family was known to be Black. The changes in his economic and social status were remarkable, and the story he tells underscores the salience of race in life's possibilities. The primary reason, then, that stories, or narratives, are deemed important among CRT scholars is that they add necessary contextual contours to the seeming "objectivity" of positivist perspectives.

Third, CRT insists on a critique of liberalism. Crenshaw (1988) argues that the liberal perspective of the "civil rights crusade as a long, slow, but always upward pull" (p. 1334) is flawed because it fails to understand the limits of current legal paradigms to serve as catalysts for social change and its emphasis on incrementalism. CRT argues that racism requires sweeping changes, but liberalism has no mechanism for such change. Rather, liberal legal practices support the painstakingly slow process of arguing legal precedence to gain citizen rights for people of color.

Fourth, and related to the liberal perspective, is the argument posed by CRT that Whites have been the primary beneficiaries of civil rights legislation. For example, although under attack throughout the nation, the policy of affirmative action has benefited Whites, a contention that is validated by the fact that the actual numbers reveal that the major recipients of affirmative action hiring policies have been White women (Guy-Sheftall, 1993). One might argue, then, that many of these White women have incomes that support households in which other Whites live – men, women, and children. Thus, these women's ability to find work ultimately benefits Whites, in general.

In contrast, let us look at some of the social benefits African Americans have received due to affirmative action policies. Even after twenty years of affirmative action, African Americans constitute only 4.5 percent of the professoriate (Hacker, 1992). In 1991 there were 24,721 doctoral degrees awarded to US citizens and noncitizens who intended to remain in the USA, and only 933 or 3.8 percent of these doctorates went to African American men and women. If every one of those newly minted doctorates went into the academy, it would have a negligible effect on the proportion of African Americans in the professoriate. In addition, the majority of the African Americans who earn PhDs earn them in the field of education, and of that group, most of the degrees are in educational administration where the recipients continue as school practitioners (Hacker, 1992).

Thus, CRT theorists cite this kind of empirical evidence to support their contention that civil rights laws continue to serve the interests of Whites. A more fruitful tack, some CRT scholars argue, is to find the place where the interests of Whites and people of color intersect. This notion of "interest-convergence" (Bell, 1980, p. 94) can be seen in what transpired in Arizona over the Martin Luther King, Jr Holiday commemoration.

Originally, the state of Arizona insisted that the King Holiday was too costly and therefore failed to recognize it for state workers and agencies. Subsequently, a variety of African American groups and their supporters began to boycott business, professional, and social functions in the state of Arizona. When members of the National Basketball Association and the National Football League suggested that neither the NBA All-Star Game nor the Super Bowl would be held in Arizona because of its failure to recognize the King Holiday, the decision was reversed. Hardly anyone is naive enough to believe that the governor of Arizona had a change of heart about the significance of the King Holiday. Rather, when his position on the holiday had the effect of hurting state tourist and sports entertainment revenues, the state's interests (to enhance revenue) converged with that of the African American community (to recognize Dr King). Thus, converging interests, not support of civil rights, led to the reversal of the state's position.

In a recent compilation of CRT key writings (Crenshaw *et al.*, 1995) it is pointed out that there is no "canonical set of doctrines or methodologies to which [CRT scholars] all subscribe" (p. xiii). But, these scholars are unified by two common interests – to understand how a "regime of white supremacy and its subordination of people of color have been created and maintained in America" (p. xiii) and to change the bond that exists between law and racial power.

In the pursuit of these interests, legal scholars, such as Patricia Williams (1991) and Derrick Bell (1987, 1992), were among the early critical race theorists whose ideas reached the general public. Some might argue that their wide appeal was the result of their abilities to tell compelling stories into which they embedded legal issues.[3] This use of story is of particular interest to educators because of the growing popularity of narrative inquiry in the study of teaching (Connelly and Clandinin, 1990; Carter, 1993). But, just because more people are recognizing and using story as a part of scholarly inquiry does not mean that all stories are judged as legitimate in knowledge construction and the advancement of a discipline.

Lawrence (1995) asserts that there is a tradition of storytelling in law and that litigation is highly formalized storytelling, though the stories of ordinary people, in general, have not been told or recorded in the literature of law (or any other discipline). But this failure to make it into the canons of literature or research does not make the stories of ordinary people less important.

Stories provide the necessary context for understanding, feeling, and interpreting. The ahistorical and acontextual nature of much law and other "science" renders the voices of dispossessed and marginalized group members mute. In response, much of the scholarship of CRT focuses on the role of "voice" in bringing additional power to the legal discourses of racial justice. Indeed, Delgado (1990) argues that people of color speak with experiential knowledge about the fact that our society is deeply structured by racism. That structure gives their stories a common framework warranting the term "voice." Consequently, critical race theorists are attempting to interject minority cultural viewpoints, derived from a common history of oppression, into their efforts to reconstruct a society crumbling under the burden of racial hegemony (Barnes, 1990).

The use of voice or "naming your reality" is a way that CRT links form and substance in scholarship. CRT scholars use parables, chronicles, stories, counter-stories, poetry, fiction, and revisionist histories to illustrate the false necessity and irony of much of current civil rights doctrine. Delgado (1989) suggests that there are at least three reasons for "naming one's own reality" in legal discourse:

1   much of "reality" is socially constructed;
2   stories provide members of outgroups a vehicle for psychic self-preservation; and
3   the exchange of stories from teller to listener can help overcome ethnocentrism and the dysconscious (King, 1992) drive or need to view the world in one way.

The first reason for naming one's own reality involves how political and moral analysis is conducted in legal scholarship. Many mainstream legal scholars embrace universalism over particularity. According to Williams (1991), "theoretical legal understanding" is characterized, in Anglo-American jurisprudence, by the acceptance of transcendent, acontextual, universal legal truths or procedures. For instance, some legal scholars might contend that the tort of fraud has always existed and that it is a component belonging to the universal system of right and wrong. This worldview tends to discount anything that is nontranscendent (historical), or contextual (socially constructed), or nonuniversal (specific) with the unscholarly labels of "emotional," "literary," "personal," or false (Williams, 1991).

In contrast, critical race theorists argue that political and moral analysis is situational – "truths only exist for this person in this predicament at this time in history" (Delgado, 1991, p. 11). For the critical race theorist, social reality is constructed by the formulation and the exchange of stories about individual situations (see, for example, Matsuda, 1989). These stories serve as interpretive structures by which we impose order on experience and it on us (Delgado, 1989).

A second reason for the naming one's own reality theme of CRT is the psychic preservation of marginalized groups. A factor contributing to the demoralization of marginalized groups is self-condemnation (Delgado, 1989). Members of minority groups internalize the stereotypic images that certain elements of society have constructed in order to maintain their power. Historically, storytelling has been a kind of medicine to heal the wounds of pain caused by racial oppression. The story of one's condition leads to the realization of how one came to be oppressed and subjugated, thus allowing one to stop inflicting mental violence on oneself.

Finally, naming one's own reality with stories can affect the oppressor. Most oppression, as was discussed earlier, does not seem like oppression to the perpetrator (Lawrence, 1987). Delgado (1989) argues that the dominant group justifies its power with stories, stock explanations, that construct reality in ways that maintain their privilege. Thus, oppression is rationalized, causing little self-examination by the oppressor. Stories by people of color can catalyze the necessary cognitive conflict to jar dysconscious racism.

The "voice" component of CRT provides a way to communicate the experience and realities of the oppressed, a first step in understanding the complexities of racism and beginning a process of judicial redress. For example, the voice of people of color is required for a deep understanding of the educational system. Delpit (1988) argues one of the tragedies of the field of education is how the dialogue of people of color has been silenced. Delpit begins her analysis of the process-oriented vs the skills-oriented writing debate with a statement (or story) from an African American male graduate student at a predominantly White university who is also a special education teacher in an African American community:

> There comes a moment in every class where we have to discuss "The Black Issue" and what's appropriate education for Black children. I tell you, I'm tired of arguing with those White people, because they won't listen. Well, I don't know if they really don't listen or if they just don't believe you. It seems like if you can't quote Vygotsky or something, then you don't have any validity to speak about your own kids. Anyway, I'm not bothering with it anymore, now I'm just in it for a grade.
>
> (p. 280)

The above comment and numerous other statements found in Delpit's analysis illustrate the frustration of teachers of color that is caused by being left out of the dialogue about how best to educate children of color. Further, Delpit raises several very important questions:

> How can such complete communication blocks exist when both parties [Black and Whites] truly believe they have the same aims? How can the bitterness and resentment expressed by educators of color be drained so that all sores can heal? What can be done?
>
> (p. 282)

Critical race theory and citizenship

One of the places to begin understanding CRT is to examine how conceptions of citizenship and race interact. Although connections of CRT and citizenship are numerous and complex, in this chapter I will attempt to detail only one of the central connections that is important in understanding the relationship of this scholarship to educational issues. That central connection is the "property issue" (Ladson-Billings and Tate, 1995). CRT scholars assert that the USA is a nation conceived and built on property rights (Bell, 1987; Harris, 1993). In the early history of the nation only propertied White males enjoyed the franchise. The significance of property ownership as a prerequisite to citizenship was tied to the British notion that only people who *owned* the country, not merely those who *lived* in it, were eligible to make decisions about it.[4]

The salience of property often is missed in our understanding of the USA as a nation. Conflated with democracy, capitalism slides into the background of our understanding of the way in which US political and economic ideology are entangled and read as synonymous. But it is this foundation of property rights that make civil rights legislation so painfully slow and sometimes ineffective. Civil rights are wedded to the construction of the rights of the individual. Bell (1987) argues that "the concept of individual rights, unconnected to property rights, was totally foreign to these men of property," (p. 239) in his explanation of how men who expressed a commitment to liberty and justice could uphold the repression of African Americans, the indigenous peoples who inhabited the land, and women.

African Americans represented a particular conundrum because not only were they not accorded individual civil rights because they were not White and owned no property, but also that they were constructed *as* property! However, that construction was only in the sense that they could be owned by others. They possessed no rights of property ownership. Whites, on the other hand, according to Harris (1993), benefited from the construction of whiteness as the ultimate property. "Possession – the act necessary to lay basis for rights in property – was defined to include only the cultural practices of Whites. This definition laid the foundation for the idea that whiteness – that which Whites alone possess – is valuable and is property" (p. 1721).

This thematic strand of whiteness as property in the USA is not confined to the nation's early history. Indeed, Andrew Hacker's (1992) exercise with his college students illustrates the material and social value the students place on their possession of whiteness. Hacker uses a parable to illustrate that although the students insist that "in this day and age, things are better for Blacks" (p. 31), none of them would want to change places with African Americans. When asked what amount of compensation they would seek if they were forced to "become Black," the students "seemed to feel that it would not be out of place to ask for $50 million, or $1 million for each coming Black year" (p. 32). According to Hacker:

> And this calculation conveys, as well as anything, the value that white people place on their own skins. Indeed, to be white is to possess a gift whose value can be appreciated only after it has been taken away. And why ask so large a sum? . . . The money would be used, as best it could, to buy protection from the discriminations and dangers white people know they would face once they were perceived to be black.
>
> (p. 32)

Thus, even without the use of a sophisticated legal rhetorical argument, Whites know they possess a property that people of color do not and that to possess it confers, aspects of citizenship not available to others. Harris's (1993) argument is that the "property functions of whiteness" (p. 1731) – rights of disposition, rights to use and enjoyment, reputation and status property, and the absolute right to exclude – make the American dream of "life, liberty, and the pursuit of happiness" a more likely and attainable reality for Whites as citizens. This reality also is more likely to engender feelings of loyalty and commitment to a nation that works in the interests of Whites. Conversely, Blacks, aware that they will never possess this ultimate property, are less sanguine about US citizenship.

Patricia Williams (1995) explains these differential notions of citizenship as being grounded in differential experiences of rights because "one's sense of empowerment defines one's relation to law, in terms of trust–distrust, formality–informality, or right–no rights (or 'needs')" (pp. 87–8). An example of this differing relation (in this case to commerce) was shared in one of my classes. We were discussing McIntosh's (1990) article on "White privilege." One White woman shared a personal experience of going into a neighborhood supermarket, having her items rung up by the cashier, and discovering that she did not have her checkbook. The cashier told her she could take her groceries and bring the check back later. When she related this story to an African American male friend, he told her that was an example of the privilege she enjoyed because she was White. Her White property was collateral against the cart full of groceries. She insisted that this was the store's good neighbor policy, and the same thing would have happened to him. Determined to show his friend that their life experiences were qualitatively different, the young man went shopping a few days later and pretended to have left his checkbook. The young woman was standing off to the side observing the interaction. The same cashier, who had been pointed out by the woman as the "neighborly one," told the young African American man that he could push the grocery items to the side while he went home to get his checkbook. The White woman was shocked as the African American male gave her a knowing look.

These daily indignities take their toll on people of color. When these indignities are skimmed over in the classrooms that purport to develop students into citizens, it is no wonder students "blow off" classroom discourse. How can students be expected to deconstruct rights, "in a world of no rights" (Williams, 1995, p. 98) and construct statements of need "in a world of abundantly apparent need?" (p. 89).

African Americans, thus, represent a unique form of citizen in the USA – property transformed into citizen. This process has not been a smooth one. When Chief Justice Taney concluded in the *Dred Scott* decision that African Americans had no rights that Whites were required to respect, he reinscribed the person-as-property status of African Americans. Later in *Plessy* vs *Ferguson* the high court once again denied full citizenship rights to African Americans as a way to assert White property rights – rights to use and enjoy and the absolute right to exclude.

Even the laudable decision of *Brown* vs *Board of Education* comes under scrutiny in the CRT paradigm. Lest we misread *Brown* vs *Board of Education* as merely a pang of conscience and the triumph of right over wrong, it is important to set *Brown* in context. First, historically the *Brown* decision helped the USA in its struggle to minimize the spread of communism to so-called Third World nations. In many countries, the credibility of the USA had been damaged by the widely broadcast inequitable social conditions that existed in the USA in the 1950s. Both the government and the NAACP lawyers argued the *Brown* decision would help legitimize the political and economic philosophies of the USA with these developing nations (Bell, 1980).

Second, *Brown* provided reassurance to African Americans that the struggle for freedom and equality fought for during the Second World War might become a reality at home. Black veterans faced not only racial inequality, but also physical harm in many parts of the South. And, the treatment of African Americans after the war in concert with the voice of African American leaders such as Paul Robeson may have greatly influenced the *Brown* decision. Robeson argued:

> It is unthinkable . . . that American Negroes [*sic*] would go to war on behalf of those who have oppressed us for generations . . . against a country [the Soviet Union] which in one generation has raised our people to the full human dignity of mankind.
>
> (Foner, 1978, pp. 17–18)

According to Bell (1980), it is not unreasonable to assume that those in positions of power would recognize the importance of neutralizing Robeson and others who held similar views. Robeson's comments were an affront to the "national interests." Thus, racial decisions by the courts were pivotal in softening the criticism about the contradiction of a free and just nation that maintained a segment of its citizenry in second-class status based on race. Finally, there were White capitalists who understood that the South could be transformed from an Agrarian society to an industrialized sunbelt only when it ended the divisive battle over state-supported segregation. Here, segregation was read as a barrier obstructing the economic self-interest of US profit makers.

At this writing, the electorate of California have passed Proposition 209, calling for an end to "preferential treatment" in state employment and state university admission policies based on race or gender. The trope of preferential treatment has help create a perception that ending affirmative action will lead to a more fair and equitable society, while, in reality, the proposition will be used to instantiate the hierarchical relations of power that once again privilege whiteness as the most valued property. Citizenship for people of color remains elusive.

Critical race theoretical approaches to education

Thus far in this chapter I have attempted to explain the meaning and historical background of CRT in legal scholarship and the role of property rights in understanding citizenship. However, educators and researchers in the field of education will want to know what relevance CRT has to education. The connections between law and education are relatively simple to establish. Since education in the USA is not outlined explicitly in the nation's constitution, it is one of the social functions relegated to individual states. Consequently, states generate legislation and enact laws designed to proscribe the contours of education.

One of the earliest legislative attempts was Massachusetts' "old deluder Satan" act that required citizens of the state to provide education for its children to insure they received moral and religious instruction. In the modern era the intersection of school and law provided fertile ground for testing and enacting civil rights legislation. Thus, the landmark *Brown* decision generated a spate of school desegregation of Central High School in Little Rock, Arkansas, the New Orleans Public Schools, the University of Mississippi, the University of Alabama, and the University of Georgia. By the 1970s, school desegregation/civil rights battles were being fought in northern cities. The fight for school desegregation in Boston schools was among the most vicious in civil rights annals.

One recurring theme that characterized the school/civil rights legal battles was "equal opportunity." This notion of equal opportunity was associated with the idea that students of color should have access to the same school opportunities, that is, curriculum, instruction, funding, facilities as White students. This emphasis on "sameness" was important because it helped boost the arguments for "equal treatment under the law" that were important for moving African Americans from their second-class status.

But what was necessary to help African Americans to "catch up" with their White counterparts? Beyond equal treatment was the need to redress pass inequities. Thus, there was a move toward affirmative action and the creation of African Americans and other marginalized groups as "protected classes" to insure that they were not systematically screened out of opportunities in employment, college admission, and housing. If we look at the way that public education is currently configured, it is possible to see the ways that CRT can be a powerful explanatory tool for the sustained inequity that people of color experience. I will use the areas of curriculum, instruction, assessment, school funding, and desegregation as exemplars of the relationship that can exist between CRT and education.

Curriculum

CRT sees the official school curriculum as a culturally specific artifact designed to maintain a White supremacist master script. As Swartz (1992) contends:

> Master scripting silences multiple voices and perspectives, primarily legitimizing dominant, white, upper-class, male voicings as the "standard" knowledge students need to know. All other accounts and perspectives are omitted from the master script unless they can be disempowered through misrepresentation. Thus, content that does not reflect the dominant voice must be brought under control, *mastered*, and then reshaped before it can become a part of the master script.
> (p. 341)

This master scripting means stories of African Americans are muted and erased when they challenge dominant culture authority and power. Thus, Rosa Parks is reduced to a tired seamstress instead of a long-time participant in social justice endeavors as evidenced by her work at the Highlander Folk School to prepare for a confrontation with segregationist ideology. Or, Martin Luther King, Jr becomes a sanitized folk hero who enjoyed the full support of "good Americans" rather than a disdained scholar and activist whose vision extended to social justice causes throughout the world and challenged the USA on issues of economic injustice and aggression in Southeast Asia.

The race-neutral or colorblind perspective, evident in the way the curriculum presents people of color, presumes a homogenized "we" in a celebration of diversity. This perspective embraces a so-called multicultural perspective by "misequating the middle passage with Ellis Island" (King, 1992, p. 327). Thus, students are taught erroneously that "we are all immigrants," and, as a result, African American, Indigenous, and Chicano students are left with the guilt of failing to rise above their immigrant status like "every other group."

But it is not just the distortions, omissions, and stereotypes of school curriculum content that must be considered, it also is the rigor of the curriculum and access to what is deemed "enriched" curriculum via gifted and talented courses and classes. As Jonathan Kozol (1991) describes:

> The curriculum [the white school] follows "emphasizes critical thinking, reasoning and logic." The planetarium, for instance, is employed not simply

for the study of the universe as it exists. "Children also are designing their own galaxies," the teacher says.

(p. 96)

In my [Kozol's] notes: "Six girls, four boys. Nine White, one Chinese. I am glad they have this class. But what about the others? Aren't there ten Black children in the school who could *enjoy* this also?"

This restricted access to the curriculum is a good illustration of Harris's (1993) explanation of the function of property in terms of use and enjoyment.

Instruction

CRT suggests that current instructional strategies presume that African American students are deficient. As a consequence, classroom teachers are engaged in a never-ending quest for "*the* right strategy or technique" to deal with (read: control) "at-risk" (read: African American) students. Cast in a language of failure, instructional approaches for African American students typically involve some aspect of remediation.

This race-neutral perspective purports to see deficiency as an individual phenomenon. Thus, instruction is conceived as a generic set of teaching skills that should work for all students. When these strategies or skills fail to achieve desired results, the students, not the techniques, are found to be lacking.

Fortunately, new research efforts are rejecting deficit models and investigating and affirming the integrity of effective teachers of African American students.[5] This scholarship underscores the teachers' understanding of the saliency of race in education and the society, and it underscores the need to make racism explicit so that students can recognize and struggle against this particular form of oppression.

Examples of counterpedagogical moves are found in the work of both Chicago elementary teacher Marva Collins and Los Angeles high school mathematics teacher Jaime Escalante. While neither Collins nor Escalante is acclaimed as a "progressive" teacher, both are recognized for their persistence in believing in the educability of all students. Both remind students that mainstream society expects them to be failures and prod the students to succeed as a form of counterinsurgency. Their insistence on helping students achieve in the "traditional" curriculum represents a twist on Audre Lorde's notion that one cannot dismantle the master's house with the master's tools. Instead, they believe one can only dismantle the master's house with the master's tools.

Assessment

For the critical race theorist, intelligence testing has been a movement to legitimize African American student deficiency under the guise of scientific rationalism (Gould, 1981; Alienikoff, 1991). According to Marable (1983), one purpose of the African American in the racial/capitalist state is to serve as a symbolic index for poor Whites. If the working-class White is "achieving" at a higher level than Blacks, then they feel relatively superior. This allows Whites with real power to exploit both poor Whites and Blacks. Throughout US history, the subordination of Blacks has been built on "scientific" theories (e.g. intelligence testing) that depend on racial stereotypes about Blacks that make their condition appear appropriate. Crenshaw (1988) contends that the point of controversy is no longer that these stereotypes were developed to rationalize the oppression of Blacks, but rather, "[T]he extent to which these stereotypes serve a hegemonic function by perpetuating a mythology about both Blacks and Whites even today, reinforcing an illusion of a White community that cuts across ethnic, gender, and class lines" (p. 1371).

In the classroom, a dysfunctional curriculum coupled with a lack of instructional innovation (or persistence) adds up to poor performance on traditional assessment measures. These assessment measures – crude by most analyses – may tell us that students do not know what is on the test, but fail to tell us what students actually know and are able to do. A telling example of this mismatch between what schools measure and what students know and can do is that of a 10-year-old African American girl who was repeatedly told by the teacher that she was a poor math student. However, the teacher was unaware that the girl was living under incredible stresses where she was assuming responsibilities her drugaddicted mother could not. To ward off child welfare agents the child handled all household responsibilities, including budgeting and paying all the household bills. Her ability to keep the household going made it appear that everything was fine in the household. According to the teacher, she could not do fourth-grade math, but the evidence of her life suggests she was doing just fine at "adult" math!

School funding

Perhaps no area of schooling underscores inequity and racism better than school funding. CRT argues that inequality in school funding is a function of institutional and structural racism. The inability of African Americans to qualify for educational advancements, jobs, and mortgages creates a cycle of low educational achievement, underemployment and unemployment, and standard housing. Without suffering a single act of personal racism, most African Americans suffer the consequence of systemic and structural racism.[6]

Jonathan Kozol's *Savage inequalities* (1991) created an emotional and ethical stir within and beyond the education community. White colleagues talked of how moved both they and their students were as they read Kozol's descriptions of inequity in school settings. Some talked of being "moved to tears" and "unable to read more than a few pages at a time." Others talked of how difficult it was for their students to read the book. Interestingly, many African American colleagues indicated that although Kozol had been precise and passionate in his documentation, he had not revealed anything new about the differences that exist between African American and White schools. But, Kozol's research did give voice to people of color. His analysis of funding inequities provides insight into the impact of racism and White self-interest on school funding policies.

CRT argues that the import of property provides another way to consider the funding disparity. Schooling, as a function of individual states, is differentially administered by the various state legislatures. But, one of the most common aspects of these fifty different schooling agencies is the way they are funded. Almost every state funds schools based on property taxes. Those areas with property of greater wealth typically have better funded schools. In the appendix of Kozol's book are comparisons showing the disparities within three different areas. In the Chicago area, for the 1988–89 school year, the funding disparity was an almost a $4,000 per pupil difference. Chicago schools were spending $5,265 per pupil, while the suburban Niles Township High School District was spending $9,371. In the New Jersey area the differences between Camden Schools and

Princeton Schools was about $4,200 in per pupil spending. In the New York City area the difference was almost $6,000 in per pupil spending.

Talking about the disparity between per pupil spending often invites the critique that money doesn't matter. Studies as far back as Coleman *et al.* (1966) and Jencks *et al.* (1972) have argued that family and individual effects are far more powerful than schools in determining poor school performance. Whether or not school spending is a determining factor in school achievement, no one from the family and individual effects camp can mount an ethical case for allowing poor children to languish in unheated, overcrowded schools with bathrooms that spew raw sewage while middle-income White students attend school in spacious, technology rich, inviting buildings. If money doesn't matter, then why spend it on the rich?

CRT takes to task school reformers who fail to recognize that property is a powerful determinant of academic advantage. Without a commitment to redesign funding formulas, one of the basic inequities of schooling will remain in place and virtually guarantee the reproduction of the status quo.

Desegregation

Although desegregation is not occurring in every school district, its impact on the national level is important enough to be included with the more common school experiences of curriculum, instruction, assessment, and funding. Despite the recorded history of the fight for school desegregation, CRT scholars argue that rather than serving as a solution to social inequity, school desegregation has been promoted only in ways that advantage Whites (Bell, 1990).

Lomotey and Staley's (1990) examination of Buffalo's "model desegregation" program revealed that African American students continued to be poorly served by the school system. African American student achievement failed to improve, while suspension, expulsion, and dropout rates continued to rise. What, then, made Buffalo a model desegregation program? In short, the answer is the benefits that Whites derived from the program and their seeming support of desegregation. As a result of the school desegregation program, Whites were able to take advantage of special magnet school programs and free extended childcare. Thus, the dominant logic is that a model desegregation program is one that insures that Whites are happy (and do not leave the system altogether).

The report of school desegregation in Buffalo is not unlike the allegorical story presented by CRT dean, Derrick Bell (1987). The story, entitled "The sacrificed Black children," illustrates how the failure to accept African American children into their community schools causes a White school district to ultimately end up begging the students to come because their presence was intimately tied to the economic prosperity of the community. It is this realization that civil rights legislation in the USA always has benefited Whites (even if it has not always benefited African Americans) that forms the crux of the CRT argument against traditional liberal civil rights legislation. The CRT argument provides an important segue into the final section of this chapter – the need for caution in proceeding with the integration of CRT into educational research.

Words of caution

It is the pattern in educational research for a new idea or innovation to take hold and proliferate. Sometimes an idea takes a while to take root, but once it does, most likely its creators lose control of the idea. Consider what happened with the notion of cooperative learning. When Cohen and Roper (1972) proposed cooperative classroom structures to equalize the status of White and African American students, their work held great promise for helping teacher to develop curricular and instructional strategies for improving the academic performance of all children in desegregated classrooms. However, somehow their findings got distilled into day-long workshops and five-step lesson plans. School systems throughout the USA were adopting cooperative learning without any thought to improving the performance of children of color.

A similar transmutation of theory is occurring in the area of multicultural education. Although scholars such as James Banks, Carl Grant, and Geneva Gay[7] began on a scholarly path designed to change schools as institutions so that students might be prepared to reconstruct the society, in its current practice iteration, multicultural education is but a shadow of its conceptual self. Rather than engage students in provocative thinking about the contradictions of US ideals and lived realities, teachers often find themselves encouraging students to sing "ethnic" songs, eat ethnic foods, and do ethnic dances. Consistently, manifestations of multicultural education in the classroom are superficial and trivial "celebrations of diversity."

What, then, might happen to CRT in the hands of educational researchers and school personnel? Well, to be honest, like Lani Guinier, I doubt if it will go very far into the mainstream. Rather, CRT in education is likely to become the "darling" of the radical left, continue to generate scholarly papers and debate, and never penetrate the classrooms and daily experiences of students of color. But, students of color, their families, and communities cannot afford the luxury of CRT scholars' ruminations any more than they could afford those of critical and postmodern theorists, where the ideas are laudable but the practice leaves much to be desired.

As excited as I may be about the potential of CRT for illuminating our thinking about school inequity, I believe educational researchers need much more time to study and understand the legal literature in which it is situated. It is very tempting to appropriate CRT as a more powerful explanatory narrative for the persistent problems of race, racism, and social injustice. If we are serious about solving these problems in schools and classrooms, we have to be serious about intense study and careful rethinking of race and education. Adopting and adapting CRT as a framework for educational equity means that we will have to expose racism in education *and* propose radical solutions for addressing it. We will have to take bold and sometimes unpopular positions. We may be pilloried figuratively or, at least, vilified for these stands. Ultimately, we may have to stand, symbolically, before the nation as Lani Guinier and hear our ideas distorted and misrepresented. We may have to defend a radical approach to democracy that seriously undermines the privilege of those who have so skillfully carved that privilege into the foundation of the nation. We will have to adopt a position of consistently swimming against the current. We run the risk of being permanent outsiders, but, as Wynter (1992) suggests, we must operate from a position of *alerity* or *liminality* where we may "call into question the rules of functioning on whose basis the United States conceptualizes itself as a generically 'White' nation, and elaborate its present system of societal self-knowledge" (p. 19). But, I fear we (educational researchers) may never assume the liminal position because of its dangers, its discomfort, and because we insist on thinking of ourselves as permanent residents in a *nice* field like education.

Notes

1   For a richer description of CRT, see Tate (1997).
2   Scholars such as Peggy McIntosh (1990) and Ruth Frankenberg (1993) have begun to deconstruct whiteness through their position of otherness as women. Their work suggests possibilities for Whites to deploy a CRT analysis.
3   Williams is known for her Benetton story where she was locked out of the trendy clothing store in New York because of her race. Some doubted the "generalizability" of Williams story until television personality Oprah Winfrey reported a similar incident. Bell's "Space Traders' " story is an allegorical tale that suggests that White America would gladly "give away" African Americans to space aliens if the aliens made a good enough trade.
4   Of course in America the concept of "ownership" of the land has to be contested by the indigenous people's rights to that land. However, that discussion is beyond the scope of this one.
5   See for example, Foster and Newman (1989), Henry (1992), and Ladson-Billings (1995).
6   The impact of racism generally is tied to the everyday lives of poor and underclass people of color. Recently, revelations of major US corporations (e.g. Texaco and Avis) indicate that they systematically perpetuate racism in hiring, promotion, and customer service.
7   Banks, Grant, and Gay are but a few of the notables who were in the forefront of the intellectual genesis of multicultural education. Gwendolyn Baker, Carlos Cortez, and Margaret Gibson are others. Any attempt to name them all would fall short.

References

Alienikoff, T. A. (1991). A case for race-consciousness. *Columbia Law Review*, 91, 1060–1125.
Barnes, R. (1990). Race consciousness: the thematic content of racial distinctiveness in critical race scholarship. *Harvard Law Review*, 103, 1864–71.
Bell, D. (1980). *Brown* and the interest-convergence dilemma. In D. Bell (ed.), *Shades of Brown: New Perspectives on School Desegregation* (pp. 90–106). New York: Teachers College Press.
—— (1987). *And We are Not Saved: The Elusive Quest for Racial Justice.* New York: Basic Books.
—— (1992). *Faces at the Bottom of the Well.* New York: Basic Books.
Carter, K. (1993). The place of story in the study of teaching and teacher education. *Educational Researcher*, 22 (1), 5–12.
Cohen, E. G. and Roper, S. S. (1972). Modification on interracial interaction disability: an application of status characteristics theory. *American Sociological Review*, 37, 643–57.
Coleman, J. S., Campbell, E. G., Hobson, C. J., McPartland, J., Mood, A. M., Weinfeld, F. D. and York, R. L. (1966). *Equality of Educational Opportunity.* Washington, DC: US Government Printing Office.
Connelly, F. M. and Clandinin, D. J. (1990). Stories of experience and narrative inquiry. *Educational Researcher*, 19 (5), 2–14.
Crenshaw, K. (1988). Race, reform, and retrenchment: transformation and legitimation in antidiscrimination law. *Harvard Law Review*, 101 (7), 1331–87.
Crenshaw, K., Gotanda, N., Peller, G., and Thomas, K. (eds.) (1995). *Critical Race Theory: The Key Writings that Formed the Movement.* New York: Free Press.
Delgado, R. (1989). Symposium: Legal storytelling. *Michigan Law Review*, 87, 2073.
—— (1990). When a story is just a story: does voice really matter? *Virginia Law Review*, 76, 95–111.
—— (1991). Brewer's plea: critical thoughts on common cause. *Vanderbilt Law Review*, 44, 1–14.
—— (ed.). (1995). *Critical Race Theory: The Cutting Edge.* Philadelphia: Temple University Press.

Delpit, L. (1988). The silenced dialogue: power and pedagogy in educating other people's children. *Harvard Educational Review*, 58, 280–98.

Foner, P. (ed.). (1978). *Paul Robeson Speaks*. New York: Citadel Press.

Foster, M. and Newman, J. (1989). "I don't know nothin' about it": Black teachers' code-switching strategies in interviews. *Working papers in educational linguistics* (WPEL). Philadelphia: Graduate School of Education, University of Pennsylvania.

Frankenberg, R. (1993). *White Women, Race Matters: The Social Construction of Whiteness*. Minneapolis: University of Minnesota Press.

Gordon, R. (1990). New developments in legal theory. In D. Kairys (ed.), *The Politics of Law: A Progressive Critique* (pp. 413–25). New York: Pantheon Books.

Gould, S. J. (1981). *The Mismeasure of Man*. New York: W. W. Norton.

Gramsci, A. (1971). Selections from the prison notebooks. Q. Hoare and G. N. Smith (eds. and trans.) New York: International Publishers.

Guinier, L. (1991). No two seats: the elusive quest for political equality. *Virginia Law Review*, 77, 1413–514.

—— (1994). *The Tyranny of the Majority: Fundamental Fairness is Representative Democracy*. New York: Free Press.

Guy-Sheftall, B. (1993 April). *Black Feminist Perspective on the Academy*. Paper presented at the annual meeting of the American Educational Research Association, Atlanta.

Hacker, A. (1992). *Two Nations: Black and White, Separate, Hostile, Unequal*. New York: Ballantine Books.

Haney López, I. (1995). White by law. In R. Delgado (ed.), *Critical Race Theory: The Cutting Edge* (pp. 542–50). Philadelphia: Temple University Press.

Harris, C. (1993). Whiteness as property. *Harvard Law Review*, 106, 1707–91.

Henry, A. (1992). African Canadian women teachers' activism: recreating communities of caring and resistance. *Journal of Negro Education*, 61, 392–404.

Jencks, C., Smith, M., Acland, H., Bane, M. J., Cohen, D., Gintis, H., Heyns, B., and Michelson, S. (1972). *Inequality: A Reassessment of the Effect of Family and Schooling in America*. New York: Basic Books.

King, J. (1992). Diaspora literacy and consciousness in the struggle against miseducation in the Black community. *Journal of Negro Education*, 61, 317–40.

—— (1995). Culture-centered knowledge: Black studies, curriculum transformation, and social action. In J. Banks and C. M. Banks (eds.), *Handbook of Research on Multicultural Education* (pp. 265–90). New York: Macmillan.

Kozol, J. (1991). *Savage Inequalities*. New York: Basic Books.

Ladson-Billings, G. (1995). "But that's just good teaching!" The case for culturally relevant teaching. *Theory Into Practice*, 34, 159–65.

Ladson-Billings, G. and Tate, W. F. (1995). Toward a critical race theory of education. *Teachers College Record*, 97, 47–68.

Lawrence, C. (1987). The id, the ego, and equal protection: reckoning with unconscious-racism. *Stanford Law Review*, 39, 317–88.

—— (1995). The word and the river: pedagogy as scholarship and struggle. In K. Crenshaw, N. Gotanda, G. Peller, and K. Thomas (eds), *Critical Race Theory: The Key Writings that Formed the Movement* (pp. 336–51). New York: Free Press.

Lee, S. M. (1993). Racial classifications in the US census: 1890–1990. *Ethnic and Racial Studies*, 16, 75–94.

Lomotey, K. and Staley, J. (1990, April). *The Education of African Americans in Buffalo Public Schools*. Paper presented at the annual meeting of the American Research Association, Boston.

Lopez, I. H. (1995). The social construction of race. In R. Delgado (ed.), *Critical Race Theory: The Cutting Edge* (pp. 191–203). Philadelphia: Temple University Press.

McIntosh, P. (1990). White privilege: unpacking the invisible knapsack. *Independent School*, Winter, 31–6.

Marable, M. (1983). *How Capitalism Underdeveloped Black America*. Boston: South End Press.

Matsuda, M. (1989). Public response to racist speech: considering the victim's story. *Michigan Law Review*, 87, 2320–81.

Monaghan, P. (1993, June 23). "Critical race theory" questions the role of legal doctrine in racial inequity. *Chronicle of Higher Education*, A7, A9.

Morrison, T. (1992). *Playing in the Dark: Whiteness and the Literary Imagination.* Cambridge, MA: Harvard University Press.

Omi, M. and Winant, H. (1993). *Racial Formation in the United States from the 1960s to the 1990s* (2nd ed.). New York: Routledge.

O'Neill, M. (1992). Teaching literature as cultural criticism. *English Quarterly,* 25 (1), 19–24.

Roediger, D. (1991). *The Wages of Whiteness: Race and the Making of the American Working Class.* London: Verso.

Swartz, E. (1992). Emancipatory narratives: rewriting the master script in the school curriculum. *Journal of Negro Education,* 61, 341–55.

Tate, W. (1997). Critical Race Theory and education: history, theory, and implications. In M. Apple (ed.), *Review of Research in Education,* 2 (pp. 191–243). Washington, DC: American Educational Research Association.

West, C. (1992, Aug. 2). Learning to talk of race. *New York Times Magazine,* 24, 26.

—— (1993). *Keeping Faith.* New York: Routledge.

Williams, G. H. (1995). *Life on the Color Line.* New York: Plume.

Williams, P. (1991). *The Alchemy of Race and Rights: Diary of a Law Professor.* Cambridge, MA: Harvard University Press.

—— (1995). Alchemical notes: reconstructing ideals from deconstructed rights. In R. Delgado (ed.), *Critical Race Theory: The Cutting Edge* (pp. 84–94). Philadelphia: Temple University Press.

Wynter, S. (1992). *"Do not call us Negros": How Multicultural Textbooks Perpetuate Racism.* San Francisco: Aspire.

PART II

IDENTITIES
Race, ethnicity, class, gender, sexuality

CHAPTER 5

DYSCONSCIOUS RACISM
Ideology, identity, and the miseducation of teachers

Joyce E. King

In Lynda Stone (ed.) *The Education Feminism Reader*, New York: Routledge, pp. 336–48, 1991

They had for more than a century before been regarded as . . . so far inferior . . . that the negro might justly and lawfully be reduced to slavery for his benefit. . . . This opinion was at that time fixed and universal in the civilized portion of the white race. It was regarded as an axiom in morals as well as in politics, which no one thought of disputing . . . and men in every grade and position in society daily and habitually acted upon it . . . without doubting for a moment the correctness of this opinion.

(Dred Scott vs *Sanford*, 1857)

Racism can mean culturally sanctioned beliefs which, regardless of the intentions involved, defend the advantages whites have because of the subordinated positions of racial minorities.

(Wellman, 1977, p. xviii)

The goal of critical consciousness is an ethical and not a legal judgement about the social order.

(Heaney, 1984, p. 116)

Celebrating diversity

The new watchwords in education, "celebrating diversity," imply the democratic ethic that all students, regardless of their sociocultural backgrounds, should be educated equitably. What this ethic means in practice, particularly for teachers with little personal experience of diversity and limited understanding of inequity, is problematic. At the elite private Jesuit university where I teach, most of my students (most of whom come from relatively privileged, monocultural backgrounds) are anxious about being able to deal with all the diversity in the classroom. Not surprisingly, given recent neoconservative ideological interpretations of the problem of diversity, many of my students also believe that affirming cultural difference is tantamount to racial separatism, that diversity threatens national unity, or that social inequity originates with sociocultural deficits and not with unequal outcomes that are inherent in our socially stratified society. With respect to this society's changing demographics and the inevitable "browning" of America, many of my students foresee a diminution of their own identity, status, and security. Moreover, regardless of their conscious intentions, certain culturally sanctioned beliefs my students hold about inequity and why it persists, especially for African Americans, take White norms and privilege as givens.

The findings presented herein will show what these beliefs and responses have to do with what I call "dysconscious racism" to denote the limited and distorted understandings my students have about inequity and cultural diversity – understandings that make it difficult for them to act in favor of truly equitable education. This chapter presents a qualitative analysis of dysconscious racism as reflected in the responses of my teacher education students to an open-ended question I posed at the beginning of one of my classes during the fall 1986 academic quarter to assess student knowledge and understanding of social inequity. Content analysis of their short essay responses will show how their thinking reflects internalized ideologies that both justify the racial status quo and devalue cultural diversity. Following the analysis of their responses and discussion of the findings, I will describe the teaching approach I use to counteract the cognitively limited and distorted thinking that dysconscious racism represents. The concluding discussion will focus on the need to make social reconstructionist liberatory teaching an option for teacher education students like mine who often begin their professional preparation without having ever considered the need for fundamental social changes (see also Ginsburg and Newman, 1985; and Ginsburg, 1988).

Critical, transformative teachers must develop a pedagogy of social action and advocacy that really celebrates *diversity*, not just random holidays, isolated cultural artifacts, or "festivals and food" (Ayers, 1988). If dysconscious racism keeps such a commitment beyond the imagination of students like mine, teacher educators need forms of pedagogy and counterknowledge that challenge students' internalized ideologies and subjective identities (Giroux and McLaren, 1986). Prospective teachers need both an intellectual understanding of schooling and inequity as well as self-reflective, transformative emotional growth experiences. With these objectives in mind, I teach my graduate-level Social Foundations of Education course in the social reconstructionist tradition of critical, transformative, liberatory education for social change (see Freire, 1971; Searle, 1975; Shor, 1980; Heaney, 1984; Gordon, 1985; Giroux and McLaren, 1986; Sleeter and Grant, 1988). In contrast to a pedagogy for the oppressed, this course explores the dynamics of a liberatory pedagogy for the elite. It is designed to provide such teacher education students with a context in which to consider alternative conceptions of themselves and society. The course challenges students' taken-for-granted ideological positions and identities and their unquestioned acceptance of cultural belief systems that undergird racial inequity.

Thus, the course and the teaching methods I use transcend conventional social and multicultural Foundations of Education course approaches by directly addressing societal oppression and student knowledge and beliefs about inequity and diversity. By focusing on ways that schooling, including their own miseducation, contributes to unequal educational outcomes that reinforce societal inequity and oppression, students broaden their knowledge of how society works. I offer this analysis of dysconscious racism and reflections on the way I teach to further the theoretical and practical development of a liberatory praxis that will enable teacher education students to examine what they know and believe about society, about diverse others, and about their own actions.

Discovering dysconscious racism

Dysconsciousness is an uncritical habit of mind (including perceptions, attitudes, assumptions, and beliefs) that justifies inequity and exploitation by accepting the existing order of things as given. If, as Heaney (1984) suggests, critical consciousness "involves an ethical judgement" about the social order, dysconsciousness accepts it uncritically. This lack of critical judgment against society reflects an absence of what Cox (1974) refers to as "social ethics"; it involves a subjective identification with an ideological viewpoint that admits no fundamentally alternative vision of society.[1]

Dysconscious racism is a form of racism that tacitly accepts dominant White norms and privileges. It is not the *absence* of consciousness (i.e. not unconsciousness) but an *impaired* consciousness or distorted way of thinking about race as compared to, for example, critical consciousness. Uncritical ways of thinking about racial inequity accept certain culturally sanctioned assumptions, myths, and beliefs that justify the social and economic advantages white people have as a result of subordinating diverse others (Wellman, 1977). Any serious challenge to the status quo that calls this racial privilege into question inevitably challenges the self-identity of white people who have internalized these ideological justifications. The reactions of my students to information I have presented about societal inequity have led me to conceptualize dysconscious racism as one form that racism takes in this post-civil rights era of intellectual conservatism.

Most of my students begin my Social Foundations course with limited knowledge and understanding of societal inequity. Not only are they often unaware of their own ideological perspectives (or of the range of alternatives they have not consciously considered), most are also unaware of how their own subjective identities reflect an uncritical identification with the existing social order. Moreover, they have difficulty explaining "liberal" and "conservative" standpoints on contemporary social and educational issues and are even less familiar with "radical" perspectives (King and Ladson-Billings, 1990). My students' explanations of persistent racial inequity consistently lack evidence of any critical ethical judgment regarding racial (and class/gender) stratification in the existing social order; yet, and not surprisingly, these same students generally maintain that they personally deplore racial prejudice and discrimination. Wellman (1977) notes, however, that this kind of thinking is a hallmark of racism. "The concrete problem facing white people," states Wellman "is how to come to grips with the demands made by blacks and whites while at the same time *avoiding* the possibility of institutional change and reorganization that might affect them" (p. 42). This suggests that the ability to imagine a society reorganized without racial privilege requires a fundamental shift in the way white people think about their status and self-identities and their conceptions of black people.

For example, when I broach the subject of racial inequity with my students, they often complain that they are "tired of being made to feel guilty" because they are white. The following entries from the classroom journals of two undergraduate students in an education course are typical of this reaction:[2]

> With some class discussions, readings, and other media, there have been times that I feel guilty for being white which really infuriates me because no one should feel guilty for the color of their skin or ethnic background. Perhaps my feelings are actually a discomfort for the fact that others have been discriminated against all of their life because of their color and I have not.

How can I be thankful that I am not a victim of discrimination? I should be ashamed. Then I become confused. Why shouldn't I be thankful that I have escaped such pain?

These students' reactions are understandable in light of Wellman's insights into the nature of racism. That white teacher education students often express such feelings of guilt and hostility suggests they accept certain unexamined assumptions, unasked questions, and unquestioned cultural myths regarding both the social order and their place in it. The discussion of the findings that follows will show how dysconscious racism, manifested in student explanations of societal inequity and linked to their conceptions of black people, devalues the cultural diversity of the black experience and, in effect, limits students' thinking about what teachers can do to promote equity.

The findings

Since the fall academic quarter 1986, I have given the student teachers in my Social Foundations course statistical comparisons such as those compiled by the Children's Defense Fund (Edelman, 1987) regarding black and white children's life chances (e.g. "Compared to White children, Black children are twice as likely to die in the first year of life"; see Harlan, 1985). I then ask each student to write a brief explanation of how these racial inequities came about by answering the question: "How did our society get to be this way?" An earlier publication (King and Ladson-Billings, 1990) comparing student responses to this question in the fall 1986 and spring 1987 quarters identifies three ways students explain this inequity. Content analysis of their responses reveals that students explain racial inequity as either the result of slavery (Category I), the denial or lack of equal opportunity for African Americans (Category II), or part of the framework of a society in which racism and discrimination are normative (Category III). In the present chapter, I will again use these categories and the method of content analysis to compare student responses collected in the 1986 and 1988 fall quarters. The responses presented here are representative of 22 essay responses collected from students in 1986 and 35 responses collected in 1988.

Category I explanations begin and end with slavery. Their focus is either on describing African Americans as "victims of their original (slave) status" or they assert that black/white inequality is the continuing result of inequity that began during slavery. In either case, historical determinism is a key feature; African Americans are perceived as ex-slaves, and the "disabilities of slavery" are believed to have been passed down intergenerationally. As two students wrote:

> I feel it dates back to the time of slavery when the Blacks were not permitted to work or really have a life of their own. They were not given the luxury or opportunity to be educated and *each generation passed this disability on* [italics added].
> (F6-21)[3]

> I think that this harkens back to the origin of the American Black population as slaves. Whereas other immigrant groups started on a low rung of our economic (and social class) ladder and had space and opportunity to move up, Blacks did not. They were perceived as somehow less than people. This view may have been passed down and even on to Black youth.
> (F8-32)

It is worth noting that the "fixed and universal beliefs" Europeans and white Americans held about black inferiority/white superiority during the epoch of the Atlantic slave trade, beliefs that made the enslavement of Africans seem justified and lawful, are not the focus of this kind of explanation. The historical continuum of cause and effect evident in Category I explanations excludes any consideration of the cultural rationality behind such attitudes; that is, they do not explain *why* white people held these beliefs.

In Category II explanations the emphasis is on the denial of equal opportunity to black people (e.g. less education, lack of jobs, low wages, poor health care). Although students espousing Category II arguments may explain discrimination as the result of prejudice or racist attitudes (e.g. "Whites believe blacks are inferior"), they do not necessarily causally link it to the historical fact of slavery or to the former status of black people as slaves. Rather, the persistently unequal status of African Americans is seen as an *effect* of poverty and systemic discrimination. Consider these two responses from 1986 and 1988:

> Blacks have been treated as second class citizens. Caucasians tend to maintain the belief that Black people are inferior . . . *for this reason* [italics added] Blacks receive less education and education that is of inferior quality . . . less pay than most other persons doing the same job; [and] live in inferior substandard housing, etc.
>
> (F6-3)

> Because of segregation – overt and covert – Blacks in America have had less access historically to education and jobs which has led to a poverty cycle for many. *The effects described are due to poverty* [italics added], lack of education and lack of opportunity.
>
> (F8-7)

In addition, some Category I and Category II explanations identify negative psychological or cultural characteristics of African Americans as effects of slavery, prejudice, racism, or discrimination. One such assertion is that black people have no motivation or incentive to "move up" or climb the socioeconomic ladder. Consequently, this negative characteristic is presumed to perpetuate racial inequality: like a vicious cycle, whites then perceive blacks as ignorant or as having "devalued cultural mores." The following are examples of Category II explanations; even though they allude to slavery, albeit in a secondary fashion, the existence of discrimination is the primary focus:

> Blacks were brought to the U.S. by Whites. They were/are thought to be of a "lower race" by large parts of the society . . . society has impressed these beliefs/ideas onto Blacks. [Therefore] Blacks probably have lower self-esteem and when you have lower self-esteem, it is harder to move up in the world. . . . Blacks group together and stay together. Very few move up . . . partly because society put them there.
>
> (F6-18)

> Past history is at the base of the racial problems evident in today's society. Blacks have been persecuted and oppressed for years. . . . Discrimination is still a problem which results in lack of motivation, self-esteem and hence a lessened "desire" to escape the hardships with which they are faced.
>
> (F8-14)

In 1986 my students' responses were almost evenly divided between Category I and Category II explanations (10 and 11 responses, respectively, with one Category III response). In 1988 all 35 responses were divided between Category I (11) and Category II (24) responses, or 32 and 68 percent, respectively. Thus, the majority of students in both years explained racial inequality in limited ways – as a historically inevitable consequence of slavery or as a result of prejudice and discrimination – without recognizing the structural inequity built into the social order. Their explanations fail to link racial inequity to other forms of societal oppression and exploitation. In addition, these explanations, which give considerable attention to black people's negative characteristics, fail to account for white people's beliefs and attitudes that have long justified societal oppression and inequity in the form of racial slavery or discrimination.

Discussion

An obvious feature of Category I explanations is the devaluation of the African American cultural heritage, a heritage that certainly encompasses more than the debilitating experience of slavery. Moreover, the integrity and adaptive resilience of what Stuckey (1987) refers to as the "slave culture" is ignored and implicitly devalued. Indeed, Category I explanations reflect a conservative assimilationist ideology that blames contemporary racial inequity on the presumed cultural deficits of African Americans. Less obvious is the way the historical continuum of these explanations, beginning as they do with the effects of slavery on African Americans, fails to consider the specific cultural rationality that justified slavery as acceptable and lawful (Wynter, 1990). Also excluded from these explanations as possible contributing factors are the particular advantages white people gained from the institution of racial slavery.

Category II explanations devalue diversity by not recognizing how opportunity is tied to the assimilation of mainstream norms and values. These explanations also fail to call into question the basic structural inequity of the social order; instead, the cultural mythology of the American Dream, most specifically the myth of equal opportunity, is tacitly accepted (i.e. with the right opportunity, African Americans can climb out of poverty and "make it" like everyone else). Such liberal, assimilationist ideology ignores the widening gap between the haves and the have nots, the downward mobility of growing numbers of whites (particularly women with children), and other social realities of contemporary capitalism. While not altogether inaccurate, these explanations are nevertheless *partial* precisely because they fail to make appropriate connections between race, gender, and class inequity.

How do Category I and Category II explanations exemplify dysconscious racism? Both types defend white privilege, which, according to Wellman (1977), is a "consistent theme in racist thinking" (p. 39). For example, Category I explanations rationalize racial inequity by attributing it to the effects of slavery on African Americans while ignoring the economic advantages it gave whites. A second rationalization, presented in Category II explanations, engenders the mental picture many of my students apparently have of equal opportunity, not as equal access to jobs, health care, education, etc. but rather as a sort of "legal liberty" that leaves the structural basis of the racial status quo intact (King and Wilson, 1990). In effect, by failing to connect a more just opportunity system for blacks with fewer white-skin advantages for whites, these explanations, in actuality, defend the racial status quo.

According to Wellman, the existing social order cannot provide for unlimited (or equal) opportunity for black people while maintaining racial privileges for whites (p. 42). Thus, elimination of the societal hierarchy is inevitable if the social order is to be reorganized, but before this can occur, the existing structural inequity must be recognized as such and actively struggled against. This, however, is not what most of my students have in mind when they refer to "equal opportunity."

Category I and Category II explanations rationalize the existing social order in yet a third way by omitting any ethical judgment against the privileges white people have gained as a result of subordinating black people (and others). These explanations thus reveal a dysconscious racism that, although it bears little resemblance to the violent bigotry and overt white supremacist ideologies of previous eras, still takes for granted a system of racial privilege and societal stratification that favors whites. Like the whites of Dred Scott's era, few of my students even think of disputing this system or see it as disputable.

Category III explanations, on the other hand, do not defend this system. They are more comprehensive, and thus more accurate, because they make the appropriate connections between racism and other forms of inequity. Category III explanations also locate the origins of racial inequity in the framework of a society in which racial victimization is *normative*. They identify and criticize both racist ideology and oppressive societal structures without placing the responsibility for changing the situation solely on African Americans (e.g. to develop self-esteem) and without overemphasizing the role of white prejudice (e.g. whites' beliefs about black inferiority). The historical factors cited in Category III explanations neither deny white privilege nor defend it. I have received only one Category III response from a student at the beginning of my courses, the following:

> [Racial inequity] is primarily the result of the economic system . . . racism served the purposes of ruling groups; e.g., in the Reconstruction era . . . poor whites were pitted against Blacks – a pool of cheap exploitable labor is desired by capitalists and this ties in with the identifiable differences of races.
>
> (F6-9)

Why is it that more students do not think this way? Given the majority of my students' explanations of racial inequity, I suggest that their thinking is impaired by dysconscious racism – even though they may deny they are racists. The important point here, however, is not to prove that students are racist; rather, it is that their uncritical and limited ways of thinking must be identified, understood, and brought to their conscious awareness.

Dysconscious racism must be made the subject of educational intervention. Conventional analyses – which conceptualize racism at the institutional, cultural, or individual level but do not address the cognitive distortions of dysconsciousness – cannot help students distinguish between racist justifications of the status quo (which limit their thought, self-identity, and responsibility to take action) and socially unacceptable individual prejudice or bigotry (which students often disavow). Teacher educators must therefore challenge both liberal and conservative ideological thinking on these matters if we want students to consider seriously the need for fundamental change in society and in education.

Ideology, identity, and indoctrination are central concepts I use in my Social Foundations of Education course to help students free themselves from miseducation and uncritically accepted views that limit their thought and action. A brief description of the course follows.

The cultural politics of critiquing ideology and identity

One goal of my Social Foundations of Education course is to sharpen the ability of students to think critically about educational purposes and practice in relation to social justice and to their own identities as teachers. The course thus illuminates a range of ideological interests that become the focus of students' critical analysis, evaluation, and choice. For instance, a recurring theme in the course is that of the social purposes of schooling, or schooling as an instrument of educational philosophy, societal vision, values, and personal choice. This is a key concept about which many students report they have never thought seriously. Course readings, lectures, media resources, class discussions, and other experiential learning activities are organized to provide an alternative context of meaning within which students can critically analyze the social purposes of schooling. The range of ideological perspectives considered include alternative explanations of poverty and joblessness, competing viewpoints regarding the significance of cultural differences, and discussions of education as a remedy for societal inequity. Students consider the meaning of social justice and examine ways that education might be transformed to promote a more equitable social order. Moreover, they are expected to choose and declare the social changes they themselves want to bring about as teachers.

The course also introduces students to the critical perspective that education is not neutral; it can serve various political and cultural interests, including social control, socialization, assimilation, domination, or liberation (Freire, 1971; Cagan, 1978; O'Neill, 1981). Both impartial, purportedly factual information as well as openly partisan views about existing social realities such as the deindustrialization of America, hunger and homelessness, tracking, the "hidden" curriculum (Vallance, 1977; Anyon, 1981), the socialization of teachers, and teacher expectations (Rist, 1970) allow students to examine connections between macrosocial (societal) and microsocial (classroom) issues. This information helps students consider different viewpoints about how schooling processes contribute to inequity. Alongside encountering liberal and conservative analyses of education and opportunity, students encounter the scholarship of racial educators such as Anyon (1981), Freire (1971), Kozol (1981), and Giroux and McLaren (1986), who have developed "historical identities" (Boggs *et al.*, 1979) within social justice struggles and who take stronger ethical stances against inequity than do liberals or conservatives. These radical educators' perspectives also provide students with alternative role models; students discuss their thoughts and feelings about the convictions these authors express and reflect upon the soundness of racial arguments. Consequently, as students formulate their own philosophical positions about the purposes of education, they inevitably struggle with the ideas, values, and social interests at the heart of the different educational and social visions that they, as teachers of the future, must either affirm, reject, or resist.

Making a conscious process of the struggle over divergent educational principles and purposes constitutes the cultural politics of my Social Foundations course. In this regard my aim is to provide a context within which student teachers can recognize and evaluate their personal experiences of political and ethical indoctrination. In contrast to their own miseducation, and using their experience in my course as a point of comparison, I urge my students to consider the possibilities liberatory and transformative teaching offers. To facilitate this kind of conscious reflection, I discuss the teaching strategies, which I myself model in my efforts to help them think critically about the course content, their own worldview, and the professional practice of teaching (Freire and Faundez, 1989). To demonstrate the questions that critical, liberatory teachers must ask, and to make what counts as "school knowledge" (Anyon, 1981) problematic, I use Freire's (1971) strategy of developing "problem-posing" counterknowledge. For example, I pose biased instructional materials as a problem teachers address. Thus, when we examine the way textbooks represent labor history (Anyon, 1979) and my student teachers begin to realize all they do not know about the struggles of working people for justice, the problem of miseducation becomes more real to them. Indeed, as Freire, Woodson (1933), and others suggest, an alternative view of history often reveals hidden social interests in the curriculum and unmasks a political and cultural role of schooling of which my student teachers are often completely unaware.

Analysis of and reflection on their own knowledge and experience involves students in critiquing ideologies, examining the influences on their thinking and identities, and considering the kind of teachers they want to become. I also encourage my students to take a stance against mainstream views and practices that dominate in schools and other university courses. Through such intellectual and emotional growth opportunities, students in my course reexperience and reevaluate the partial and socially constructed nature of their own knowledge and identities.

My approach is not free from contradictions, however. While I alone organize the course structure, select the topics, make certain issues problematic, and assign the grades, I am confident that my approach is more democratic than the unwitting ideological indoctrination my students have apparently internalized. For a final grade, students have the option of writing a final exam in which they can critique the course, or they may present (to the class) a term project organized around an analytical framework they themselves generate.

Toward liberatory pedagogy in teacher education

Merely presenting factual information about societal inequity does not necessarily enable preservice teachers to examine the beliefs and assumptions that may influence the way they interpret these facts. Moreover, with few exceptions, available multicultural resource materials for teachers presume a value commitment and readiness for multicultural teaching and antiracist education that many students may lack initially (Brandt, 1986; Sleeter and Grant, 1988; Bennett, 1990). Teacher educators may find some support in new directions in adult education (Mezirow, 1984) and in theories of adult learning and critical literacy that draw upon Freire's work in particular (Freire and Macedo, 1987). This literature offers some useful theoretical insights for emancipatory education and liberatory pedagogy (Heaney, 1984). For example, the counterknowledge strategies I use in my Social Foundations course are designed to facilitate the kind of "perspective transformation" Mezirow (1984) calls for in his work. It is also worth noting that a tradition of critical African American educational scholarship exists that can be incorporated into teacher preparation courses. Analyses of miseducation by Woodson (1933), DuBois (1935), and Ellis (1917) are early forerunners of critical, liberatory pedagogy. This tradition is also reflected in contemporary African American thought and scholarship on education and social action (see Perkins, 1986; Childs, 1989; Gordon, 1990; Lee *et al.*, 1990; Muwakkil, 1990).

As Sleeter and Grant (1988, p. 194) point out, however, white students sometimes find such critical, liberatory approaches threatening to their self-concepts and identities. While they refer specifically to problems of white males in this regard, my experience is that most students from economically privileged, culturally homogeneous backgrounds are generally unaware of their intellectual biases and monocultural encapsulation. While my students may feel threatened by diversity, what they often express is guilt and hostility. Students who have lived for the most part in relatively privileged cultural isolation can only consider becoming liberatory, social-reconstructionist educators if they have both an adequate understanding of how society works and opportunities to think about the need for fundamental social change. The critical perspective of the social order offered in my course challenges students' worldviews as well as their self-identities by making problematic and directly addressing students' values, beliefs, and ideologies. Precisely because what my students know and believe is so limited, it is necessary to address both their knowledge (that is, their intellectual understanding of social inequity) and what they believe about diversity. As Angus and Jhally (1989, p. 12) conclude, "what people accept as natural and self-evident" is exactly what becomes "problematic and in need of explanation" from this critical standpoint. Thus, to seriously consider the value commitment involved in teaching for social change as an option, students need experiential opportunities to recognize and evaluate the ideological influences that shape their thinking about schooling, society, themselves, and diverse others.

The critique of ideology, identity, and miseducation described herein represents a form of cultural politics in teacher education that is needed to address the specific cultural rationality of social inequity in modern American society. Such a liberatory pedagogical approach does not neglect the dimension of power and privilege in society, nor does it ignore the role of ideology in shaping the context within which people think about daily life and the possibilities of social transformation. Pedagogy of this kind is especially needed now, given the current thrust toward normative schooling and curriculum content that emphasizes "our common Western heritage" (Bloom, 1987; Hirsch, 1987; Gagnon, 1988; Ravitch, 1990). Unfortunately, this neoconservative curriculum movement leaves little room for discussion of how being educated in this tradition may be a limiting factor in the effectiveness of teachers of poor and minority students (King and Wilson, 1990; Ladson-Billings, 1991). Indeed, it precludes any critical ethical judgment about societal inequity and supports the kind of miseducation that produces teachers who are dysconscious – uncritical and unprepared to question white norms, white superiority, and white privilege.

Myths and slogans about common heritage notwithstanding, prospective teachers need an alternative context in which to think critically about and reconstruct their social knowledge and self-identities. Simply put, they need opportunities to become conscious of oppression. However, as Heaney (1984) correctly observes: "Consciousness of oppression can not be the object of instruction, it must be discovered in experience" (p. 118). Classes such as my Social Foundations course make it possible for students to reexperience the way dysconscious racism and miseducation victimize them.

That dysconscious racism and miseducation of teachers are part of the problem is not well understood. This is evident in conventional foundations approaches and in the teacher education literature on multiculturalism and pluralism that examine social stratification, unequal educational outcomes, and the significance of culture in education but offer no critique of ideology and indoctrination (Gollnick and Chinn, 1990; Pai, 1990). Such approaches do not help prospective teachers gain the critical skills needed to examine the ways being educated in a racist society affects their own knowledge and their beliefs about themselves and culturally diverse others. The findings presented in this chapter suggest that such skills are vitally necessary. The real challenge of diversity is to develop a sound liberatory praxis of teacher education that offers relatively privileged students freedom to choose critical multicultural consciousness over dysconsciousness. Moving beyond dysconsciousness and miseducation toward liberatory pedagogy will require systematic research to determine how teachers are being prepared and how well those whose preparation includes critical liberatory pedagogy are able to maintain their perspectives and implement transformative goals in their own practice.

Notes

1 It should be noted that dysconsciousness need not be limited to racism but can apply to justifications of other forms of exploitation such as sexism or even neocolonialism – issues that are beyond the scope of the present analysis.
2 I want to thank Professor Gloria Ladson-Billings, who also teaches at my institution, for providing these journal entries. See her discussion of student knowledge and attitudes in *The Journal of Negro Education*, 60, 2, 1991.
3 This and subsequent student comment codes used throughout this chapter identify individual respondents within each cohort. "F6-21," for example, refers to respondent 21 in the fall 1986 academic quarter.

References

Angus, I. and S. Jhally (eds.) (1989). *Cultural Politics in Contemporary America*. New York: Routledge.
Anyon, J. (1979). Ideology and U.S. history textbooks. *Harvard Educational Review*, 49, 361–86.
—— (1981). Social class and school knowledge. *Curriculum Inquiry*, 11, 3–42.
Ayers, W. (1988). Young children and the problem of the color line. *Democracy and Education*, 3(1), 20–6.
Bennett, C. (1990). *Comprehensive Multicultural Education: Theory and Practice*. Boston: Allyn & Bacon.
Bloom, A. (1987). *The Closing of the American Mind*. New York: Simon & Schuster.
Boggs, J., G. L. Boggs, F. Paine and L. Paine (1979). *Conversations in Maine: Exploring our Nation's Future*. Boston: South End Press.
Brandt, G. (1986). *The Realization of Anti-Racist Teaching*. Philadelphia: The Falmer Press.
Cagan, E. (1978). Individualism, collectivism, and radical educational reform. *Harvard Educational Review*, 48, 227–66.
Childs, J. B. (1989). *Leadership, Conflict, and Cooperation in Afro-American Social Thought*. Philadelphia: Temple University Press.
Cox, G. O. (1974). *Education for the Black Race*. New York: African Heritage Studies Publishers.
DuBois, W. E. B. (1935). Does the Negro need separate schools? *Journal of Negro Education*, 4, 329–335.
Edelman, M. W. (1987). *Families in Peril: An Agenda for Social Change*. Cambridge, MA: Harvard University Press.
Ellis, G. W. (1917). Psychic factors in the new American race situation. *Journal of Race Development*, 4, 469–86.
Freire, P. (1971). *Pedagogy of the Oppressed*. New York: Harper & Row.
Freire, P. and A. Faundez (1989). *Learning to Question: A Pedagogy of Liberation*. New York: Continuum.

Freire, P. and D. Macedo (1987). *Literacy: Reading the Word and the World*. South Hadley, MA: Bergin & Garvey.

Gagnon, P. (1988, November). Why study history? *Atlantic Monthly*, pp. 43–66.

Ginsburg, M. (1988). *Contradictions in Teacher Education and Society: A Critical Analysis*. Philadelphia: Falmer Press.

Ginsburg, M. and K. Newman (1985). Social inequalities, schooling and teacher education. *Journal of Teacher Education*, 36, 49–54.

Giroux, J. and P. McLaren (1986). Teacher education and the politics of engagement: the case for democratic schooling. *Harvard Educational Review*, 56, 213–38.

Gollnick, D. and P. Chinn (1990). *Multicultural Education in a Pluralistic Society*. Columbus, OH: Merrill.

Gordon, B. (1985). Critical and emancipatory pedagogy: an annotated bibliography of sources for teachers. *Social Education*, 49(5), 400–2.

—— (1990). The necessity of African-American epistemology for educational theory and practice. *Journal of Education*, 172(3), 88–106.

Harlan, S. (1985, June 5). Compared to White children, Black children are . . . *USA Today*, 9-A.

Heaney, T. (1984). Action, freedom, and liberatory education. In S. B. Merriam (ed.), *Selected Writings on Philosophy and Education* (pp. 113–22). Malabar, Fla.: Robert E. Krieger.

Hirsch, E. D. (1987). *Cultural Literacy: What Every American Needs to Know*. New York: Houghton Mifflin.

King, J. and G. Ladson-Billings (1990). The teacher education challenge in elite university settings: developing critical and multicultural perspectives for teaching in a democratic and multicultural society. *European Journal of Intercultural Studies*, 1(2), 15–30.

King, J. and T. L. Wilson (1990). Being the soul-freeing substance: a legacy of hope in Afro humanity. *Journal of Education*, 172(2), 9–27.

Kozol, J. (1981). *On Being a Teacher*. New York: Continuum.

Ladson-Billings, G. (1991). Beyond multicultural illiteracy. *Journal of Negro Education*, 60(2), 147–57.

Lee, C. D., K. Lomotey and M. J. Shujaa (1990). How shall we sing our sacred song in a strange land? The dilemma of double consciousness and complexities of an African-centered pedagogy. *Journal of Education*, 172(2), 45–61.

Mezirow, J. (1984). A critical theory of adult learning and education. In S. B. Merriam (ed.), *Selected Writings on Philosophy and Adult Education* (pp. 123–40). Malabar, Fla.: Robert E. Krieger.

Muwakkil, S. (1990). Fighting for cultural inclusion in the schools. *In These Times*, 14(37), 8–9.

O'Neill, W. F. (1981). *Educational Ideologies: Contemporary Expressions of Educational Philosophy*. Santa Monica, CA: Goodyear.

Pai, Y. (1990). *Cultural Foundations of Education*. Columbus, OH: Merrill.

Perkins, U. E. (1986). *Harvesting New Generations: The Positive Development of Black Youth*. Chicago: Third World Press.

Ravitch, D. (1990). Diversity and democracy. *The American Educator*, 14, 16–20.

Rist, R. (1970). Student social class and teacher expectations. *Harvard Educational Review*, 40, 411–51.

Searle, C. (ed.). (1975). *Classrooms of Resistance*. London: Writers and Readers Publishing Cooperative.

Shor, I. (1980). *Critical Teaching in Everyday Life*. Boston: South End Press.

Sleeter, C. and C. Grant (1988). *Making Choices for Multicultural Education: Five Approaches to Race, Class and Gender*. Columbus, OH: Merrill.

Stuckey, S. (1987). *Slave Culture: Nationalist Theory and the Foundations of Black America*. New York: Oxford University Press.

Vallance, E. (1977). Hiding the hidden curriculum: an interpretation of the language of justification in nineteenth-century educational reform. In A. Bellack and H. Kliebard (eds.), *Curriculum and Evaluation* (pp. 590–607). Berkeley, CA: McCutchan.

Wellman, D. (1977). *Portraits of White Racism*. Cambridge: Cambridge University Press.

Woodson, C. G. (1933). *The Miseducation of the Negro*. Washington, D.C.: Associated Publishers.

Wynter, S. (1990, September 9). *America as a "world": A Black Studies Perspective and "cultural model" Framework*. [Letter to the California State Board of Education.]

CHAPTER 6

IDENTITY TRAPS OR HOW BLACK* STUDENTS FAIL

The interactions between biographical, sub-cultural and learner identities

Deborah Youdell

British Journal of Sociology of Education, 24(1), 3–20, 2003

Introduction

This chapter is concerned with understanding the continued inequities of school experiences and outcome experienced by African-Caribbean students. In developing this understanding, the chapter explores the performative constitution of identity constellations inside schools, showing the complex interactions between multiple identities within shifting discursive frames. Specifically, the analysis demonstrates how the privilege associated with African-Caribbean identities within student subcultures is recouped and deployed within organisational discourse as 'evidence' of these students' undesirable, or even intolerable, identities as learners. As such, the analysis adds to understandings of the processes of institutional racism inside schools.

The experiences of African-Caribbean students in UK schools have been the subject of research for some years. Recent reviews of research undertaken in the UK in the last two decades showed that African-Caribbean students attain persistently lower outcomes at age 16 than their White classmates; that the gaps between African-Caribbean and White students have grown; and that African-Caribbean students are significantly more likely to be excluded (suspended or expelled) from school than White students (Gillborn and Gipps, 1996; Gillborn and Mirza, 2000). During the period covered by these reviews, scholars have been concerned to better understand the processes involved in producing these outcomes. Such research has sought to resist prevailing 'deficit' notions of African-Caribbean students, their families and communities. Instead, attempts have been made to understand experiences of schooling from the perspective of African-Caribbean students and develop new explanations for African-Caribbean students' disproportionately low educational outcomes.

Additive understandings of the subordination of particular social groups were a key feature of this research during the 1980s. For instance, Fuller's (1984) research was predicated on the understanding that African-Caribbean girls would be 'doubly subordinated' along axes of gender and ethnicity. Similarly, Mac an Ghaill (1988) used an additive notion of 'triple subordination' – along axes of race, class and gender.

At the time of Fuller's (1984) and Mac an Ghaill's (1988) research, as now, African-Caribbean girls tended to fare better in school than African-Caribbean boys – outcomes which are contrary to the notion of double or triple subordination. While at the time neither Fuller (1984) nor Mac an Ghaill (1988) fundamentally questioned the additive model itself, both offered partial explanations for this apparent lack of fit. In trying to make sense of this apparent contradiction, Fuller (1984) made an important contribution to understandings of African-Caribbean students' school experiences. She suggested that African-Caribbean girls were simultaneously pro-education and anti-school, a position that she saw as being 'intimately connected with their positive identity as black and female' (Fuller, 1984, p. 84). Mac an Ghaill (1988) developed this notion to explain why triple subordination could be 'only partially successful' (Mac an Ghaill, 1988, p. 19) and show how African-Caribbean girls' 'strategies of institutional survival' (Mac an Ghaill, 1988, p. 11) could be understood as 'resistance within accommodation' (Mac an Ghaill, 1988, p. 9).

While African-Caribbean girls' resistances were seen to be located within an accommodation of schooling, African-Caribbean boys were seen to resist 'institutional incorporation' (Mac an Ghaill, 1988, p. 110) and create 'anti-school male sub-cultures' (1988, p. 9). These subcultures rejected 'Englishness' and fore-grounded African-Caribbean identities, thereby offering 'collective protection and survival' (Mac an Ghaill, 1988, p. 102).

While early research identified the significance of teachers' practices (Driver, 1977), more recently theorisations of institutional racism have been crucial to advancing understandings of African-Caribbean students' school experiences. Mac an Ghaill's (1988) study was framed by the understanding that

> racism operates both through the existing institutional framework that dis-criminates against all working class youth and through 'race'-specific mecha-nisms, such as the system of racist stereotyping, which are also gender-specific. There may be no conscious attempt to treat black youth in a different way to white youth, but the unintended teacher effects result in differential responses, which work against black youth.
>
> (Mac an Ghaill, 1988, p. 34)

Gillborn's (1990) study was underpinned by such an understanding of institutional racism. Gillborn argued that the school context was framed by teachers' formal and informal constructions of an 'ideal client' (Gillborn, 1990, p. 26 after Becker, 1970), incorporating classed, gendered, and raced notions of 'appropriate pupil behaviour' (Gillborn, 1990, p. 25). This ideal client of schooling was seen to have particular implications for African-Caribbean boys.

Gillborn (1990) argued that teachers' interpretations of and responses to the behaviours of African-Caribbean boys sustained a '*myth of an Afro-Caribbean challenge to authority*' (Gillborn, 1990, p. 19, emphasis in original as title). This could be seen in relation to culturally specific behaviours as well as those that were common across student groups. For instance, Gillborn suggested that a particular way of walking common amongst African-Caribbean boys in the school was a cultural practice *interpreted* by the school as a challenge to authority. As such, it became a racialised site for institutional disciplinary practices and African-Caribbean boys' contestation of this. Gillborn asserted that

> in the day-to-day life of the school almost any display of Afro-Caribbean ethnicity was deemed inappropriate and was controlled, either officially

(in the case of non-uniform dress) or informally (in the case of speech or the style of walking noted above).

(Gillborn, 1990, p. 29)

This is not to suggest that African-Caribbean boys' contestations were unmediated. Gillborn (1990) stressed that African-Caribbean boys' adaptations to schooling included a multitude of practices of resistance *and* accommodation which had varied and shifting meanings and functions. Nor is this to suggest *intentional* racism on the part of teachers. Gillborn (1995) described institutional racism inside schools as 'a dynamic and complex facet of school life . . . in which routine institutional procedures and teachers' expectations may be deeply implicated' (Gillborn, 1995, p. 36). Nevertheless, Gillborn's understanding of racism as institutional does not render teachers inactive in its continuation. Rather, Gillborn argued that 'teachers play an active (although usually unintentional) role in the processes that structure the educational opportunities of minority students' (Gillborn, 1995, p. 42).

Research by Gillborn and Youdell (2000) reiterated the importance of understandings of institutional racism in analyses of African-Caribbean students' school experiences and outcomes. This study showed how institutional discourses of ability and race coalesced to exclude African-Caribbean students from educational opportunities rationed through practices of 'educational triage' (Gillborn and Youdell, 2000, p. 133).

The notion of institutional racism, then, offers important insights into how African-Caribbean students can attend schools which appear to have developed and be implementing equal opportunities policies and still be significantly *more* likely to be excluded (suspended or expelled) and *less* likely to attain benchmark educational outcomes than their counterparts from other racial or ethnic groups.

This chapter takes up the notion of institutional racism, understood to be cited and inscribed through multiple discursive frames, and deploys this alongside particular post-structural understandings of the discursive constitution of identities. The possibilities offered to understandings of race and ethnic identity by post-structural theories have begun to be developed and some significant insights have been offered (see Mac an Ghaill, 1996; Zack, 1997; Jacobson, 1998; Miron, 1999). Nevertheless, these more nuanced understandings of the constitution of race and ethnic identities have not been taken up broadly in educational research. This chapter aims to make a further contribution to understandings of how the minutiae of everyday life in schools constitutes African-Caribbean students as undesirable learners. The evidence presented in the remainder of this chapter offers a detailed account of the 'identity traps' which go some way to explaining 'how Black students fail'.

Theory to practices

This analysis is underpinned by a Foucauldian understanding of discourse. This theorisation implies a subject who is constituted through the productive power of discursive practices; that is, the meanings through which the 'world' and the 'self' are made knowable and known are imputed through discourse (Foucault, 1990, 1991). The work of Judith Butler is also central to the analytical frame developed here. Drawing on the work of Foucault, Butler (1993) explores the notion of performativity, which she defines as 'that discursive practice that enacts or produces that which it names' (Butler, 1993, p. 130). That is, discursive practices which appear to *describe* (pre-existing) subjects are not, in fact, simply descriptive. Rather they are *productive*.

More recently, Butler (1997a) has offered a revised understanding of performatively constituted subjects. In this work, Butler departs from Austin (1962) to argue that the performative is necessarily 'citational' – in order to be intelligible, discursive practices cite prior discursive practices – and its effects are 'non-necessary' – the potential for a performative to mean something else is embedded in the impossibility of fixing meaning (Butler, 1997a, p. 39, after Derrida, 1988). Butler adapts Althusser's understanding of interpellation (Althusser, 1971), interpreting interpellation as a potential performative, in order to suggest that '[b]eing called a name' (Butler, 1997a, p. 2) is a prerequisite for being *'recognizable'* (Butler, 1997a, p. 5, original emphasis) as a subject. She also takes up Bourdieu's notion of habitus and suggests that the dispositions of the bodily habitus might be understood as 'tacit performative[s]' that are formed by and *formative of* ritual and convention (Butler, 1997a, p. 159–60). Understood in this way, Bourdieu's (1990) practical sense of the habitus is understood as a tacit awareness of the potential performative force and limits of bodily practices.

Butler's understanding of performative interpellation and performative habitus have particular implications for making sense of agency. This framework suggests that the subject who has been named is able to name another – he/she has 'linguistic agency' (Butler, 1997a, p. 15). *This is not the agency of a sovereign subject who exerts her/his will. Rather, this agency is derivative, an effect of discursive power.* The linguistic agency of this performatively interpellated subject is simultaneously enabled and constrained through discourse. This subject retains intent and can seek to realise this through the deployment of discursive practices. The effects of such deployments, however, are never guaranteed due to the citationality and historicity of discursive practices.

This theoretical framework offers important tools for enhancing understandings of how African-Caribbean students are constituted in and through schooling. Those data analysed in the remainder of this chapter were generated through a school ethnography which focused on Year 11 students (age 15–16) in a co-educational, multi-ethnic, outer London secondary school, 'Taylor Comprehensive', during the 1997/98 academic year. The study brought together research approaches developed within the tradition of school ethnography (see Atkinson and Delamont, 1995; Hammersley and Atkinson, 1995) and more recent adaptations of qualitative methods informed by post-structural theory (see Silverman, 1997).

In presenting data, sociological transcription conventions are combined with the conventions of a theatrical script to offer a series of 'episodes'. This presentational style is adopted to underline and expose the complex, contextual, interactive and ongoing nature of discursive practices; facilitate detailed analysis of the deployment of multiple discourses, as well as their intersections and contradictions; demonstrate the analytical approach being taken; and leave the data open, as far as possible, to further, alternative analyses.

Constituting Black sub-cultural identities

My analysis within this section shows how race and subcultural identities are constituted through students' bodily and linguistic practices. It also begins to indicate how these subcultural identities are recouped and redeployed – are constituted *again differently* – within the school's organisational discourse. As noted earlier, I will use the term 'Black' in my discussion of these data. This reflects the self-naming practices of the African and Caribbean students in the study whose sameness to each other, and difference from other ethnic groups, is constituted through this naming.

Episode 1 Black and other names

DY (*the researcher, mid/late twenties, woman, White*)
MARCELLA (*year 11 student, girl, Black*)
MOLLY (*year 11 student, girl, White*)
JULIET (*year 11 student, girl, Mixed-race*)
JASMINE (*year 11 student, girl, Mixed-race*)

Sitting in a group around a table in the Year Base (Home Room). The discussion takes place while the rest of the tutor group is in a lesson. The group is in the process of recounting a conflict with RACHEL, *another girl in year 11, that resulted in* MARCELLA *being excluded from school for a fixed term (suspended).*

MARCELLA: I went to maths and I confronted her and I got excluded for it. She's just something!
MOLLY: You called her 'Popadom'.
ALL: (*laugh*)
[. . .]
MARCELLA: I hit her a bit, buffed her out a bit, so she learned sense!
   (*simultaneously*) JULIET: Duffed her up a bit.
   (*simultaneously*) MOLLY: Called her a few names.
MARCELLA: And when I used to see her I pushed her a bit and called her abusive names . . . I know the reasons sound silly but I have my reasons, (*trailing off*) she's just, one, a . . . (*agitated, with heightened 'Black accent'*) She thinks she's Black! Come on! She thinks she's Black! She thinks she's Black! She thinks she's Black!
   (*simultaneously*) ALL: Yeah.
MARCELLA: (*parody of 'Black' accent*) She talks to me, she talks to me like that, what a damn talk?
[. . .]
DY: What do you mean 'she thinks she's Black'?
JULIET: The way she acts.
MOLLY: The way she talks.
JULIET: Everyone knows, every one knows here that she's . . . (*interrupted*)
   (*simultaneously*) MOLLY: (*to DY*) Even you know.
MARCELLA: (*interrupting* JULIET) I know there's not a certain way for a Black person to present, but there *is*.
JULIET: No, but there is.
MARCELLA: Yeah, that's the thing, there *is*, that's what . . . I know . . . I have to say this, there *is*, that's what, I have to say, but there *is*.
JULIET: The hairstyles and stuff.
MARCELLA: Yeah, but there *is*, there *is*, I know there's not a Bla . . . (*laughs*) know what I mean!
ALL: (*laugh, someone claps*)
   (*simultaneously*) MOLLY: (*quoting*) 'There is'!

MOLLY:	(*imitating mature, rational tone*) That's the way it is in this kind of society.
MARCELLA:	And you know Coolie right, she's *Indian*, a proper Indian right, I have Indian next door neighbours so I know what they look like, right.
	(*simultaneously*) GROUP MEMBER: (*laughs*)
	(*simultaneously*) GROUP MEMBER: (*a sharp intake of breath*)
MARCELLA:	She, right, you know when a Black person and an Indian person makes a baby they call the baby *Coolie* because its got half Black and half Indian, she goes round saying that that's what she is because she's ashamed of what, where she comes from.
DY:	So where is she from?
JULIET:	She's Indian, yeah.
MARCELLA:	Indian.
[. . .]	
DY:	So what are you saying? That she *acts* like she thinks she's Black?
MARCELLA:	Blacker than me, I know this sounds funny but she does, she uses words that I'm not even ready for yet!
DY:	What sort of words?
MARCELLA:	I forgot what.
MOLLY:	like 'gwarnin' or something like that, in'it?
ALL:	(*laugh*)
	(*simultaneously*) JASMINE: Not ready!
MARCELLA:	She just, I don't know, she's just something else she is. And also cos she goes out with Black boys it gets to my head you see, so she gets a bit . . .
MOLLY:	Do they actually *know* she's Indian?
JASMINE:	No probably not.
	(*simultaneously*) MARCELLA: No.
	(*simultaneously*) JULIET: I don't think so you know.
MARCELLA:	Cos [boy] thought that she was Coolie.
JASMINE:	When she rings up [girl], she said he asked her 'What are you?' and she goes 'Coolie'.
ALL:	Yeah.
DY:	So she tells people that she's got a Black parent and an Indian parent?
MARCELLA:	Yeah, Coolie.

Episode 1 illustrates how race identities are performatively constituted and contested through their naming and designation. Furthermore, it shows the discursive practices through which races are constituted as discrete, authentic and hierarchical. The group draws on a number of names that might be understood as race identities. Some of these are familiar – Black, Indian, White. Others are perhaps more recognisable as terms of abuse – 'Coolie', 'Popadom'. Drawing on Butler's notion of performative interpellation, these names are not understood as descriptive. Rather, the deployment of these names is taken as a moment in the constitution both of race identities and individual subjects within these terms. All of these names are permeated by an understanding of race as a discrete and authentic marker of identity.

Marcella strenuously and repeatedly asserts the existence of a particular way of being that is quintessentially Black, and the rest of the group recognise and concur with this assertion. Despite illustrations such as Marcella's own exaggerated mode of speech and the group's discussion of language, behaviour and modes of bodily adornment, the girls do not pin down the exact nature of the Black way of being that they are asserting. This does not suggest, however, that the group's assertion is spurious. Rather, it may well be the very impossibility of specifying the minutiae of the composite 'parts' of Blackness that give the claim its force. When Molly asserts that I share this understanding, at a certain level it is true. I do share the group's tacit knowledge of Black, despite also being aware that an attempt to define this risks crude generalisation, essentialism, racism and, ultimately, failure. When Marcella first makes her assertion, she precedes it with a disclaimer: 'I know there's not a certain way for a Black person to present . . . '. Marcella is at least implicitly aware that such assertions have been and continue to be used to denigrate Black people and legitimate their subjugation. Yet, in the context of this disclaimer, she asserts that 'there is' and the rest of the group concur.

It may be possible to understand the Black that the group is referring to in terms of bodily habitus (Bourdieu, 1990, 1991). By adopting Butler's suturing of Bourdieu's theory of habitus with Foucault's notion of discourse, it is possible to understand the Black asserted by the group as a constellation of discursively constituted dispositions, imbued with particular forms of discursive capital, that are deeply inscribed and exceed conscious choice or sovereign agency (Butler, 1997a).

In naming and asserting this specific Black race identity, the group is not simply reporting fact or offering a description. They are citing an enduring discourse of race which simultaneously inscribes and performatively interpellates race identities. A key feature of these discursive practices is a continued citation of an enduring discourse of race phenotypes or physiognomies. While there seems to be some oscillation between a discourse of essential races and a discourse of culturally constructed races, race remains self-evident and unproblematised (if problematic). At the core of the group's understanding there appears to be an implicit assertion of racial authenticity; individuals are *a* race – whether Black, Coolie, Indian or White – which is determined by the race of parents, is enduring, and can be identified. This recourse to authenticity carries with it at least a residual acceptance of race as natural and based in essences – race identity remains a biological fact.

The Hierarchy within the Other

The group does not explicitly state that hierarchical relations exist between races, yet such a hierarchy is implicit in their discussion. This hierarchy appears to be concerned, not with the relationship between Black and White race identities, but with the hierarchical relations between race and ethnic identities other than White.

Rachel's (imagined) desire to be Coolie, or even Black, implies a common, tacit understanding that these race identities are more desirable than the 'real' Indian race identity that is designated to her (which she is performatively interpellated as being). That Popadom appears to simultaneously constitute and denigrate an Indian race identity suggests that the former is of a lower status than the latter. Rachel's (alleged) 'thinking' she is Black appears to cause greater outrage than her (perceived) 'false' claim to be Coolie. This may be taken to imply that the former carries particularly high status, it may also reflect the greater plausibility of the latter claim within a discourse of race phenotypes or physiognomies. The inference that Black boys are particularly desirable as boyfriends is further indication of the high relative status of Black. The inference that Rachel's claim to a Coolie race identity enables her to establish relationships with Black boys, and the related inference that these boys would not go out with Rachel if they 'knew' her 'real' race, conveys the implicit hierarchy of Black > Coolie > Indian. Taken together, then, the discursive practices within the group constitute an underlying race

Episode 2 Raced heterosexual desire

DY (*the researcher, mid/late twenties, woman, White*)
NAOMI (*year 11 student, girl, Black*)
SARAH (*year 11 student, girl, South East Asian*)
STEVE (*year 11 student, boy, White*)

The Episode takes place during a Science lesson. DY is sitting at a table with this group of students. SARAH listens to the conversation but also regularly looks up at the teacher who is giving instructions for the lesson. NAOMI is looking through STEVE's school diary and hands it to DY to read.

DY:	(*reading from a 'Commendations' page in* STEVE's *school diary*) 'For having a massive dick. Angel'. 'For being the best fuck. Moan Baby'.
NAOMI and SARAH:	(*laugh*)
STEVE:	(*resigned protest*) Arrg . . .
DY:	Who wrote that?
STEVE:	My girlfriend.
NAOMI:	(*laughing*) Steve's loved out!
[. . .]	
STEVE:	I've got a thing for Mixed-race girls.
DY:	Yeah?
NAOMI:	His last two girlfriends have been.
STEVE:	Black girls like Black boys.
NAOMI:	I wouldn't go out with a White boy.
DY:	Really?
STEVE:	Think about it, you don't often see a White boy and a Black girl together.
NAOMI:	White girls like Black boys and Black boys like White girls.
STEVE:	Yeah, but Black girls don't like White boys.
NAOMI:	We like them . . .
STEVE:	(*interrupting, matter-of fact*) Yeah, but you don't go out with them.
[. . .]	
DY:	So who do Mixed-race boys go out with?
NAOMI:	White girls, or Mixed-race girls.
STEVE:	and Mixed-race girls go out with . . . (*smiles*)
ALL:	(*laugh*)

Hierarchy within the Other of Black > Coolie > Indian > Popadom. This hierarchy cites and inscribes the relative status of particular race identities within broader discourses of youth/street culture – discourses which performatively constitute ethnic and race identities in particular ways.

Episode 2 offers an account of legitimate inter- and, in some cases, intra-race relationships. This account begins to suggest a Schema of raced hetero-sex which confirms and adds a further (hetero-)sexualised dimension to the Hierarchy within the Other (Figure 6.1). In Episode 2 Black boys are indicated as Black girls' only sexual object. While, Steve obliquely implies that he may want to go out with Black girls, he simultaneously acknowledges that this is not reciprocal and may transgress the boundaries of appropriate inter-race sexual objects and relationships. No boys of other races are identified as wanting to go out with Black girls. This appears to leave Black girls with only one legitimate raced relationship 'choice' – Black boys. In the context of the 'hierarchy within the other' this might appear counter-intuitive – a correspondence between high status and high desirability might be expected. And this is the case for Black boys (see later). The exclusively intra-race nature of Black girls' appropriate relationships exposes the highly gendered nature of the Hierarchy within the Other and Black girls' position at the pinnacle of this. Black girls' position is protected and inscribed by their only going out with boys *also* at this pinnacle – Black boys. Going out with less well-placed boys might threaten Black girls' own status. Furthermore, understood as potentially reproductive relationships, these exclusively intra-race relationships can be seen as constituting Black girls as the guardians of Blackness – a constitution that cites and inscribes discourses of authentic races, racial integrity and female reproductive responsibility coupled with paternal ownership. The disavowal of Black

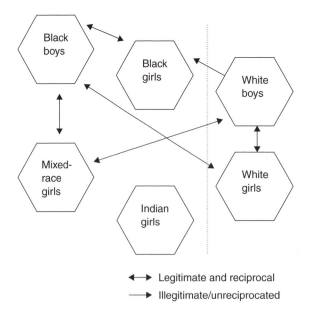

Figure 6.1 Schema of raced hetero-sex (*Note:* this Schema is partial and is intended to suggest constitutions of legitimate desire and not actual relationship practices)

girls' inter-race relationships, therefore, protects and inscribes Black status and the integrity of Black.

In contrast, it appears that Black boys' status is inscribed through their almost universal desirability. In Episode 2 it is stated that Black boys and White girls share reciprocal desire. The same is implied for Black girls but is not explicitly stated. Episode 1 suggested that Black boys and Coolie girls share a reciprocal desire. As Coolie appears to act in this context as a particular specification of 'Mixed-race', it seems reasonable to extrapolate that the same will be true in relation to 'other' Mixed-race girls. Conversely, Episode 1 shows the disavowal of inter-race relationships between Black boys and Indian girls, even as 'Coolie' testifies to this reciprocal, if illegitimate, desire.

Black boys are, then, the most legitimately desired and desiring of all boys. They share reciprocal positions as legitimate sexual partners with White girls as well as girls of all races, with a degree of privilege in the terms of the Hierarchy within the Other. It seems that Black boys' status is not compromised by inter-race relationships in the way seen for Black girls. Indeed, it is possible that inter-race relationships with White girls (and the expropriation of White masculine propriety this infers) *contribute* to this status. This gendering of legitimate inter-race relationships is borne out by research evidence which suggests that Black men are twice as likely to cohabit with White partners as Black women (Office for National Statistics, 1996).

However, this legitimated desire and desirability is not without cost. While the status of Black boys at the pinnacle of the students' and popular cultures' race hierarchy is preserved through these discourses, the (imagined) overwhelming desire for Black boys cites and inscribes a discourse of Black hyper-masculinity steeped in the historicity of discourses of Black savagery and sexual incontinence. This is a discourse which sustains notions of the Black man's 'threat' to White masculinities, White femininity and the 'purity' of Whiteness.

It is noteworthy that the Hierarchy within the Other and the Schema of raced hetero-sex suggested here do not distinguish between African and Caribbean race identities. Rather, the students' discursive practices assert a singular Black identity – a constitution which may reflect the simultaneous cultural hybridity (Hall, 1992) and homogenisation (Burbules and Torres, 2000) that are features of globalised subcultures. At the same time, and in an apparent tacit inversion of discourses of White racial purity and proscribed miscegenation, Mixed-race identities are constituted through the Hierarchy and Schema as lesser to, and a lessening of, Blackness.

By demarcating which inter-race relationships are acceptable and which are not, the Schema of raced hetero-sex cites and inscribes notions of miscegenation and the exotic Other, themselves predicated on understandings of phenotypic or physiognomic races. The historicity of these notions is so deeply sedimented that discourses of sexuality appear as intrinsically raced: as Jacobson (1998) notes, '[t]he policing of sexual boundaries – the defence against hybridity – is precisely what keeps a racial group a racial group' (Jacobson, 1998, p. 3).

Touching

The bodily contact and synchronised movement of Scene 1 of Episode 3 is a moment in the bodily constitution of gender, sexual, subcultural, race and learner identities. While the bodily chain in this Scene seems to be relatively uncommon in the school, many girls link arms as they walk around the corridors. This is a practice that is

Episode 3 Black bodies

Scenes are drawn from observations in the school.

Scene 1: Touching
A school corridor during morning break. Marcella, Naomi and Marcia (Year 11 girls, Black) walk slowly around a corner. Marcella is in the middle flanked by the other girls. She has an arm around the back of the neck of each of the other girls, her lower arm and hand hanging over the front of each girl's shoulder. Both Naomi and Marcia have their near side arm around Marcella's lower back, their hands lightly clasping her at the side of the waist/hip. All of the girls are around the same height. Marcella's arms, therefore, are pushed upwards from the armpit in order to reach the other girls' necks and the other girls are leaning/pulled inwards and down slightly to facilitate Marcella's reach. Movement is facilitated by the girls walking slowly and in time with one another. Marcella makes eye contact with me, smiles and calls "Hi Miss, I want you to meet my friends!".

Scene 2: Slouching
Year 11 Maths lesson. The lowest of the stratified year 11 maths teaching groups, it is a relatively small class. A number of students are absent. The majority of students are boys. One group of boys (Black, Mixed-race and White) is seated spread out around a large desk. They have lots of space, with empty seats separating some of the boys. These boys sit low in their chairs, bums at the front of the seats. They lean back with legs either outstretched resting on heels or bent at the knees with legs wide apart and feet flat on the floor. Some sit with their chair at a right angle to the desk, rest one elbow on the table and raise the forearm and hand on which the head then rests. Alternatively, they rock back on the rear legs of the chair, bracing themselves by knees on the underside of the table top or feet caught around the far legs of the table.

---

unseen among and criticised by boys. Furthermore, while there is no official rule that prohibits such consensual bodily contact, teachers regularly censure this behaviour on grounds that it is a cause of congestion and a potentially hazardous obstacle.

The bodies in the Scene cite and inscribe the bodily intimacy of girls' friendships and implicitly cite and contribute to the prohibition of such bodily intimacy between boys. Moving around in a chain of bodies is difficult and uncomfortable. That these girls move rhythmically and in time is constitutive of a femininity positioned as natural and sexually desirable; it is also potentially constitutive of their raced femininity and position in the Schema of raced hetero-sex. The chain displays the inaccessible Black-heterosexual-feminine body to a (multiply raced-) heterosexual-masculine audience. This chain of bodies *does* create an obstacle that other students must navigate. In this way it is indicative and formative of the group's location at the pinnacle of the Hierarchy within the Other, a location which is itself constituted as incommensurable with official school norms. That such a bodily chain is likely to be censured if seen by a teacher cites and inscribes the girls' irreverence for school norms. Whether the girls share intent, and whether this intent is concerned with mounting a bodily challenge to school norms and/or inscribing the unity of the group and its subcultural status, these girls' bodies are acting their place in discourse.

Slouching

The postures of the boys in Scene 2 of Episode 3 are counter to the school's known expectations for deportment inside the classroom. The ideal student, even the tolerable student, does not slouch, rest his head as if asleep, or rock on the back legs of his chair. In terms of the official school discourse these postures cite and constitute the boys' negative school orientation. The school also constitutes these students' identities in terms of their educational 'ability' – this class is at the bottom of a hierarchy of eight stratified teaching sets. A disproportionate number of the boys in this group are Black and Mixed-race. I have discussed elsewhere the impact of such set allocations as an element of educational triage that appear to be particularly damaging for Black boys (see Gillborn and Youdell, 2000). In terms of the student subculture, the boys' bodies cite heterosexual masculinity, the privilege of Blackness, irreverence for the school and high subcultural status, all of which are intimately linked. In seeming contradiction to these bodily practices, these boys not only continue to attend this lesson, they participate – they ask and answer questions and express concern over forthcoming external examinations. It appears that the boys' bodily practices provisionally offset the diminished status – or even humiliation – associated with their location in the lowest teaching group. The subcultural cool of these masculine bodies counteracts the (marginally) pro-school identities implied through continued attendance at, and participation in, this lesson. There appears to be a tacit agreement amongst these boys – if the masculinity of subcultural privilege and irreverence to school norms is maintained bodily, then the concomitant negative school orientation can be temporarily suspended, and continued attendance at and participation in the lesson can be legitimised. In saying that this is a tacit agreement I am suggesting that it is a necessarily collective practice, but one which is unlikely to have been discussed or verbally agreed on. Rather, the boys have a practical sense of the value of their bodily dispositions in this context and deploy these as second nature in ways that sustain both their masculine identities *and* their legitimate participation in education.

The boys' postures go unacknowledged and unchallenged by the teacher. It seems that the teacher understands (at least tacitly) the contradiction between the boys' subcultural and learner identities. That is, she is aware that these boys might well have opted not to 'risk' their subcultural identities and stopped attending this lesson. She may also anticipate (again, at least tacitly) that the masculine bodies that the school censures may be acceptable, or even valued, in the likely (assumed) post-school destinations of these boys. The teacher appears willing, then, to forgo the school's usual expectations of deportment. In another teaching context (perhaps a higher teaching set) such bodily practices would be designated so anti-school that they would constitute the students as undesirable. Indeed, such designations may have contributed to these boys' trajectories into the lowest teaching group.

The Schema of raced hetero-sex and the Hierarchy within the Other demonstrate some of the discursive processes through which Black students are privileged in the student subculture. Yet as Episode 3 begins to show, beyond the reach and influence of the discourses of youth/street culture, this privilege may have limited value. In terms of Bourdieu's (1990) capital, in the context of the student culture, these students have capital of high market value. In the context of the school's institutional culture, and hegemonic culture more broadly, the value of such capital shifts.

For Bourdieu, the market value of a given form of capital is not intrinsic but varies across contexts or market locations (Bourdieu, 1990, 1991). By conceiving of forms of capital as discursive, both their values *and* meanings are seen to be mobile and formative. The markets in which discursive capital circulates are also discursively constituted – the meanings, limits and legitimacy of these markets are constituted through discourse. As such, forms of discursive capital can be understood to circulate within discursive markets. Adopting this understanding, it appears likely that students' youth/street culture privilege will be inversely related to their privilege in the discursive markets of the school. Indeed, for Black boys, the dispositions and capitals that secure them the pinnacle of the 'hierarchy within the other' and Schema of raced hetero-sex, may not only be devalued but also, extending Bourdieu's economic analogy, may be the very practices that constitute their negative equity in discursive markets dominated by hegemonic culture. It is to these issues that the remainder of this chapter will turn.

Identity traps – constituting Black learners

These performatively constituted Black identities are not without risk and cost. If we accept Althusser's understanding of subjection (Althusser, 1971), the position of subject always entails cost – subjection is simultaneously formative and regulative. In this sense, the subject who is constituted as a subject by turning to the hail is necessarily 'self-incarcerating' (Butler, 1997b, p. 32). The notion of the self-incarcerating subject is useful for understanding how *the subcultural privilege of students' Black identities may become a discursive trap.*

The analysis offered here suggests that identity constellations frequently bring with them particular limits as well as further constitutions that are unforeseen, undesirable or even counter to those identities that the subject intentionally or tacitly seeks. That is, it may be the very practices that constitute privilege in the Hierarchy and Schema which organisational discourse recoups and redeploys in ways that constrain the sorts of learners that Black students can be.

Black subcultural identities: (mythical) challenge or discursive entrapment?

Students' subcultural constitutions of Blackness and organisational constitutions of Blackness are deeply entwined. The moment of practice in which Black students constitute themselves within the terms of the student subculture may also be the moment of practice in which the school organisation constitutes them as a challenge to authority. Drawing on the theoretical tools outlined earlier, the analysis that follows shows how the apparently mundane bodily practice of leaving a room contributes to the constitution of Black students as intrinsically at odds with, and a challenge to, school authority. Furthermore, I suggest that it is the very success of these students' Black youth/street-cultural identities that entraps them within institutional and broader discourses of the Black challenge to White hegemony.

The school's discursive relationship with and constitution of Blackness

Blackness is censured within and through the discursive practices of the school organisation. This is not an explicit censure, nor is it a censure of some innate or intrinsic Blackness. Rather it is an implicit censure of particular youth/street subcultural constitutions of Black identity. That is, at the level of the institution, discursive practices of Black youth/street culture are tacitly mediated through discourses that constitute these practices as inherently challenging to the school's (or individual teacher's) authority and, by extension, the broader White hegemony. This is not simply a rejection of the subcultural meanings of discursive practices of Blackness. It is a mediation that, in rejecting these subcultural meanings, constitutes particular (and denigrated) Black learner identities.

The school's constituting interpretations of Black subcultural identities as intrinsically anti-school and a challenge to authority are tacit. It is unlikely that any racialised or racist *intent* underpins these constitutions. Rather, the racialised and racist nature of these constitutions can be understood in terms of common sense and institutional racism. Such racism operates through the historicity – the sedimented meanings – of unrecognised and unacknowledged organisational and common sense discourses which cite and inscribe the biological and/or cultural deficiency, hyper-sexuality, deviance and threat of Blackness – the discourse of a Black challenge to White hegemony.

At the level of the body, discourses of phenotypic or physiognomic races, which insist on bodily race that is observable and classifiable, contribute to the ongoing constitution of Black identities (Alcoff, 2001). As an assemblage of students is subjected to the surveillent gaze of the teacher, the endurance and authority of these discourses ensures that the teacher sees these Black students – students who, through an array of further raced discourses are classified as 'trouble', a challenge to authority – as needing to be kept under closer surveillance in order to be subjected to greater control.

Black students' practices, then, are mediated through organisational and common sense discourses that designate these subcultural and race identities as inherently counter to the school organisation and culture. Black students' discursive constitutions of race and subcultural identity are at once *censured* by the school organisation as undesirable and simultaneously *deployed* as 'proof' of this undesirability. In this way, it is the very cultural capital within the student milieu of Black subcultural identities that renders these identities undesirable at the level of the institution. Furthermore, in the moment of institutional censure and deployment, the school organisation also contributes to the ongoing constitution of these subcultural identities *and* the incommensurability of these with desirable learner identities.

The school's constituting mediations of Black learner identities can be seen in Episode 4. The Head of Year stands looking out over an assembly of students seated on the hall floor. His position optimises the capacity of his surveillent gaze; this is a moment in the deployment of technologies of disciplinary power (Foucault, 1991). These Black boys may or may not be being more disruptive/less attentive than other students, but any disturbance is minimal – it is not apparent to me. Out of a largely White student population it is a group of Black boys who are subjected to particular and continued surveillance and, ultimately, ejected from the hall. This is not because the Head of Year is deliberately discriminating against Black boys. It is because those sedimented discourses through which the Head of Year classifies the student population to ensure that these boys are identified as being a challenge to authority and, therefore, in need of greater surveillance and control.

This analysis might seem to suggest that if Black students were able or prepared to jettison practices of Black subcultural identities then they would not be subjected to the surveillance and control of this tacit racism. Yet to suggest that it

Episode 4 Black bodies walking

Year 11 Assembly.
The majority of the year group (predominantly White), group tutors
(All White, predominantly women), and DY *are present. The Head of Year*
(man, White) is addressing the year group.

The Head of Year pauses and looks out to the back of the assembled students.
A few minutes later, looking in the same part of the audience, he calls out
a short string of boys' names and instructs them to pay attention. A minute or
so later he stops mid-sentence and calls: "OK Daniel, outside my office
please". There is a pause. Daniel (boy, Black) slowly gets to his feet, shaking
his head as he does so. He takes his time as he leaves the hall, there is a sway
and spring to his gait. The head of year continues his address. Through the
rest of the address the Head of Year sends a further two Black boys from the
same group to wait outside his office. Each boy exits in a similar
manner to Daniel. As the final boy walks towards the door, the head of year
continues to chastise him. The boy makes a short tutting sound, which is
audible to those towards the front of the hall, as he walks out of the door.

---

might be Black students who should modify themselves in order to be constituted
as desirable learners seems vulnerable to being recouped by discourses of cultural
difference and *deficit* which the school's constituting practices cite and inscribe.
Butler (1997a) suggests that the promise offered by the performative is the possibility for identities to mean something else or to endure in contexts where they
have not belonged – a possibility which she calls a politics of performative resignification. My preceding discussion suggests that these constitutions of Blackness
cannot be reinscribed – made to mean differently – through any simple act of personal presentation.

The practices of Black students are by no means uniform, yet students who do
not fit enduring constitutions of Blackness are frequently overlooked or constituted as exceptional (for instance, especially talented; middle class not working
class; African not Caribbean). See, for example, Mac an Ghaill, 1988; Gillborn,
1990, 1995; Sewell, 1997. Enduring discourses of visible, classifiable race and the
Black challenge to White hegemony bound the intelligible subject positions available to Black students. These discourses are inscribed once again by constituting
explanations for difference which foreground 'gifts' and 'talents' or biographical
specificities. This analysis does not imply that Black young people cannot reinscribe
their identities, but it does begin to map the limits of a politics of performative
resignification.

Black students' constitutions of self and
relationships with the school

In a racialised school context, students know, at least tacitly, that their Blackness
renders them undesirable learners. These Black students cannot have both a pro-
school, positively oriented learner identity *and* a high status Black subcultural
identity. This is not simply because these Black students refuse such dual identities.

Rather it is because these identities are constituted, in part, through their incommensurability and opposition. In this context, the Black identities at stake are self-consciously racialised *and* politicised. Irrespective of the fact that these identities trap students in discourses of authentic races and the incommensurability of Blackness and desirable learners, these identities are (at least partially and tacitly) a response to and resistance of White hegemony.

It also seems likely that Black students' subcultural identities play a significant role in the maintenance of their self-esteem or even their sense of self. These Black students cannot be 'pro' the very institution that they understand themselves to be subjugated by, and experience themselves to be discriminated against within, without substantial cost. While this does not mean they must be *anti*-school, the historicity embedded in the discourses through which these identities are constituted forecloses the viability of the simultaneity of Black subcultural status *and* pro-school. The 'Uncle Tom' which might be one alternative identity available to these students does not promise a markedly better relationship with the school and seems to insist on a markedly worse relationship with the self and peers. It is perhaps useful to understand this in terms of Althusser's subjection through the turn to the Law (Butler, 1997b, citing Althusser, 1971). If the school organisation is positioned as the Law that hails these students, then the students turn through their desire for subjectivity (albeit also subjection) and tacit 'guilt' over their contestation of the subjugating authority of the Law. That students turn at this hail is further explained by the fact that the subjectivity which proves (constitutes) their guilt in the school context is also the subjectivity that constitutes their value in other (subcultural) contexts.

This analysis suggests that the school organisation and Black students are engaged in a complex series of performative constitutions of identities that present something of a double bind to Black students. Namely, if these students want the protection (Mac an Ghaill, 1988) afforded by the status of a Black subcultural identity (and it is unsurprising that they do as the alternatives available appear extremely limited), then the cost of this is the concomitant constitution of an inherently challenging learner identity that must *be at once censured and deployed* by the school organisation.

This is illustrated by my analysis of the practices of the boys as they leave the hall in Episode 4. The way that the boys walk seems much like the Black boys' walk discussed by Gillborn (1990). The boys in Episode 4 are not disciplined *for* walking in this way (as in Gillborn, 1990), rather, they walk in this way *after having been disciplined*. I suggest that the meaning(s) of this walk, and the non-verbal utterance of the final boy, are constituted by and constitutive of both Black subcultural and learner identities. These bodily practices are not intrinsic markers of either Blackness or a Black challenge to school authority. It is the congealed institutional meanings designated, but not once and for all fixed, to these bodily practices which constitutes these practices as a challenge to school authority. These meanings are not inaugurated within the episode, they are citational. They are imbued with an embedded historicity which the Head of Year and these Black boys as well as other staff and students are well aware of (at least tacitly). The performative force lent to these bodily practices by this historicity, as well as the institutional authority of the school, constrains tightly the possibilities of alternative meanings within this context.

This is not to suggest that, at the level of the boys' intent, they are simply leaving the room with some neutral gait that at once cites and forms their bodily habitus. While the boys' gait may well be understood as a disposition of bodily habitus, in this context it is unlikely that it exceeds the boys' conscious choice. It is important to consider the boys' status within the student subculture, as well as their audience in understanding the implications of the way they leave the room. These boys are positioned at the pinnacle of both the Hierarchy within the Other and the Schema of raced hetero-sex. These subcultural identities are publicly threatened by their ejection from the hall – high-status masculinity is denied as these boys are provisionally constituted as student-child and forced to submit to the authority of the teacher-adult. The boys' walk, and the final boy's non-verbal utterance (constituted here as irreverently 'kissed teeth', but equally plausibly an expression of frustration at being ejected from the hall (again)?), might be understood as attempts to recoup this provisional constitution. The boys' bodily practices cite and inscribe their subcultural identities, reasserting and confirming their status despite its denial by the school. As such, it is a further moment in the ongoing constitution of these identities. Yet, as I have already shown, within the school's institutional discourse these bodily citations and inscriptions of subcultural identity and status, and their potential to recoup the 'student-child' which being ejected from the hall entails, simultaneously cite and inscribe a Black challenge to White hegemony.

These boys are trapped in a double bind which is the effect of two realms of constituting discourses, that of the student and street/youth culture and that of the school organisation. I suggest that the boys know that such an exit from the hall will be understood by the Head of Year, other staff and students as a challenge to the authority of the Head of Year and the school more generally. To walk out of the room in this manner, within the discursive frame that permeates and constrains this context, is a clearly recognised assertion of a Black subcultural identity that is constituted as oppositional to the school. That is, it is constitutive of an intolerable learner identity. Yet by walking out of the room in this way, and uttering a (particular) non-verbal exclamation on exit, in the case of the final boy, the boys are able to acquiesce to the Head of Year's discipline while simultaneously reasserting a high status subcultural identity which is inscribed by the school even as it is constituted as intrinsically at odds with the school institution. It seems likely that these boys are well aware of this double bind and actively choose to prioritise a Black subcultural identity. To do otherwise in this discursive frame would be to (hopelessly) attempt to constitute themselves as desirable learners. Such an attempted constitution would be hopeless because this is a learner identity from which these boys are barred through the school's organisational discourses *as well as* their own discursive practices through which they challenge this constituting bar.

Conclusion

This chapter shows how it is through the most apparently trivial moments of everyday life in school that African-Caribbean students' identities as learners come to be constituted as undesirable, intolerable, far from 'ideal', within the terms of the hegemonic discourses of the school organisation.

The body and its apparently mundane movements constitute students in particular ways – in the case of African-Caribbean students it seems that the school organisation deploys these bodies to the severe detriment of the students themselves. This indicates the importance of understanding the ways in which the body is involved in the constitution of identities. My analysis suggests that these potentially performative bodily activities are an integral part of the discursive constitution of identities. They do not supplement the discursive – accessible and meaningful only through discourse, they are already discursive. This underlines the importance of making a particular distinction between the linguistic and the discursive. The linguistic and the discursive are not one and the same. The discursive field is constituted by and constitutive of representations whether these are linguistic, textual, visual, bodily or otherwise. Bodily practices are not somehow inherently White/Black, masculine/feminine, pro-/anti-school, imbued with particular degrees of subcultural status. Rather, bodies are designated within these terms through discourse – their meanings are cited and inscribed. Just as the historicity of discourse is sedimented through its citation within linguistic practices, so it is sedimented through its citation within bodily practices be these intentional, tacit or unintentional.

Identities are constrained within mobile discursive chains that can act to trap particular identities in ways that are counter to or at odds with the intent or desire of the individual subject. Constellations of identities are connected in and constituted through discursive chains that render some identities accessible and some identities inaccessible or even unintelligible. Of particular significance are the ways in which discursively embedded relationships between biographical or subcultural identities and learner identities trap students within particular learner identities which seem almost impossible to escape. Specifically, African-Caribbean subcultural identities are deployed within organisational discourse as evidence of (to constitute) undesirable learners.

These connections are not new. The analytic tools offered here, however, significantly enhance understandings of the relationships between learner, biographical and subcultural identities. This offers further insight into the processes through which institutional racism impacts on the educational experiences and outcomes of African-Caribbean students.

Note

* The term 'Black' is used here to refer to African-Caribbean students. In my introductory and concluding discussions I use the widely accepted term African-Caribbean. My discussion of those data presented uses the term Black – the term that students who might also be identified as African and Caribbean, and whose experiences and accounts are drawn on in this chapter, used to refer to themselves.

References

Alcoff, L. M. (2001) Towards a phenomenology of racial embodiment, in: R. Bernasconi (ed.) *Race: Blackwell Readings in Continental Philosophy* (Oxford, Blackwell).

Althusser, L. (1971) Ideology and ideological state apparatuses, in: B. Brewster (trans.) *Lenin and Philosphy* (London, Monthly Review Press).

Atkinson, P. and Delamont, S. (1995) *Fighting Familiarity: Essays on Education and Ethnography* (Cresshill, NJ, Hampton Press Inc.).

Austin, J. L. (1962) *How To Do Things With Words* (Cambridge, MA, Harvard University Press).

Becker, H. S. (1970) *Sociological Work: Methods and Substances* (New Brunswick, NJ, Transaction Books).

Bourdieu, P. (1990) *The Logic of Practice* (Stanford, CA, Stanford University Press).

—— (1991) *Language and Symbolic Power* (Cambridge, MA, Harvard University Press).

Burbules, N. C. and Torres, C. A. (eds) (2000) *Globalisation and Education: Critical Perspectives* (London, Routledge).

Butler, J. (1990) *Gender Trouble: Feminism and the Subversion of Identity* (London, Routledge).

—— (1993) *Bodies That Matter: On the Discursive Limits of 'Sex'* (London, Routledge).

—— (1997a) *Excitable Speech: A Politics of the Performative* (London, Routledge).

Butler, J. (1997b) *The Psychic Life of Power: Theories in Subjection* (Stanford, CA, Stanford University Press).

Connell, R. W. (1995) *Masculinities* (Cambridge, Polity Press).

Derrida, J. (1988) Signature Event Context, in: J. Derrida (ed.) *Limited Inc* (Elvanston, IL, Northwestern University Press).

Driver, G. (1977) Cultural competence, social power and school achievement, *New Community*, 5(4), 353–60.

Foucault, M. (1990) *The History of Sexuality Volume 1: An Introduction* (London, Penguin).

—— (1991) *Discipline and Punish: The Birth of the Prison* (London, Penguin).

Fuller, M. (1984) Black girls in a comprehensive school, in: M. Hammersley and P. Woods (eds) *Life in School: The Sociology of Pupil Culture* (Milton Keynes, Open University Press).

Gillborn, D. (1990) *'Race' Ethnicity and Education: Teaching and Learning in Multi-ethnic Schools* (London, Unwin Hyman).

—— (1995) *Racism and Antiracism in Real Schools: Theory, Policy, Practice* (Buckingham, Open University Press).

Gillborn, D. and Gipps, C. (1996) *Recent Research on the Achievements of Ethnic Minority Pupils, Report for the Office for Standards in Education* (London, HMSO).

Gillborn, D. and Mirza, H. S. (2000) *Educational Inequality: Mapping Race, Class and Gender – A Synthesis of Research Evidence* (London, Office for Standards in Education).

Gillborn, D. and Youdell, D. (2000) *Rationing Education: Policy, Practice, Reform and Equity* (Buckingham, Open University Press).

Hall, S. (1992) The question of cultural identity, in: S. Hall and T. McGrew (eds) *Modernity and its Futures* (Buckingham, Open University Press).

Hammersley, M. and Atkinson, P. (1995) *Ethnography: Principles in Practice*, 2nd edn (London, Tavistock Publications).

Jacobson (1998) *Whiteness of a Different Color: European Immigrants and the Alchemy of Race* (Cambridge, MA, Harvard University Press).

Mac an Ghaill, M. (1988) *Young, Gifted and Black* (Milton Keynes, Open University Press).

—— (1996) *Understanding Masculinities: Social Relations and Cultural Arenas* (Buckingham, Open University Press).

Miron, L. F. (1999) Postmodernism and the politics of race identities, in: R. D. Torres, L. F. Miron and J. X. Inda (eds) *Race, Identity and Citizenship* (Oxford, Blackwell).

Office for National Statistics (1996) *Social Focus on Ethnic Minorities* (London, HMSO).

Sewell, T. (1997) *Black Masculinities and Schooling: How Black Boys Survive Modern Schooling* (Stoke on Trent, Trentham Books).

Silverman, D. (ed.) (1997) *Qualitative Research: Theory, Method and Practice* (London, Sage).

Zack, N. (ed.) (1997) *Race/Sex: Their Sameness, Difference and Interplay* (London, Routledge).

CHAPTER 7

LOOSE CANONS
Exploding the myth of the 'black macho' lad

Tony Sewell

In D. Epstein *et al.* (eds) *Failing Boys?* Buckingham: Open University Press, pp. 111–27, 1998

Not all black boys are the same. This may seem a simple or common-sense assertion but in terms of teacher perception and the popular discourses that underpin 'black masculinity' there is evidence of an acceptance of cultural and ethnic essentialism. This chapter is written with data drawn from an ethnographic study of an inner city boys' school. It seeks to challenge the homogenization of black (i.e. African-Caribbean) boys into one big lump of rebellious, phallocentric underachievers. I want to point to the differences between those who conform to the requirements of schooling and those who do not. Within this, I want to show the fluid, multifarious, shifting and hybrid constructions of black masculinities that operated in this school. I will argue that a more heterogeneous perspective of black boys has been missing from the literature which has failed to look at class, context and the complex intersections of masculinity and ethnicity. Emancipation from the canon of 'black masculinity' gives us a more sophisticated understanding of 'underachievement' and the survival strategies of these children. Those teachers who were most successful with African-Caribbean boys were aware that too many boys were tagged with the label of 'black machismo'. Their success was not in the ignoring of masculinity and ethnicity but in realizing the complex identities of the boys in a context where racism worked on a number of levels.

The key part of my empirical evidence is drawn from Township School, an inner-city boys' comprehensive school in the Greater London area. The school faced an ongoing battle to avoid closure. It had a roll of 500 but this had been falling over the last five years. The school was unpopular because of its exam results and reputation of having a poor discipline record. It is located in a rich suburb, uncomfortably nestling between a number of public (i.e. private) schools. The appointment of the school's first African-Caribbean head teacher marked a new start for the school with the expectation that this new leader would change its fortunes.

At the time of research there were 61 students of Asian origin, 63 of African origin, 140 of African-Caribbean origin, 31 mixed-race students, 127 white boys and 23 others. African-Caribbean boys were six times more likely to be excluded from school compared to other groups. In spite of this disproportionate amount of punishment, African-Caribbean boys adopted various strategies to survive the problems of racism and the inadequacies of teaching and management in the school. In order to understand the range of responses I reworked Merton's (1957)

Table 7.1 Reworking of Merton's typologies

Typology	Meaning
Positioned	Discourse and cultural forms of the school and the way they are perceived as goals and means.
Position themselves	Communities and subculture; producing discourses of acceptance or resistance.
Categories	From a multiplicity of axes for the production of possibly conflicting subject positions and potential practices and interactions.

typology of the four ways in which subjects negotiated their schooling. These were: the 'conformists' who accept both the means and goals of schooling; the 'innovators' who accept the goals but reject the means of schooling; the 'retreatists' who reject both; and the 'rebels' who reject both but replace them with their own agenda. I was aware that Merton's typology could easily be seen as four stereotypes. The Merton model presupposes that student behaviour can be regimented into these fixed categories. I argue to the contrary, that students are decentred subjects changing their social identity depending on the context and their role(s) within it.

There is a need to look at positions around different discourses and cultural forms and regard Merton's categories not as fixed entities but as rooted in positions that come from an acceptance or resistance to the various discourses and cultural forms of the school and the boys' subculture. A reworked model would be as in Table 7.1.

It is impossible to talk of 'goals' and 'means' without first unpacking the cultural influences or relationships available to different students. The 'categories' then become the result of different discourses and cultural forms and the way individuals are positioned and position themselves in relation to them.

The conformists: the ultimate sacrifice or doing your own thing?

By far the largest single category (41 per cent) was conformist. This meant that most African-Caribbean boys were not rebelling against school and most accepted its means and goals. There has been a concentration in the literature on so-called 'black underachievement' and black conflict with school but little on those boys who say they like school and do relatively well. Therefore we have the danger of perceiving African-Caribbean boys as a single entity who are all disillusioned with schooling. 'Conformist students' were united through the conflict between the 'black fictive culture' (Fordham, 1988, p. 56) of the peer group and the goals, values and expectations of the school. It was this characteristic which helped me develop the conformist type. This is not necessarily the boy who does very well academically but from observation and their own perceptions we get a picture of boys who feel that they cannot embrace both the values of school and those of their own black peer group.

Conformists tended to have a mixture of friends from different ethnic backgrounds, unlike the exclusively black peer group of the rebels. Some of these conformists tended to go to the extreme in their break from the collective, so much so that the discourse borders on the racialized. Kelvin, who is a Year 9 student, gives this 'individualistic' perspective as the reason why he has avoided exclusion:

TS: Do you belong to a gang or posse?
Kelvin: No, because my mum says I shouldn't hang around students who get into trouble. I must take my opportunity while I can.
TS: What students in this school do you avoid?
Kelvin: They are fourth years, you can easily spot the way they walk around in groups, they are mostly black with one or two whites. They're wearing baseball hats and bopping [black stylized walk].
TS: Don't you ever 'bop'?
Kelvin: Sometimes for a laugh, but it's really a kind of walk for bad people. I might walk like this at the weekend with my mates but not in school in front of the teachers. It sets a bad example.

Kelvin has not only linked group or community dynamics with bad behaviour, but is also using a racialized discourse. It is this perceived anti-school subculture of African-Caribbean fourth years that Kelvin links with 'bad people'. He cannot reconcile an 'innocent' cultural expression, which he shares even if it is only on weekends, with the values and norms of being a 'good' student. There is a cost to doing well in Township and that sacrifice is made by Kelvin and his mother.

Fordham (1988) describes the collective identity that Kelvin resists as 'fictive-kinship'. In her study of black American children she looks at how a sense of racialized 'brotherhood' and 'sisterhood' affects their attitude to schooling. This desire to flee from the black collective and cut an individual path is shown not only in attitudes to work but in music and cultural tastes. Kelvin echoes this in his comments on black music:

TS: What music do you like?
Kelvin: I like UB 40 and Meatloaf.
TS: What do you think of rap and ragga music?
Kelvin: It's not my favourite because some of the rappers are offensive to women and cuss. It makes you want to dance to the beat, but the words about women are bad. It's not fair.
TS: What do the rest of the kids in your year think about your musical tastes?
Kelvin: They think I'm weird, but I say to them 'I don't have to listen to the same music or dress up like you.' I am my own person. My mum told me to be my own person and not copy other people. I just follow that.

In Fordham's study, the students who conformed to the schooling process also felt they could not share the same music as the students who were anti-school. Although Kelvin does express some of these attitudes, he is too complex an individual to be categorized simply as 'acting white' in order to progress. The information from his parents could easily be interpreted as a 'survival' or 'tactical' strategy in a racist context as distinct from an act of self-denial or what Fordham calls 'racelessness'. The problem with Kelvin's rationale is that he sees little that is good in the black collective identity. It is perceived as oppositional to schooling and therefore bad. One of the most important attributes of fictive-kinship is the blanket of security it gives in a hostile context. Weis (1985, p. 125) notes this ambivalence when she argues that being a conformist is more than just an act of individual will:

> The ethic of co-operation is deeply rooted among the urban poor, and individuals do not break these ties easily. While individualism may be a desired goal, it may be impossible to live out in a context of scarce resources. It must be stressed that the desire for dominant culture embodies its own contradictions: while dominant culture may be desired on one level, it is white, not black. Given that student cultural form at Urban College [located in the urban ghetto of a city in the north-east of the United States] acts largely to reproduce the urban underclass, success in school represents a severe break with the underclass community. Since the collective offers the only security students have, the individual must carefully weigh his or her chances for success against the loss of security that the community provides.

There was in Township a capacity among many of the conformist students to work at a compromise between the tensions that Weis describes. The tragedy in Township is that too many of these students did not have the capacity or the 'luck' to fine-tune the balance between keeping their distance and at the same time staying 'in' with their friends.

This tension was not just an example of student weaknesses; often there were times when conformist students would attempt to claim the 'individual' ground but this was taken away by negative teacher expectation. Stephen, an African-Caribbean Year 10 student, was determined not to be linked with the 'posse' (African-Caribbean gang) but his teachers were not prepared to separate him from the group when it came to punishments. Stephen shows some similarity to Gillborn's (1990) student, Paul Dixon:

> Like the members of the clique discussed earlier, Paul Dixon recognised and rejected the negative image which some staff held of him. Rather than reacting through a glorification of that image within a culture of resistance, however, Paul channelled his energies into succeeding against the odds by avoiding trouble when he could and minimising the conflicts which he experienced with his teachers.
>
> (Gillborn, 1990, p. 63)

Like Paul Dixon, Stephen was too often perceived as being in the same category as the anti-school students, despite his efforts to claim individual ground. This individuality was also challenged by his peer group and, most strongly, by the Year 10 posse:

TS:	What do the 'posse' think of you?
Stephen:	I think they think I'm part of them, even though I'm doing my own things now. When I go to my class and they bunk off, they will say to me I'm a goody goody. But I turn to them and say that when I get my flash car and you're begging for money then you wished you had behaved like me.
TS:	What do they say when you tell them this?
Stephen:	They call me a pussy.

Being called a 'pussy' Stephen suffers the ultimate attack for being a conformist, which is a charge against his masculinity. Being pro-school cannot be reconciled with the machismo of the subculture. Mac an Ghaill (1994) comments on how some anti-school African-Caribbean boys have linked academic achievement with being gay or effeminate (see also, Epstein, 1998).

The category of 'conformist student' becomes, in Township, a fluid context with these students positioning themselves and being positioned by others. Their own stance in school may come from a series of influences: parental, class and even religion. However, no conformist student was really allowed to 'be himself'. In fact this 'individualistic' stance was seen to be most objectionable not only by the fictive-kinship of the peer group but ironically by many teachers. Although these boys claimed to share the dominant ethos of the school, which saw black peer grouping as a negative, many were still perceived as part of a wider African-Caribbean challenge. They could never really escape the castle of their skins and gender. However, the important point is that many of them wanted to. The kind of escape path that many of them desired was not a denial of their race and gender but from the restrictive 'positioning' that came from the teachers and the peer group. Loury (1993, pp. 6–7), a black American academic, talks about this challenge to the 'black psyche':

> I now understand how this desire to be regarded as genuinely black, to be seen as a 'regular brother,' has dramatically altered my life. It narrowed the range of my earliest intellectual pursuits, distorted my relationships with other people, censored my political thought and expression, informed the way I dressed and spoke, and shaped my cultural interests. Some of this was inevitable and not all bad, but in my experience the need to be affirmed by one's racial peers can take on a pathological dimension. Growing into intellectual maturity has been, for me, largely a process of becoming free of the need to have my choices validated by 'the brothers.' After many years I have come to understand that until I became willing to risk the derision of the crowd I had no chance to discover the most important truths about myself or about life. I have learned that one does not have to live surreptitiously as a Negro among whites in order to be engaged in a denial of one's genuine self for the sake of gaining social acceptance. This is a price that blacks often demand of each other as well.

Innovators: learning to balance on the tightrope or a step too far for 'mankind'

The second largest grouping (35 per cent) of African-Caribbean boys surveyed came under the category of innovation. This category accepted the goals of schooling but rejected the means. The origins of their pro-school values are mostly parental. However, they reject the means of schooling. At the heart of 'innovation' is a conflict; you are positive about the wider values of education but you cannot cope with the schooling process. I arrived at this category by looking first at the research done on black girls. Fuller (1980, p. 59) has shown how the black girls in her study managed subtly to resolve this dichotomy. She describes their attitude as 'pro-education' and not 'pro-school'. They managed to distance themselves from conformists (keeping themselves close to their peer groups) and yet achieve academic success.

The category of innovation as applied to the boys in Township is really about their 'desire' or 'struggle' rather than a successful accomplishment of this positioning. In other words we need to examine why black girls have been more successful at 'innovation' compared to African-Caribbean boys?

Frank Sinclair was a Year 10 student and a key member of the clique in his year called the 'posse'. He was expelled from two schools before coming to Township. He has already had five short-term exclusions since he has been at his new school:

> TS: What did your mum say when she found out about your latest exclusion?
>
> Frank: She just sent me to my Dad's house. And my Dad would talk long, long, long.
>
> TS: What did he say?
>
> Frank: He says it would be harder for me to get a job than a white man. He's always talking about this; it's like when he starts he can never finish. Most of the time I go up on Saturdays, get my pocket money – I only want to speak to him. He would just keep on about education. Then as I'm about to go he would get a book out and I would have to sit down and do some weird maths. And if I can't do a sum he would start getting mad.
>
> TS: Do you think it is worth coming to school?
>
> Frank: Yes, I have some friends who are about 21 and they're just loafing around. I just want to go to college do a B-Tec National [a vocational qualification for students of 16+] and go and work in a bank.

Frank is representative of many boys at Township School who were positive about education but rejected the schooling process. These boys were unable/disabled to fine-tune these two opposing instincts in order to avoid open conflict with teachers.

One popular reason given for why 'innovation' may never be successfully accomplished is that black boys face greater pressure and teacher racism compared to girls. This might be the case, but the work of Mirza (1992) shows black girls, too, having to work against the racist discourses of their teachers and experiencing more exclusions compared to their white counterparts.

Another popular reason given is the power and pressure of a peer group that demands an anti-school hypermasculinity. Mac an Ghaill (1994, pp. 87–8) points to this pressure:

> The Black Macho Lads were particularly vindictive to African-Caribbean academic students who overtly distanced themselves from their anti-school strategies. In response, the Black Macho Lads labelled them 'batty men' [a homophobic comment]. As Mercer and Julien (1988, p. 112) point out, a further contradiction in subordinated Black Masculinities occurs, 'when Black men subjectively internalise and incorporate aspects of the dominant definitions of masculinity in order to contest the conditions of dependency and powerlessness which racism and racial oppression enforce.' Ironically the Black Macho Lads, in distancing themselves from the racist school structures, adopted survival strategies of hyper-masculine heterosexuality that threatened other African-Caribbean students, adding further barriers to their gaining academic success.

These two popular reasons for the difficulty of 'innovation' can both be reduced to notions of underachievement and hypermasculinity. However, there is a danger of overplaying the achievement of black girls and making an exaggerated comparison. Also, Mac an Ghaill's analysis needs to be balanced by the fact that there were boys who did successfully negotiate the pressures of peer group and the demands of school. For them there was no psychic pressure between the so-called 'two worlds'. To use a cliché they 'worked hard and played hard'.

In Township a combination of teacher racism and peer-group pressure led to 'innovation' being a tightrope that many, but not all, of these boys failed to cross. What we need to take from the innovators is not simply an analysis of them as victims, but their reasons for feeling that the 'means' of schooling cannot work for them. In many cases, these reasons centred on individual teachers' class management, and a curriculum irrelevant to them and their interests.

'Retreatism': an invisible resistance or glad to be unnoticed?

There were a minority of African-Caribbean students in my sample who can be classified as 'retreatist' (6 per cent). These are students who reject both the goals and means of schooling but for whom these are not replaced by the subculture. In fact schooling is replaced with no significant alternative: their task is simply to reject work. The characteristics behind this typology stem from a psychological perspective where a student is marginalized within the margin. In Township we have already established that the black male presence itself could be perceived by some teachers as threatening. For 'retreatism' to be successful it needs an additional characteristic to 'accommodate' this negative teacher expectation. Therefore the African-Caribbean boys who best avoided exclusion were those who were perceived as non-threatening. In physical terms they were either very slight or very overweight and usually had special educational needs.

Joseph is a third-year student. He spends most of his day walking around the corridors. He claims never to have been 'picked up' by his class teachers who regard him as a 'slow learner'.

TS:	Why do you spend so much time outside lessons?
Joseph:	It's just boring and the teachers that I have are weak and they can't control the class.
TS:	Do you ever hang around with the 'posse'?
Joseph:	You must be joking. I hate them. They go around trying to bully students and get their dinner money. They just want to start trouble.
TS:	Have you ever been excluded?
Joseph:	No.
TS:	Why?
Joseph:	Because I'm not that rude when I'm around teachers.
TS:	How long can you get away with not turning up to lessons?
Joseph:	Weeks. Teachers sometimes see me on the corridor but they don't say anything. They don't think I'm a bad boy because I'm not aggressive.

Joseph is not only opposed to teachers; he also hates the subculture of the 'posse'. It is because he is not visibly rejecting the schooling process that he avoids open conflict with teachers. Retreatists are never seen in groups of more than two and they resist schooling through subversion. For example, they might walk the corridors pretending that they are on an errand for a teacher. In Township it was significant that this form of resistance was open to only a minority of black boys. However, it is more evidence of the qualitative difference of the 'black masculine' experience in the school. Joseph was overweight for his age and the teachers perceived him as 'soft and cuddly' (to quote his form teachers). The physically aggressive signals that teachers picked up from the posse were not present in a student like Joseph. He was therefore more likely to be ignored because he was perceived as non-threatening.

In the case of the retreatists, their experience was not one of a phallocentric charged rebellion. They resisted school through subversion. They add another complex layer to any notion of a uniform 'black masculine' experience in Township school. Even their relationship to the dominant values of the black peer group is different from that of many other boys; they refuse to give the posse any legendary status. They claim an invisible ground marginalized by the schooling process and despised by the dominant peer group.

Rebels: phallocentric revenge or exploding black canons?

At the heart of some black feminist critique (e.g. hooks, 1992) is a debate about the motivation and consequences of black male rebellion to racist oppression. It is suggested that because of the sexualized way in which black males are excluded from mainstream society, the only way they can find an alternative power is in an exaggerated phallocentricity which exploits women. What is interesting about this debate is that there are some black scholars (e.g. Staples, 1982) who read this as an 'understandable' response and others, like bell hooks (1992, p. 112), who feel that this is an internalized oppression:

> If Black men no longer embraced phallocentric masculinity, they would be empowered to explore their fear and hatred of other men, learning new ways to relate. How many Black men will have to die before Black folks are willing to look at the link between the contemporary plight of Black men and their continued allegiance to patriarchy and phallocentrism?

It is my argument that neither Staples nor hooks have allowed for the complex nature of black male rebellion, particularly when it manifests itself in the context of school. Rebellion in Township was really a rather damp squib affair. There were a number of boys who did translate their experience into a phallocentric discourse but there were other forms of rebellion which were more sophisticated and were not a form of internalized oppression. Those boys who did fit into bell hooks' category I call 'hedonist'. They replaced the goals and means of schooling with their own agenda. They were frequently excluded and found comfort in an anti-school black machismo. One afternoon, I showed a video of a programme by the comedian, Lenny Henry, to a group of Year 9 and 10 African-Caribbean students, in which Henry plays the feckless Delbert who makes his living doing scams. This was their response:

TS: Why does Delbert have to keep using 'scams'?
Michael: It's the only way he, as a black youth, can survive.
Donald: Check it, no one is going to give him a job, he has to do a bit of illegal business or else he's going to go hungry.
Michael: Most black kids do scams.
TS: Why?
Dennis: It's how we are – we have to go crooked because the system is like that.
TS: What do you mean?

Dennis: The police and employers, let's face it, they don't like black people.

Allan: I don't think it's just black kids that pull scams. Loads of white boys always do it. They just do it differently.

TS: What do you mean?

Allan: Yes, the black kids do it up front and they don't care.

TS: Do you think that the white boys are more clever with their sneaky scams?

Allan: No way, the white boys are just pussies, they haven't got the balls like a black man, most of them go on as if they are batty men [homosexual].

TS: Do you all agree with that?

[There is universal agreement.]

These responses do confirm an attitude that has internalized oppression and that sees black masculinity in a narrow patriarchal and phallocentric framework. What is particularly interesting is the contemptuous attitude that these boys have for white boys. This again must be contextualized, with many black students having close relationships with white students. However, as part of the construction of hedonistic rebellion, white students are perceived as effeminate and featuring low in terms of the values of the dominant peer group (see also, Epstein, 1998).

African-Caribbean boys constituted just under one-third of the school (at 31 per cent of the school roll), while white boys constituted the second largest ethnic group with over a quarter of the school (at 28 per cent); however, many of the white boys thought that the school was 90 per cent black. As one white boy said to me 'to get on in this school you have to act black'. This point is made by Hewitt (1996, p. 40):

> For some white English pupils, the celebration of cultural variety actually seems to include all cultures that are not their own. It is not surprising that white children – especially, it seems, young people from working class homes – experience themselves as having an invisible culture, even of being cultureless.

My problem with this analysis is that a neutral culture can also stand for the normal or the unproblematic. All too often 'ethnic minority' or 'African-Caribbean' is linked with deprivation or underachievement.

Although there was no overt racial tension between black and white students, the white boys operated in a discreet manner. Their racism was kept between themselves or with their white friends outside of school. The rebels were aware that they were admired by some white boys who felt that 'acting black' was being anti-school and this was fuelled by a masculinity that they envied. Therefore there were the white 'wannabees' who hung around the fringe of the posse, yet they would also confess to having white friends who were involved in racist attacks. As Hebdige (1979) noted, the impact of African-Caribbean youth culture on white youth was ambiguous but not progressive – as, for example, skinheads in the 1960s incorporated Jamaican music to bolster their white nationalism. However, it is admiration of a phallocentric black masculinity that most disturbs the psyche of white youths, as remarked by Back (1994, p. 179) in his essay, 'The "White Negro" revisited':

> For white young men, the imaging of black masculinity in heterosexual codes of 'hardness' and 'hypersexuality' is one of the core elements which attracts them to black masculine style. However, the image of black sexuality as potent and 'bad'

is alarmingly similar to racist notions of dangerous/violent 'black muggers'. When racist ideas are most exposed, in situations where there is intimate contact between black and white men, stereotypical ideas can be reproduced, 'dressed up' as positive characteristics to be emulated. White identification with black people can become enmeshed within the discourse of the 'noble savage', which renders blackness exotic and reaffirms black men as a 'race apart'.

(Back, 1994, pp. 178–9)

Black phallocentrism has a mirror effect on the black male subject. He positions himself in phallocentric terms and this is confirmed by the obsessive jealousy of other groups. African-Caribbean boys are not passive subjects in the face of racialized and gendered stereotyping. They are active agents in discourses which appear to be seductively positive but are in essence racist. This leads to a strong confirmation of an identity that has its source in the dislocation of black and white masculinity. It points to a more complex formation of black masculinity that relies often on 'reputation' rather than substance and has its roots not in a crisis among black boys but an 'insecurity' in white masculinity.

The Lenny Henry response also points to the need, in schools, to deconstruct stereotypes of black males; I do not mean by swapping 'bad' images with 'nice' black middle-class new men. This is equally unrealistic. There is a need to look carefully at the processes that have constructed these images, in particular, a need for an analysis of the media and how it has exploited black male sexuality. The ways in which these boys have been gendered within the school context has left some of them both alienated from 'caring' and 'responsible' notions of masculinity, and victims of the commodification of black culture. This is an argument that Gilroy (1993, p. 228) develops in his book *Small Acts*:

The popularity of materialism and misogyny is partly a result of the fact that those images of blackness are the mechanisms of the 'crossover' relationship. They are in a sense the most comfortable representations of blackness. They are the images that the dominant culture finds easiest to accept, process and take pleasure in. So often the medium of their transmission is a discourse on black masculinity that constructs black men as both sources of pleasure and sources of danger to white listeners and spectators.

The problem with Township is that no one had the insight or courage to take on the issue of how black masculinity is constructed and its influence on the wider society. The nearest that the students came to any sort of discussion about these issues was when the new black head teacher (Mr Jones) took a group of boys for their personal and social education class; however, he failed to grasp the opportunity. He felt too threatened by the boys' phallocentric subculture:

TS: What do you think about the African-Caribbean boys' attitude to women?

Mr Jones: During a social education class, we were talking about children's reading books and we were trying to identify stereotypes. I told them I had 10-year-old twins, one boy, one girl, and my wife and I decided we would not create this gender divide in the twins. Then one of the boys in the class said to me, 'You've only got two kids sir?' I said 'Yes, that's right.' He then asked, 'What about the others back in Jamaica?' I said, 'I've only got two children.' He said, 'Well sir, you're not really a true Yard Man!'

The term 'Yard Man' is a reference to Jamaicans who are from 'back home' or affectionately the 'back yard'. He is linked with a street 'hard-man' lifestyle and he is notorious for fathering many children with different mothers and taking no responsibilities for his actions. Mr Jones had an ideal opportunity to deconstruct the 'Yard Man' and examine the cultural process that goes into his construction. Instead, he saw this as just more evidence of lost youth, who have become irresponsible and who worship destructive role models.

Rebellion in Township was not just phallocentric; there were those who articulated their rebellion on a political level. Calvin is a Year 10 pupil. His dad died, leaving his mum to raise five boys. He has good contacts and a strong network of friends outside school who are a lot older. This helps to bolster his reputation in the posse as a man who does business with 'big people'. He has most conflict with a white teacher named Ms Kenyon. In one class, Calvin was sharing a joke with a group of boys at the back of the class. Ms Kenyon's response was to seek confrontation in a battle of the wills:

Ms Kenyon: Calvin, will you shut up. I don't know why you come to my lessons because you're not interested in doing any work.
Calvin: I would do if you didn't give us rubbish work. Look around, half the class haven't got a clue what you're on about.
Ms Kenyon: And you have, have you?
Calvin: The lesson is boring and so are you.

Calvin does not see a link between schooling and getting a good job. He has already set up his own small business as a 'mobile barber', cutting hair at people's homes. He said he could make up to £300 a week. He carries a mobile phone in school so that clients can make appointments:

TS: How important is it for you to own your own business?
Calvin: It is important for black people to make money because white people don't take us seriously because we're poor.
TS: Is education important to you?
Calvin: Not really, I know what I need to know from the street. I'll give it 3 years and I bet no one will bother with school. There ain't no jobs for no one and they don't want to give jobs to black people.

The national figures on levels of unemployment for black youths compared to white confirmed Calvin's claims that job prospects were bleak for school-leavers. Calvin has rejected the world of schooling and replaced it with his alternative source of income and his most valued contact with the adult world in his community. He spoke about 'real' education which gave black people economic independence and pride in their race.

Calvin has contempt for what Dhondy (1978, p. 46) calls the functions of school:

The reaction of Black youth to discipline, grading and skilling processes is substantially different and potentially more dangerous to schools. And it is precisely because the education of Black youth starts and continues within the communities of which they are still a part.

Although Calvin exercises individualism in terms of his contempt for many of his peers and his desire to be his own boss, he looks positively towards his local black community for inspiration, guidance and success. He has not distanced himself from power and knowledge; it is school knowledge that he despises. He firmly believes that knowledge can be used for collective action and the eventual betterment of the condition of black people, showing that students in this category do not necessarily close off the possibility of pursuing an emancipatory relationship between knowledge and dissent. He has realized that there are other sources of knowledge which meet his material and psychological needs and they can be found within his community.

The emphasis on framing all the rebels as phallocentric is incorrect. Indeed, much theory and analysis of phallocentrism seems always to point to black boys and ignores the sexist and misogynistic attitudes which have been the inspiration for white working-class rebellion. Furthermore, many teachers seem to find these problems only with black boys. The category of rebel has a wide spectrum, much of which is political and pedagogic. It is simply an analysis and rejection of an education system that works against many black boys. This more sophisticated response has often been silenced by the 'obsessive' preoccupation with the dynamics of the black phallus.

Conclusions

In this chapter I have tried to unpack some of the oversimplifications that exist in the current debate about boys' underachievement. African-Caribbean boys are seen in research (e.g. Mac an Ghaill, 1994) and popular discourse as the tip of the iceberg in a general doomsday scenario of male disillusionment with school. This analysis links gender identity to an anti-school attitude. Boys, the argument runs, try to show their maleness by being as unfemale as possible and, in doing so, contrast themselves with girls, who are generally more committed to school work. This has been made worse by peer-group pressure which boys are highly sensitive to, and this allows generalizations to be made about boys as a group. African-Caribbean boys have been seen in this context as a unified lump, who underachieve academically and are driven by a phallocentric revenge impulse to repair their oppressed maleness. There is a need to question seriously this overall pessimism of boys' alleged failure and in particular examine the complex, ambivalent and contradictory male identities that are constructed in school.

I have stressed that there are a number of costs and benefits to the boys in occupying each ideal position and this impacts on other relations (i.e. with male and female teachers, parents, other black boys and white boys). If we look at the parents of conformist students we see them divided on the issue of whether Kelvin should 'bop' (black stylized walk) in front of the teachers. I put the example to many black parent groups and it divides them. Some say he should curb his cultural style in order to 'get on' and not draw attention to himself, while others are adamant that for teachers to see his cultural expression as a threat is really racist and the teachers should change their attitudes. This example shows that even when African-Caribbean boys occupied the ideal of conformist, it was not unproblematic.

What we can say which goes against the tide of pessimism is that there was no evidence that boys were less positive towards school work than girls. Most of the African-Caribbean boys positioned themselves in the pro-school categories of conformist and innovation, while only 24 per cent saw themselves as rejecting the goals and means of schools. Even those boys who could be categorized as rebels were not a simplified and unified group. Rebellion was complex and was not solely based on a phallocentric revenge as in many cases the boys had adopted a political position to explain their rejection of school.

In trying to solve the problems of teaching black boys, teachers need to avoid two falsehoods. The first is to deny that African-Caribbean boys face a disproportionate amount of punishment in school which is based on a wider myth of a greater African-Caribbean male challenge. Second, that African-Caribbean boys are a homogenous lump of rebellious phallocentric underachievers. There are a number of particular areas of school policy and practice which would merit attention, which I will mention briefly here. (See Sewell, 1997 for a fuller discussion.)

In practical terms, schools and teachers need to confront the ways in which they confirm African-Caribbean boys as 'rebellious, phallocentric underachievers'. A start would be a school policy on social justice that was democratically developed and not tokenistic. Another practical approach for schools is for teachers and pupils to learn the art of conflict resolution. This will entail teachers being mindful of their own contribution to the negative behaviours of some African-Caribbean boys. In particular, it would be useful if teachers were to:

- avoid negative comments on cultural styles (e.g. hair styles and dress);
- respect students' personal space;
- use friendly gestures, not aggressive ones;
- use the students' preferred name;
- get on their level physically (e.g. by kneeling or bending down, ask questions rather than make accusations);
- deal with problem behaviour in private;
- listen carefully when students speak.

The respect factor is not only important when teachers are relating to students. What is also crucial is that students learn that there is an appropriate behaviour for a particular context – the idea that all situations do not deserve the same response.

Finally, the creative adaptation of the National Curriculum is needed to take on the interests and perspectives of African-Caribbean boys. Personal and social education should have courses that examine how identities are constructed, particularly on the level of race and gender. Many white teachers have complained that they are not equipped on the level of resources or experience to engage black children with their own culture. My response to teachers who say this to me is usually a question: 'What topic work are you doing with your children?' They may answer, 'The Greeks'. My response is 'Are you an Ancient Greek?' Clearly in order to do this work they have to research and prepare. It is now probably easier to find resources to do a topic called the 'Caribbean people' than it is to find material on the Greeks. What the teachers also often forgot is that the best resource is the children themselves.

The use of black male mentors and other outreach initiatives remain important but must never undermine the particular context of each school. Indeed, the notion that black boys need a black male presence in order for them to learn because they cannot learn from women (Holland, 1996) remains problematic. It assumes that all boys are turned off school, which is not true, and that the cause of this disillusionment is solely rooted in their inability to relate their 'maleness' to female teachers. There is a need to acknowledge the particular needs of boys – especially in relation to reading – but this should never make us resort to policies and practices that reinforce patriarchy and sexism.

References

Back, L. (1994) The 'White Negro' Revisited: race and masculinities in south London, in A. Cornwall and N. Lindisfarne (eds) *Dislocating Masculinity, Comparative Ethnographies*. London: Routledge.

Dhondy, F. (1974) The black explosion in schools. *Race Today*, 6(2): 44–50.

Epstein, D. (1998) Real boys don't work: 'underachievement', masculinity, and the harassment of 'sissies', in D. Epstein, J. Elwood, V. Hey and J. Maw (eds) *Failing Boys? Issues in Gender and Achievement* (pp. 96–108). Buckingham: Open University Press.

Fordham, S. (1988) Racelessness as a factor in black students' school success: pragmatic strategy or Pyrrhic victory? *Harvard Educational Review*, 58(1): 54–84.

Fuller, M. (1980) Black girls in a London comprehensive school, in R. Deem (ed.) *Schooling for Women's Work*. London: Routledge and Kegan Paul.

Gillborn, D. (1990) *Race, Ethnicity and Education*. London: Unwin Hyman.

Gilroy, P. (1993) *Small Acts: Thoughts on the Politics of Black Cultures*. London: Serpent's Tail.

Hebdige, D. (1979) *Subculture: The Meaning of Style*. London: Routledge.

Hewitt, R. (1996) *Routes of Racism: The Social Basis of Racist Action*. Stoke-on-Trent: Trentham Books.

Holland, S. (1996) Interview on Choice FM Radio, London.

hooks, b. (1992) *Black Looks: Race and Representation*. London: Turnaround.

Loury, G. (1993) Free at last? A personal perspective on race and identity in America, in G. Early (ed.) *Lure and Loathing: Essays on Race, Identity and the Ambivalence of Assimilation*. New York: Penguin.

Mac an Ghaill, M. (1994) *The Making of Men: Masculinities, Sexualities and Schooling*. Buckingham: Open University Press.

Mercer, K. and Julien, I. (1988) Race, sexual politics and black masculinity: a dossier, in R. Chapman and J. Rutherford (eds) *Male Order: Unmasking Masculinity*. London: Lawrence and Wishart.

Merton, R. (1957) *Social Theory and Social Structure*. Chicago: Free Press.

Mirza, H. S. (1992) *Young, Female and Black*. London: Routledge.

Sewell, T. (1997) *Black Masculinity and Schooling: How Black Boys Survive Modern Schooling*. Stoke-on-Trent: Trentham Books.

Staples, R. (1982) *Black Masculinity: The Black Man's Role in American Society*. San Francisco: Black Scholar Press.

Weis, L. (1985) *Between Two Worlds: Black Students in an Urban Community College*. London: Routledge and Kegan Paul.

CHAPTER 8

THE SOULS OF WHITE FOLK
Critical pedagogy, whiteness studies, and globalization discourse

Zeus Leonardo

Race Ethnicity and Education, 5(1), 29–50, 2002

Globalization literature is filling up bookshelves in bookstores and libraries. One can buy Mander and Goldsmith's (1996) activist-oriented collection of essays on the global economy, a critical geographer's response to the current economic restructuring in David Harvey's (1989) *The Condition of Postmodernity*, and Jaggar and Rothenberg's (1993) popular *Feminist Frameworks* includes a global feminist perspective in its third edition. Of course, who can forget Marshall McLuhan's coining of the phrase, "global village," to describe fast technology's capacity to link the backroads of rural China to the potholes of New York. One can expect that the arrival of *Globalization for Dummies* should be right around the corner.[1] In education, there is a burgeoning engagement with the shifting purpose of schools in a world economy. Recently, *Educational Theory* (2000) devoted an entire volume to globalization. School reform has taken on a global face in *International Handbook of Educational Change* by Hargreaves *et al.* (1998), and Peter McLaren (2000) reinvigorates the pedagogical lessons of "el Che" in international socialist struggles against capital.

However, as this chapter argues, there has not been a pronounced attempt to integrate globalization discourse with whiteness studies. The excellent introduction to the different social and educational theories on globalization by Wells *et al.* (1998) documents the dominant concern with the economy in globalization literature. Ricky Lee Allen (2000), following the example of Immanuel Wallerstein, has launched a critique of the white educational left for announcing globalism through a curious neglect of the past hundreds of years of global colonialism by largely European forces, a process that is neither novel nor come lately. This chapter takes a different tack on the relationship between the twin towers of globalization and whiteness. Just as Blackmore (2000) finds it problematic that gender issues are not incorporated into the discourse of educational reform and globalization, this chapter asserts that race, and in particular whiteness, must be situated in the global context. It appropriates the concepts of globalization – such as multinationalism, fragmentation, and flexibility – and applies them for the study of whiteness. In short, it argues that, like the economy, whiteness as a privileged signifier has become global.

We are witnessing the globalization of capital through new strategies. Flexible accumulation, contract and part-time work, smaller batches of production, and exportation of labor to Third World nations represent some of capital's late modus operandi. Multinational corporations encourage "friendly" trade relations for the mutual benefit of the global bourgeoisie. Such a diversification of the capitalist venture produces, much to Lukacs's (1971) chagrin, the fragmentation of consciousness, or the inability to grasp the totality of experience. This condition leads to the false impression that the "class situation" within a given nation is improving because much of the manufacturing and hard labor remains out of sight and out of mind. Meanwhile, the *maquiladora* factory workers of Mexico and rural women in the Philippines suffer the daily exploitation that harks back to the brutal labor conditions of industrial capitalism. As the world economy evolves, we witness the incredible flexibility of capitalism to respond to crises and recessions. Yet, its imperative is no different today than when Marx first started writing about it. Capitalism bears a certain permanent trait but not the one that its proponents prefer to promulgate. Rather, as Blackmore (2000) reminds us, "Markets are based upon inequality, envy, greed, desire, and choice . . . Exchange relations are valued by market, while nonexchange relations (voluntary school work, domestic labor, and emotion work) in the 'private' are ignored" (p. 478). As the material conditions change, so does capitalism. Its sophistication is marked by its ability to flex according to, accommodate, and exploit current global conditions. Yet, it is unchanging in its essential feature of the extraction of surplus value and the mystification of the process that makes this possible. Critical scholars have organized around explaining the latest mutations of capitalism in a global context. Because we know that capital is intimate with race, a close relationship exists between economic exploitation and racial oppression.

Since the publication of David Roediger's (1991) book, *The Wages of Whiteness*, there has also been a parallel development in the engagement of whiteness studies (McIntosh, 1992; Frankenberg, 1993, 1997; Allen, 1994, 1997; Ignatiev, 1995; Delgado and Stefancic, 1997; Lipsitz, 1998). Whiteness is now regarded as a critical point of departure in a pedagogy of demystification. The critically acclaimed collection of Kincheloe *et al.* (1997), *White Reign*, advocates an assault on white privilege by exposing whiteness as a socially constructed signifier and rearticulating it through a "critical pedagogy of whiteness" (Kincheloe and Steinberg, 1997, p. 12; see also McLaren, 1995, 1997; Fine *et al.*, 1997; Giroux, 1997). Whiteness studies has achieved such momentum and currency, the ever popular journal, *Educational Researcher*, devoted substantial attention to it in the December 2000 issue consisting of critical responses to Rosa Hernandez Sheets's (2000) book reviews of the "white movement in multicultural education" (Dilg, 2000; Howard, 2000; McIntyre, 2000). Clearly, the issues of globalization and whiteness are critical components of a pedagogy attempting to understand the oppressive structures that distort clear knowledge. These structural features filter into micro-interactions between students and teachers. This chapter offers a neo-abolitionist global pedagogy by linking whiteness with globalization processes.

Neo-abolitionist pedagogy suggests that teachers and students work together to name, reflect on, and dismantle discourses of whiteness. This does not mean dismantling white people, as McLaren (1995) has pointed out. But it does mean disrupting white discourses and unsettling their codes. The complementary goal is to dismantle race without suggesting to students of color that their racial experiences are not valid or "real." However, it necessitates a problematization of race at the conceptual level because there is a difference between suggesting that race, as a concept, is not real and affirming students' racialized and lived experiences as "real." Students of color benefit from an education that analyzes the implications of whiteness because they have to understand the daily vicissitudes of white discourses and be able to deal with them. That is, in order to confront whiteness, they have to be familiar with it. In the process, they also realize that their "color-ness" is relational to whiteness's claims of color-blindness and both are burst asunder in the process. Thus, the goal is for students of color to engage whiteness while simultaneously working to dismantle it. White students benefit from neo-abolitionism because they come to terms with the daily fears associated with the upkeep of whiteness. In so far as whiteness is a performance (Giroux, 1997), white students possess a vulnerable persona always an inch away from being exposed as bogus. Their daily white performance is dependent on the assertion of a false world built on rickety premises.

Before we embark on a study of whiteness, two concepts must be clarified: whiteness and white people. "Whiteness" is a racial discourse, whereas the cate-gory "white people" represents a socially constructed identity, usually based on skin color. For practical purposes, we are born with certain bodies that are inscripted with social meaning (Leonardo, 2000). Most people do not radically alter their physical identity throughout their lifetime. However, that white students act on the world does not suggest they accomplish this from the perspective of a white racial paradigm; in fact, they could be articulating their life choices through non-white discourses or strategies of anti-whiteness. To the extent that a man can be feminist, whites can be anti-white. Likewise, students of color (an identity) could live out their life through whiteness (Hunter and Nettles, 1999). Thus, it can be said that whiteness is also a racial perspective or a worldview. Furthermore, whiteness is sup-ported by material practices and institutions. That said, white people are often the subjects of whiteness because it benefits and privileges them. As a collection of everyday strategies, whiteness is characterized by the unwillingness to name the contours of racism, the avoidance of identifying with a racial experience or group, the minimization of racist legacy, and other similar evasions (Frankenberg, 1993). White people have accomplished many great things; the issue is whether or not they have asserted whiteness. Many white subjects have fought and still fight on the side of racial justice. To the extent that they perform this act, they dis-identify with whiteness. By contrast, historically, the assertion of a white racial identity has had a violent career. Roediger (1994) grasps these distinctions when he claims that whiteness is not just oppressive and false, it is "*nothing but* oppressive and false" (p. 13; italics in original). That is, whenever whiteness, as an imagined racial collective, inserts itself into history, material and discursive violence accompanies it. Or to mimic Stephanie Spina (2000), we must come to terms with the whiteness of violence and the violence of whiteness.

In this sense, whiteness is not a culture but a social concept. White people prac-tice everyday culture when they consume Coke, fries, and a Big Mac. Non-white people all over the world also have access to McDonalds but this is not indigenous to their culture. Whites also partake in formal cultural events, such as Protestant wed-dings. These practices are functional and are not harmful by themselves; they are part of what we call white culture. As a racial category, whiteness is different from white culture but connected to it through historical association. Aspects of white culture assume superiority over others and it is this historical record that must not fade from our memory (see Spring, 2000). However, whereas some facets of white culture are benign or even liberatory, such as critical traditions of the Enlightenment, whiteness is nothing but false and oppressive. Although not exclusively, whiteness has historically stratified and partitioned the world according to skin color (see Hunter, 1998), or the modern sense of race as the politics of pigmentation. The assertion of the white race is intimate with slavery, segregation, and discrimination. White culture, on the other hand, is an amalgamation of various white ethnic practices. Whiteness is the attempt to homogenize diverse white ethnics into a single category (much like it attempts with people of color) for purposes of racial domination.

Multinational whiteness: the hegemony of white images

As whiteness becomes globalized, white domination begins to transcend national boundaries. Without suggesting the end of nations or their decreased significance for racial theory, multinational whiteness has developed into a formidable global force in its attempt to control and transform into its own image almost every nook and cranny of the earth. W. E. B. Du Bois (1989) once commented that American Negroes attempting to escape white racism will fail to find a place on earth untouched by the long arms of European colonization.[2] At the turn of the twentieth century, the Philippines, Hawaii, and West Indies were added to global colonization by white Europeans and Americans. Thus, the point was not to flee the American social landscape, but to change it. From the video, "*Color of Fear*," Victor, an African-American man, supports this view when he lashes out against David, a white American man, for his naive suggestion that every man should carve out his place in society and stand on his own ground (Wah, 1994).[3] Victor reminds us that whites have stood on someone else's ground for centuries. A pedagogical critique of whiteness must transcend its national articulations and link knowledge of whiteness to global processes of (neo)colonization whereby apparently separate white nations share common histories of domination over non-white peoples. This is an important educational lesson because students learn that the white diaspora has, to a large extent, created a global condition after its own image, a condition that whites are generally ill-equipped to understand. Or as Ricky Lee Allen (2000) says, "Whites may have created the world in their own image, however they completely *misunderstand* the world that they have created" (p. 14; italics in original).

Both white and non-white students understand that a multinational critique of whiteness transcends limitations found in discourses which deal with race exclusively at the national level. For example, when discussing the effects of racism within any given nation, the common refrain of "Well, why don't _____ just go back to their country if they're not happy here?" (fill the blank with an ethnic or racial group) exposes several faulty assumptions. One, it assumes that students who voice opposition to white racism do not belong in the nation they seek to improve by ridding it of racism. Two, it frames the issue of racism as the problem or realm of non-whites who are dissatisfied with their lot in life rather than a concern for the humanity of all people, including whites. Three, as Du Bois has already articulated, whiteness is a global phenomenon and there is very little space on the globe unaffected or unpartitioned by white power. Fourth, it assumes white ownership of racialized territories; whites rarely tell other whites to "go back to Europe." Freire (1993) agrees when he says, "The oppressor consciousness tends to transform everything surrounding it into an object of its domination. The earth, property, production, the creations of people, people themselves, time – everything is reduced to the status of objects at its disposal" (p. 58).

Today, the European Community (EC) is more than an economic strategy to consolidate money currency or friendly trade relations between European nations. Since we know that economic development is also coterminous with the evolution of whiteness, the EC represents late capitalism's partnership with multinational whiteness. With the technological revolution, late white movements are able to connect via websites and the Internet, just as easily as the Zapatistas were able to utilize e-mail technology for their own revolution in Chiapas, Mexico.[4] The UK joins the EC, Asians create the Asian Pacific Economic Community (APEC), and an international indigenous people's movement mark the reconfiguration of global politics (Porter and Vidovich, 2000). A critical pedagogy of whiteness must cut whiteness across national boundaries. In doing so, dialectical forms of pedagogy provide students with a discourse emphasizing what Mills (1997) calls a "transnational white polity" (p. 29) as well as transnational resistance to the Racial Contract. Critical forms of education must come to grips with global white supremacy in order for students to understand that race is both a product and producer of differences in a Herrenvolk ethics of justice for "just us" (whites) (Mills, 1997, p. 110). Of course, it should be made clear that this is a vocation that requires collaboration between whites as race traitors (Ignatiev and Garvey, 1996a), or whites who dis-identify with whiteness, and non-white resisters. In an increasingly multinational condition where we can talk about the global assembly line, what often fades to black is the global color line.

Whiteness is guilty of a certain "hidalguismo," or son of God status, in its quest to exert its brand of civilization on non-white nations. As Nilda Rimonte (1997) explains, "Hidalguismo is the obsessive pursuit of status and honor, the alpha and omega of the hidalgo's life" (p. 42). Whiteness stamps its claims to superiority, both morally and aesthetically speaking, on its infantilized Other by claiming to speak for people who apparently speak in gibberish. It aims to comprehend a people better than it comprehends itself. For example, California's Proposition 227, which challenged bilingual programs, consolidates English as the only language of instruction in schools. Although parents can request a waiver to continue their children's participation in bilingual programs, Proposition 227 struck a blow to the legitimacy of bilingual education. In the USA, the common white supremacist argument goes something like this: in Mexico, immigrant students are asked to speak Spanish. Why can't the United States ask the same? We can answer such charges in several ways.

First, the fact that bilingual education is a difficult program to implement is confused with immigrants' lack of desire to speak English. Mexicans, Asians, and other students from non-English speaking nations are (re)constructed as resistant to speaking English rather than acknowledging the formidable challenge to attaining a second language. Second, that Mexico may desire a monolingual educational system (if this is empirically the case) does not suggest that this is the ethically preferred vision for schools in general. Notice that monolingual instruction is naturalized by appealing to an external example, as if the way another nation conducts its education justifies one's own. Gramsci's concept of hegemony explains this instance as a subject's ability to confuse common sense with good sense. Third, the argument obscures the global privilege of English as the international language of business. Mexico (as well as other non-English speaking societies) may promote their own language, but they would surely welcome a student's ability to speak English since this would put the country in a better economic position in the global market. Learning English in a non-English speaking nation is not comparable to learning Spanish in California. Hidalguismo blinds whiteness to its own position in the world by projecting its specific rationalizations onto the general population.

Another mainstream discourse that obscures the multinational nature of whiteness is the attempt to construct white supremacist groups as "outside" of mainstream society. At best, the liberal discourse acknowledges white crimes against humanity as an ugly part of our past. In this pedagogy of amnesia, students are encouraged to think of the "founding fathers" as benign, national heroes who were products of their social milieu. Indeed, Thomas Jefferson and Abraham Lincoln, just to name two, lived in a time when slavery was legal. However, that Jefferson owned slaves and Lincoln rejected racial integration or equality (see McLaren, 1997) seem to be peripheral to their development as leaders of the nation. That is, their participation in racist practices occupies the fringes of our historical memory inasmuch as neo-fascist organizations are constructed as fringe groups in society. This does not negate the fact that Jefferson and Lincoln were also responsible for creating certain liberatory institutions (or helping destroy them, as in the case of slavery). That said, to speak of them as caught up in the logic of the times disregards the fact that at any given historical juncture, there are white traitors who speak up against racial oppression. In other words, it is not the case that white subjects have no choice about the matter of racism.

Participation is very much within the realm of choice and whites have been able to speak against the dehumanizing structures of racism even against their own immediate interests. The example of Sartre (1963) should remove doubts about positive white participation in decolonial struggles. Barthes's semiology proffers people a "methodology of the oppressed" in their attempts to understand, as Fanon also suggested, the way that colonial relations become sedimented at the level of meaning and signification (Sandoval, 1997). Memmi's (2000) unrelenting critique of racism in Tunisia and other national contexts shows us how he understood, as well as or better than any Third World subject, the crippling and dehumanizing effects of "heterophobia," or fear of difference (p. 43). In many ways, Sartre, Barthes, and Memmi's project parallels Freire's (1993) pedagogy of the oppressed. As a white Brazilian, Freire understood the centrality of struggles against racism as the existential analog of class exploitation (see McLaren and Leonardo, 1996). Whiteness is less of an essence and more of a choice.

Conceptually, constructing white supremacist organizations as "fringe" groups is problematic. Students learn inadvertently that multinational racism sits at the margins of society, whereas racial democracy exists at the center. Therefore, neo-fascist groups are not considered a significant threat and can be dismissed as irrational whites. As Mills (1997) notes, this kind of logic makes an exception out of racism, an aberration of white supremacy, and a deviation from the norm in Western development. A counter-pedagogy would suggest otherwise. Despite the racial progress we have experienced through the Civil Rights Movement in the USA and the fight against apartheid in South Africa, white normativity remains central to the development of both Western and non-Western nations. Anti-hate groups, civil rights agendas, and racial dialogue maintain their marginal status in the inner workings of schools and society. Critical forms of multiculturalism have made significant progress in globalizing education (i.e. representing non-white cultures) but whiteness still remains at the center of many national curricula or culture. It is racialization which remains at the center, with deracialization staying at the margins.

In the Filipino diaspora, white or mestiza/o physical traits are considered beautiful (Root, 1997). In Brazil, color-blind discourse disables the nation's ability to locate white privilege in exchange for an imagined racial paradise of mixing, matching, and miscegenation (Warren, 2000). On European soil, the neo-Nazi Progress Party in Norway came in second during the presidential race, while Belgium, France, and Austria are witnessing an increase in white supremacist hopefuls in the government (Flecha, 1999). In the USA, whites feel minimized under the sign of multiculturalism, victimized by affirmative action, and perceive that they suffer from group discrimination despite the fact that white women are the largest beneficiaries of such policies (Marable, 1996; Tatum, 1997), and the utter lack of empirical evidence for "imaginary white disadvantage" (Winant, 1997, p. 42; see also Kincheloe and Steinberg, 1997, pp. 14–16). Nevertheless, whites react with both intellectual and nationalist nativism, as evidenced by the reassertion of Eurocentric, humanist curricula and the Thatcherist brand of xenophobia to make Britain Great once more (Hall, 1996; Hesse, 1997).[5]

Fragmentation of consciousness and global racism

Such misconceptions fail to be explained at purely the empirical level. This state of affairs is nowhere more illuminated than white students who feel disadvantaged or victimized by civil rights legislation or racially motivated educational policies; they perceive themselves as institutionally "oppressed." Their understanding of the nature of racial advantage suffers from globalization's ability to fragment further our total understanding of race and racism. The appeal to white disadvantage is "real" to the extent that whites who believe in their perceived victimization act in a way that is consistent with such a worldview. Teachers may design lesson plans or respond to students' queries about such matters in a way that is empirically misinformed, and appeals to the evidentiary state of affairs can only go so far. In other words, for the white person who feels victimized, evidence of the utter lack of reality to white disadvantage fails to convince them. Students (of all ages) benefit from an ideological critique of whiteness so that they understand the total, global implications of whiteness, a sensibility that links the local with the global processes of racial privilege. But as long as white perspectives on racial matters drive the public discourse, students receive fragmented understandings of our global racial formation.

Ramon Flecha (1999) mobilizes the concept of "postmodern racism" to describe a condition wherein racial and ethnic differences become incommensurable and subjects fail to address the important issue of equality in the face of difference. As Flecha distinguishes, "Modern racism occurs when the rules of the dominant culture are imposed on diverse peoples in the name of integration. Postmodern racism occurs when people deny the possibility of living together in the same territory" (p. 154). Postmodern racism assumes the guise of tolerance only to be usurped by relativism, a proliferation of differences rather than a leveling of power relations. That is, according to Flecha, postmodern racism fragments educators and students' ability to discern the difference between democracy and dictatorship, the difference being a certain will to power rather than truth or virtuosity. In contrast, the dialogical methods of Habermas and Freire offer a viable alternative to postmodern thought because they recognize the value of rationality and critical consensus through criticism (see also Sirotnik and Oakes, 1986).

Dialogical approaches represent a counter-strategy to the fragmenting effects of white consciousness, perhaps most recently exhibited by postmodern theories that emphasize incommensurability of worldviews. The incommensurability argument that affects racial dialogue suggests that we are all different and should be valued as such. Without critical attention to the ways that asymmetrical relations of power inscribe difference, Flecha finds that ludic postmodernism degrades into a relativistic discourse and fails to integrate disparate peoples within a given territory. Or as McLaren *et al.* (2001) assert, ludic multiculturalism – which should not be confused with critical forms of multiculturalism – refers to the flattening out of difference, as if they were equal and transitive. This reasoning allows for the mistaken claim that whites suffer from discrimination (e.g. reverse affirmative action) just as blacks have suffered from it "in the past."

The fragmenting effects of the global economy work in tandem with the fragmenting tendencies of whiteness. As a perspective, whiteness is historically fractured in its apprehension of racial formations. In order to "see" the formation in full view, whites have to mobilize a perspective that begins with racial privilege as a central unit of analysis. Since starting from this point would mean whites engage in a thorough historical understanding of "how they came to be" in a position of power, most whites resist such an undertaking and instead focus on individual merit, exceptionalism, or hard work. The act of interpreting the totality of racial formations is an apostasy that white students and educators must undertake but one which does not come easy or without costs. The costs are real because it means whites would have to acknowledge their unearned privileges and disinvest in them. This is a different tack from saying that whites benefit from renouncing their whiteness because it would increase their humanity. Whites would lose many of their perks and privileges. So, the realistic appraisal is that *whites do have a lot to lose* by committing race treason, not just something to gain by forsaking whiteness. This is the challenge.

In his discussion of gender and race, Terry Eagleton (1996) provokes a distinction between identity politics and class relations. He calls class position relational in a way that gender and race are not, because possessing a certain skin color or body configuration does not prevent another person from owning such traits. By contrast, a landless laborer occupies a material position because the gentleman farmer owns the land or property. Eagleton goes on to say that being black does not mean one is of a different species from a white person. Pigmentation is not definitive of a general human experience in the same way that freckle-faced people do not constitute an essentially different human category. In this, Eagleton exposes the racist and patriarchal imagination by highlighting its contradictions and illogics. However, his analysis leaves out a more powerful explanation of how racism actually works. Like most oppressive systems, racism functions through an illogical rationalization process. For instance, the one-drop rule, or the Rule of Hypodescent, demarcates blacks from whites by drawing an artificial and arbitrary line between them in order to both create more slaves and limit people's power to achieve whiteness. Thus, the power of whiteness comes precisely from its ability to usurp reason and rational thought, and a purely rationalistic analysis limits our understanding of the way it functions. Despite its contradictions, the contours of racism can be mapped out and analyzed and this is what Cheryl Harris (1995) attempts when she compares whiteness to owning property.

First, whiteness becomes property through the objectification of African slaves, a process which set the precondition for "propertizing" human life (Harris, 1995, p. 279). Whiteness takes the form of ownership, the defining attribute of free individuals which Africans did not own. Second, through the reification and subsequent hegemony of white people, whiteness is transformed into the common sense that becomes law. As a given right of the individual white person, whiteness can be enjoyed, like any property, by exercising and taking advantage of privileges co-extensive with whiteness. Third, like a house, whiteness can be demarcated and fenced off as a territory of white people which keeps Others out. Thus, calling a white person "black" was enough reason, as late as 1957, to sue for character defamation; the same could not be said of a black person being mistaken for "white." This was a certain violation of property rights much like breaking into someone's house. In all, whites became the subjects of property, with Others as its objects.

As Charles Mills (1997) explains, the Racial Contract is an agreement to misinterpret the world as it is. It is the implicit consensus that whites frequently enter into, which accounts for their fragmented understanding of the world as it is racially structured. When confronted with the reality of racial oppression, according to Hurtado, whites respond with:

> I will listen to you, sometimes for the first time, and will seem engaged. At critical points in your analysis I will claim I do not know what you are talking about and will ask you to elaborate *ad nauseam*. I will consistently subvert your efforts at dialogue by claiming "we do not speak the same language."
> (cited in McLaren *et al.*, 2001, pp. 211–12; italics in original)

The frequent detours, evasions, and detractions from the circuits of whiteness cripple our understanding of the racio-economic essence of schools and society. It is a distortion of perfect communication in Habermas's (1984) sense of it which creates what I call an altogether "ideological speech situation." That is, communication is ideological to the extent that the "ideal speech situation" is *systematically* distorted, which is different from saying that it is always a bit distorted. As Hurtado plainly describes, radical communication about the Contract meets apathy and indifference, perhaps a bit predictably. Admitting the reality of white racism would force a river of centuries of pain, denial, and guilt that many people cannot assuage.

In several instances, both in colleagues' courses as well as mine, white students have expressed their emotions and frustrations through tears when white privilege is confronted. In fact, Rains (1997) has described the same event occurring in her courses. Although it might seem cynical or unfeeling to analyze critically such an occurrence, it is important to deploy such a critique in the name of political and pedagogical clarity. It is imperative to address the local moment and "be there" for all students but in slicing through the pathos, one also benefits from reflection on the moment in its larger, global significance. The times when I have confronted this scenario can be described as the honest interrogation of racial power engaged by both white and non-white students. At certain moments, some anger has been expressed, sometimes frustration. In general, the milieu is emotional and politically charged. How can it not be? In one particular case, I witnessed a situation where a black student interrogated the issue of racial privilege and questioned a white colleague's comments for failing to do the same. By the end of the exchange, the white student left the room crying and the discussion halted. In another case, an earnest discussion took place about racism and ways to address it in schools. A white student cried because she felt frustrated and a little helpless about how she comes into the fold of becoming an anti-racist educator. After a minute of pause, students of color returned to the discussion at hand, not breaking their stride. In a third instance, in the midst of discussing the importance of building solidarity between teachers against racism, a white student cries and asks her colleagues to remember that they must stay cohesive and support each other as comrades in struggle. A colleague reports a fourth instance where, during a dialogue about the experiences of women of color, a white woman repeatedly insisted that the real issue was class, not race, because her experiences as a woman were similar to the women of color. When a faculty of color informed her that she was monopolizing the discussion and in the process invalidated the voices of women of color, the white woman cried and was unable to continue. In all these cases, we observed the guilt of whiteness prompting the women to cry in shame. Made to recognize their unearned privileges and confronted in public, they react with tears of admission.

Discussing (anti)racism is never easy and is frequently suppressed in mainstream classroom conditions. The establishment of the right conditions is precious but often precarious. In the first case, we must keep in mind that it was the black student who felt dehumanized and subsequently felt enough courage to express her anger about comments she perceived to be problematic. The act of crying by the white student immediately positioned the black student as the perpetrator of a hurt and erased/deraced the power of her charge. A reversal of sorts had just occurred. The white student earned the other students' sympathy and the professor followed her to the hallway to comfort her, while the black student nursed her anger by herself. Likewise, I could not help but feel for the white student. Upon reflection, an important difference needs to be discussed. In the act of crying, the student attenuated the centuries of hurt and oppression that the black student was trying to relay. In the act of crying, the student transformed racism into a local problem between two people. I couldn't help feeling that other students in the class thought the black person was both wrong and racist, erasing/deracing the institutional basis of what she had to say. The room's energy suddenly felt funneled to the white student.

Clearly, there are more "harmonious" ways of teaching the topic of race and racism. However, they also often forsake radical critique for feelings. Feelings have to be respected and educators can establish the conditions for radical empathy. That said, anger is also a valid and legitimate feeling; when complemented by clear thought, anger is frighteningly lucid. Thus, a pedagogy of politeness only goes so far before it degrades into the paradox of liberal feel-good solidarity absent of dissent, without which any worthwhile pedagogy becomes a democracy of empty forms. White comfort zones are notorious for tolerating only small, incremental doses of racial confrontation (Hunter and Nettles, 1999). This does not suggest that educators procure a hostile environment, but a pedagogical situation that fails to address white racism is arguably already the conduit of hostility. It fragments students' holistic understanding of their identity development through the ability of whiteness to deform our complete picture of the racial formation. It practices violence on the racialized Other in the name of civility and as long as this is the case, racial progress will proceed at the snail pace of white racial consciousness. White race traitors and progressive Others shall piece together a whole from the fragmentary pieces that whiteness has created out of this world.

The Contract challenges educators of the new millennium to explain the untruth of white perspectives on race, even a century after Du Bois's initial challenge. Obviously, this does not mean that whites cannot grasp the Contract; many do, but they cannot accomplish this from the white point of view, a worldview which, according to Gibson, projects a "delusional world," "a racial fantasyland," and "a consensual hallucination" (cited in Mills, 1997, p. 18). With the rise of globalization, education – which prides itself for inculcating into students knowledge about the real world – struggles to represent the world in the most real way possible. White epistemology can be characterized as fragmentary and fleeting because white livelihood depends on this double helix. It is fragmentary because in order for whiteness to maintain its invisibility, or its unmarked status, it must by necessity mistake the world as non-relational or partitioned (Dwyer and Jones, III, 2000). This allows the white psyche to speak of slavery as "long ago," rather than as a legacy which lives today; it minimizes racism toward non-white immigrants today through a convenient and problematic comparison with white immigrants, like the Irish or Jews. It is also fleeting because it must deny the history of its own genesis and the creation of the Other. It can only be concerned with "how things are and not how they got to be that way."

As a socio-spatial epistemology, whiteness sees the world upside-down. Mills (1997) and I agree when he says:

> *Thus on matters related to race, the Racial Contract prescribes for its signatories an inverted epistemology, an epistemology of ignorance, a particular pattern of localized and global cognitive dysfunctions (which are psychologically and socially functional), producing the ironic outcome that whites will in general be unable to understand the world they themselves have made.*
>
> (p. 18; italics in original)

According to Mills, whiteness concerns itself with racial details and misses the totality of the Racial Contract. Like the way it partitions the world according to its own image, whiteness constructs history as separate racial details without coherence. As a result, it fails to provide our students the language to link together California's Proposition 187 (anti-immigrant), 209 (anti-affirmative action), and 227 (anti-bilingualism) as related to white hegemony. With the exception of particular Asian ethnic groups (to which I will return later), all three legislations limit the rights of students of color. Fortunately, white and non-white activists have countered such measures with unrelenting protests and public organizing because, as Hopson *et al.* (1998) remind us, "[R]ecognizing and valuing language varieties and multiple ways of speaking among students is a precondition to understanding how to teach them" (p. 5). As a racial epistemology, whiteness is necessarily idealist in order to construct the Other as abstract, rather than concrete. Enslavement, discrimination, and marginalization of the Other work most efficiently when they are constructed as an idea rather than as people. They can be more easily controlled, aggregated as the same, or marked as unchanging and constant when textbooks idealize them as inconsequential to the history and evolution of humankind. In effect, whiteness eggs us on to yoke together different peoples around the globe under the sign of sameness.

Flexible whiteness and accommodation of the Other

Clearly, whites can no longer hide behind the façade of a color-blind discourse. Not that this stops many whites from doing so. However, with the increasing interrogation of whiteness as a social construction, an unearned center, and its spurious claims to superiority, it becomes more difficult to assert its invisibility (Winant, 1997). Through certain social developments, whites are coming to see themselves as racialized whites, not merely as individuals. In fact, invisibility has been its historical double bind. As a sort of Foucauldian (Foucault, 1979) racial panopticon, whiteness remained cloaked in darkness while marking those with darker complexion for purposes of effective surveillance. As a marker of the Other, whiteness was able to dodge relative scrutiny as a positionality, a morally conditioned, socially informed perspective. Instead, whiteness has long reserved the privilege of making everyone but itself visible, lest it be exposed as a position within a constellation of positions. At the same time, whiteness becomes the ubiquitous marker of all that is right because it is associated with being white.

Like finance capital, whiteness becomes more abstract and harder to locate. Whiteness, as a discourse, and whites as the subjects of such discourse have had to respond to this *ongoing* crisis, much like late capitalism, with whiteness studies only its recent challenge. In order to maintain its racial hegemony, whiteness has always had to maintain some sense of flexibility. That is, like late capital, white domination must work with scope, not scales, of influence, especially in times of crisis. It must accommodate subjects previously marked as Other in order to preserve its *group power*. In other words, for it to remain dominant, whiteness has to seduce allies, convince them of the advantages of such an alliance, and sometimes be able to forsake immediate advantages for long-term goals of domination. Nowhere is this more pronounced than the literature on the induction of the Irish into the white race. To a lesser extent, one can trace some of the same tendencies in the recent incorporation of Asians into the American racial polity.

Whiteness has had to show signs of flexibility in its ongoing quest for global domination. In the 1800s, white domination in the USA was introduced to a new problem: the Irish. As an oppressed group in western Europe, Irish people immigrated to the USA first to escape racial oppression and religious persecution on their homeland (Takaki, 1993). However, with the coming of the potato famine, Irish emigration from their beloved land became one of survival and simple existence. On American soil, the Irish were regarded as "black niggers" who were initially perceived as being closer to blacks than whites on the chain of being. Similar epithets and descriptions were leveled against Irish people as those used against blacks. They were called "a race of savages" with a low "level of intelligence," "lacking self control," and sexually animalistic (Takaki, 1993, p. 149). Negroes referred to them as "a Negro turned inside out" (Takaki, 1993, p. 153).[6] The "great educator" of the nineteenth century, Horace Mann, was greatly concerned about education's ability to civilize the Catholic and lazy-perceived Irish. In his comparisons between Irish racial oppression in Ireland and African and Indian racial oppression in the USA, Theodore Allen (1994) finds many intersecting themes in the groups' treatment by their oppressors. For example, he writes:

> *The essential elements of discrimination against the Irish in Ireland, and against the African-Americans, which gave these respective regimes the character of racial oppression, were those that destroyed the original forms of social identity, and then excluded the oppressed groups from admittance into the forms of social identity normal to the colonizing power.*
>
> (p. 82; italics in original)

The Irish, like North American Indians, became strangers in their own land through slow deculturalization campaigns by their oppressors. In Ireland, British rule outlawed the practice of Catholic holidays and the Irish language, beginning with the edict of Henry VIII in 1541 (Purdon, 1999). On US soil, colonists "civilized" Indians through English instruction and Protestant conversion (Spring, 2000). Like African slaves, the Irish, though not enslaved *en masse* and considered as free labor, suffered extreme labor exploitation as indentured servants and wage laborers. With respect to education, Charter Schools for Irish children in Ireland bear the imprints of colonial education, complete with paltry material conditions, neglect, and low levels of literacy.

However compelling the similarities may appear, Irish people eventually *became* white whereas blacks and Indians remain non-white. In addition, their racial oppression does not follow the modern sense of race as a form of skin color stratification. Moreover, the Irish embraced whiteness as a path to social mobility and economic independence. Takaki (1993) documents the shift from Irish abolitionism when in Ireland to acceptance of slavery upon arrival in the USA. This ironic twist highlights the contradiction in whiteness's ability to modify its own "purity" in order to retain group power. What it previously marked as subhuman, it later accepts as brethren. Irish ascendancy also shows the wicked flexibility of whiteness to offer broader membership for newcomers in exchange for allegiance to the white nation state. It marks the general transition of the Irish from green to white (Ignatiev, 1995), a process of both push and pull factors.

As competition for labor intensifies, the Irish are pushed away from working-class solidarity with blacks in order for the (white) bourgeoisie to disrupt class cohesion. At the same time, the Irish are pulled into white identity in order to maintain their privileges as white inductees. A purely economistic analysis fails to ask why Irish people vehemently competed with blacks for labor, rather than with Germans and Italians, who outnumbered free black laborers. In fact, as Roediger (1991) puts it, competition with Irish people for unskilled jobs was most felt from other arriving Irish people. Irish labor became increasingly regarded as white labor and as such would promote greater white solidarity and the naturalized expectations that came with this new found social position. Race and class make strange bedfellows when racial solidarity confounds class politics (see McLaren *et al.*, 2000). Were the Irish to align themselves with black labor, an intersectional coalition threatens both white supremacy and bourgeois power. Because we know whiteness is partner-in-crime with capital, it makes sense that the whitening of the Irish subverts both racial and class equality.

White flexibility works in tandem with capital's flexibility. They are the hour and minute hands of a clock, so predictable that it should not surprise the critical educator that where you find one, the other lurks closely behind. A global pedagogy of neo-abolitionism understands that whiteness is a nodal point in the triumvirate with capitalist exploitation and patriarchy. Thus, it makes little rhetorical sense to pose the question of, for a people persecuted on their own land, how could the Irish choose to oppress another group? Such a question betrays a certain politics of surprise about the reality of racial power. Whiteness conjures up a fictive solidarity when this is deemed convenient. To explain the Irish question as an instance of the bourgeoisie duping an unsuspecting slice of the working class overlooks the racial analysis that is mobilized by the transitional white group. It is a bit like a white family choosing to enroll their children into a school that boasts a weak or mediocre academic curriculum over a superior school because the latter is populated by too many Others, be they black or otherwise (Holme, 2000). At first glance, the rationalist or economic analysis suggests that the family in question forsakes its own immediate interests through an irrational thinking process. Upon further reflection, the family advances the long-term and global imperatives of white supremacy by encouraging racial segregation and white racial solidarity.

In many parts of the USA, today's Asian-American student is commonly touted as the "model minority." When discussing race relations, we must keep in mind that this favorable image is a commentary on the perception of African-American and Latino students as less than ideal students. Thus, it has been asserted that the apparently favorable status accorded Asian-Americans is a ploy to discipline their non-white counterparts. Also, it must be noted that although not all Asian-American groups benefit from such status in the same way, such as Hmong or Cambodian refugees, there is a general perception of Asians as the "intelligent minority." Dubbed as "whiz kids," "probationary whites," "honorary whites," or "Asian whites," Asian-Americans have prompted Hernnstein and Murray (1994) to revisit the eugenics debate to find proof of the genetic make-up of Asian intelligence. The authors also make claims on the African lag behind the Asian wonders. Citing a combination of hereditary and environmental factors, Hernnstein and Murray earned their controversy by raising the specters of de Gobineau or Binet. Neither their genetic nor environmental assertions are new. The main controversy surrounds their *reaffirmation* of the hereditary, essentialist argument about intelligence that many but a few scholars have refuted, dating back to Boas's (2000) study of the problems in more or less biological explanations of race.

For this present study, the Asian-American case is instructive because it exposes the social construction of whiteness and its political consequences. Historically degraded as "brown monkeys," "heathen Chinee," or "pagan," Asian-Americans and their educational ascendancy in the USA now signify their approach toward whiteness. This is not as impossible as it sounds when we keep in mind that certain south-east Asian groups have already claimed Aryan status based on geographical and linguistic roots (Mazumdar, 1989). This should not be confused with the position that Asian-Americans *are* white, but rather, *approaching* whiteness. Moreover, it is not necessarily the case that whites think Asian-Americans are white or, for that matter, that the latter consider themselves white. There are too many differences between whites and Asian-Americans to suggest that this is happening, ranging from cultural practices to certain forms of ethnic nationalism. However, this shows again the flexibility of whiteness to incorporate groups into its borders previously thought of as well outside of it. President George W. Bush's multicultural cabinet is a perfect example of the attempt to represent people of color within the confines of color-blind discourse.[7] President Bush's cabinet selections are honorary members of the neo-conservative project's inability to confront the race question, let alone the white question. Black and brown masks do not necessarily translate into progressive minds when it comes to racial discourse.

The favored status of Asian-Americans reminds us that whiteness mutates according to historical conditions. Amidst consistent criticisms of racial oppression in the USA, enter the bleaching of Asian-Americans. White supremacist discourse presents their particular position in the USA as proof that immigrant children can succeed in schools and thrive in society. As latecomers after the 1965 Immigration Act, Asian-Americans, as a racial group, provide more than enough evidence for the endorsement of US opportunity structure. Anyone can succeed; moreover, anyone can be white. With much effort and heart, African-Americans, Latinos, and Native Americans can also realize the American dream . . . of being white. But as we have seen in the Irish case study, becoming white is a two-way process. Not only must the structure provide the space for a group to become white, the group in question must desire whiteness. It is questionable whether such a two-way process is happening for non-whites today. There are some key differences.

With British imposition of English in Ireland, indigenous languages, like Gaelic, remain secondary for many Irish people. Thus, unlike the Irish, many Asian students speak a language other than English. Unlike the Irish, most blacks bear skin tones darker than most whites. And unlike the Irish, Native Americans have never considered themselves Euro-Americans. The incorporation of non-white students into the discourse of whiteness is tenuous at best. However, this does not suggest that it is impossible at worst. There are certain characteristics about Asian-Americans, for example, that suggest at least a compatibility with whiteness. One, certain Asian-American communities have developed a pattern of avoiding racial analysis of their lives (Sethi, 1995), opting instead for the discourse of hard work. Two, Portes and Rumbaut's (1990) research finds that Asian immigrants, by and large, arrive in the USA with a different class status and different material resources from their Latino counterparts. As a result, they comprise a selective group of immigrants and have a different contact experience with American class structures which puts them closer to white experience. In schools, Asian-American students are tracked with their white classmates and away from other racial groups, giving them an educational experience closer to whites. With respect to global expansion, China and Japan's imperialist histories resemble European military occupations all over the world. Clearly, the whitening of Asian peoples in the USA is a struggle without a verdict. The prerequisites have been s/cited but they are insufficient to suggest that Asians are making the transition from yellow to white.

Future directions in pedagogy, whiteness, and globalization studies

Within Marxist debates, the advent of Western or neo-Marxism inaugurated the cultural arm of social analysis. Lukacs, Frankfurt critical theory, and Gramsci emphasized the role of consciousness, subjectivity, and consent to explain what the blind spot of orthodox Marxism neglected. Rejecting both the determinism and teleology of Leninist varieties of historical materialism, neo-Marxism opted for a more variegated and nuanced theory of the social formation. It even engaged bourgeois culture and thought, suggesting that revolutionary theory must come to grips with high culture and art in order to map out the general superstructural features of social life. Likewise, in race theory, whiteness studies may be called a form of *neo-race theory*. More orthodox accounts of the racial formation traced white racism's effect on the lives of people of color through studies of slavery, discrimination, and school segregation. By contrast, neo-race theory finds it imperative to peer into the lives and consciousness of the white imaginary in attempts to produce a more complete portrait of global racism and ways to combat it. Recent themes of neo-race theory include white privilege, genesis of the white race, and white abolitionism (Roediger, 1991, 1994; McIntosh, 1992; Allen, 1994, 1997).

This new development in social and educational theory has been extremely productive and provides educators and students a critical vernacular with which to dismantle racist practices and chip away at white supremacist institutions. In our rush to consume such frameworks, bell hooks (1997) warns against neglecting the lessons learned from more orthodox explanations of racism's effect on people of color (see also, Morrison, 1970). As hooks explains, in the black imagination, whiteness is a form of "terror" (p. 169) that haunts all black people, regardless of their class position or politics (p. 175). With much attention being devoted to deconstruction of the white center, experiences on the margin fade to black. Nonetheless, any problematization of the margin necessitates a similar assault on its supplementary center. Said (1979) says as much in his study of Orientalism whereby the Orient is written into history by the Occident. Simultaneously, the Occident invents itself by inventing its Other.

White students do not disinvest in whiteness by claiming "I'm not white," since this is how whiteness currently operates. By and large, whites already believe they are individuals and not a racial group. The abolition of whiteness would counter this process. Neo-abolitionism is not the process of denying one's whiteness because white power is efficiently maintained through strategies of invisibility. White students must first own their racialization by naming its source in whiteness and recognizing it as fundamental to their development as alienated human beings. For whiteness, as a global formation, is alienating to its subjects and objects. As such, the global formation of whiteness is the target of critique. Abolishing race is mutually dependent with abolishing whiteness (Ignatiev and Garvey, 1996b) because the "possessive investment in whiteness" (Lipsitz, 1998) is arguably the strongest form of racialization, contrary to popular beliefs about minority identity politics. The English-only movement, anti-immigrant nativism, and Western-centric curricula represent white identity politics. It is responsible not only for the racialization of white subjects but also of non-white people. Moreover, a "critical race pedagogy" (Lynn, 1999) cannot be guided by a white perspective, which is not to say that it cannot include white experiences as points of departure. Although experiences do not speak for themselves, interpretation always begins with their lived dimensions (Sleeter, 1995). Taking its cue from critical race theory, critical race pedagogy does for education what critical race theory accomplishes for law: the interrogation of racially structured rules for social participation (Solorzano and Yosso, 2000). Global studies of whiteness work in partnership with critical race theories to arrive at the racialized core of knowledge production in schools.

A critical pedagogy of whiteness must be dialectical in order to avoid the reductive notion that whiteness is only bad (Giroux, 1997) or that white choices are reduced to the double bind of whites as either enemies or allies of students of color (Ellsworth, 1997). Taken literally, Giroux's suggestion appears to lack historical support since, as Roediger has suggested, whiteness as a racial category seems nothing but false and oppressive. When whites have articulated their choices through whiteness, the results have been predictable. Taken strategically, critical pedagogy must forge a third space for neo-abolitionist whites as neither enemy nor ally but a concrete subject of struggle, an identity which is "always more than one thing, and never the same thing twice" (Ellsworth, 1997, p. 266). This new positionality will be guided by non-white discourses. Again and to reiterate, there is a difference between white people, white culture, and whiteness. Students would do well to recognize the point that as they work against whiteness, they are undoing the self they know and coming to terms with a reconstructed identity. Like the abolitionists of the nineteenth century, white subjects of the twenty-first century commit one of the ultimate acts of humanity: race treason. This act of repudiation must be accompanied by a racial project of rearticulation whereby whites and students of color actively work to dismantle the material basis of white privilege (Winant, 1997). In other words, global pedagogy and neo-abolitionism are not only acts of free speech but of praxis.

Acknowledgments

I would like to thank my reviewers for their critical and gracious commentaries on my work. It was a pleasure to include their suggestions in the spirit of comradeship. Also, special thanks to REE editor, Professor David Gillborn, for working with me on the document from start to finish.

Notes

1 In the USA, a slew of books has been designed for beginners in specific subjects, such as *Weddings for Dummies* and *Homebuying for Dummies*. They provide an introduction to such topics and are not designed to be critical. Unlike the introductory but critical book by Anderson *et al.* (2000), *Field Guide to the Global Economy*, the fictive book, *Globalization for Dummies*, would offer uncritical analysis of global processes.
2 I use "Negroes" to observe DuBois's terminology. African-American or black will be used for more contemporary arguments.
3 *Color of Fear* has become a popular instructional video in the USA. It is a dialogue about race relations between nine men representing Latinos, blacks, Asians, and whites.
4 The Zapatistas of Chiapas, Mexico are a group of indigenous revolutionary guerillas who have banded together against the Mexican Government in order to protect their land and human rights. Their symbolic leader is Subcomandante Insurgente Marcos whose assistance has allowed the group to use the Internet for relaying their communiqués on a global scale (see Juana Ponce de León, 2001).
5 For nativism American style, see Hopson *et al.*, 1998, pp. 6–10.
6 Again, I use Negroes to observe terminology of the time.
7 US President George W. Bush's cabinet is a multicultural group, comprised of representatives from different ethnic and racial groups but each bringing a right-wing agenda to government: e.g. Secretary of State Colin Powell (African-American), Secretary of Education Rod Paige (African-American), National Security Adviser Condoleezza Rice (African-American), Transportation Secretary Norman Mineta (Japanese-American), Labor Secretary Elaine Chao (Chinese-American), Energy Secretary Spencer Abraham (Lebanese-American), White House Counsel Alberto Gonzales (Latino-American).

References

Allen, R. L. (2000) The globalization of white supremacy, paper presented at the *Annual Conference of the National Council for the Social Studies*.
Allen, T. (1994) *The Invention of the White Race*, vol. 1 (London, Verso).
—— (1997) *The Invention of the White Race*, vol. 2 (London, Verso).
Anderson, S., Cavanagh, J., Lee, T., and Enrenreich, B. (eds) (2000) *Field Guide to the Global Economy* (New York, The New Press).
Blackmore, J. (2000) Warning signals or dangerous opportunities? Globalization, gender, and educational policy shifts, *Educational Theory*, 50, 467–86.
Boas, F. (2000) Instability of human types, in: R. Bernasconi and T. Lott (eds) *The Idea of Race* (Indianapolis, IN, Hackett Publishing Co. Inc.).
De León, J. P. (2001) Traveling back for tomorrow, in: J. P. De León (ed.) *Our Word is Our Weapon: Selected Writings Subcomandante Insurgente Marcos*, pp. xxiii–xxxi (New York, Seven Stories Press).
Delgado, R. and Stefancic, J. (eds) (1997) *Critical White Studies* (Philadelphia, PA, Temple University Press).
Dilg, M. (2000) Response to Rosa Hernandez Sheets's review of *Race and Culture, Educational Researcher*, 29(9), 24–6.
DuBois, W. E. B. (1989) *The Souls of Black Folk* (New York, Penguin).
Dwyer, O. and Jones, J. P. III (2000) White socio-spatial epistemology, *Social and Cultural Geography*, 1, 209–22.
Eagleton, T. (1996) *Postmodernism and its Illusions* (Oxford, Blackwell).
Ellsworth, E. (1997) Double binds of whiteness, in: M. Fine, L. Weis, L. C. Powell, and L. Mun Wong (eds) *Off White: Readings on Race, Power and Society*, pp. 259–69 (New York, Routledge).
Fine, M., Weis, L., Powell, L. C., and Mun Wong, L. (eds) (1997) *Off White: Readings on Race, Power and Society* (New York, Routledge).
Flecha, R. (1999) Modern and postmodern racism in Europe: dialogical approach and anti-racist pedagogies, *Harvard Educational Review*, 69, 150–71.
Foucault, M. (1979) *Discipline and Punish* (New York, Vintage).

Frankenberg, R. (1993) *White Women, Race Matters: The Social Construction of Whiteness* (Minneapolis, MN, University of Minnesota Press).
—— (ed.) (1997) *Displacing Whiteness* (Durham, NC, Duke University Press).
Freire, P. (1993) *Pedagogy of the Oppressed* (New York, Continuum).
Giroux, H. (1997) *Channel Surfing* (New York, St Martin's Press).
Habermas, J. (1984) *The Theory of Communicative Action*, vol. 1 (Boston, MA, Beacon Press).
Hall, S. (1996) What is this "black" in black popular culture? in: D. Morley and K. Chen (eds) *Stuart Hall*, pp. 465–75 (New York, Routledge).
Hargreaves, A., Lieberman, A., Fullan, M., and Hopkins, D. (eds) (1998) *International Handbook of Educational Change* (Dordrecht, Kluwer).
Harris, C. (1995) Whiteness as property, in: K. Crenshaw, N. Gotanda, G. Peller, and K. Thomas (eds) *Critical Race Theory*, pp. 276–91 (New York, The New Press).
Harvey, D. (1989) *The Condition of Postmodernity* (Cambridge, MA, Blackwell).
Hernnstein, R. and Murray, C. (1994) *The Bell Curve* (New York, Free Press).
Hesse, B. (1997) White governmentality: urbanism, nationalism, racism, in: S. Westwood and J. Williams (eds) *Imagining Cities: Scripts, Signs, Memory*, pp. 86–103 (London, Routledge).
Holme, J. J. (2000) The role of ideology and social networks in residentially-based school choices: a précis, paper presented at a meeting of the *Sociology of Education Association*.
hooks, B. (1997) Representing whiteness in the black imagination, in: R. Frankenberg (ed.) *Displacing Whiteness*, pp. 165–79 (Durham, NC, Duke University Press).
Hopson, R., Green, P., Yeakey, C., Richardson, J., and Reed, T. (1998) Language and social policy: an analysis of forces that drive official language politics in the United States, *Chicago Policy Review*, 2(2), 1–24.
Howard, G. (2000) Reflections on the "white movement" in multicultural education, *Educational Researcher*, 29(9), 21–3.
Hunter, M. (1998) Colorstruck: skin color stratification in the lives of African American women, *Sociological Inquiry*, 68, 517–35.
Hunter, M. and Nettles, K. (1999) What about the white women? Racial politics in a women's studies classroom, *Teaching Sociology*, 27, 385–97.
Ignatiev, N. (1995) *How the Irish Became White* (New York, Routledge).
Ignatiev, N. and Garvey, J. (eds) (1996a) *Race Traitor* (New York, Routledge).
—— (1996b) Abolish the white race by any means necessary, in: N. Ignatiev and J. Garvey (eds) *Race Traitor*, pp. 9–14 (New York, Routledge).
Jaggar, A. and Rothenberg, P. (eds) (1993) *Feminist Frameworks*, 3rd edn (Boston, MA, McGraw Hill).
Kincheloe, J. and Steinberg, S. (1997) Addressing the crisis of whiteness: reconfiguring white identity in a pedagogy of whiteness, in: J. Kincheloe, S. Steinberg, N. Rodriguez and R. Chennault (eds) *White Reign*, pp. 3–29 (New York, St Martin's Griffin).
Kincheloe, J., Steinberg, S., Rodriguez, N., and Chennault, R. (eds) (1997) *White Reign* (New York, St Martin's Griffin).
Leonardo, Z. (2000) Betwixt and between: introduction to the politics of identity, in: C. Tejeda, C. Martinez, and Z. Leonardo (eds) *Charting New Terrains of Chicana(o)/Latina(o) education*, pp. 107–29 (Cresskill, NJ, Hampton Press).
Lipsitz, G. (1998) *The Possessive Investment in Whiteness* (Philadelpia, PA, Temple University Press).
Lukacs, G. (1971) *History and Class Consciousness* (Cambridge, MA, MIT Press).
Lynn, M. (1999) Toward a critical race pedagogy: a research note, *Urban Education*, 33, 606–26.
Mander, J. and Goldsmith, E. (eds) (1996) *The Case against the Global Economy* (San Francisco, CA, Sierra Club Books).
Marable, M. (1996) Staying on the path to racial equality, in: G. Curry (ed.) *The Affirmative Action Debate*, pp. 3–15 (Reading, MA, Addison-Wesley).
Mazumdar, S. (1989) Race and racism: South Asians in the United States, in: G. Nomura, R. Endo, S. Sumida, and R. Long (eds) *Frontiers of Asian American Studies: Writing, Research, and Commentary*, pp. 25–38 (Pullman, WA, Washington State University Press).

McIntosh, P. (1992) White privilege and male privilege: a personal account of coming to see correspondences through work in women's studies, in: M. Andersen and P. H. Collins (eds) *Race, Class, and Gender*, pp. 70–81 (Belmont, CA, Wadsworth Publishing).

McIntyre, A. (2000) A response to Rosa Hernandez Sheets, *Educational Researcher*, 29(9), 26–7.

McLaren, P. (1995) *Critical Pedagogy and Predatory Culture: Oppositional Politics in a Postmodern Era* (New York, Routledge).

—— (1997) *Revolutionary Multiculturalism: Pedagogies of Dissent for a New Millennium* (Boulder, CO Westview Press).

—— (2000) *Che Guevara, Paulo Freire, and the Pedagogy of Revolution* (Lanham, MD, Rowman and Littlefield).

McLaren, P. and Leonardo, Z. (1996) Paulo Freire, in: E. Cashmore (ed.) *Dictionary of Race and Ethnic Relations*, 4th edn, pp. 134–6 (New York, Routledge).

McLaren, P., Leonardo, Z., and Allen, R. L. (2000) Epistemologies of whiteness: transforming and transgressing pedagogic knowledge, in: R. Mahalingam and C. McCarthy (eds) *Multicultural Curriculum: New Directions for Social Theory, Practice, and Policy*, pp. 108–23 (New York, Routledge).

McLaren, P., Carrillo-Rowe, A., Clark, R., and Craft, P. (2001) Labeling whiteness: decentering strategies of white racial domination, in: G. Hudak and P. Kihn (eds) *Labeling: Pedagogy and Politics*, pp. 203–24 (New York, Falmer Press).

Memmi, A. (2000) *Racism* (Minneapolis, MN, University of Minnesota Press).

Mills, C. (1997) *The Racial Contract* (Ithaca, NY, Cornell University Press).

Morrison, T. (1970) *The Bluest Eye* (New York, Plume).

Portes, A. and Rumbaut, R. (1990) *Immigrant America: A Portrait* (Berkeley, CA, University of California Press).

Porter, P. and Vidovich, L. (2000) Globalization and higher education policy, *Educational Theory*, 50, 449–65.

Purdon, E. (1999) *The Story of the Irish Language* (Dublin, Mercier Press).

Rains, F. (1997) Is the benign really harmless? Deconstructing some "benign" manifestations of operationalized white privilege, in: J. Kincheloe, S. Steinberg, N. Rodriguez, and R. Chennault (eds) *White Reign*, pp. 77–101 (New York, St Martin's Griffin).

Rimonte, N. (1997) Colonialism's legacy: the inferiorizing of the Filipino, in: M. Root (ed.) *Filipino Americans*, pp. 39–61 (Thousand Oaks, CA, Sage).

Root, M. (ed.) (1997) *Filipino Americans* (Thousand Oaks, CA, Sage).

Roediger, D. (1991) *The Wages of Whiteness* (London, Verso).

—— (1994) *Toward the Abolition of Whiteness* (London, Verso).

Said, E. (1979) *Orientalism* (New York, Random House).

Sandoval, C. (1997) Theorizing white consciousness for a post-empire world: Barthes, Fanon, and the rhetoric of love, in: R. Frankenberg (ed.) *Displacing Whiteness*, pp. 86–107 (Durham, NC, Duke University Press).

Sartre, J.-P. (1963) Preface to *Wretched of the Earth* (New York, Grove Press).

Sethi, R. (1995) Smells like racism, in: P. Rothenberg (ed.) *Race, Class, and Gender in the United States: An Integrated Study*, pp. 89–99 (New York, St Martin's Press).

Sheets, R. (2000) Advancing the field or taking center stage: the white movement in multicultural education, *Educational Researcher*, 29(9), 15–21.

Sirotnik, K. and Oakes, J. (1986) Critical inquiry for school renewal: *Liberating Theory and Practice*, in: K. Sirotnik and J. Oakes (eds) *Critical Perspectives on the Organization and Improvement of Schooling*, pp. 3–93 (Boston, MA, Kluwer-Nijhoff).

Sleeter, C. (1995) Reflections on my use of multicultural and critical pedagogy when students are white, in: C. Sleeter and P. McLaren (eds) *Multicultural Education, Critical Pedagogy, and the Politics of Difference*, pp. 415–37 (Albany, NY, SUNY Press).

Solorzano, D. and Yosso, T. (2000) Toward a critical race theory of Chicana and Chicano education, in: C. Tejeda, C. Martinez, and Z. Leonardo (eds) *Charting New Terrains of Chicana(o)/Latina(o) Education*, pp. 35–65 (Cresskill, NJ, Hampton Press).

Spina, S. (2000) The psychology of violence and the violence of psychology, in: S. Spina (ed.) *Smoke and Mirrors: The Hidden Context of Violence in Schools and Society*, pp. 177–209 (Lanham, MD, Rowman & Littlefield).

Spring, J. (2000) *Deculturalization and the Struggle for Equality*, 3rd edn (Boston, MA, McGraw-Hill).

Takaki, R. (1993) *A Different Mirror* (Boston, MA, Little Brown).

Tatum, B. D. (1997) *Why Are All the Black Kids Sitting Together in the Cafeteria?* (New York, Basic Books).

Wah, L. M. (Producer/Director) (1994) *The Color of Fear* (Video) (Oakland, CA, Stir-fry Productions).

Warren, J. (2000) Masters in the field: white talk, white privilege, white biases, in: F. Winddance Twine and J. Warren (eds) *Racing Research, Researching Race: Methodological Dilemmas in Critical Race Studies*, pp. 135–64 (New York, New York University Press).

Wells, A., Carnochan, S., Slayton, J., Allen, R. L., and Vasudeva, A. (1998) Globalization and educational change, in: A. Hargreaves, A. Lieberman, M. Fullan, and D. Hopkins (eds) *International Handbook of Educational Change*, pp. 322–48 (Dordrect, Kluwer).

Winant, H. (1997) Behind blue eyes, in: M. Fine, L. Weis, L. C. Powell, and L. Mun Wong (eds) *Off White: Readings on Race, Power and Society*, pp. 40–53 (New York, Routledge).

PART III

PRACTICES
Life in school

CHAPTER 9

GOOD, BAD AND NORMAL TEACHERS

The experiences of South Asian children

Ghazala Bhatti

In *Asian Children at Home and at School*, London: Routledge, pp. 178–206, 1999

Introduction

Much has been written about the effects of school processes on school children. Researchers have been interested in exploring student responses to different teaching styles and school ethos. In terms of this study, it is important to look particularly at ethnographic studies of those secondary schools that have an ethnically mixed intake including Asian children.

Wright's (1986) ethnographic study was quite significant in the way it drew attention to the African Caribbean experience of racism within secondary schools. It was not able to focus on the Asian experience. Mac an Ghaill's (1988) study focused on the theme of 'resistance within accommodation' which was how some Asian and African Caribbean young people in his sample reacted to their experiences of racism at school and college. Asian and African Caribbean girls were united, and known as 'The Black Sisters'. They were able to use the school in a way that was 'instrumental, that is, knowledge is not valued for its own sake but as a means to an end, that of gaining qualifications'. But Asian and African Caribbean boys experienced and 'resisted' school rather differently. The 'Rasta Heads' openly rejected school values and school curriculum, whereas Asian boys, 'The Warriors' as a working-class subcultural group, put up resistance and 'carried on their anti-school practices covertly'. The latter's resistance remained largely invisible to their teachers, who took more notice of African Caribbean boys. Although Mac an Ghaill has looked at some of the aspects of social class, 'race' and gender, his focus on racism to the near exclusion of other factors can give the impression that if this aspect is rectified somehow *all* other problems would be resolved for the young people. My research suggests a far more complex picture. Undoubtedly racism is a very powerful constraining factor, but although Mac an Ghaill had negotiated access to these children's homes, the study did not consider the children's home-related concerns, such as the differences between African Caribbean and Asian girls' responses to gender-specific preoccupations. No analysis was presented of the young people's linguistic and cultural heritage, their interactions with parents, nor was there a serious discussion of staff room and within-class ethnography.

Another secondary school based ethnographic study which looked at Asian children's experiences is that of Gillborn's (1990). He concentrated on Asian male pupils, mainly under the heading of differentiation and polarisation within the school, and found that

> in terms of their academic careers the Asian males in City Road experienced school in ways which resembled the careers of their white rather than their Afro-Caribbean peers.
>
> (Gillborn 1990, p. 100)

But the similarity in terms of the academic careers of white and Asian boys needs to be studied with more detailed knowledge of their social class, ethnic and linguistic backgrounds, and their numbers/percentages in particular schools. Middle-class children's experiences of schooling, for instance, may be qualitatively different from working-class Indian Bangladeshi children's. Gillborn did not study Asian girls' views and experiences within the mixed comprehensive school. Wade and Souter (1992) studied British Asian girls, but not British Asian boys.

Drawing on Asian children's accounts of their daily encounters with their teachers and peers, this chapter will attempt to address some of the omissions from previous studies by focusing on Asian children's experiences of and expectations from Cherrydale. It begins by describing children's categories of 'good', 'bad' and 'normal' teachers, drawing attention to those vivid instances which caused particular distress to children and those which Asian children quoted as examples of racism. The chapter then explores children's feelings about school more generally and looks at what they wanted from school in their own terms. The effect of gender is also considered.

Asian children and their teachers

Like other children in Cherrydale School, Asian children described some of their teachers in graphic detail. Some of the instances include the experiences which they shared with the whole class. But they talked often in emotional terms about other events which they experienced individually. All this had implications for the categories in which children placed their teachers.

Before presenting details of teachers who fall into different categories, it is important to explain how these categories were derived from children's conversations and questionnaires and how they all fit together. Some children used words such as 'caring', 'kind hearted' and 'helpful' and 'not-caring', 'mean' and 'unfair' whereas others used words such as 'racist', 'non-racist' and 'plain normal'. All children claimed to know which teachers liked children. Unlike their parents many Asian children did not assume that most teachers liked all children. Asian children were clear in their own minds about what distinguished a good teacher from a bad one. The most frequently used words throughout the sample were 'good' and 'bad' and 'just normal'. These three main categories cover all the teachers in the school. The children's category system was not always simple and straightforward. For instance whereas all racist teachers were 'bad' teachers, not all non-racist teachers were automatically 'good' teachers. Most non-racist teachers were 'just normal' unless they displayed other attributes. These qualities are described in the next section. It was easier to detect from children's individual accounts the qualities of 'bad' teachers than it was to immediately tell the difference between 'good' and 'normal' teachers. This was a difficult task and I had to confirm my understanding of Asian children's categories several times before arriving at the following conclusions from questionnaires and conversations.

There were altogether sixty teachers in Cherrydale school; fifteen of these were consistently described as 'bad' teachers. Of the 'bad' ones five were 'racist' teachers. There were eight 'good' teachers in school and all the rest, that is thirty-seven, were 'just normal'. There was widespread consensus about this. Obviously not all children were taught by every single teacher but the reputations of the 'good' and the 'bad' teachers travelled through the school and children could explain the differences quite vividly. It is possible that some children could have been prejudiced (for or against) some teachers by knowing about them before actually meeting them. It must be said at the outset that children on whom I relied for most of the information in this chapter were not themselves ethnographers. They related recent and long remembered accounts of what they experienced as their realities.

Woods (1993, pp. 15–19) has discussed research on pupils' conception of the 'good' and the 'bad' teachers. Most of the pupils in previous studies like those in my sample thought that good teachers should be able to teach and make children work and keep control. Some children in my study expressed a preference for a strict teacher so long as he or she made them work hard. The role played by humour in teacher–student relationships has been discussed by many researchers including Woods (1976), Walker and Goodson (1977) and Stebbins (1980). The children in my sample described the kind of humour they did not like. As in many previous studies (see Gannaway, 1976; and Furlong, 1977) 'soft' teachers were seen as ineffective and described as 'bad' teachers.

'Good' teachers

Asian children had a clear idea of who a good teacher was. This was a combination of their perceptions of the teacher's teaching abilities and the teacher's general attitudes towards them. What follows is an 'ideal type' of the good teacher. Obviously not every good teacher had all these qualities. A good teacher was somebody who could control the class and make all children work. She or he was somebody with a sense of humour which did not touch on racist or sexist topics, neither would it verge on sarcasm. Children, irrespective of ethnicity and gender, were offended by three particular teachers who were frequently sarcastic. Sarcasm was always equated in children's minds with arrogance and misuse of power. A good teacher was a fair-minded teacher who preferably told children off in private and did not make a spectacle of them in public in front of their peers (see also Docking, 1987, p. 79.) Such a teacher would in addition praise children too and smile and not look serious all the time. Such teachers explained things very slowly so that everyone could understand them. They would not ask one child to explain things back to the whole class knowing full well that the child had not understood. A good teacher did not have one favourite but many favourites, each for a different occasion:

> Take Mrs Nicholas, she likes Tom for carrying things, Jill for cleaning the board, me for giving things out, Sammy for tidying her table. Mr Thomas, now he is a different sort. He only chooses girls.
>
> (Sunil: 33, taped conversation)

A good teacher gave clear instructions and did not scold individual children but reprimanded the whole class. A good teacher displayed every child's work at some time. A good teacher did not need to shout. Asian children, together with other children, made fun of teachers who shouted at them frequently. Shouting caused silent hysteria at the back of the class in the case of those teachers who were not considered to be particularly effective at controlling children. Some children offered to take me to good and bad teachers' classes, an invitation I could not resist but could not always accept.

Good teachers gave out notes to children who had missed their work because of absence or illness and did not often make them copy things from somebody else because that would make that person feel very important. Good teachers were supposed to set a little bit of homework from time to time, which they marked promptly, but they were forgiven if they did not. Children looked forward to their lessons. Good teachers were described by many children as 'X' (excellent), 'brill' (brilliant) and 'ace'.

Above all, good teachers did not send many children in detention or in the annexe and they did not need to 'go running to the deputy head for cover' (Yusuf: 12). Good teachers confiscated sweets and chewing gum but returned them to the children at the end of the class or made the child share them with everyone else including the teacher. Good teachers liked children. They were interested in cricket and football results and in television programmes such as *EastEnders* and *Neighbours*. Children could talk to them about 'normal things' (Mala: 20).

A good teacher was someone who went out of the way to help those children who were having problems. Instances of such help quoted to me were a teacher intervening with other teachers on behalf of the students to let them have extra time to hand in an assignment, giving up lunch breaks to help children, occasionally visiting children at home without complaining about them to their parents about mischief done at school. This category was a personal one for individual children and was linked to the teachers' general attitude to the whole class as well as their attitude to the individual.

Among Asian children it was interesting to note that the words 'caring teachers' within the 'good' category were most often mentioned by the Bangladeshi newcomers to Britain. They were grateful for any kind of help which was offered to them, most particularly help with English. They were the most appreciative of any children in the sample as far as relationships with teachers were concerned. Any negative encounters they may have had with their white peers were offset against the help that teaching assistants and ancillary staff offered them mostly within the class. They were not withdrawn from their normal classes for extra lessons. They were equally happy about any rare home visits they received from teaching assistants. They did not differentiate between teachers and teaching assistants. So long as they helped them with their English, Bangladeshi children treated them with equal respect. They were shocked at the noisy behaviour of the rest of the class and thought that children were not taught to respect their teachers in Britain. This would just not happen in Bangladesh.

> They are so naughty. They *swear* you know, about their teachers. I think that is very bad. Very, very bad.
>
> (Hasina: 50, field notes)

> They are lucky. They have nice building and things to do here . . . and they don't like teachers, some of them. I don't understand that.
>
> (Nazar: 44, taped conversation)

These children had experienced deprivation and could see the contrast between the school they attended in Bangladesh and the school they were attending in Cherrytown. They found it difficult to understand the attitude of some children in their classes. They held particularly negative opinions about their Asian peers' disobedience. They felt very ashamed (they told me) if another Asian child misbehaved in school because that 'spoilt the name of all' Asians. They were rarely in top sets. They never participated in whole class discussions or in anything which required a team effort at class level; they were thus heavily dependent on teachers for most of their interactions in English. By contrast, they excelled in Bengali classes. Success in Bengali helped to build their confidence. These particular Bangladeshi children could not believe that teachers could be racist towards them. They did not understand or failed to recognise how that could be possible.

> Teachers are there to help you. If you are good, teacher will help you. If you are naughty, what can teacher do? Racist, you mean rude? How can teacher be rude? Children are rude.
>
> (Saghar: 19, taped conversation)

From the other children, there were by comparison fewer examples of caring acts which teachers had performed. It could be argued that the criteria described by Bangladeshi newcomers to Britain were not applicable to all the rest. Even so, I did hear examples of some individual teachers, who had, in the children's opinions, helped them greatly.

> Well Mr McLaren you see . . . he is caring. He will always stop and ask how the lesson was and if things are OK at home and he looks worried when I miss his lesson . . . and he gives out notes to me and that is very kind.
>
> (Qasim: 2, taped conversation)

> Mr Jones actually talked to my father and made him let me go on a trip. He said he would look after me and make Mrs Smith personally responsible . . . my father listened. No one else is so good in this school, not for me anyway. Most teachers are plain normal.
>
> (Parveen: 8, taped conversation)

The reputation of being a good and caring teacher mostly had to be earned through personal one-to-one interaction.

'Bad' teachers

Again, what follows is an 'ideal type'. Bad teachers could neither control children nor teach them. They were boring people. They did not like children and should be teaching old-age pensioners who would 'sit deaf and dumb to listen to boringness' (Manzar: 3). They shouted all the time and got very red in the face. They had 'pokey' and 'squeaky' voices and they could not respond to a joke from the children. They felt they were there to teach and everything else was a waste of time including cricket and football and television programmes like *Grange Hill* and *Neighbours*. Bad teachers liked one person in the whole class whom the rest of the class made fun of. Children often sat and discussed what kind of a human being had married or was going to marry such a boring teacher.

Maahin: She'd [the teacher] probably feed him spinach soup everyday.
Shama: Yuck and cabbage and brussels sprout *salan* [curry]. Yuck yuck.

(Taped conversation)

Sohel: He [the teacher] will spend all his time looking grumpy. He'll never buy his wife a treat. He never gives us sweets not even [at] end of term.

(Taped conversation)

Food was important to children of this age. It was interesting however that Maahin and Shama thought in terms of the female teacher feeding her partner/ husband and Sohel thought in terms of him buying her presents. Bad teachers could not control naughty children. They could not make their lessons interesting. They were predictable in their behaviour and the work they set. They never went out on school trips with the children. They were unfair people who picked on individuals lesson after lesson. Once they made up their mind about individual children they did not change their opinion easily. These teachers were caricatured with tremendous zeal and did not seem real when they were described eloquently with a mixture of passion and humour. There were, time and time again in conversations with both boys and girls, vivid instances and live demonstrations of humour as a coping strategy:

Once old grumpoo don't like you, he never never *can* like you. TOUGH! [shrug of one shoulder and a wink copying a teacher: this teacher often said 'tough']

(Asad: 5, field notes)

Bad teachers were not open to reasoning. Children could not talk them out of their apparently perpetual bad mood. Bad teachers were also moody people who did not tell the children what exactly the children had done to deserve the bad mood. They were adults with whom children could not make amends. They did not tell the children anything about their personal life. Bad teachers were more likely than good teachers to have a nickname. Asian children used the same names which the rest of the children used. In Cherrydale School these were 'Slow torture' (boring long lessons), 'Speedy' (latecomer to class), 'Dracula' (shouted to frighten children), 'Uniformy' (wore the same clothes to school daily), 'Suede Shoes' (wore worn-out leather shoes, not suede) and 'Postman Pat' (sent complaint letters home and put many children on report, that is, children had to get a piece of paper signed for good behaviour by every teacher for a week).

Racist teachers were always 'bad'. They stereotyped Asian children. They thought, several children separately told me, that most Asian girls got married at 16 or soon after and most Asian boys were noisy male chauvinists. (Although I heard some comments from teachers which would confirm the fairly widely held view about girls, I did not hear comments which would confirm the opinion held about boys.) These were teachers who always looked serious and wore a scowl on their faces; according to the children they did not have any sense of humour. They actually managed to hurt the children by their attitude both by saying things and by not saying things and pretending not to notice hurtful behaviour which was being perpetrated against Asians and African Caribbeans. Children told me they could always sense if a teacher fell in the racist category. There was a possibility of some children calling those teachers racist in whose lessons they were having

Table 9.1 Incidents of alleged teacher racism

Instances quoted of teachers' racist behaviour	Number of occurrences reported by different children
Not given the chance to answer questions in class	23 = 19 boys, 4 girls
Not given any responsibility in class (giving out books etc.)	15 = 12 girls, 3 boys
Being singled out for punishment or admonishment	35 = 33 boys, 2 girls
Not being helped in class	25 = 14 boys, 11 girls
Being ignored	12 = 10 boys, 2 girls
Teachers not believing complaints against white peers	21 = 21 boys
Teachers being racially abusive of other students in their absence (all references about five particular teachers)	16 = 5 boys, 11 girls

particular difficulties. It was difficult to ascertain whether some children were blaming the teacher as a figure of authority for their own problems or whether their accounts were wholly true. Racist incidents and the number of times they were mentioned to me by different individual children are set out in Table 9.1. They were mentioned repeatedly in connection with particular teachers whose classes I was not able to observe often. In my presence the teachers whom the children put in the racist category did not do the kinds of things that Asian children said they normally did. This is not altogether surprising, given my presence as an identifiable Asian adult.

I repeatedly asked the children for concrete evidence to support their references to teachers' racism, such as perhaps the atmosphere in the classroom. This was not always an easy topic for the children to broach, as many instances might sound ambiguous and unprovable. The powerful feelings expressed like the ones indicated in the following sections made it difficult to deny their negative impact. If the children felt upset about an incident it had a dimension of subjective truth for them which had to be taken into account and dealt with very sensitively.

A significant point, which came up very frequently, was that most Asian children in Cherrydale School did not remember having been taught by *any* Asian mainstream teachers in Britain. Those who were taught by the first mainstream, non-white, African Caribbean teacher at Cherrydale School found her strict but good because she forced them to do their best and because she was really angry when they missed school. Most Asian children whom she taught thought she was caring and they put her in the 'good' category even though two Asian girls admitted that they were terrified of her. They also admitted they had tried to 'wind her up'. Only two children mentioned having been taught for one term by an Asian business studies teacher.

'Normal' teachers

The normal teachers, who were most numerous in Cherrydale, were situated between the two extremes described as 'good' and 'bad'. They did not have any outstanding negative attributes. They were sometimes caricatured in the names which children bestowed upon them and yet they seemed to be on the whole nondescript. The children had little to say about them and they did not spend much time talking about them but to say things to the effect that: 'If you don't hassle him he don't hassle you' (Yusuf: 12). Another interesting and highly original use of descriptive language for the normal teacher was that used by the confident bilingual Uzma (9). 'He is OK. What can I say? Not very warm, not very cold, just *kunkuna* [lukewarm]!' A normal teacher was mostly a harmless, fair-minded person who would occasionally do peculiar things like 'phoned my father, just imagine! To ask if he'd come to parents' evening. Mostly he's normal. Mostly he doesn't do that' (Asad: 5). Children's general opinions about what kinds of pupils teachers liked best were mostly based on their interactions with their normal teachers.

All children had an opinion about what sorts of pupils were the ones that the teachers liked and what kinds of pupils were the ones the teachers disliked and why. They could tell me with touching honesty which teachers they themselves were good to and which ones they did not much care about or were disobedient with, and why. Predictably they were on their best behaviour with the good teachers and had different coping strategies to deal with the bad ones. With normal teachers they claimed to behave normally.

Distress caused by teachers

There were many instances of Asian children reporting individual teachers who 'picked' on them and made an example of them and African Caribbean children rather than white children.

> Last week David kept talking to me in maths and he never said anything to him for ages. When I turned around to tell him to shut up I got sent out. That's not fair is it? If you answer back he [the teacher] goes mad.
>
> (Tahir: 39, taped conversation)
>
> I think Mr Hawkins is racist you know because each time I put my hand up or another Black or Asian kid does, he doesn't ask us. He *always* asks a white kid. You come and see for yourself.
>
> (Shakeel: 35, taped conversation)

In another incident I was told that

> You know when you get stuck in your work and you put your hand up to ask for help, she *never* comes. And if you moan then she will come very near the bell time and then you stay behind [in your lesson] don't you, till the next lesson, because all the white kids will have done it and you won't. This happens [to me] so many times. And what can I do about it? Can't tell other teachers.
>
> (Sunil: 33, taped conversation)

Incidents repeatedly brought up in conversations are summarised in Table 9.1.

There were ten children who individually explained to me what exactly made them feel so uncomfortable with certain teachers. A random selection of incidents which hurt the children, and which they considered racist but too petty to mention to their parents or other teachers, are reported here. I was not present at any of these incidents.

It was when we were going to draw pictures of our teacher in art and he said 'Oh no you can't draw me in shorts, you can't do that I'm Muslim and Muslims don't show their legs!'

(Parveen: 8, field notes)

This was said to a Muslim girl in front of the whole class, who laughed at her. There is implied sexism in the remark, besides the allusion to Muslims.

In cooking we were talking one day about recipes and different dishes and one teacher said if we had ever eaten nignogs because that was one of the things written in a book she had, called *Good Housekeeping*. Karen [African Caribbean child] was not in the class then.

(Tasneem: 11, taped conversation)

Tasneem knew that the comment would have hurt Karen a lot. What saddened her was that of all the dishes in the book the teacher made it a point to mention this one. They did not make that particular dish in the end.

It was that French teacher. All of us [Asian] children get into trouble with her sooner or later. She goes on and bloody on about how French is the best language in the world, and how some people speak funny sounding languages.

(Qasim: 2, taped conversation)

Qasim's Urdu was quite good and he tended to speak Urdu with two friends. He felt that she was talking about Asian languages in particular. African Caribbean girls too told me about this particular teacher's 'stupid, dumb' behaviour. This was further confirmed by white children who attended her class and who felt that she was unduly harsh with children from ethnic minority backgrounds. Yet the children felt that she did not actually do anything outrageous enough for them to report her to anyone.

But you can *see* racist teachers are like that. You can't actually prove anything about them often . . . They just *are* {racist}.

(Saira: 38, taped conversation)

The important common factor in all these reported incidents was that the girls and boys did not feel able to do anything about it. Although the children were hurt by the experiences, they felt that these incidents were too petty to report to anyone. It became obvious that even if they wanted to talk about this to someone, they would not know which particular person in school they should talk to. Besides, there was at that time no equal opportunities policy statement in the school and no statement of pupils' rights which could be referred to. It was all very ambiguous, so that when such incidents occurred the children did not know how seriously to take them, or who to turn to. They talked to their friends about it, they told me, and left it at that.

Racism and the teaching staff

The incidents mentioned here were different in degree and kind from the incidents the children considered much more serious, which were consistently mentioned about particular 'bad' teachers. One of these was lack of action on the teachers' part when children were being racist towards each other in the teachers' presence. One typical incident reported to me in this connection was by a friend of the boy who was 'picked on'.

> One day after the test Mrs Hinds was calling out names of kids who got high marks. Someone asked who got the lowest marks and the teacher said 'Zafar Ali'. Someone shouted at the back 'All Pakis are dumb'. Everyone laughed. *Everyone* heard it, even Mrs Hinds . . . She didn't do nothing. She pretended she never heard it. There was no punishment, no . . . Then the same damn teachers tell you to ignore it, just like *they* do.
>
> (Salman: 25, experience related in fourth year, taped conversation)

Zafar was not the only one who said that some teachers were good at pretending not to hear offensive racist remarks which were aimed at particular children. Zafar was so incensed about the way no reprimand followed the comment from his classmate, that he did not go to school for two whole days. He just sat in the park, nursing his pride. He said he had got low marks because he had been ill the previous week and did not know they were going to have a test, otherwise he would have been better prepared. He did not talk to his parents about it because he said he did not want to worry them. His paternal grandmother had died around that time and his father was very anxious about going away to Pakistan to take part in the burial. It was *his* battle. The school was not told about Zafar's other pressures at home because he felt that the school was

> Good at kicking you when you are down, if they can't help me with studies how can they help in other things?
>
> (Zafar: 32, taped conversation)

He was convinced that he had to learn to be a 'strong man' and would have to solve any problems on his own.

Some children called out offensive names, then, at a lack of response, those children hurled bags across the floor to trip up children who were not responding to the provocation. As this mostly happened during lunch breaks and after school teachers tried not to notice. Now and then, some Asian children told me, things got out of hand.

> *Tahir*: They call us Paki, bingo, curry chappati, curly worly {reference to hair, aimed at both African Caribbean and Asian children}.
>
> *Bilal*: Yeah and umm . . . curtain, greasy {oily hair} and when we are in a gang we call them honky tonky, pagan, red necks, piggy wiggy . . . If we are not in a gang, tough luck ain't it!
>
> (Taped conversation)

It was difficult to be sure how far teachers were aware of the prevalence of racial abuse. Not a single teacher during the course of this research once mentioned it to me as one of his or her main worries. It never formed the subject of serious discussion in the staff room during all the time I was there, though it was clearly a major daily battle for many Asian and African Caribbean children.

When teachers did take action it was often seen sarcastically by the Asian children as an act of tokenism, not real concern or reassurance. Such critical incidents were more often mentioned by boys. The following is a typical example where the teacher's intervention was seen by Asian boys in the class as 'a real good pretending to care'. It was reported to me by Nazim's friend Amir.

> In class that day one boy was giggling and pulling faces at Nazim. Then he called Nazim Paki, so Nazim told Jimmy that he'll get him after school. I don't know how Cole {form teacher} got to know about it. He was not in class at the time, he had gone to get the stapler. When Cole asked Jimmy Manders he said 'I wasn't calling him Paki. I was making jokes about them other Asian peoples that's all.' You know what Cole did? He told Jimmy Manders not to do that again and made them shake hands . . . Ha! . . . Jimmy wasn't put in detention. Now he's going around doing it to other little kids.
>
> (Amir: 36, taped conversation)

There were instances quoted to me by African Caribbean and Asian children, of spiral provocation between white and non-white boys, on both sides, which ended in the African Caribbean or Asian boys being put in detention or being sent to 'the annexe' (a form of solitary confinement during class time). The teachers who witnessed the final act, saw it as the last straw, did not always seem to explore details about the build up behind the particular incident which led to the Asian child's punishment. The following incident is an illustration of this. The child who was eventually punished was seen as the loser in the event by his opponent and his peers, thus adding insult to injury. Whenever the teachers punished an Asian or African Caribbean child in such circumstances it was construed by the punished child as a racist act *because* in the child's estimation the white child got away scot free. Teachers did not appear to be fair minded from these elaborate accounts.

> It was going on and on between us for days, in maths, in English then in PE Kevin beat me with a hockey stick on my legs during the games lesson. I told him to stop it. After the lesson I asked him why he did it. He said he'd do it again. So my mate grabbed him and I hit him. Williams and Hicks {teachers} annexed me and my mate all day. They said they will expel me if I'm caught again! Nobody asked *him* why he hit me with the hockey stick! These are good racist teachers . . . huh, and they knew!
>
> (Dilip: 42, taped conversation)

Asian boys in these instances expected more fairness from their teachers because they were adults. In the event of that not happening in the boys' estimation, it was seen as collusion between white people at the expense of Asians, and added a kind of subterranean tension which the teachers did not seem to do anything about.

Although it is very rare for examples of racism by teachers to occur openly in an Asian or African Caribbean researcher's presence during ethnographic research, one instance that could be interpreted in this way did occur in my presence when the tape recorder was left running and I was making notes. This was construed as racism on the part of the teacher by the Asian boy who was unfairly punished. It was the only incident of its kind which I witnessed in several months of fieldwork, and it occurred during a typically misguided, mismanaged, noisy, uncontrolled humanities class, which always seemed to start five to seven minutes late. The teacher Amanda Paine (AP) used to enter looking harassed and leave even more harassed. Time passed very slowly, even for a researcher, in her lessons, and the children had nicknamed her 'slow torture'. I was sitting behind Asad and Shakeel at the back of the class. The following account is based on a transcript of my tape of the lesson, supplemented by field notes.

> The boys always sat at the back of the class concentrated in the left half of the room. The girls mostly sat in the front rows. (Fifteen minutes into the lesson)

> *AP*:   You must work out what you were doing from last week. Then you can do today's work.
> *Paul*:   But Miss what were we doing last week?
> *John*:   {shouting} Yea. He don't know nothing Miss.
> *Chloe*:   It was them graph things with the blue ink.

> Noise level was rising slowly. Shakeel sitting in front of me laughed aloud. Miss Paine fixed him with a stare.

> *Paul*:   But Miss, Miss, ask John to stop it this minute.

> John was sitting behind Paul on Shakeel's right at an adjacent table and was trying to pull Paul's bag lying on the floor towards himself, using his foot as an aid. Asad was sitting on Shakeel's left.

> *Asad*:   Fancy footwork, John. {tape}
> *John*:   Shut up Asad. You keep out of this. (John and Asad look at each other)
> *Ann*:   Miss can I borrow a sharpener?

Ann walked across to Liz's table without waiting for an answer. With her back to Miss Paine she put a smartie in her mouth, winked at me and went away with the sharpener. Ann put her hand up looking at me. 'Miss can somebody help me?' Miss Paine nodded. I walked across to Ann's table to help her. It seemed Miss Paine had no intention of getting up. Noise level was quite high. Miss Paine was reading the book to herself. Some children, mostly girls and one African Caribbean boy, were trying desperately to concentrate on their work.

When I got back approximately ten minutes later to my previous place there was an argument going on between Asad and Shakeel on the one hand and John and Paul on the other (field notes). In the general noise of the classroom the conversation had not been audible from Ann's table. Something had flared up in the few minutes I was away. The following is a transcript of the tape recording.

> *Shakeel*:   Your referee cheats in cricket any way.
> *John*:   Pakis are always playing foul. Now *you* should know that.
> *Shakeel*:   {looking at me} Did you hear that?
> *John*:   What can *she* do? The whole world knows. I saw it with me own eyes on telly. {Reference to the Shakoor Rana and Mike Gatting incident in Faisalabad, Pakistan. It was cricket season.}

The atmosphere was getting charged. Miss Paine was busy writing the date on the blackboard. Lot of general noise in class which sounds incoherent on tape. Shakeel looking very provoked, shoved the book aside and pushed the chair back. Lull in noise level.

> *John*:   Look at him! Paki Pakora {Latter said in a near whisper but audible to Shakeel, Asad and me}

Shakeel:	I'll smash your face in, you clown {said very loudly}
AP:	{turning around} Right that's enough. Shakeel leave the class this minute. (field notes and tape recording)
Shakeel:	But Miss . . .
AP:	Out! Go and stand outside . . . God these boys!

I wrote in my field notes that Shakeel made a lot of noise collecting things and putting them in his bag. There was a look of great satisfaction on John's face. There was pin-drop silence in the class. Ann and Teresa and Huma looked sympathetically at Shakeel who walked out showing a fist to John.

After the lesson I asked Shakeel what he would do. He said that the teacher was racist and should be sacked but that he would sort things out with John eventually. I had tried to ask John what would happen to him, but he just pushed me aside as he walked away when the bell rang. Miss Paine's decision to send an Asian boy out instead of punishing both boys was racist in its outcome if not in intention. Had both boys been Asian or white the matter might not have had racist connotations. The incident led next day to a fight between three white and three Asian boys outside school premises and outside school hours. Both Shakeel and John were involved. Shakeel's friends told me about the fight. They did not tell their teachers.

When Shakeel was sent out of the class it had seemed an irrational, impulsive act on the teacher's part. Other children had also been making a noise and not just Shakeel. It had seemed surprising to me at the time that Miss Paine did not keep the quarrelling parties behind to try and ascertain the circumstances which had led to the incident. Miss Paine did not leave the classroom to explore what had happened. She did not send either of the two boys to detention classes. She did not to my knowledge discuss the incident with a more senior teacher. If she had brought it out into the open, my presence in the classroom as a researcher, together with comments from their peers who saw the whole event, could have been used to establish a fairer outcome for the boys. At the time it had seemed puzzling that she did not discuss the incident with me. One possible explanation for this could be that she was not accountable to me and did not consider me worthy of discussing the incident with. She may not have discussed the incident with me either because she knew I was quite close to some of the children, or because it might have amounted to acknowledging that she had failed to maintain discipline in her class. She might have been aware of my need to keep what I had observed confidential. I am not sure whether she would have discussed it with a male researcher or a white researcher. It is possible that Miss Paine was tired that day and wanted to go home. It was the second last period on a Thursday afternoon. Perhaps she had had a difficult day or had taught unusually demanding classes on that particular day. It is hard to believe that Miss Paine thought the matter would end there as far as the boys were concerned. She had even seen John's rude behaviour towards me and had not admonished him. Perhaps she did not feel responsible for the boys' behaviour.

As a teacher she could have done a number of things. She could have asked the whole class to be quiet for some time. She could have changed the boys' places. If she felt that she had to send Shakeel out she could have sent him on an errand instead of sending him out as a punishment. She could have read something to the whole class. She could even have asked me to go and find a senior member of staff. Miss Paine did none of these things. She did make some comments to me in passing immediately after the lesson about rude children. She did not once acknowledge that her style of teaching and lack of classroom control had something to do with what happened. She thought the boys in her class were the worst she had ever seen and blamed them for making things difficult by wasting her time. She could not believe Shakeel could ever be good in any class. I told her about how good he always was in Urdu classes. She looked surprised and unconvinced. She did not mention John's rudeness. It is just possible that she did not see it, but that does not seem very likely. Miss Paine did not once mention that she could improve her class management. The reason she let me come into her classes was that she knew I was following Huma, Paul and Asad in different classes.

I felt very uneasy at the end of each of these lessons and after this particular incident considered asking one of the deputy heads to come to the children's rescue. In the end I did not because I felt that the news of my indiscretion would travel through the teaching staff and would put an end to my access to other classes. It was a most difficult decision.

When those Asian girls who were better achievers than Shakeel spoke of racism, it was never in the context of physical incidents or physical violence, but in terms of implied allusions. It was as though the girls began to categorise in their own minds as racist, incidents which had happened to them in the past as well as noticing those which occurred now. These girls spoke bitterly of being 'used by the teachers when the teachers needed *my* help but not helping me out when I needed their help' (Saira: 38). Asian girls were hardly ever excluded or punished at Cherrydale in the way that boys were. Asian girls were seen by most of their teachers as passive quiet creatures who were 'really well brought up', according to a maths teacher. Nevertheless, they were bitter when they realised what had happened to them along the way. One incident which captures the feelings of being 'used' is set out below:

> Each time they wanted to worm things out about Asian children they asked other Asian children. Me? I was *always* called in to translate for them, you know, for parents who only speak Punjabi. At that time I felt very important of course. I thought look Miss asked *me* from the whole school. Miss Ellis told me I was so intelligent and reliable! But when it came for the time for me to apply to university they did not believe I would get the grades. They could have said earlier, I would have brushed up my revision better . . . I was stupid. I believed the school was on my side! I think they were racist, don't you?
>
> (Parveen: 8, taped conversation)

Parveen's story raises several points. The school did not have or did not want to maintain close contact with a member of staff, or with somebody at the Multicultural Centre whose help could be sought when needed. Instead the school had to rely on children, who were not really in a position to refuse. At most it shows a lack of sensitivity. It was difficult on the basis of available data to ascertain whether Miss Ellis actually said that Parveen was intelligent and reliable. Assuming words to such effect were used by the teacher, it is possible that they were used only in the context of translation and not as a general statement. I did not have access to Parveen's predicted grades or to her progress reports over the years to check her achievements against teachers' predictions. It could be the case that Parveen assumed she would be able to gain entry into a university very easily and it turned out to be harder than she had imagined. By her own admission she had not revised as well as she could have. Miss Ellis had left the school by the time I learnt Parveen's story, so I could not hear Miss Ellis's account of the same. To call the school racist on the strength of Parveen's story alone would seem premature.

If such incidents occurred repeatedly among Asians and African Caribbeans as opposed to white working-class students, then there would be reason to think that Cherrydale was intentionally discriminating against such students. I do not have comparable data. However, incidents like these can be racist in outcome if secondary schools like Cherrydale fail to monitor their policy and practice.

Another incident quoted to me of being 'used' was one related by a bus driver's daughter. The same incident was quoted to me by a white parent who later became a local councillor and was present on the occasion one year before I started the research, thus confirming Saira's account. Saira said she had reached the sixth form by the time it dawned on her what had been happening.

> You would not believe it! There I was dumbo idiot standing in front of so many people in the hall, telling them all white black and all {prospective parents} what a good school Cherrydale was and how all Asian parents should send their children to it because here we could wear our own dress and LOOK here we could study what we liked! Bloody hell! Two years after that I discovered that the same school didn't care a toss! They forgot, *forgot* to tell me I needed biology O levels to get into medicine! Mr Hill helped me but he never used me. To them {rest of the school} I am just Muslim, just a bus driver's daughter. *That* to me is real racism . . . You can never quite prove it, right? They all defend each other. You should have seen them when they needed my help! I feel so sick I can't bear to think what an idiot I have been. God!!
>
> (Saira: 38, taped conversation)

When I enquired about Saira at school, especially from teachers who she said had 'used' her, there was an uncomfortable silence. Whereas previously they had been talking happily, teachers dropped their gaze and looked away. One of her previous teachers said 'Saira was all right; she had never needed much help.' It is difficult to verify whether teachers forgot to advise Saira or she was advised about biology and she forgot. Perhaps the particular teachers whom Saira came across were ignorant about entry requirements. Saira singled out one teacher who came to her rescue and wrote to medical colleges on her behalf. He was the head of history. Apart from him all other teachers had fallen in Saira's estimation. When Saira was asked to talk to people about her school in public she was very flattered. It was only when she failed to gain admission to a medical college that she became self-conscious and put it down to teachers' alleged prejudices about her social class and religious background. It may be that teachers had simply not thought about her as a potential university student and had not considered what subjects she needed to take for a particular university course. It is also possible that had Saira not encountered any difficulties with her intended course she might not have felt that most teachers were being racist towards her.

It is significant that not a single Asian boy related a similar incident to me where he felt 'used'. Asian girls, it would seem, are 'used' more than Asian boys.

Teachers and the gender effect

Asian girls and boys interpreted school processes differently. Each had a lot to say about the way teachers treated the other. Asian boys thought that Asian girls were treated leniently whereas Asian girls thought that Asian boys were ostentatious and therefore often got themselves into trouble.

Asian boys' accounts

Almost all children – boys and girls, regardless of ethnicity – said that girls could get away with breaking 'small rules' (Oliver, white 14-year old) more easily than the boys, and that teachers were particularly partial towards Asian girls. This opinion was first brought to my attention by white boys, who felt that they were 'got at' (Simon, white 14-year old) by teachers more often than girls were. There was an informal hierarchy among those who were caught.

> They [Asian girls] can come in late, even ten minutes late into science and get away with it. Teachers are real softies with Asian girls . . . Take that Amina. She will look at her shoes and mumble something and walk away. Dead cool like . . . You watch me when I try mumbling into *my* shoes . . . oh boy, oh boy Goggles will annexe me if I do that.
>
> (Joseph, white 14-year old, taped conversation)

There were several examples quoted in this vein by boys, Asian, African Caribbean and white. According to them Asian girls in particular were excused more easily if they failed to hand in their work on time, or if they truanted. If they were caught they were let off lightly. They were not scolded for misbehaving in class nor for answering back. They were not reprimanded for copying work from the girl sitting next to them in class. They were seldom caught while talking in class.

Asian boys also mentioned arranged marriages when they spoke of teachers' attitudes towards Asian girls.

> It is very simple. They [teachers] feel sorry for you. You are doomed. You are an Asian girl with arranged marriage written on your face . . . Of course if you are a boy you can *never* never have arranged marriage . . . oh no.
>
> (Nazim: 7, taped conversation)

This seemed to be a particularly sore topic with both Asian girls and boys. Girls felt that the teachers stereotyped them. Boys felt that teachers were not concerned about them.

Something else emerged from talking to boys: Pakistani and Indian boys felt neglected. They told me in great detail how in their opinion teachers treated Bangladeshi newcomers to England differently from the way they themselves were treated.

> *Manzar:* They say nothing to you if they can feel pity for you. 'Oh poor thing Bengali boy, you're new to our wonderland we better pity you, we better not tell you off!!' [said in a high pitched tone, mimicking a teacher] that is what they say to themselves. But if you are good in speaking English they don't try to make you better, get you gooder marks. They think you're fine!
> *Dilip:* Yes. Once you speak English, you don't get real help no more.
>
> (Taped conversation)

It was true that the school had no provision for offering second stage help in English as a second language. It was significant, however, that boys like Manzar and Dilip were able to diagnose their own needs. Asian girls did not talk about favouritism or about teachers' patronising attitudes towards newly arrived Bangladeshi girls. This does not rule out the occurrence of such incidents among Bangladeshi girls.

Asian boys, like boys in general, said they could not respect teachers who failed to control the classes and make the children work. They had more contempt for 'soft' male teachers than for 'soft' female teachers. The boys, both Asian and white, related instances where

> Downs just stands and smiles! I mean Jeff throws books around. Peter pulls faces. And there is Old Softie smiling!
>
> (Kevin, white 14-year old)

Softie teachers whose class management allowed disruptive noise to rise to the detriment of classroom activities were especially despised.

Asian girls' accounts

Those girls who saw themselves as 'just normal, not very thick not very clever,' (Halima: 48) seemed to be judging themselves according to the ability band in which they were placed by most of their subject teachers, though it was difficult to say so with absolute certainty because of lack of access to children's records. These girls and those whom their peers expected to get into university or college said similar things. They thought that boys were forced to prove themselves to their male friends in a peculiar kind of combat, and that girls did not labour under that sort of pressure.

> You know how it is, each boy has to show off to his friends about how strong he is. So he must belong to a gang to *look* strong. Girls don't have to do that. They can if they want to, but they don't *have* to.
>
> (Naz: 1, taped conversation)

Many girls, Asian, white and African Caribbean, felt that boys on the whole got into more trouble with teachers than they themselves did. They did not think that Asian boys got into more trouble than white boys did, a point disputed heatedly by Asian boys. This happened according to most of the girls because boys were more mischievous and they knew they could get away with less drastic consequences than girls could as far as their parents were concerned.

> They won't be *made* to stay at home to help at home will they? I mean if anything goes wrong . . . [if they overstep the limit at school] . . . if you are a girl it will be quite bad. You may not be able to go to college.
>
> (Amina: 13, taped conversation)

The gossip factor mentioned earlier was evoked again and again in this context. In terms of teachers' attitudes, girls complained that many of their teachers assumed that they would be married off young. They said that the ghost of arranged marriage was more often mentioned by their male than their female teachers.

> 'Your sister got married then? Was it last weekend? When will you get married, Kalsoom?' he says. He has no business saying that to me.
>
> (Kalsoom: 24, taped conversation)

Asian girls were much more aware of an audience, of peers overhearing comments made by teachers about them. They were far more self-conscious than Asian boys were. Many Asian girls mentioned arranged marriage as a vexed topic.

It is difficult to say much, on the strength of available data, about the extent to which white teachers' assumptions about Asian girls' early arranged marriages negatively affected their expectations of them academically. This topic needs to be researched systematically. This would probably affect more the life chances of those Asian girls who were placed in lower and middle ability bands. Six Asian girls and two Asian boys in particular spoke bitterly about the low academic expectations that their teachers had of them. This was mostly, though not always, true of the first child in the family, through whom the education system was being tested by the parents (see Bhatti (1999), chapter 3).

In classroom observation it was not always possible to tell the differences between those girls who were keen to study on and those who might have been waiting to get married, as all Asian girls were quiet in their classes most of the time. By comparison Asian boys appeared to be less quiet. Stanley (1986) has written about the way in which girls deliberately keep quiet and do not always draw attention to themselves. Asian girls in my sample excelled at this. Some Bangladeshi girls were struggling in their English lessons and suffered from a great deal of consternation at having to stand in front of the whole class and perform short plays and even to read aloud. Their teachers did not make allowances for what they saw as acts of timidity.

Teachers' alleged lower academic expectations of Asian children

Many Asian children who found themselves retaking exams in the sixth form felt that teachers did not press Asian pupils as much as they could have. I was not able to verify whether teachers pressed white pupils more than Asian pupils. More detailed data would be required to explore this further. Cherrydale School, however, was aware that its pupils did not obtain as high grades as another school in the city.

Elaborate explanations were often offered by Asian children of why teachers behaved in the manner they did.

> One dirty fish spoils the whole pond they say in Punjabi. It is the same here, isn't it? If there is one stupid Asian boy or girl in class they [teachers] think we are all the same.
>
> (Parminder: 49, field notes)

I asked this sixth former to explain exactly what she was implying. She thought that teachers did not expect Asian children to do well at school because there were some disobedient Asian children in the school (alluded to in the above proverb) who spoilt everyone else's chances. She felt that as a consequence all Asian children had to bear the brunt. I also learnt that she, together with the three other Asian girls who were retaking exams, felt that they had not been 'stretched enough' in secondary school in the first place, otherwise they would not have had to retake examinations.

Parminder's view was typical of Asian sixth formers, several of whom told me their teachers should have set them more homework which they should have marked. They felt generally that if they had been put under more pressure they would have achieved better exam results. One of the girls explained to me her feelings of anger and disillusion with a teacher who upon her failing to get into a medical college said, 'What, a B and still whinging!' (Uzma: 9). She was upset because she thought with a little more help and pressure she could have got the grades she needed instead of which she was being told that she should be grateful for what she did get.

> I went home and cried. He would have been happy if I failed everything I suppose. I now go around telling everyone to work hard for A levels from the very first day and not treat it like . . . baby exams. Nobody told us A levels were so different from other exams.
>
> (Uzma: 9, oldest child, taped conversation)

It was difficult to say for sure whether these children were able to see the whole picture clearly or whether they were taking account of their own lack of best effort in obtaining the grades they retrospectively felt they could have got 'with some extra pushing'. Others who retook exams felt that they had not tried their very best consistently and that they were in large noisy classes which made it difficult for them to concentrate. They also felt that when they met the same teachers in the sixth form they were treated very differently from the way they had been treated in previous years. They thought that their teachers had 'improved'. Asian children did not make any explicit connections in their conversations about teachers' changed attitude as a direct response to their having got older.

Other experiences of education

Besides the experiences which have been described so far Asian children spoke about other matters related to schooling and education. These are discussed briefly in this section.

Educated in two countries

Seven newly arrived children from Bangladesh and two Pakistani children who found themselves moving between Bangladesh and Pakistan, had the experience of being educated in two countries (see Bhatti, 1999, pp. 270–1). Except in one case the Bangladeshi children had fathers on low incomes. These families had undergone much stress as they had only recently been reunited after several years. These children were grateful that they could attend school. One of the children with whom I was having a group discussion told me in a matter of fact voice one day 'my parents are not educated. That is why we are in a mess' (Zeeba: 22).

Zafar (32), Shakeel (35) and Aslam (43) had attended schools both in Britain and Pakistan. Their perceptions of education in the two countries were interesting, even though these children were a small minority in the sample.

> You are taught *loads and loads* in Pakistan. You get *loads* of homework and heavy books, yeh? You are afraid if you don't finish it. I had four homework books in Gujarat. You have to buy them yourself and cover them with brown paper so they don't get dirty . . . If you drop your book on the floor because it is full of **ilm** [knowledge] you have to kiss the book . . . otherwise you will remain **budhu** [stupid] [laughter]. If the teacher calls out your name over

there you have to listen with attention or he'll get mad . . . here you can mess about, yeh?

(Aslam: 43, taped interview)

They felt that they learnt more in Pakistan but they enjoyed and 'messed about' more in lessons in Britain. Classroom observations of the boys quoted above confirmed their statements.

'Repeaters'

'Repeaters' has a negative connotation in the subcontinent because it refers to those who do not pass their examinations and are obliged to stay down a year. There were six children, mostly boys, who by their own account were likely to be 'repeaters'. They were mostly Pakistani boys who felt that they did not manage to achieve what they wanted and they would use the sixth form or a college of further education for instrumental purposes to try and 'learn again, new things if I can' (Shakir: 10). These children felt let down by school:

> I wish they had pushed me more at school. Mr Collins should have *made* me do it like he made me practise for football matches.
>
> (Maqbool: 40, field notes)

Children like Maqbool were more likely than the rest of the sample to join the college of further education.

In a group discussion I had with five Pakistani boys, one boy had this to say to his peers and me about his older brother's experiences at Cherrydale. He classes himself as a future 'repeater' and began to see schooling as an instrumental process.

> But Mr Richards said he should be able to find some apprenticeship. They gave him admission [re-admission at the sixth form] because he was quiet like, had given them no serious trouble and when he did well enough to get into college no one was surprised. Sajid said Mr Richards would've been pleased if he failed again. So he [Sajid] says you should use school as a repeater if you fail. No point liking it or trying to enjoy it. Just slog, like.
>
> (Tahir: 39, taped conversation)

Reading

This generation of Asian children had gone through Cherrydale School without having cultivated the habit of reading at home. They said they did not bring books to read at home on a regular basis, and they had passed the stage of reading aloud daily to their teachers. They were not regular users of the public library even though they remembered having had library cards at some point in their lives. Only three children out of fifty made use of the public library, roughly on a monthly basis. They said they spent some time during the school holidays in the public library when they accompanied their mothers to the shops. The main public library was located in the main shopping centre. On the whole their written English would have benefited immensely from extra reading and writing. This was something that some of the children realised when they approached their school leaving age. They found it difficult to fill in forms. In more than half of the cases I filled in the questionnaires for them while they spoke lucidly and looked on. They said they would have found it easier to complete them at home in their own time. They preferred to talk things through rather than fill the answers in a form. One of the tasks they found most difficult was writing essays at home, they told me. Only four children had dictionaries at home. Two out of the four reported actually using them at home.

Problems with homework

By the time girls and boys were old enough to join Cherrydale School, the responsibility for completing homework lay on their own shoulders. There was a pattern of diminishing interest in school matters which they shared with me. Once an Asian child entered the secondary school and found himself or herself running into difficulties with subjects like science and English, the next logical step was to try and approach the subject teacher for extra tuition. When that and 'home help' failed to materialise, life was very difficult for those who were determined to make a success of it at any cost. It needed considerable determination to succeed. It would have been very useful to have had access to these children's maths, science and English results for three years during which I was involved in the fieldwork and to have compared that with the rest of the children in their year groups, but this was not possible because I was not granted access to such information. The members of staff whom I approached did not find time to sit and talk to me specifically on this matter and also told me that they did not see any point in it as all the children were treated

> in exactly the same way and all the teachers try their best to let all children realise their full potential.
>
> (head of CDT, field notes)

A 'colour blind' approach is apparent from this rhetorical comment (see also Bhatti, 1999, chapter 8).

Feeling invisible at school

Many Asian children, mostly those in the fifth year and in the sixth form, told me that they felt invisible in school. Their mainstream teachers did not celebrate their presence, their festivals, their culture or their achievements. If someone from their background had done very well academically, the school did not acknowledge it. When I asked whether the same teachers acknowledged other children's achievements better and pointed out that I had not seen other children's photographs on the walls either, I was told vehemently by the sixth formers that three teachers continuously gave examples of high achievers who were white who had got good grades in the previous year but they never during the course of the whole year mentioned Asian young people who had got into a university in the past. They said any positive comments about successful Asian students who had previously attended the sixth form would have encouraged them enormously. Asian children felt that if they did well they too would soon be forgotten. They then began to wonder if the school cared about them even while they were there.

Others who were not in the sixth form felt invisible too. I was told that in the third year their PE teachers for instance did not let them rest and not do PE during *Ramadan* (the Muslim month of fasting) unless they brought letters from home every day. Nine children who did not have older brothers and sisters who could write fluent letters in English said they had to forge letters and signatures because their parents could not write in English. They would not dream of bringing letters written in Urdu or Bengali into school, because they knew there was 'no one in school who could read that anyway'. They felt that if the school had not had one particular deputy headteacher (Mrs Fisher) who cared about them they would have been even more 'unwanted and invisible'. They also felt that the school did not really make any effort to invite their parents in. The school never during the course of this research told parents that there would always be someone there who would be able to explain matters to them in Punjabi or Bengali. All these things made Asian children feel invisible in school even though they looked different from white children because of their colour and on that account were highly visible. In addition they were also noticeable because of their names, religion, culture and so on.

Several children felt that their teachers did not make any effort to pronounce their names properly and because of that they were called a name which bore no resemblance to their real name at home. This sometimes resulted in their friends, including their Asian friends at school, calling them something completely different from the name their parents called them at home, reinforcing yet again the difference between home and school.

Some said they had got used to it. Six children said they felt invisible because they had to please their teachers but their teachers did not have to please them. They knew that this was also the case with many of their white peers and that this was what school was all about. As Saira once said to me drily, 'at home parents are always right, at school teachers are always right'. They themselves dwelt somewhere in between and had to learn to negotiate their own space. Twenty-six children said they had at different times asked the school to help them get in touch with home teachers and told me that unlike their primary and middle schools, which kept telephone numbers of such people, only two of the teachers at Cherrydale seemed to know what these children were talking about. Their Cherrydale teachers were similarly, they felt, not prepared to give them extra tuition even when the children said they needed them and some were ready to pay.

> The woman thought I was a raving lunatic! All I said was I didn't understand the physics experiments she was teaching us and wanted the name of a home teacher who could teach me a bit!
>
> (Qasim: 2, taped conversation)

Qasim said he did not ask again.

The kinds of children teachers liked

Children thought that teachers liked polite, good-mannered, well-behaved children who were, according to a widespread opinion, 'hard working and brainy and who did what they were told' (Maqbool: 40). The words mentioned frequently were bright, brainy, intelligent, good and 'goodie'. Teachers also liked children who did not miss their lessons and who did not 'creep'. More girls than boys felt that teachers liked children who cared about their work and offered to help their teachers. Six boys told me their teachers were scared of boys who 'gave an attitude back' and who lived in Lawley. These boys did not live in Lawley themselves. Teachers liked children who were well dressed and rich and those who agreed with everything the teacher said and did not argue back. To the question 'I think most of my teachers care about me', ten said yes, sixteen said no, eight said that they did not know and sixteen did not answer. Most of the fifty Asian children did not openly say they felt that teachers really cared about them. Of the ten who thought teachers cared about them, eight were girls.

Expectations and aspirations

Many young people in the sample said they wanted to carry on with some form of further education or training after leaving school. Some could see the discrepancy between what they ideally wanted to do with their lives and what they might have to settle for (see Bhatti, 1999, pp. 273–5). In order to find out how far they actually achieved their aspirations, one would have to do a longitudinal study of these young people and their families. In their study Eggleston *et al.* found that

> In their fifth year at school, more black than white children were expected to undertake a one year sixth form course, usually to enhance O level or CSE stocks.
>
> (Eggleston *et al.* 1986, p. 280)

Asians are included among black children in this reference. What the children told me about themselves seems to indicate the existence of the same trend in Cherrydale School as the one reported by Eggleston and colleagues. It is significant nevertheless that only eight children mentioned employment as their immediate future plan upon leaving school. Seven did not know what they wanted to do. All the rest wanted to study on or receive some kind of vocational training, either at a college of further education or at a university.

Eggleston *et al.* made two observations which were also found in my data. They found that 'fathers of children with South Asian family backgrounds were more likely to be in unskilled or partly skilled jobs' than in other jobs and also that in the case of children

> It is probable that some of the enthusiasm to continue full-time education sprang from a lack of confidence about employment and a desire not to face negative experiences.
>
> (ibid., p. 280)

Whatever the reason the children in my sample had, they saw education on the whole as something to aspire for. They thought that they would be in a college of further education if need be and if the school refused to let them stay on.

When they had to address the question as to what in their opinion they would actually be doing, altogether nineteen children did not know what their future would turn out to be. Seven girls (four Bangladeshi and three Pakistanis) mentioned marriage as a real possibility, but the hurdle of dowry had to be overcome first in some families. It was far more likely that these girls would have to start looking for employment rather than walk straight into marriage and domesticity as some of their teachers assumed.

Summary

Asian children's perceptions of their teachers helped to place them in three different categories. There were good, normal and bad teachers. Children could describe in minute detail the distress caused on occasion by their teachers. The most poignant memories were those associated with racism. Several incidents which caused children much concern have been discussed in this chapter including the effect which gender had on teacher–student interactions. Boys thought teachers were very lenient with Asian girls, whereas Asian girls complained that teachers held stereotypical opinions about them. Some Asian children felt that teachers held lower academic expectations of them as compared to their white peers. It was not possible to verify this. Many children felt they knew what sorts of students teachers liked. Many Asian children aspired to further and higher education and wanted to have the opportunity to achieve that goal. From most of their accounts, young people's hopes and aspirations did not receive a proportionate level of practical help and encouragement from their teachers and they were to a large extent responsible for their own destiny.

References

Bhatti, G. (1999) *Asian Children at Home and at School: An Ethnographic Study*, London, Routledge.

Docking, J. W. (1987) *Control and Discipline in Schools: Perspectives and Approaches*, London, Harper and Row.

Eggleston, J., Dunn, D., Anjali, M. and Wright, C. (1986) *Education for Some: The Educational and Vocational Experiences of 15–18 Year Old Members of Minority Ethnic Groups*, Stoke-on-Trent, Trentham.

Furlong, J. V. (1977) 'Anancy goes to school; a case study of pupils' knowledge of their teachers', in P. Woods and M. Hammersley (eds) *School Experience*, London, Croom Helm.

Gannaway, H. (1976) 'Making sense of school', in M. Stubbs and S. Delamont (eds) *Explorations in Classroom Observation*, London, Wiley.

Gillborn, D. (1990) *'Race', Ethnicity and Education*, London, Unwin Hyman.

Mac an Ghaill, M. (1988) *Young, Gifted and Black: Student–Teacher Relations in the Schooling of Black Youth*, Milton Keynes, Open University Press.

Stanley, J. (1986) 'Sex and the quiet school girl', *British Journal of Sociology of Education*, vol. 7, no. 3, pp. 275–86.

Stebbins, R. (1980) 'The role of humour in teaching: strategy and self expression', in P. Woods (ed.) *Teacher Strategies*, London, Croom Helm.

Wade, B. and Souter, P. (1992) *Continuing to Think: The British Asian Girl*, Clevedon, Multilingual Matters.

Walker, R. and Goodson, I. (1977) 'Humour in the classroom', in P. Woods and M. Hammersley (eds) *School Experience*, London, Croom Helm.

Woods, P. (1976) 'Having a laugh, an antidote to schooling', in M. Hammersley and P. Woods, *The Process of Schooling*, London, Routledge and Kegan Paul.

—— (1993) *Pupil Perspectives and Cultures*, E208 Unit 12, Milton Keynes, Open University Press.

Wright, C. (1986) 'School processes – an ethnographic study', in J. Eggleston, D. Dunn, M. Anjali and C. Wright, *Education for Some: The Educational and Vocational Experiences of 15–18 Year Old Members of Minority Ethnic Groups*, Stoke-on-Trent, Trentham.

CHAPTER 10

HOW WHITE TEACHERS CONSTRUCT RACE

Christine E. Sleeter

In C. McCarthy and W. Crichlow (eds) *Race Identity and Representation in Education*, New York: Routledge, pp. 157–71, 1993.

In the education literature one finds frequent reference to the fact that the teaching population in the US is becoming increasingly white while the student population becomes increasingly racially diverse. The significance of teacher race is usually framed in terms of the degree to which a white teaching force is appropriate for students of color. For example, educators discuss teachers' expectations for and interactions with children of color (Aaron and Powell, 1982; Simpson and Erickson, 1983; Irvine, 1991), teachers as role models (Baez and Clarke, 1990), and the gap between the cultures of the community and the classroom (Tewell and Trubowitz, 1987; Metz, 1990). One can read most discussions of teacher race as tacitly assuming that the system of education is basically as it should be but that it functions most effectively when there is cultural congruence between teachers and students. To help address issues related to congruence between students and teachers, some educators strongly advocate recruiting more teachers of color (Justiz and Kameen, 1988; Haberman, 1989; Contreras and Engelhardt, 1991).

Many educators concentrate on the need to make teacher-education course work critical and multicultural, without specifically interrogating the racial identities of a predominantly white teaching force (Shor, 1986; Lee, 1989; Liston and Zeichner, 1990). In such discussions congruence between teachers and students of color is less an issue than is the orientation toward social justice issues that teachers bring, an orientation that presumably can be cultivated in anyone regardless of race.

In this chapter I will argue that it is terribly inadequate to address racism in education primarily by trying to educate white teachers. Teacher race *does* matter, and for reasons that include and extend beyond issues of cultural congruence in the classroom. I locate this chapter within a body of literature that examines how schools reproduce structures of inequality and oppression and that advocates schools undergo fundamental restructuring for all students (see e.g. Oakes, 1985; Cummins, 1986; Grant and Sleeter, 1986; Sleeter and Grant, 1988; Banks and Banks, 1989; Nieto, 1992). I will argue that teachers bring to the profession perspectives about what race means, which they construct mainly on the basis of their life experiences and vested interests. I will examine specifically perspectives of teachers of European descent in order to argue that a predominantly white teaching force in a racist and multicultural society is not good for anyone, if we wish to have schools reverse rather than reproduce racism.

Theoretical perspectives about racism

To "solve" racism by educating whites is to locate racism mainly in biased individual actions, which in turn are assumed to stem from ideas and assumptions in people's heads: prejudiced attitudes, stereotypes, and lack of information about people of color. A psychological view of racism assumes that if we can change and develop what is in the heads of white people, they in turn will create significant changes in institutions. Viewing racism as prejudice and misperception assumes "that racist attitudes are very rarely rational. Even in those cases where the attitudes are regarded as rational, they are not considered to be in the interests of the person expressing them" (Wellman, 1977, p. 14). Prejudice and misperception can be corrected by providing information. With more information, white people will abandon racist ideas and behaviors and (presumably) work to eliminate racism.

Educational approaches to addressing racism usually adopt this theoretical perspective. However, educators who try to teach white people about racism often experience tenacious resistance. For example, based on a study of twenty-three white preservice students who experienced intensive course work that involved both instruction about concepts and issues related to multicultural education and over 100 hours of experience with low-income minority children in schools, Haberman and Post observed "the remarkable phenomenon of students generally using these direct experiences to selectively perceive and reinforce their initial preconceptions" (1992, p. 30). Teacher education reinforced, rather than reconstructed, how the white students viewed children of color. Results of other studies of preservice and in-service education about multicultural teaching are only slightly more encouraging. While some studies find white students' attitudes to improve somewhat immediately after receiving instruction, studies do not report lasting changes in whites' perspectives and/or behavior patterns (e.g. Baker, 1977; Redman, 1977; Bennett, 1979; Grant, 1981; Washington, 1981).

By contrast, a structural analysis views racism not as misperception but as a structural arrangement among racial groups. Racist institutions, according to Frederickson, are controlled by whites, who restrict the access of nonwhites to "power and privileges" (1981, p. 240), in order to retain and regulate "a reservoir of cheap and coercible labor for the rest of the country" (p. 245). While a psychological analysis of racism focuses on what is in people's heads and asks how to change it, a structural analysis focuses on distribution of power and wealth across groups and on how those of European ancestry attempt to retain supremacy while groups of color try to challenge it. A structural analysis assumes that how white people view race rests on their vested interest in justifying their power and privileges. White people's common sense understandings of race "are ideological defenses of the interests and privileges that stem from white people's position in a structure based in part on racial inequality" (Wellman, 1977, p. 37).

A structural analysis of racism suggests that education will not produce less racist institutions as long as white people control them. As Beverly Gordon has argued, expecting white educators to reconstruct racist institutions ignores the fact that they face

> the sticky dilemma of attempting to educate the masses in a way that allows them accessibility to high status knowledge and places them on an equal footing to compete. Most assuredly in time, they will compete with our children and ostensibly with us for a share of the power and the reallocation of resources. And while most people do have good intentions, when our social

status is threatened, we tend to become even more conservative in order to protect our material gains.

(1985, p. 37)

In what follows, I will discuss data from a study of a staff development program to illustrate how white teachers process education about race. I will argue that it is important to educate white people as well as people of color about racism, but not with the assumption that white people on their own will then reconstruct racist institutions. As a white teacher educator, I do not believe most of us will do that. After discussing how white teachers construct race, I will then attempt to refocus discussion about the implications of the "whitening" of the teaching force and the role of teacher education.

A study of teachers

In 1987 a colleague and I secured funding to offer what became a voluntary two-year staff development project for thirty teachers in schools in which at least one-third of the students were from low-income or racial minority (mostly African American or Latino) families. Twenty-six of the teachers were Euroamerican, three were African American, and one was Mexican American. They taught in grade levels ranging from preschool through high school (most taught grades one–six); seven taught special education, two taught English as a second language, and the rest taught in the general education program.

The teachers attended nine all-day staff development sessions during the first year of the study and five sessions during the second year. The sessions were conducted by a series of outside consultants and addressed a variety of topics such as demographic changes, culture and learning style, curriculum, working with parents, and cooperative learning. My main role was to conduct classroom observations and interviews with the teachers over the two-year period to find out what they were learning, what sense they were making of the sessions, and how they were relating the material to their teaching and their understanding of their students. The staff development sessions, research methods, and findings are described in detail elsewhere (Sleeter, 1992).

The teachers taught in two contiguous school districts located in two small cities in the Rust Belt that had developed as industrial manufacturing centers. Both cities – New Denmark and Gelegenheit (pseudonyms) – were established in the mid-1880s, when "Old Immigrants" from northern and western Europe and the British Isles, as well as Yankees from New England, came to the area to better their lives, in the process pushing Native people off the land. In the early 1900s a second wave of "New Immigrants" from southern and eastern Europe were encouraged to come to the area to work as industrial laborers. Throughout most of the 1900s descendants of the second wave of immigrants engaged in various forms of conflict with descendants of "Old Immigrants"; for example, they unionized; they combated prejudice and disdain in the community; and they created community organizations to resist attempts to "Americanize" them (Buenker, 1976, 1977). Many teachers in the community were descendants of both waves of immigrants and could draw on their own family histories to understand how mobility is achieved in the United States.

Although small numbers of African Americans and Mexican Americans had lived in the communities since the 1800s, these groups did not begin to grow significantly until the 1960s. By the late 1980s New Denmark's population was about eighteen percent African American and eight percent Latino, and Gelegenheit's was about six percent African American and six percent Latino, both minority groups growing much more rapidly than the white population. To most residents, African Americans and Mexican Americans were simply the latest (and not too welcome) newcomers in a series of immigrant groups and would have to engage in the same process of self-help, assimilation, and perseverance that previous groups had experienced.

New Denmark School District had instituted a school desegregation plan in the mid-1970s, accompanied by a series of multicultural education workshops; Gelegenheit School District had not begun to do this. On various indicators, African American and Latino students were experiencing large problems in the schools. For example, in New Denmark a series of newspaper articles (published after the conclusion of this study) reported that white students in one of the cities received a progressively disproportionate share of the "A" grades, from eighty-seven percent in the sixth grade to ninety-one percent in the twelfth (students in the district were sixty-nine percent white). By then "the percentage of Hispanic and Black students who received four or more D's and F's remained above sixty percent. For majority [white] students, that rate was thirty percent" (Taylor, 1990, p. 5A). However, neither district engaged in much open discussion about this kind of racial problem, even after the series of articles was published.

The dominant discourse around issues of race during the late 1980s was quite conservative. Nationally the media stressed the United States' loss of undisputed world hegemony. Schools were blamed for being too lax and spreading a "rising tide of mediocrity" (National Commission on Excellence in Education, 1983). News magazines and news programs discussed the most recent immigrants, suggesting that racial and cultural diversity posed new problems for the United States; most of the discussion centered around trying to identify what we have in common in order to promote national unity (see, e.g. Henry, 1990). The media frequently connected African Americans and Latinos with social problems that many Americans regarded as the result of moral depravity: drug use, teen pregnancy, and unemployment. Asian Americans were hailed as the "model minority," portrayed as achieving success in the United States through hard work and family cohesiveness (Suzuki, 1989), following the same route to success that many whites believed their ancestors had followed. Most school reforms that were discussed emphasized raising standards and requiring students to work harder, and the "at risk" discourse emerged to describe those who were falling behind (who were mainly children of color and children from low-income backgrounds). In New Denmark and Gelegenheit School Districts, problems students of color faced in schools were generally conceptualized through a cultural-deficiency perspective in which the main causes of their difficulties were located in their homes and communities (such as parental attitudes, gang influence, and "deficient" language skills), and supplementary programs were provided to remedy presumed deficiencies.

As David Wellman (1977) has discussed, a paradox of white consciousness is the ability not to see what is very salient: the visible markers of social categories that privilege people of European ancestry. Racial boundaries and racial privileges, highly visible and ubiquitous in the United States, were becoming increasingly so in New Denmark and Gelegenheit. One had only to turn on the TV or drive through the community to see people of European ancestry dominating mainstream institutions and the most desirable resources, while people of non-European ancestries were clustered and compartmentalized into the least desirable spaces and rendered through media as either invisible or satisfied with or deserving of their lot.

White people usually seek to explain persistent racial inequality in a way that does not implicate white society. In this chapter, I will focus on how the twenty-six white teachers viewed race.

Race = European ethnicity

Most of the white teachers in the program interpreted race and multicultural education through the European ethnic experience. As Michael Omi and Howard Winant explain,

> ethnicity theory assigned to blacks and other racial minority groups the roles which earlier generations of European immigrants had played in the great waves of the "Atlantic migration" of the nineteenth and early twentieth centuries.
>
> (1986, p. 20)

Ethnicity theory holds that the social system is open and that individual mobility can be attained through hard work. Over time, ethnic ancestry will disappear as a determinant of life chances.

Equating race with European ethnicity provided white teachers with a way to explain mobility in US institutions. A few made direct reference to their own ethnic backgrounds; for example, a daughter of Italian immigrants commented,

> One of my pet peeves, that I know if you want to work, you can work. . . . I know what my father did when he was in need, . . . and we didn't have the free lunches and we didn't have the clothes that other kids wore.
>
> (Teacher interview, December 15, 1987)

I asked twenty-two of the white teachers about their fathers' occupations: four fathers had held jobs that normally require college education, two had owned small businesses, and the other sixteen had worked as laborers of various sorts. The teachers had attained upward mobility by earning college degrees and becoming teachers; their own families' life experiences had taught them that mobility is attainable, but not necessarily easy.

Ethnicity theory denies the significance of visible, physiological marks of ancestry and of the history of colonization and harsh subjugation that Europeans and Euroamericans extended over other peoples (Omi and Winant, 1986; Ringer and Lawless, 1989). In so doing it denies white social institutions any complicity in the subordinate status of people of color. White teachers of students of color need some way of understanding why people of color have not done as well in society as whites have. Teachers generally like their students – including their students of color – and wish to help them. How do white teachers explain racial inequality without either demeaning their students or questioning their own privileges? I observed two strategies: denial of race altogether, and defining students of color as "immigrants."

Denying the salience of race

> What's the big hangup, I really don't see this color until we start talking about it, you know. I see children as having differences, maybe they can't write their

numbers or they can't do this or they can't do that, I don't see the color until we start talking multicultural. Then, oh yes, that's right, he's this and she's that.

(Teacher interview, May 16, 1988)

I really believe that elementary teachers feel that kids are kids. . . . People would say, "Well, what's your minority breakdown?" And teachers would really have a rough time saying, you know, it was like asking how many of your kids are wearing glasses.

(Teacher interview, December 15, 1987)

White teachers commonly insist that they are "color-blind": that they see children as children and do not see race (Rist, 1978). Many of the twenty-six white teachers began the program with a "color-blind" perspective, and throughout the two years, seven steadfastly maintained it; by the second year, these teachers' attendance at sessions dwindled because of the program's focus on race. What does it mean to construct an interpretation of race that denies it?

Francisco Rios (1992) asked sixteen teachers in an inner-city high school to think aloud about twelve classroom scenes and then analyzed their responses in terms of the salience of three scene characteristics: student gender, student race, and type of action (instructional, disciplinary, and personal). He found that student race was the only statistically significant characteristic; student gender and type of action were not. In other words teachers' responses varied with student race, but not with student gender. While teachers may deny that race is important, race is still quite salient to them.

People do not deny seeing what they actually do not see. Rather, they profess to be color-blind when trying to suppress negative images they attach to people of color, given the significance of color in the United States, the dominant ideology of equal opportunity, and the relationship between race and observable measures of success. Many of the white teachers in our study associated people of color – and particularly African Americans and Latinos – with dysfunctional families and communities, and lack of ability and motivation. Several expressed these associations rather freely in discussions of their students and their parents; for example:

I have a very close family, . . . [my husband and I] have been very strong disciplinarians and we encourage the work ethic . . . . I realize how foolish and presumptuous [it is] to think all these kids are coming from the same thing . . . . Just to have a totally helter-skelter house where there is nothing regular and the people who are your parent figures come and go. . . .

(Teacher interview, May 16, 1988)

All these blacks, they're coming to school late every day. Well, nobody takes care of these children, you know, they have to get up and everything like that.

(Teacher interview, December 7, 1988)

For the most part, teachers took for granted that the US social structure is fairly open (after all, they "made it"). Some reacted angrily to suggestions that it is not.

I am wrestling with the last two sessions . . . where the women's issue was brought up, and also the issue of the blacks. From my standpoint, I left those two meetings so depressed, because I started teaching in the '60s when we were told to instill pride in these people, treat them as adults, I'm speaking now of blacks, women, you know . . . . I've walked away from those meetings thinking I've wasted twenty-five years now, and I got shot down again, and once again, as a teacher, it's my fault . . . . I thought we were doing well.

(Teacher interview, February 22, 1988)

The three ladies up there telling us about their experiences as multicultural people in an all-white class and so on, how they interpreted things, and how it stuck with them today, . . . I couldn't understand why they . . . couldn't understand now that most of those kinds of days are gone . . . . These are things they are hanging on to years ago. I don't think it is that way any more.

(Teacher interview, February 23, 1988)

These examples to the contrary, most of the white teachers did not focus directly on the distribution of resources across groups or the ideology of equal opportunity. Instead they conceptualized racism as the unfair application of (probably) accurate generalizations about groups to individuals, in a way that biases one's treatment of them. Individuals should be able to succeed or fail on their own merit and should not be held back by "deficiencies" of their race as a whole. As long as a teacher does not know for certain which students will be held back by "cultural deficiencies," it is best to treat them as if one did not see their skin color. Therefore, in an effort not to be racist themselves and to treat all children equally, many white teachers try to suppress what they understand about people of color, which leads them to try not to "see" color.

Trying not to see what is obvious (color) and to suppress the negative and stereotypical imagery with which one is bombarded requires considerable psychological energy. Education about race conflicts with many white teachers' strategies of denial, compounding the psychological energy they must expend to continue being "blind" to color. Many simply avoid such discussions or staff development programs. Some of the teachers who participated in this two-year program did so with ambivalence and resented the attention given in sessions to African Americans and Latinos:

I've had a lot on multicultural, you know, I taught in an inner-city school, and we had a lot about habits of the Hispanic, habits of the blacks, so probably that's kind of redoing it.

(Teacher interview, March 24, 1988)

To me, all of the speakers were slanted for blacks or Hispanics only, and I think that's an injustice. . . . Get Indian children, get their views as to what they feel about American playgrounds and classrooms.

(Teacher interview, May 18, 1988)

The teachers perceived staff development on multicultural education as useful if it gave them new information about groups they did not already "know all about," or if it reaffirmed what they were doing in the classroom. However, since they did not perceive that there would be anything worthwhile to learn about African Americans and Latinos, or about racism, and since constant and direct attention to these groups brought their own negative associations, as well as white guilt, to the surface, some of the white teachers stopped coming. Of the pool of teachers in both districts who had been invited to participate, I assume many did not apply precisely because they did not see value in acknowledging their own negative associations with people of color, or any suggestion that racism still exists.

Using culture to ease the process of assimilation

Most of the white teachers who participated in the staff development sessions, and who did not vigorously assert a "color-blind" stance, believed that some degree of mutual cultural adaptation between the school and immigrant and minority communities would ease the transition of minority students into the dominant culture. While they did not view the dominant culture or its institutions as a problem, they recognized that cultural differences can interfere with the successful transition from one cultural context to another and sought adaptations in their own routines that might facilitate the process for some of their students. As one teacher put it,

> At least we can make a dent in the problem by the methods that we're using in teaching and like changing the style a little bit and trying to adapt to the students, rather than expecting them to make the swing and adapt to the way that we're teaching.
>
> (Teacher interview, May 18, 1989)

Several of the staff development sessions provided material from which teachers drew for adaptations, such as two sessions on culture and cognitive style, two sessions on parent involvement, and a session on cooperative learning. Teachers came away from these sessions with a variety of insights about cultural compatibility. Some began to reinterpret students' behavior as cultural rather than as simply "wrong."

> It kind of answers some questions as to why do I have certain students who can't seem to stay in their seats and pay attention . . . . And why I have some that are a little bit more, you know, quiet and withdrawn . . . . It doesn't always help me to know exactly what to do with them, but at least I have a little better understanding.
>
> (Teacher interview, May 17, 1988)

Several teachers added to their repertoire additional strategies for communicating with parents, such as sending or telephoning home positive messages or translating messages into Spanish. A few stopped insisting that students look them in the eye. Many teachers were intrigued by the possibility that students might enjoy and learn more from cooperative learning than from whole-class or individual teaching strategies.

> I remember the first time that I heard that different kinds of different cultures learned in different ways, it made me remember and think about how some of my kids would be reacting in class sometimes, you know, where they would be helping each other and a couple of instances where kids may have just been helping each other instead of copying. I concluded that they were copying, or cheating.
>
> (Teacher interview, February 28, 1988)

Increased use of cooperative learning was the greatest observable impact the staff development program had on the teachers' classroom behavior. By the end of the two-year period about half had begun to use this method. And as we found out in the classroom observations, the proportion of teaching time in which children engaged in cooperative learning and other group work had jumped from eleven to thirteen percent in the first observations to thirty percent in the last. Teachers attributed their own interest in cooperative learning to its connection with learning style; the fact that colleagues in their buildings had been trained in it and could provide help; students' positive reactions to it; and their perception that cooperative learning can be broken down into steps to master. Several teachers also liked the fact that cooperative learning could be incorporated into the form and structure of their teaching without changing other things too much.

These kinds of adaptations do have considerable value, reducing the stress students of color must deal with when the culture of the classroom conflicts with their home culture and building on strengths and preferences students have for learning. The teachers appear to have accepted the validity of such adaptations because they fit within ethnicity theory, according to which "newcomers" face difficulties due to cultural differences and these difficulties can be eased during the process of transition. I should emphasize that several of the staff development facilitators were African Americans who did not adhere to ethnicity theory and did not regard changes in school process as temporary bridges to ease cultural assimilation. Nevertheless, the facilitators focused on presenting useful strategies, and this had some success in that it led to greatly increased use of cooperative learning.

However, there seemed to be a difference between the goals the facilitators had in mind and those most white teachers accepted. An African American facilitator explicitly voiced her commitment to promoting high achievement among students of color. However, in none of the sessions was there rigorous discussion of what should constitute high achievement. When, in one interview, I asked a teacher to compare the achievement of her school with that of a predominantly white suburban school, she interpreted my question as changing the subject from multicultural education to something else (and said of course, the achievement in her school was lower, what else would one expect?). Since the time of this study my attempts to get groups of white teachers in local schools to define exactly what should constitute a standard for high achievement in inner-city schools have become an interesting study in avoidance behavior. Teachers say, for example, that success is different for different children, that existing measures of achievement are biased and therefore do not count, or that it is irrelevant how they define achievement because their efforts will be undone by the homes or the next teacher students have. Relatively few white teachers argue that inner-city students can and should be attaining the same levels of achievement as white suburban students, a pattern that is consistently found in studies of schools (e.g. Anyon, 1981; Grant and Sleeter, 1986; Fine, 1991).

Schools are one of the main gatekeepers in the allocation of social resources. I suspect that most white teachers are at once unsure how much intelligence students of color (and poor white students) can actually display, fearful that well-educated African American, Latino, and Native American students might launch a bold critique of white institutions and white people, and aware that parity in achievement across groups would threaten a major advantage white people and their children currently enjoy. But few teachers will admit to these fears, and they may not even be conscious of them. Instead, many try to implement strategies that might reduce failure and make the system of schooling work more smoothly, and they regard their support for these actions as evidence that they are not racist. From the perspective of ethnicity theory, such actions help those on the bottom to gain mobility in an open system. From the perspective of a theory of racial oppression, however, such actions may serve mainly to mask the oppressiveness of the education system.

Culture as symbolic of family and individual differences

Using interviews, Richard Alba (1990) investigated the symbolic meaning white Americans attached to ethnicity in the 1980s. He was interested in why Euroamericans continue to express interest in ethnicity in spite of the belief that European ethnicity in the United States no longer structures life chances to any significant degree. What he found describes very well the meanings with which many white teachers infuse multicultural education when they try to work with it in the classroom.

Alba argues that Euroamericans view participation in ethnic identity as an individual choice. Euroamericans stress the commonality of ethnic immigrant histories and value expressions of ethnicity that can be shared across ethnic lines: food was the most widespread expression mentioned; holidays, festivals, and related activities were also mentioned. Many whites in his sample equated ethnicity with one's private family history, rather than viewing it as a group's collective experience. Whites rarely connected ethnicity with social structures, such as neighborhood, friendship group, occupation, or political organizations. The symbolic meaning Euroamericans attach to ethnicity today upholds the ideology of individuality and mobility within an open system and the myth that everyone came to the United States in search of a better life and had to work equally hard to better themselves. It attempts to place all groups on an equal status in which ethnicity is a private matter and otherwise not very important. In so doing, this meaning averts a structural analysis of racism and inequality in contemporary US society, implicitly reaffirming the superior position of Euroamericans.

If white teachers wish to regard race and ethnicity in a positive manner, and if they wish to try to reduce tensions among students in multiracial schools, the Euroamerican ethnic experience provides a repertoire of concepts to use, focusing on customs a group brought from the "old" country. About half of the white teachers in my study encoded Alba's symbolic expressions of ethnicity into lessons they occasionally added to the "regular" curriculum. Essentially these lessons tried to teach students that one should be proud of family and individual differences and not stereotype others negatively.

Some teachers taught lessons oriented around family heritage. Typically such lessons began with a discussion of where (what country) their families came from, and what customs the family has retained.

> We are talking a lot about their heritage and they have gone back and found all these neat things that are going on in their families, and now they've started bringing in recipes because we're going to make a recipe book from some recipes that have been handed down in their families.
>
> (Teacher interview, May 16, 1988)

Several white teachers incorporated food, music, and holidays from different countries into their teaching, although these lessons tended to retain a Eurocentric bias. For example, a music teacher developed a "Children Around the World" concert that was very creative but included more countries from Europe than from any other continent and represented Africa in terms of animals and Tarzan whoops. Some teachers developed lessons comparing the customs of different groups. For example, an English teacher concluded the discussion of a story about a Puerto Rican family with a comparison of customs in New York with those in Puerto Rico, and an ESL (English as a Second Language) teacher had immigrant students compare customs for celebrating holidays in their countries with customs for celebrating Christmas in the United States.

Even Native American experience was interpreted within the ethnicity paradigm. For example, a fifth-grade teacher taught a social studies lesson about how Indians immigrated over the land bridge from Asia, and later in the year her students read a story about the dancer Maria Tallchief's success in ballet and retention of her Indian name because of pride in her ancestry.

Prejudice and stereotyping were the focus of a few lessons I observed. In these lessons, teachers viewed prejudice and stereotyping as resulting from generalizations individuals incorrectly apply to other individuals and groups. For example, one teacher had students consider how labels can hurt and limit options. Another taught an extensive unit about prejudice, focusing on the Holocaust and *The Diary of Anne Frank*. Prejudice was interpreted as an irrational feeling with damaging consequences; from the unit, students should gather that they should not harbor prejudice toward others.

Several teachers taught lessons about individual differences and self-concepts, connecting these loosely with race and ethnicity. For example, an elementary teacher had students create personal coats of arms that expressed various positive images about themselves and their families. Another teacher created a classroom flower in which each petal included the name of a student and positive words other students had written about her/him. Role models were another theme of several lessons and classroom decorations. Several teachers occasionally put up posters of famous African Americans or other Americans of color, and their textbooks occasionally featured stories about famous Americans of color. Generally white teachers use role models to instill pride in children and show them that members of their group can succeed if they work hard.

At times African American students resisted participating in lessons about ethnic origins, and this puzzled the teachers. For example, a teacher who taught a lesson about family heritage remarked that,

> I only have three black students in my room and they have not gone back further than Mississippi, and it's been, no way are they going to go back further . . . . The one little boy said, "we didn't come from Africa," that was the first thing he said when we started from where our ancestors came.
>
> (Teacher interview, May 16, 1988)

When another teacher began a lesson with a discussion of where students' ancestors came from, she was similarly surprised that no African American students located their ancestry in Africa. During the two-year staff development project, none of the teachers connected such responses with the celebration of Europe and silence about Africa that the school curriculum maintains, or with the media's depiction of Europe as industrialized and "developed" and Africa as "underdeveloped" and "primitive."

I regarded many of the lessons described above as positive experiences for students, and some of them (such as the unit on the Holocaust) taught worthy material. I would critique this body of lessons mainly on the basis of their huge silences and collective implications. By omission they implied that race no longer structures access to resources in the United States, and that America's racial groups stand in equal status to one another, differentiated only by customs in which anyone can participate. Lessons added token representations of Americans of color (mainly by adding personal knowledge about the students in the classroom) to a curriculum that heavily favored Europe and Euroamericans, without reconstructing students' interpretations of the histories of Americans of color, or their knowledge of Africa, contemporary Latin America, or the pre-Columbian Americas. Even depictions of role models, by focusing on an individual's achievements and ignoring her or his difficulties in attaining them, can suggest that the system is open equally to anyone who will try.

Americans of color were lumped with immigrants who were collectively defined as "other," bringing customs that are, at best, interesting to learn about and share when there is time. "Whiteness" was taken as the norm, as natural. When teachers told me about "multicultural lessons" or "multicultural bulletin boards," what they usually drew my attention to was the flat representations of people of color that had been added; multidimensional representations of whiteness throughout the school were treated as a neutral background not requiring comment. In a discussion of Rosaldo's (1989) concept of "cultural stripping," McLaren critiques whites' naturalization of their identities: "Being white is an entitlement, not to preferred racial attributes, but to a raceless subjectivity. That is, being white becomes the invisible norm for how the dominant culture measures its own civility" (1991, p. 244). Whites so internalize their own power and taken-for-granted superiority that they resist self-questioning. Whites appropriate the idea of culture to mean "sub-categories of whiteness (Irishness, Jewishness, Britishness)" (Dyer, 1988, p. 46), which can be fleshed out in personal subjective meanings or residual expressions of life in other countries and other times. This provides a "positive" as well as nonthreatening template for whites to apply to discussions of race.

Beginnings of analyses of white supremacist institutions

None of the white teachers constructed a strong critique of white-supremacist institutions during the two-year period, but three of the twenty-six (as well as all four teachers of color) expressed insights that would lead in that direction. One white special education teacher, who had described racism as an attitudinal problem early in the study, began to draw connections between racism and the structure of special education.

> [I'm] seeing basically how our system is set up, the value system our whole society is set up on. And it makes me feel like we are here because of a lot of suffering.
>
> (Teacher interview, May 19, 1988)

Later in a paper she wrote, "Many cultures and governmental systems have been established on the idea that some people were meant to rule and live in luxury and some were meant to serve and live in poverty and suffering." I did not see her translate these insights into her teaching practice, however, and she dropped the program after the first year.

A second white teacher developed similar insights, locating the beginning of her awareness of racism in her teaching in a predominantly black school in a university town, when she realized that the town tried very hard to ignore the existence of the school and its needs. Part of her job as a preschool teacher involved working with parents, and she gradually began to identify with them. After the conclusion of this study she became angry about the district's apparent disinterest in programs for low-income and minority parents, and she began talking about organizing the parents to speak out.

A third white teacher taught several social studies lessons for high school special education students about civil rights and labor issues. I observed her teach a lesson about civil disobedience, focusing on the 1960s; the lesson included ideas such as freedom riders, Black Muslims, lunch counter sit-ins, and racial riots in Detroit and Watts.

Why did these three teachers begin to focus their attention on various aspects of racism and institutional discrimination rather than cultural customs and individual differences? Two taught special education and one taught in a state-funded preschool program; all three occupied positions in the school structure that served populations that schools marginalize, where they found themselves waging battles on behalf of their students against conservative bureaucracies and, often, resistant colleagues. In the last interview, when I asked teachers how much power they believed those who participated in the staff development program had to change the school system, two of these three were the only teachers to discuss organizing and exerting pressure; the others all advocated individual solutions. I would suggest that their experience working in marginalized programs, coupled with participation in the staff development program, helped to politicize frustrations they were experiencing.

Conclusion

The staff development program spanned two years. I have not organized this chapter sequentially because I did not see most white teachers construct a qualitatively new understanding of race over the two-year period. Instead, I saw them select information and teaching strategies to add to a framework for understanding race that they took for granted, which they had constructed over their lifetimes from their position as white people in a racist society.

White people are aware of the efforts they and their families and friends have made to better themselves, and they are aware of the problems they encounter in everyday life. It is in their interest to assume that the problems they face are not unique and that the efforts all people make pay off according to the same rules. "Given the racial and class organization of American society, there is only so much people can 'see.' Positions they occupy in these structures limit the range of their thinking. The situation places barriers on their imaginations and restricts the possibilities of their vision" (Wellman, 1977, p. 235). Spending most of their time with other white people, whites do not see much of the realities of the lives of Americans of color nor encounter their viewpoints in any depth. Nor do they really want to, since those viewpoints would challenge practices and beliefs that benefit white people.

Faced with the paradox of liking and helping students of color while explaining away the subordination of people of color and adhering to social structures that benefit themselves and their own children, the white teachers I studied responded in patterned ways. Many simply refused to "see" color. Others searched for "positive" associations with race by drawing on the European ethnic experience, which points toward petrified vestiges of immigrant culture that add texture to the fabric of everyday life. Discussing race or multiculturalism meant discussing "them," not the social structure. The staff development program provided material they could draw from; like the program studied by Haberman and Post (1992), it did not reconstruct their basic interpretation of race.

I write this chapter as a Euroamerican person who has struggled with my own understanding of race and who for years has been in the process of learning how to teach white educators about race. It is possible for a white person's understanding of race to undergo marked transformation; I experienced a reconstruction of my own understanding over a period of years, and I know other whites who have done so. As a teacher educator, I continually seek points of access into how Euroamerican students view the world. But at the same time, while I believe whites are educable, I have gained appreciation for the strength of our resistance to change. My own color gives me a degree of comfort, privilege, and insulation that serves me in ways I continue to take for granted. It is from this position that I offer some thoughts about what to do.

I would advocate strongly working to reverse policies that propel mainly white people into the profession, such as the use of the National Teachers Exam, the lengthening of teacher education programs, and other means of defining standards in ways that penalize rather than reward strengths and resources that teachers of color could bring. Schools as they are structured currently operate in ways that largely reproduce the racial and social class structure. Various fields of discourse, such as multicultural education, emancipatory pedagogy, and Afrocentrism, express ideas and commitments for reworking schools to serve the interests of diverse populations. What I am suggesting goes beyond interaction patterns in classrooms, role models, or linking home and school cultures. I am suggesting the need to populate the teaching force with people who bring diverse worldviews and discursive fields of reference, including those that expose, challenge, and deconstruct racism rather than tacitly accepting it.

Educators of color are much more likely to bring life experiences and viewpoints that critique white supremacy than are white teachers and to engage in activities that challenge various forms of racism (Foster, 1990; Ladson-Billings and Henry, 1990). They are also less likely to "marginalize minority intellectual discourse" (Gordon, 1990, p. 103). Although Americans of color express a wide range of analyses of racism, the strongest critiques of racism tend to come from communities of color. The life experiences of people of color can be politicized to challenge racism in education more readily than can those of white people. In my own experience I have found much richer discussions of anti-racist ideas and actions to emerge from multiracial groups, in which whites are present but in the minority, than from all-white groups.

Is there a role for multicultural teacher education? I believe that there is but that it cannot substitute for making the education profession diverse. Ultimately the best solutions to racism will come from multiracial coalitions in which white people participate but do not dominate. Multicultural teacher education has somewhat different purposes for teachers of color and for white teachers.

For teachers of color it should help to politicize and develop what they know from life experience and to translate their commitments into emancipatory action in schools. For example, some teachers of color who have successfully entered the middle class accept much about the social class structure that ought to be questioned. Further, there are bodies of content knowledge and pedagogical practice that teachers of color often find very useful but do not simply know without being taught.

White people need to learn about racism, as well as about the historic experiences and creative works of American minority groups and about the wide range of implications for schooling. This means beginning their reeducation by forcing them to examine white privilege and planning long-term learning experiences that anticipate the various strategies white people use to avoid and reinterpret education about race. For example, structured immersion experiences in which a white person spends at least a month in a minority community, coupled with instruction about racism and the history and culture of that group, as well as development of some emotional bonding with members of the group, can propel serious reexamination of his or her perspective. The aim of education for white teachers would be to encourage them to work collectively with local communities of color and to construct an ongoing process of learning from and connecting with people of color.

Conceptualized as a form of political organizing, education may be a powerful vehicle to confront racism. An educator qua organizer must directly confront the vested interest white people have in maintaining the status quo, force them to grapple with the ethics of privilege, and refuse to allow them to rest comfortably in apolitical interpretations of race and multicultural teaching.

Acknowledgments

I am grateful to Martin Haberman, Renee Martin, Cameron McCarthy, Carmen Montecinos, and Francisco Rios for their helpful comments and suggestions on earlier drafts of this chapter.

References

Aaron, R. and Powell, G. (1982). Feedback practices as a function of teacher and pupil race during reading group instruction. *Journal of Negro Education*, 51 (1), 50–9.

Alba, R. D. (1990). *Ethnic Identity: The Transformation of White America*. New Haven: Yale UP.

Anyon, J. (1981). Social class and school knowledge. *Curriculum Inquiry*, 11, 3–41.

Baez, T. and Clarke, E. (1990). Reading, writing, and role models. *Community, Technical, and Junior College Journal*, 60 (3), 31–4.

Baker, G. (1977). Two preservice training approaches. *Journal of Teacher Education*, 28, 31–3.

Banks, J. A. and Banks, C. M. (eds) (1989). *Multicultural Education: Issues and Perspectives*. Boston: Allyn.

Bennett, C. T. (1979). The preparation of pre-service secondary social studies teachers in multiethnic education. *High School Journal*, 62, 232–7.

Buenker, J. D. (1976). Immigration and ethnic groups. In J. A. Newenschwander (ed.), *Kenosha County in the 20th Century* (pp. 1–50). Kenosha, WI: Kenosha County Bicentennial.

—— (1977). The immigrant heritage. In N. C. Burkel (ed.), *Racine: Growth and Change in a Wisconsin County* (pp. 69–136). Racine, WI: Racine County Board of Supervisors.

Contreras, G. and Engelhardt, J. M. (1990–91). Attracting and recruiting an ethnically diverse teaching force. *Teacher Education and Practice*, 6 (2), 39–42.

Cummins, J. (1986). Empowering minority students: a framework for intervention. *Harvard Educational Review*, 56, 18–36.

Dyer, R. (1988). White. *Screen*, 29, 44–64.

Fine, M. (1991). *Framing Dropouts: Notes on the Politics of an Urban Public High School*. Albany: State University of New York Press.

Foster, M. (1990). The politics of race: through the eyes of African American teachers. *Journal of Education*, 172 (3), 123–41.

Frederickson, G. M. (1981). *White Supremacy: A Comparative Study in American and South African History*. New York: Oxford University Press.

Gordon, B. M. (1985). Teaching teachers: "Nation at risk" and the issue of knowledge in teacher education. *The Urban Review*, 17, 33–46.

—— (1990). The necessity of African-American epistemology for educational theory and practice. *Journal of Education*, 172 (3), 88–106.

Grant, C. A. (1981). Education that is multicultural and teacher education: an examination from the perspectives of preservice students. *Journal of Educational Research*, 75, 95–101.

Grant, C. A. and Sleeter, C. E. (1986). *After the School Bell Rings*. London: Falmer.

Haberman, M. (1989). More minority teachers. *Phi Delta Kappan*, 70, 771–6.

Haberman, M. and Post, L. (1992). Does direct experience change education students' perceptions of low-income minority children? *The Midwestern Educational Researcher*, 5 (2), 29–31.

Henry, W. A., III. (1990, April 9). Beyond the melting pot. *Time*, pp. 28–31.

Irvine, J. J. (1991). *Black Students and School Failure: Policies, Practices, and Prescriptions*. New York: Praeger.

Justiz, M. J. and Kameen, M. C. (1988). Increasing the representation of minorities in the teaching profession. *Peabody Journal of Education*, 66 (1), 91–100.

Ladson-Billings, G. and Henry, A. (1990). Blurring the borders: voices of African liberatory pedagogy in the United States and Canada. *Journal of Education*, 172 (2), 72–88.

Lee, M. (1989, June). Making child development relevant for all children: implications for teacher education. *Early Child Development and Care*, 47, 63–73.

Liston, D. P. and Zeichner, K. M. (1990). Teacher education and the social context of schooling. *American Educational Research Journal*, 27 (4), 10–36.

McLaren, P. (1991). Decentering culture: postmodernism, resistance, and critical pedagogy. In N. B. Wyner (ed.), *Current Perspectives on the Culture of Schools* (pp. 232–57). Boston: Brookline.

Metz, M. H. (1990). How social class differences shape teachers' work. In M. W. McLaughlin, J. E. Talbert, and N. Bascia (eds), *The Contexts of Teaching in Secondary Schools: Teachers' Realities* (pp. 40–107). New York: Teachers College.

National Commission on Excellence in Education. (1983). *A Nation at Risk*. Washington, DC: US Government Printing Office.

Nieto, S. (1992). *Affirming Diversity: The Sociopolitical Context of Multicultural Education*. New York: Longman.

Oakes, J. (1985). *Keeping Track: How Schools Structure Inequality*. Princeton, NJ: Yale University Press.

Omi, M. and Winant, H. (1986). *Racial Formation in the United States: From the 1960s to the 1980s*. New York: Routledge.

Redman, G. L. (1977). Study of the relationship of teacher empathy for minority persons and inservice human relations training. *Journal of Educational Research*, 70, 205–10.

Ringer, B. B. and Lawless, E. R. (1989). *Race – Ethnicity and Society*. London: Routledge.

Rios, F. A. (1992). Teachers' implicit theories of multicultural classrooms. Doctoral dissertation, University of Wisconsin.

Rist, R. C. (1978). *The Invisible Children: School Integration in American Society*. Cambridge, MA: Harvard University Press.

Rosaldo, R. (1989). *Culture and Truth: The Remaking of Social Analysis*. Boston: Beacon.

Shor, I. (1986). Equality is excellence: Transforming teacher education and the learning process. *Harvard Educational Review*, 56 (4), 406–26.

Simpson, A. W. and Erickson, M. T. (1983). Teachers' verbal and nonverbal communication patterns as a function of teacher race, student gender, and student race. *American Educational Research Journal*, 20 (2), 183–98.

Sleeter, C. E. (1992). *Keepers of the American Dream: A Study of Staff Development and Multicultural Education*. London: Falmer.

Sleeter, C. E. and Grant, C. A. (1988). *Making Choices for Multicultural Education: Five approaches to Race, Class, and Gender*. Columbus: Merrill.

Suzuki, B. H. and Lou, R. (1989). Asian Americans as the "model minority": outdoing whites? or media hype? *Change*, 21 (6), 13–19.

Taylor, B. (1990). Grade gap grows as students advance through unified. *Racine Journal Times*, April 22, pp. 4A–5A.

Tewell, K. J. and Trubowitz, S. (1987). The minority group teacher. *Urban Education*, 22 (3), 355–65.

Washington, V. (1981). Impact of anti-racism/multicultural education training on elementary teachers' attitudes and classroom behavior. *The Elementary School Journal*, 81, 186–92.

Wellman, D. T. (1977). *Portraits of White Racism*. Cambridge: Cambridge University Press.

CHAPTER 11

CRITICAL MULTICULTURAL EDUCATION AND STUDENTS' PERSPECTIVES

Sonia Nieto

In Stephen May (ed.) *Critical Multiculturalism*, London: Falmer, pp. 191–215, 1999

Even under the best of circumstances, the secondary school experiences of most students are characterized by uncertainty and tension. For culturally and linguistically dominated students, whose schooling can hardly be defined as occurring under the best conditions, such tensions are almost inevitable (Olsen, 1988; Nieto, 1994; Gillborn, 1995). Aside from the normal anxieties associated with adolescence, additional pressure for culturally subordinated students may be the result of several factors, including the physical and psychological climate of the schools they attend, the low status their native languages and cultures are accorded in the societies in which they live, the low expectations that society has of them, and their invisibility in traditional curricula.

Students are the people most affected by school policies and practices, but they tend to be the least consulted about them. Consequently, they are ordinarily the silent recipients of schooling. Indeed, it has been pointed out that their role as passive beneficiaries of educational reforms is in direct contrast to the widely accepted constructivist expectations for their learning (Corbett and Wilson, 1995). Even when students are not silent, as when they resist and challenge the education they receive (Kohl, 1994), their advice is ordinarily neither sought nor heeded.

The contribution of critical pedagogy to multicultural education has been especially important in this regard. That is, the insistence that students must be involved in the process of their own education, a central tenet of critical pedagogy, has inspired the inclusion of student voices that had heretofore been missing from most treatments of multicultural education. Further, because it recognizes the fundamentally political nature of education and the need to challenge both its content and form, critical pedagogy brings to multicultural education a sharp institutional analysis that might otherwise be missing (Sleeter and McLaren, 1995). This analysis has created a more self-consciously critical assessment of racism and of the negative impact of school policies and practices on students who have been the greatest victims of school failure.

How do students themselves understand and interpret their school experiences, and what can critical multicultural education offer in terms of its analysis? In this chapter, I will place current discussions concerning critical multicultural education within the framework of the experiences and perspectives of secondary school students who have been marginalized due to their ethnicity, culture, native language, social class, or other differences perceived as deficiencies by the mainstream society in which they live. Specifically, I will explore both the *sociopolitical context* of the lives and education of two students in the United States, and their *particular experiences* in school with racism, ethnocentrism, and unresponsive curriculum and pedagogy. The chapter will emphasize the importance of attending to student perspectives in order to inform and expand critical multicultural education.

The sociopolitical context of education

Because the concept of *sociopolitical context* (Nieto, 1996) is central to my understanding of critical multicultural education, I will define what I mean by this term before addressing the question of student perspectives. A sociopolitical context in education takes into account the larger social and political forces operating in a particular society and the impact they may have on student learning. Thus, the notion of *power* is at the very centre of the concept because it concerns issues such as structural inequality and stratification due to social class, gender, ethnicity, and other differences, as well as the relative respect or disrespect accorded to particular cultures, languages, and dialects. Hence, school reform strategies that do not acknowledge such macro-level disparities are sometimes little more than wishful thinking because they assume that all students begin their educational experiences on a level playing field.

In spite of the rhetoric of meritocracy espoused in most western capitalist countries, social stratification is based on *groups*, not on individuals (Ogbu, 1994). Given this perspective, educational decisions about such policies as ability grouping, testing, curriculum, pedagogy, and which language to use for instruction are also *political* decisions (Freire, 1985). Embedded within all educational decisions are also assumptions about the nature of learning in general, the worthiness and capability of students from various social groups, and the value or lack of value of languages other than the dominant one. Thus, even seemingly innocent decisions carry an enormous amount of ideological and philosophical weight, and these are in turn communicated to students either directly or indirectly (Cummins, 1996). David Corson, following Bourdieu (cf. May, 1999), describes the impact of decisions affecting school policies and practices on the most disadvantaged students in society: 'The members of some social groups, as a result, come to believe that their educational failure, rather than coming from their lowly esteemed social or cultural status, results from their natural inability: their lack of giftedness' (1993, p. 11). This is the ultimate educational legacy of an unequal society, and a sociopolitical context helps to uncover this truth.

Before proceeding with a discussion of student perspectives, a caveat is in order. Because I will be using case studies of two young people from the United States, the chapter is necessarily limited to the sociopolitical context of the United States, and specifically to these two young people who are respectively African-American and Chicano. I do not wish to claim any general wisdom from their cases to students in other societies, to students of other backgrounds in the United States, or even to other African-American or Latino students. That being said, however, it should also be clear that the particular educational problems faced by the two young men in the case studies are not unique; unfortunately, many students in many schools in the United States and even in other societies are faced with tremendous educational challenges that are at least partly based on their sociopolitical realities, and not just on their individual differences. Thus, it is my hope that readers will be able to glean some useful lessons for their particular context from these two case studies.

Research on students' perspectives

Students' perspectives about their schooling experiences are a relatively new and growing field of inquiry. This kind of research is especially significant in multicultural education because of the inherent student-centredness of the field. Thus, listening to what students have to say about their experiences and attending to their suggestions can result in a more critical conception of multicultural education. Likewise, students' views have important implications for transforming curriculum and pedagogy and for educational reform in general. I am not advocating that students' views should be adopted uncritically, a romantic notion at best. What I am suggesting instead is that if students' views are sought through a critical and problem-posing approach (Freire, 1970), their insights can be crucial for developing meaningful, liberating, and engaging educational experiences. In essence, educators lose a powerful opportunity to learn from students when they do not encourage their involvement. Suzanne Soo Hoo (1993) found this to be the case in a project where students were co-researchers. The question that was investigated in the project ('What are the obstacles to learning?') benefited tremendously from students' perspectives, and as Soo Hoo concluded: 'We listen to outside experts to inform us, and consequently, we overlook the treasure in our very own backyards: our students' (1993, p. 390).

Consequently, recent research has sought students' views in order to benefit from their ideas for improving schools. For example, how do students feel about the curriculum they must learn? What do they think about the pedagogical strategies of teachers? Do they believe that their involvement in school matters? Are their own cultural, ethnic, gender, and other identities important considerations for them? How do they view tracking (streaming), testing, disciplinary policies, and other school practices? Although these are key questions that affect the schooling of all students, few students have the opportunity to discuss them. When they are asked, they often seem surprised that anybody is interested; that is what I found repeatedly in the student interviews in my own research (Nieto, 1992, 1996). Moreover, students' views are often on target in terms of current thinking in education: Phelan *et al.* (1992), in a two-year research project in the US designed to identify students' thoughts about school, discovered that their views on teaching and learning were remarkably consistent with specialists of learning theory, cognitive science, and the sociology of work.

In terms of the *content* of their education, students are generally eager to express their opinions about both the tangible curriculum as manifested in books and other didactic materials and the 'hidden' curriculum, that is, the covert messages that can be discerned in the physical environment, extracurricular activities, interactions with adults, and school policies. For example, Christine Sleeter and Carl Grant (1991) found that a third of the students in a desegregated junior high school they studied said that *none* of the class content related to their lives outside class. Those who indicated some relevancy cited only current events, oral history, money and banking, and multicultural content (because it dealt with prejudice, a topic in which they were keenly interested, as are most students regardless of their backgrounds). Other examples of US research in which students were able to express their views have come to similar conclusions: students frequently report being bored in school and seeing little relevance for their lives or their futures in what is taught (Farrell *et al.*, 1988; Hidalgo, 1991; Poplin and Weeres, 1992).

There is often a profound mismatch between students' cultures and the content of the curriculum. This is in stark contrast to Ira Shor's suggestion that 'What students bring to class is where learning begins. It starts there and goes places' (1992, p. 44). In fact, in many schools learning starts not with what students bring but with what is considered high-status knowledge, with its overemphasis on European and European American history, arts, and values. Without denying the importance of providing all students with the high-status knowledge that can open doors to otherwise unavailable life options for them, the case still needs to be made that it makes sense to begin with what students know. If not, rather than 'going elsewhere', students' learning often goes nowhere. Corroborating this lesson, Knapp *et al.* (1995), in the first large-scale study of the effect of using meaning-centred strategies in high-poverty classrooms in the United States, found that the *most* effective teachers were those who took active steps to connect learning to their students' backgrounds.

One way to use the experiences of students is to focus on the kinds of issues that they live with every day. In the case of disempowered students, these include such realities as poverty, racism, discrimination, and alienation. For instance, Karen Donaldson's (1996) study of an urban high school found that over 80 per cent of the students indicated that they had seen or experienced racism in their school. Yet these themes are conspicuously avoided in most classrooms, at least by teachers. Thus, Michelle Fine (1991) found that although over half of the students in the urban high school she interviewed described experiences of racism, teachers were reluctant to discuss it in class (cf. Moodley, 1999). Mary Poplin and Joseph Weeres (1992) also found that many of the students they interviewed brought up the issue of racism without being asked, while virtually none of the adults in the school even mentioned it. Perhaps this is because the majority of teachers in the United States are white Americans who are uncomfortable or unaccustomed to discussing these issues (Sleeter, 1994) because admitting that they exist challenges their most cherished ideals of democracy and equality (Tatum, 1992); perhaps it has to do with the tradition of presenting information in classrooms as if it were free of conflict and controversy (Kohl, 1993); or perhaps teachers are afraid of opening contentious discussions by involving students, as James Banks (1993) has suggested they might do, in debating such 'hot topics' as the literary canon or the extent to which Egypt might have influenced Greek civilization. Probably, the silence is a combination of all these factors.

Recent research focusing on students' views has found that they also have a great deal to say about the pedagogy they experience. Not surprisingly, students' views echo those of educational researchers who have found that teaching methods in most classrooms, and particularly those in secondary schools, vary little from traditional 'chalk and talk' methods; that textbooks are the dominant teaching materials used; that routine and rote learning are generally favoured over creativity and critical thinking; and that teacher-centred transmission models prevail (Goodlad, 1984; Cummins, 1994). In the case of my own research on students' perspectives, I found that although they often appreciated and applauded their teachers and the work they did, students were also critical of some practices and attitudes of their teachers (Nieto, 1994). Thus, I found striking agreement among students about the passive and text-based pedagogy that takes place in most classrooms: One young woman said: '. . . the teachers just, "Open the books to this page." They never made up problems out of their head. Everything came out of the book'. Another one said of her teacher 'She just does the things and sits down'. A young man said, 'They just teach the stuff. "Here," write a couple of things on the board, "see, that's how you do it. Go ahead, p. 25" '. Another young man stated that teachers can make classes more interesting if they teach from the point of view of the students: 'They don't just come out and say, "All right, do this, blah, blah, blah" . . . . They're not so *one-tone voice*'. And another clearly connected what he saw as meaningless pedagogy with lack of caring when he said, 'Some teachers, they just go inside and go to the blackboard. They just don't care'.

Finally, students can teach educators enormously important lessons about unquestioned practices – what María de la Luz Reyes (1992) has called 'venerable assumptions'. For instance, one of the students in my research, Vinh, a Vietnamese immigrant, questioned teachers' practice of praising students for what he considered poor work. In his own case, he explained that his English was not very good, but that teachers uncritically praised his efforts anyway. He suggested instead, 'If my English is not good, she has to say, "Your English is not good, so you have to go home and study" '. He perceived teachers' praise as hollow and insincere.

It is clear from just this brief review of some of the recent research on students' perceptions of their education that they can provide a great deal of food for thought for critical multicultural educators. In what follows, I will focus on two specific students in order to draw out some of these lessons.

Case studies of educational success and failure

In an effort to determine how school, home, and community experiences affect young people of different backgrounds, and to explore how multicultural education when conceptualized as critical, comprehensive, and grounded in social justice might lead to positive adaptations in schools, a number of years ago several colleagues and I interviewed ten students from a wide variety of ethnic, social class, and family backgrounds (Nieto, 1992). The original intention of these interviews was to find out what it meant to be from a particular culture, how their culture might influence their school experiences, and what they would change about school if they could. The results of the first set of interviews were reported through a series of case studies, as well as in later analyses related to school policies and practices (Nieto, 1992, 1994).

As it happened, for it was unplanned, all ten students in the original case studies were relatively academically successful. That is, although sometimes frustrated and alienated by school, they were for the most part fairly gratified with their school experiences. I was pleased it had turned out this way because research with linguistic, cultural, or ethnic minority students has consistently emphasized their failure in school rather than how they can learn despite difficult circumstances in their lives. According to Smith *et al.* (1993), in fact, the entire concept of academic failure has spawned a robust testing industry and a thriving niche in the academy, but it has done nothing to help those who are labelled as failures. In the end, they maintain, 'We must instead confront the very idea of school failure, seeing it for what it is, manifestations of classism and racism' (1993, p. 213). Significantly, a number of the students in my research were academically successful in spite of such challenges as abject poverty, lack of English-language skills when they began their schooling, single-parent families, a history of drug and alcohol dependence in their families, and the pressure of having to be cultural brokers for immigrant relatives at an early age.

Students in my research had a lot to say about the teachers they liked and disliked and why; about the overly important role that grades had acquired in school; about the tremendous faith their parents had in the promise of education and how schools could capitalize on it; and about the meaning their native languages and cultures had in their lives. The case studies implicated the need for schools to promote policies and practices that underscore diversity as a value to be affirmed rather than an obstacle to be confronted and obliterated. Notwithstanding the significant lessons that can be learned from successful students, their very academic success can be a serious limitation because these students tend to be the least marginalized in schools. They are, sadly, the exceptions to the rule of academic failure. Therefore, it is equally necessary to consider the experiences of students who have not been successful in school.

This chapter will centre on two students who had faced considerable failure in school but who were nonetheless having a more positive experience in alternative school settings at the time they were interviewed. Both are males and come from economically oppressed families. Paul is a Chicano from East Los Angeles, and Ron is an African-American who lives in Boston. Their case studies provide an in-depth examination of two young men who have been failed by schools and society.[1] Because at the time of their interviews both were attending public alternative schools where they were happier and more successful than in their previous schools, the case studies can serve as examples for what traditional schools can do to promote the academic achievement of many other young people in similar circumstances.

The fact that both of these case studies focus on young men of colour should come as no surprise. Although females in the United States are consistently victims of institutional bias in schools based on their gender, it is also true they earn higher grades as a group (Sadker and Sadker, 1994), probably due to their more docile and obedient behaviour in the classroom. Furthermore, young women of all groups, especially Latinas and African-American females, are more likely to complete high school and attend college than their male counterparts (Bennett, 1995). Add to this the fact that young men of all backgrounds, but especially African-American and Latino males, are the most likely to have academic and disciplinary problems in school and to be assigned to special education (Ford, 1996), and it is understandable why these case studies concern young men of colour who live in poverty.

The lives of Paul Chavez and Ron Morris are in some ways remarkably similar: they have both faced sustained and consistent academic failure; they were both expelled from former schools; they each reported great frustration with their education before being admitted to the alternative schools they later attended; they have both been criminally involved, one with a gang; they come from female-headed households and live with large extended families struggling to make ends meet; they both admit there are serious problems at home. They also share a passionate desire to be successful in school and to go to college (university), in part to make their mothers, who they deeply love but who they have disappointed profoundly on numerous occasions, proud of them. In spite of these similarities, however, Ron and Paul are also quite different in many respects.

Before presenting the actual case studies, I will briefly describe the sociopolitical context of education for first, African-American, and then, Chicano, students in the United States. This will be followed by descriptions of Ron and Paul and then by their own words, in which they express their frustrations, hopes, and desires concerning education and their futures.

A brief review of the education of African-American students in the United States

A voluminous amount of research has been produced concerning the education of African-American students in US schools, and the major conclusions of all the reports, studies, and investigations have been accurately and succinctly stated by Kofi Lomotey:

> A threefold message is presented. First, the underachievement of African-American students is persistent, pervasive, and disproportionate; the severity of the problem has been well documented. Second, the reasons that this situation persists are varied; there is no simple explanation. Third, there are clear examples of environments that have, over long periods of time, been successful in educating large numbers of African-American students. These models can be replicated; the situation is not hopeless.
>
> (1990, p. 9)

Leaving aside the more racist and hopeless explanations cited in the literature concerning the educational failure of African-American students (deficit explanations focusing, for instance, on their supposed 'racial' and genetic inferiority, or on the pathologies or 'cultural deprivation' of their communities and families), which will not be considered here, one is still left with a plethora of theories. The more reasonable explanations cited in the US literature have ranged from the brutal and systematic exclusion of Blacks from education altogether, and later their de jure and de facto segregation from quality schooling (Weinberg, 1977); cultural and social class characteristics that place them at risk of failure (Pallas *et al.*, 1989); the negative attitudes and behaviours of their teachers (Irvine, 1990; Taylor, 1991; New, 1996) the effects of personal and institutional racism and the implications of 'stereotype stigma' on their learning (Steele, 1992); and the oppositional culture developed by African-American students as a result of a legacy of enslavement and domination, and the subsequent 'burden of acting white' in the face of educational success (Fordham and Ogbu, 1986; Ogbu, 1994). Some of the literature also rightly focuses on the characteristics of the schools that African-American students attend. For example, a study by Lee *et al.* (1991) found that African-American students with higher than average scores on reading achievement tests were actually similar to their lower-scoring counterparts in many respects; what differed were the schools attended by the higher-scoring students, which had a more positive environment.

Given the complexity of reasons cited in the literature for the widespread failure of African-American students in US schools (some of which are the subject of vigorous debate because of their focus on student or family characteristics rather than on structural inequalities in society or on the conditions of schooling that produce failure), it makes sense to instead focus on what has *helped* students achieve. Thus, for example, the evidence affirming that African-American students who perceive that their teachers care about them will be more academically successful (Patchen, 1982; Pollard, 1989) also makes commonsense. Similarly, African-American students for whom teachers hold high expectations, from elementary school through college, meet and even surpass those expectations (Lomotey, 1990; Bempechat, 1992; Treisman, 1992; Irvine and Foster, 1996). Moreover, a consistent finding in the more recent research has been that when the culture of African-American students is understood, appreciated, and used as the basis of their education, they can reach high levels of achievement (Heath, 1983; Boateng, 1990; Irvine, 1990; Ladson-Billings, 1994). This is not to imply that a simplistic or superficial 'feel-good' Afrocentric focus is what is called for. It is frequently overlooked that Afrocentrism can mean many different things and that positions on Afrocentric education in the United States have ranged widely from extremely conservative to progressive. Each of these conceptions has implications for educational practice. Consequently, both the wholesale rejection of Afrocentric education as 'essentialist' or its wholesale acceptance as 'culturally relevant' are problematic because they are incomplete and partial analyses of distinct ideological positions (cf. May, 1999). Thus, a critical stance toward Afrocentric education both coincides with basic tenets of critical pedagogy and challenges it to become less Eurocentric in its framework (Akinyela, 1995).

Kofi Lomotey's insistence that 'the situation is not hopeless' (1990, p. 9) for the education of African-American students in the United States is noteworthy. That is, there is ample evidence that African-American students can and do succeed academically in some situations. We will next review the case study of Ron Morris to consider how a critically conceived multicultural education that is grounded in an understanding of inequality and a respect for students' cultures can promote that success.

Ron Morris

Ronald Morris is 19 years old, highly expressive, and eloquent. He lives with his mother, three sisters, three nieces, and two nephews in a housing development in Boston just a few blocks from the alternative school he was attending at the time of his interviews. An older brother was in prison and an older sister was living in a shelter for the homeless. Several months before he was interviewed, Ron was mugged and, in the process of attempting to run away, he was shot six times. Miraculously, no vital organs were hit, but his recovery took many months.

Held back twice in elementary (primary) school and in and out of several high schools, Ron was attending a public alternative school the student body of which was primarily Latino and African-American. Ironically, the counsellor at this school was the same teacher who had most inspired Ron in his previous educational experience, the one who taught what he referred to in his interview as 'the first real class I ever had', a class in African and African-American history. The school offered a variety of educational, creative, vocational, and cultural opportunities for its fifty students. For example, in addition to his regular classes, Ron was participating in a small tutorial, an advanced history class on the Cuban Missile Crisis taught by a renowned retired professor of history who had previously worked at both Harvard University and Boston University. Ron loved this class because students had the opportunity to examine primary texts such as original documents and tapes in order to come to their own conclusions about decisions they would have made about this event.

The multicultural nature of the Pantoja School (named for a Puerto Rican educational and community activist) is one of the features that made it so appealing to Ron, as was its philosophy of empowerment and democratic participation by students and staff. The school also boasted an active sports programme. In addition, staff were helping Ron with decisions about college and a profession, two goals that until now had seemed unattainable to him. His future, however, was not as positive as it had been several months before: during one of his interviews, Ron confided that he was about to become a father with two different young women. Although he seemed willing to take some responsibility for the children who were coming and he had a serious relationship with one of the young women, he was determined to continue his education. He seemed largely unaware, however, of how profoundly this change was to affect his life.

Following are some of Ron's thoughts about the meaning of education:

I didn't really like [school]. I used to always want to skip and go home or smoke or come to class and create ruckus or something. You know what you was going to class for. You was going to class to be taught really nothing. They didn't really teach anything. I went to school. I come in, you sit down, you learn. Like in history, you learn the same thing over and over and over again.

They talked about Christopher Columbus like he was some great god or something. I never felt like I learned anything. I learned about this guy in the first grade. You went through three different segments of Christopher Columbus. You're saying now, okay, he's got to be a fake. He's a fictional character. They just keep pumping him up. Then you just get tired.

You learned about explorers and Malcolm, a little bit about Malcolm X, a little bit about Martin Luther King. You learned a little bit about slavery, a little bit about this. You learned a little bit about everything. You learned it just so many times. You just want to say, 'Well, isn't it time that we learned something different?' There's more than just what's in this book, 'cause what's in this book is not gonna let us know who we really are as people.

[Teachers should] probably just see what the students like and teach it how they would understand it and so that it's more helpful to them. More discussion instead of more reading, more discussion instead of just letting things be read and then left alone. People read things and then don't understand what they read.

Like if school was more – not all fun and games – but it was more realistic than just reading and doing the work and then you leave. You sit there for 45 minutes doing nothing, just reading a whole book and the teacher is doing nothing but letting you read and she's probably reading the newspaper or eating gum. And that's why the dropout rate is why [it is] because they just come to school and they ain't teaching us nothing, so why am I gonna sit here?

When a teacher becomes a teacher, she acts like a teacher instead of a person. She takes her title as now she's mechanical. Teachers shouldn't deal with students like we're machines. You're a person, I'm a person. We come to school and we all [should] act like people.

Proud to be Afro-American? Well, yeah and no. Yeah, I'm proud to be Afro-American because I'm a black male and all this and I have so many dreams and so many ways of being, that I come from a great 'race' of kings and queens who went through slavery and our 'race' still survives and all that. And no, because I have to accept the term Afro-American because I was born in America. I wasn't born where my ancestors come from. I'm not as pure as my ancestors were because your family's been raped and developed these different things.

Even though [Whites], they sit there and white history is the basic history, they don't really know anything about white. They look at it as white people have always been on top, which is not true for about – they don't know about before, five, six thousand years ago. Nobody even knew who white people were. To me, that's crazy. Everybody's running around not really knowing who they are. People think they know who they are. They think they know what their history is.

[I felt comfortable in school only] once, in eighth grade. Just this case, a history class I had. Just made me want to come to school and made me want to, made me say, 'Okay, now that I know there are so many false things in the world and that there's so much out there for me to learn, stop bullshitting'.

It was a black African history class. It was titled that. It was just so different from the textbook style. It was no books. It was just documents and papers and commonsense questions and commonsense knowledge. You'd just sit there, be like, 'This is real!' It was basically about black people. It showed us Latinos. It showed us 'Caucasians'. It showed us the Jews and everything how we all played a part what society in any country is like today. I just sat in that class and I used to go to that class once a week 'cause it was only a once-a-week class. I'd sit and just be like, I was just so relaxed. I just felt like the realest person on earth.

[This school] is more out to help you achieve instead of just sitting there doing nothing. Now I'm not in that 'they're not teaching me nothing, why should I come to school?' type thing. You learn more. You learn differently. It's realistic and my beliefs as an Afro-American are respected. [Teachers here] understand my identity and culture. They respect it.

I'm not perfect. I wouldn't call myself a good student. I call myself an all right student. I know what's right and what's wrong. I just have to apply [myself] to it. If you'd asked me about two, three years ago, I'd a told you I didn't have the slightest idea why I came to school; it's stupid, it's boring, they don't teach me nothing, I don't learn anything, I should just stay home. But you're asking me that now in the Pantoja School. Now I think about it differently because I'm not in the Boston Public Schools. I'm here, I'm learning, I'm learning more from people who know. It's not a book. Here, it's 'I can teach you through experience, through documents, through this, through that.'

I'm trying to get into Harvard. My mother told me I could do it. She'd say things like, 'If them women [the two women pregnant with his children] really understand what it is for you to be the correct father to your children, they don't burden you. They'll let you become these things and they'll let these things happen so their kinds won't have a typical black future' as if they're still living in the same house and I'm working making $6 an hour and killing myself and child support is taking all the money.

A brief review of the education of Latinos in the United States

Although less so than in the case of African-American students, the educational failure of Latinos in the United States has also been the subject of sundry commissions, reports, and investigations. The picture that emerges from much of the research is that of unremitting and rampant educational failure (García, 1995; Nieto, 1995). This has been true of most Latinos, but is especially so of Mexican Americans (or Chicanos) and Puerto Ricans, the two Latino communities with a legacy of conquest or colonization by the United States. As aptly described by Richard Valencia, Chicano school failure is 'deeply rooted in history' (1991, p. 4). It has been characterized by a long history of negative conditions, including segregation, linguistic and cultural exclusion, racism, negative teacher–student interactions, consistent underfinancing of schools, and tracking (streaming). These same conditions have distinguished the educational history of Puerto Ricans in the United States (Walsh, 1991; Rivera and Nieto, 1993).

Latino students have frequently expressed feeling alienated and marginalized in their schools (National Commission, 1984; Frau-Ramos and Nieto, 1993; Upshur and Darder, 1993; Zanger, 1993). Furthermore, one study found that even when social class is held constant, Latinos still drop out at a higher rate than the general population (Steinberg *et al.*, 1984). The researchers concluded that this condition may exist because the prejudice that exists against Latinos is widespread and impedes their educational progress. Yet, as is also true in the case of African-American students, much of the research has concluded that despite the bleak picture, Latino students can and indeed have been academically successful in numerous situations.

The explanations offered for the disproportionate failure of Latinos in US schools have paralleled those given for African-American students. The more mean-spirited among them have focused on Latinos' supposed lack of intelligence, cultural inferiority, lack of a value orientation to education, or uncaring parents (see Nieto, 1995 for a review). Even some well-meaning explanations have emphasized immutable or difficult-to-change characteristics. Thus, factors that have been identified as placing students 'at risk' of failure have included minority group status, poverty, single-parent household, non-English background, and having a poorly educated mother (Pallas *et al.*, 1989), most of which apply to the vast majority of Latino students in the United States. Hence, their very identity – culturally, ethnically, and in other ways – places Latinos at risk. This reality has been borne out by a study of high-achieving and successful Chicano professionals by Patricia Gándara (1995). The study is more hopeful than previous research that focuses on students' identity as a risk factor because it addresses how Chicanos have been able to achieve academically in spite of what might be characterized as 'risk factors', specifically in this case, their low-income status. Here, too, however, the conditions that favoured the success of some over others would be at best difficult, or at worst impossible, to replicate for most Chicanos: light skin, attending middle- or upper-class and primarily white schools, and being tracked (streamed) in high-ability classes.

As I have argued elsewhere (Nieto, 1993), failure does not develop out of the blue, but is created partly through school policies and practices that in a very real way illustrate what a society believes its young people deserve. Thus, for instance, offering only low-level courses in schools serving Latino young people is a clear message that Latinos are not expected to achieve to high levels; labelling students 'at risk' because of their very ethnicity, native language, or social class is another sign that these students are expected to fail. Yet, research concerning what works with Latino students has consistently found that they respond positively to high expectations, educational environments characterized by caring and respect, positive and close relationships with their teachers, and interventions such as bilingual education and other educational strategies that build on rather than demolish their native language and culture (Zentella, 1992; Arias and Casanova, 1993; Nieto, 1993, 1995; García, 1994; Gibson, 1995). As we will see in the case study that follows, few of these conditions existed in most of the schools that Paul Chavez attended.

Paul Chavez

The signs that Paul Chavez, 16 years old, has already lived a lifetime of gang activity, drugs, and adversity are apparent from his style of dress, the 'tag' (tattoo) on his arm, to his reminiscences of 'homeboys' who have been killed. Paul's is the third generation of his family to be born in Los Angeles. He does not speak Spanish, but said that both his mother and grandmother do in spite of the fact that they too were born and raised in the United States.

At the time of his interviews, Paul lived with his mother, three brothers, and sister in a small one-family home in east Los Angeles. Signs of gang activity were apparent in the tags on buildings and walls (a sign that the 'turf' belongs to a particular gang); according to Paul, an outsider suspected of belonging to another gang might be jumped for just walking down the street. Paul's mother, who had dropped out of high school many years before, was studying to obtain her high school equivalency diploma. She and Paul's father, an alcoholic living in a halfway house, had been separated for several years. Paul belonged to a neighbourhood ('hood) gang, along with thirteen of his cousins and an older brother; an uncle and cousin had been killed as a result of their gang activity. Paul's parents also had been involved in a gang when they were younger.

Paul's academic and social problems in school began when he was in third or fourth grade. A few years later, he was suspended repeatedly from school for poor behaviour. The major problem had not been a lack of ability, but rather a lack of interest. He remembered Ms Nelson, his fifth grade teacher, as the only one with whom he had a meaningful relationship. In fact, he said she had been the only caring teacher he had during elementary (primary) school. Although he already wore gang-affiliated clothing and had a reputation as a troublemaker, Ms Nelson nevertheless held high expectations of him. It was in her classroom that he developed a fascination for history when he first read *The Diary of Anne Frank*.

When he began junior high school, the combination of negative peer pressure, family problems, and street violence had a decided influence on his school work. Consequently, he did very little in school, and he was expelled in eighth grade and stayed home for six months. By ninth grade, he was heavily involved in his gang. Several months later, he applied to a new alternative school, Nuestra Comunidad (Our Community) High School, designed for students who had dropped out or been expelled from other city schools. Heavily Chicano in population, the school was characterized by a multicultural curriculum that emphasized Chicano and Mexican history and it relied on students and staff for most decisions. After several months at the school, Paul was again expelled due to poor behaviour. After trying another programme and spending several months out of school, he applied again and had been in attendance for over a year at the time of his interviews. All of Paul's friends had by now quit school, and he confessed that he feared ending up like them. Since being accepted back into the programme, he had done quite well. Paul said that this school was different from any other he had attended because the entire staff cared about and encouraged the students, and because Chicano culture and history were central to the curriculum.

From his interviews, it was clear that Paul was at a crossroads. He had not quit his gang membership, and he seemed to both fear and be attracted to the lifestyle it represented. He was having success in school, and this was causing him to change some of his goals. Following are some of Paul's insights about these issues:

> I'm from a gang and that's it, and just 'cause I'm from a gang doesn't mean I can't make myself better. But me, I do care. I have a life and I want to keep it. I don't want to lose it. I have two little sisters and I want to see them grow up too, and I want to have my own family.
>
> I guess your peers . . . they try to pull you down and then you just got to be strong enough to pull away . . . . I got to think about myself and get what I got to get going on. Got to have your priorities straight.
>
> I came to [this school] and it was deep here. They got down into a lot of studies that I liked and there was a lot going on here. They get more into deeper Latino history here, and that's what I like. A lot of other, how you say, ethnic background. We had even Martin Luther King, we had Cesar Chavez. We had a lot of things.

I never used to think about [being Chicano] before. Now I do – being brown and just how our 'race' is just going out [being killed off]. You know, you don't want to see your 'race' go out like that. [In this school], they just leave the killings out and talk about how you can make it better, you know what I'm saying? Try to be more of the positive side of being a brown person, that's what I'm talking about.

[To make school better I would] talk about more interesting things, more things like that *I* would like, students would like. And I would get more involved, get more people involved. Get things going, not just let them vegetate or . . . on a desk and 'Here's a paper', teach 'em a lesson and expect them to do it. You know, get all involved. Try to find out what *we* think is important.

I'm getting out all I can get out [from this school]. There's so much to learn and that's all I want to do is just learn, try to educate my mind to see what I could get out of it. Now I take every chance I get to try to involve myself in something. Now it's like I figure if I'm more involved in school, I won't be so much involved in the gang, you know?

[I would want teachers to have] more patience and more understanding. [Teachers should] not think of a lesson as a lesson. Think of it as not a lesson just being taught to students, but a lesson being taught to one of your own family members, you know? 'Cause if it's like that, they get more deep into it, and that's all it takes. Teach a lesson with heart behind it and try to get your kids to understand more of what's going on. And don't lie to your kids, like to your students, saying, 'Everything is okay' and 'just say no to drugs, it's easy'. Let them know what's really going on. Don't beat around the bush. Let them know there's gangs, drugs.

I think they should get more of these aides, assistants, to be parents, okay? 'Cause the parents, I notice this: a parent in a school is more like they got *love*. That's it, they got love and they give it to you. They give it back to more students. I think they should get more like parents involved in the school like to teach this and that. Get more parents involved in the classroom too. Parents have a lot of things to say, I would think, about the schools.

After when I get my diploma, it's not the end of school, it's the beginning. I still want to learn a lot more after that. I basically want to go to college. Probably I would want to be either a teacher, a counsellor, something like working with youngsters to share my experience with them, you know? 'Cause I know there's a lot of people out there who talk down to youngsters, you know what I'm saying? Instead of talking *with* them, and just try to understand what they're going through.

You're gonna realize that you got to learn from day one . . . and education will never end. It's only when you stop it. I realize that now but I bet you there's a lot of kids that go to elementary school and [are] like I was. But see, me, I never really had somebody to push me. My mother pushed me and my mom, she just got tired. 'Paul, you're too much for me'. My father, he never really pushed me. He talked to me. That was like, 'Education, Paul, education', you know? And getting letters from my dad in jail, 'Stay in school', and that's all.

My mom, she's really proud of me. My friend was telling me that she was at church, at Bible study, a gathering at home of church people. And she was crying. She was proud. She said, 'Your mom was talking about you and she was crying. She's real proud'. And that's my mom, she's real sensitive. I love my mom so much it's even hard to explain.

I don't want to speak too soon, but I'm pretty much on a good road here. I'm pretty much making it. Trying to make something out of myself. I'm on that way, you know, I'm going that way. You can't talk about next month, at least at this time. I'm just today, get it done. That's it. The best I can. But I don't really like to build myself too high, because the higher you are, the harder you're gonna fall. I don't want to fall.

The case studies from a critical multicultural education perspective

Although the stories of Ron and Paul provide compelling examples of strength and resilience, they are also stories of defeat and despair within schools and in a society that hold out little hope for success for African-American and Latino students. Because their stories are vivid portraits of the complex interplay of relationships within families, communities, and schools, it may be helpful to view them from a critical multicultural education perspective.

How can the lens of critical multicultural education help us understand the case studies of Ron and Paul? Certainly, using multicultural education alone would uncover a number of important themes: the need to honour and respect students' cultures and identities; the urgency to diversify the curriculum; and the obligation to transform traditional pedagogy so that it better meets the needs of all students. Taken by themselves, however, these themes can remain within the categories of what Peter McLaren has called 'corporate' or 'liberal', in other words uncritical, multicultural education (McLaren, 1995). For instance, while it is true that using students' experiences as a basis of their schooling can help make their education more meaningful, it will not necessarily make students more critical thinkers. By the same token, adding a few characters of diverse ethnic background to the curriculum can be tremendously uplifting for students, but it may not help them critique how history is traditionally taught as unproblematic progress, regardless of the ethnic perspective. And changing pedagogical practices, while probably a good thing to do, will not likely in and of itself result in reversing the educational experiences of students such as Ron and Paul.

What I am suggesting is that multicultural education without a critical perspective can result in superficial changes that may not affect in any substantive way the life chances of students who have been as sorely miseducated as have Ron and Paul. On the other hand, applying a critical perspective to these case studies may prove helpful in understanding both the limits of multicultural education and its possibilities for transformative change. In what follows, I propose six ways in which a critical multicultural education can contribute to an understanding of the experiences of Ron and Paul and other young people who have been cast off by traditional schools.

Critical multicultural education affirms students' culture without trivializing the concept of culture itself

In the stories of Ron and Paul, it is clear that their community's culture and history, which had been glaringly missing from the curriculum in all their previous schools, has become a rich source of motivation and pride for both of them. In addition, they each expressed gratitude that the teachers in their new schools respected them and their backgrounds, a primary factor in academic success. However, a critical multicultural education perspective avoids what Anthony

Appiah has called 'the tyranny of identity', that is, a tightly scripted identity based on 'the politics of compulsion' (1994, p. 163). We will remember, for example, that it was in Ms Nelson's fifth-grade classroom that Paul became fascinated with history, and it was not because he was learning about Mexican history but because he was reading the story of Anne Frank. Similarly, Ron's favourite classes at his alternative school were the history tutorial on the Cuban Missile Crisis and Spanish, not because they were about his life as an African-American, but because he found the pedagogy compelling and because he was passionately interested in the world outside his own experience.

Students of all backgrounds are captivated by the study of difference, as we have seen in some of the literature reviewed previously. But generally they can see through a superficial focus on diversity that emphasizes only cultural titbits and ethnic celebrations. A critical multicultural education builds on students' interests without trivializing (or essentializing) the meaning of culture. This is important to remember because if we are serious about developing a truly liberating pedagogy, it means moving beyond an understanding of culture as a product or as the static symbol of a people (cf. Kalantzis and Cope; May, 1999). In the words of Frederick Erickson, 'I am concerned that our pedagogy and curriculum become genuinely transformative, not just cosmetically "relevant" ' (1990, p. 23).

Critical multicultural education challenges hegemonic knowledge

Students learn to accept much of what is taught in schools as factual knowledge. If it is written in a textbook, it acquires an even more powerful authenticity (Apple, 1992). Yet as James Banks reminds us, 'Hegemonic knowledge that promotes the interests of powerful, elite groups often obscures its value premises by masquerading as totally objective' (1995, p. 15). Ron was acutely aware of this; he was clearly fed up with studying Christopher Columbus because with each passing year, Columbus became even more enshrined in mythology and mystique. However, it was not only Columbus who he saw treated this way: Ron also challenged the hegemonic way in which such African-American icons as Martin Luther King and Malcolm X were being taught. Thus, he challenged not the importance of studying historical figures, but the static and uncritical way in which it is done.

This same critical perspective needs to be applied to the entire curriculum. Ironically, the same Ron who was critical of the trivial and unproblematic portrayals of Christopher Columbus, Malcolm X, and Martin Luther King rather uncritically boasted of the 'great "race" of kings and queens' from which he descended. Yes, it is true that a society of great kings and queens may be a sign of an advanced civilization. However, it is also often the sign of a rigidly hierarchical society stratified by class, gender, and other differences in which those who are not favoured are destined to lives of servitude. Given the 'deculturalization' (Boateng, 1990) that has generally characterized the schooling of African-Americans, Ron's response is understandable. Not only have Africans and African-Americans been omitted from most school treatments of history, but even when included, they have as a rule been presented as savage and barbaric. Although slavery is bemoaned, the sting of oppression is softened with the impression that Africans were the beneficiaries of a benevolent civilizing on the part of Whites. In this way, a hideous part of US history is distorted and romanticized. Ron's statement that he felt 'like the realest person on earth' in his African history class is compelling testimony of the power of a curriculum that contests this hegemonic tradition.

A critical multicultural perspective demands that all knowledge, not only 'official knowledge', be taught critically. Thus, any history that is presented with a surplus of hyperbole by the use of such adjectives as 'majestic', 'magnificent', 'dazzling', or 'awe-inspiring' needs to be interrogated just as critically as official US history when it is taught in this way. All students deserve the right to be treated with respect; this means, among other things, affirming their backgrounds as well as trusting their intelligence. Having said this, however, it is equally important to be critical of those who bemoan the dangers of essentialism without truly understanding or taking into account the lives of young people who have been alienated from school and society. This point is eloquently made by bell hooks (1994) when she states that it is those from dominant groups who perpetuate essentialism, not just those from marginalized groups. She goes on to say, '. . . I am concerned that critiques of identity politics not serve as the new, chic way to silence students from marginal groups' (1994, p. 83; see also May, 1999).

Critical multicultural education complicates pedagogy

There is no one right way to teach, and a critical multicultural perspective helps us to understand this. For Ron, using primary texts such as documents and tapes was engaging; for Paul, reading biographies was often inspiring. The issue is not so much the particular pedagogical strategy used as is, in the words of Lilia Bartolomé, 'the teacher's politically clear educational philosophy' (1994, p. 179). A critical multicultural education perspective complicates the question of pedagogy; it challenges teachers who are interested in transformative education to re-think what and how they teach, and to constantly question their decisions. For instance, while it is probably true that Ron and Paul benefited from a more inspired pedagogy at their alternative schools than had been the case before, some of these same strategies were no doubt used in their previous schools. The major issue is not, then, the strategy or approach itself, but the environment in which it takes place. Cooperative learning, for example, can take place in the most uncooperative and oppressive of settings, while truly extraordinary and high-level discussions can happen in classrooms with nailed-down seats in rigid rows.

What is most striking in the words of Ron and Paul is the deep care and respect they felt from their teachers. This is an important lesson for multicultural education. It is not meant to discourage new and innovative pedagogical strategies; on the contrary, pedagogy, to be effective, needs to become more humanizing (Bartolomé, 1994). But there is no set 'bag of tricks' that will accomplish this awesome task (cf. Kalantzis and Cope, 1999). What matters are the intentions and goals behind the pedagogy.

Critical multicultural education problematizes a simplistic focus on self-esteem

Much has been written about the importance of multicultural education in building the self-esteem of students (Beane, 1991). The conventional wisdom, that students cannot learn unless they feel good about themselves, brings up the chicken-or-egg question: that is, do students need to feel better about themselves before they can be successful students, or does their academic success help them develop a higher self-esteem? As pointed out by Joseph Kahne, self-esteem is at best a 'slippery concept' (1996, p. 17). A critical multicultural education perspective problematizes the simplistic focus on self-esteem. An astute observation by

Alfie Kohn is relevant here: 'Getting students to chant "I'm special!" – or to read a similar perfunctory message on cheerful posters or in prepackaged curricular materials – is pointless at best' (1994, p. 276).

Rather than think of it as a unitary concept, we need to understand that self-esteem operates *in relation to particular situations*. If self-esteem is used as an individual psychological construct, it overlooks the sociopolitical context of students' lives, downplaying or denying the racism and other oppressive behaviours that they experience. Therefore, how schools and society *create* low self-esteem in children needs to be considered. That is, students do not simply develop poor self-concepts out of the blue; rather, their self-esteem *in terms of schooling* is the result of policies and practices in schools that respect and affirm some groups while devaluing and rejecting others. Students from culturally dominated groups partially internalize some of the many negative messages to which they are subjected on a daily basis about their culture, ethnic group, class, gender, or language, but they are not simply passive recipients of such messages. They also actively resist negative messages through interactions with peers, family, and even school. This is one way of understanding Paul's connection with his gang, a relationship that raised his self-esteem but one that he began to question *once he became a more successful student*. The mediating role of families and communities, and in some cases schools, helps to contradict negative messages and to reinforce more positive and affirming ones.

Critical multicultural education encourages 'dangerous discourses'

According to Ellen Bigler and James Collins (1995), multicultural education is rightly perceived as a threat because it encourages 'dangerous discourses' and challenges existing arrangements in and out of school. Students such as Paul and Ron clearly understood this. Both, for instance, at last felt free to discuss issues that had been largely untouched in their former schools but that, as uncomfortable as they might be for teachers and other adults in their current schools, were important focal points of their learning. Why should this be the case in such schools? Unlike most traditional public schools, alternative schools are often the places where the most alienated students end up. In such schools, student alienation is generally understood not simply as pathological responses to individual circumstances but, at least partly, as the result of the sociopolitical context in which young people live.

Unfortunately, these 'dangerous discourses' have little place in most schools, as we have seen. Even in well-meaning schools where teachers have determined to develop a multicultural perspective, such discussions are usually missing because teachers are either unaware of the salience of such issues in the lives of students or they simply do not hear 'the hard questions' (Jervis, 1996) that children ask. Yet a critical multicultural perspective demands that schools become sites of freedom to learn even controversial issues. As such, critical multicultural education connects learning with democracy in a profound manner because it invites discussion and debate. It is not neat; it does not have all the answers. In this way, it is like life itself.

Multicultural education by itself cannot do it all

Multicultural education is a hopeful pedagogy. Because of this, it holds great promise for transforming the future of countless young people who would otherwise be rejected and devalued by the schools they attend and the societies in which they live. Nevertheless, a critical perspective makes it clear that multicultural education is not a panacea. For Paul and Ron, the road ahead is a difficult one. Crime, homelessness, and violence are just some of the manifestations of a society that is increasingly stratified and alienating, and massive structural changes in the economy are exacerbating the situation even further (cf. McLaren and Torres, 1999). Many young people in the United States, but especially those who are poor and black, Latino, or Native American, have little to look forward to but a life of unemployment or undemanding work in fast-food restaurants. To believe that changes in pedagogy and curriculum, or even the radical transformation of schooling itself could solve all these problems is illusory at best. The dilemmas faced by these young men obviously include far more than irrelevant curriculum and boring pedagogy, and that is why separating their reality from the sociopolitical context of society is like hiding one's head in the sand.

I do not mean to suggest that schools cannot make dramatic improvements in educating the large numbers of young people who are currently poorly served by both the educational system and by society itself. Indeed, that is what they have always promised to do: in the United States it is understood that schools have a social contract to educate *all* students, not just white, English-speaking, middle-class students who live with two parents. There have been numerous examples of teachers and schools who have provided environments of extraordinary academic success for students who might otherwise have been dismissed as possessing the 'intelligence' needed to achieve. Nevertheless, it is evident that schools alone cannot hope to achieve these results on a massive scale by themselves. In the case of Ron and Paul, their new schools were providing empowering models of education, but the limitations of such schools are evident. Poorly funded and small in number, although generally staffed by a corps of determined and dedicated teachers, alternative schools are a ray of hope where an entire constellation is needed. Social and structural barriers to learning as experienced by Ron and Paul are constant reminders that social justice cannot single-handedly be achieved even by caring, progressive teachers or by schools committed to multicultural education. What is needed, then, is committed and purposeful political activity, both within the classroom and outside of it, to ensure that the stated ideals of education in a democratic society are realized.

Conclusion

Paul and Ron are on the brink between triumph and disaster, and this is evident in the personal predicaments they talked about. Just over a year after they had been interviewed, I had the opportunity to speak with Beatriz McConnie Zapater and Mac Morante, my colleagues who had interviewed them. I was anxious to hear what had happened to Ron and Paul but I was determined not to repeat the sentimentalizing that goes on when specific educational strategies or programmes are simplistically proposed as the cure for the many difficult problems confronting schools and society. The outcomes of their specific situations again point out the need to face all such situations with a critical but hopeful perspective: Ron had dropped out of school and was living with one of the young women who had recently had his child; Harvard was a dream that would remain unfulfilled. Paul was still in school and would be graduating within a few months; he was looking forward to going to college.

In an essay on critical pedagogy, Maxine Greene (1986) asked what this kind of education might mean for teachers. She suggested that we need to begin by releasing our collective imaginations, and she continued:

> We might try to make audible again the recurrent calls for justice and equality. We might try to reactivate the resistance to materialism and conformity. We might even try to inform with meaning the desire to educate 'all the children' in a legitimately 'common school'.
>
> (1986, p. 440)

Like the words of Maxine Greene, the words of Ron and Paul were sometimes infused with a deep-seated belief in the power of education. How could this be? After all, both were prime examples of the failure of education to make good on its promise. But the ideal of social justice is powerful indeed, and the school as the site where social justice can best be achieved is a utopian vision that is irresistible. How else to explain Paul's desire to become a teacher? These young men were sometimes wise beyond their years, and they remind us of just how far we need to go in our schools and society to fulfil the promise of a life of equality and freedom for all our people.

Note

1   This chapter includes partial excerpts of the larger case studies of Ron and Paul. The names used in this chapter are pseudonyms, and other details (school names or the names of teachers or administrators) that might identify them, have also been changed. Paul Chavez was interviewed by Dr Mac Lee Morante, a mental health therapist and school psychologist in the Anaheim City School District, and Ron Morris was interviewed by Beatriz McConnie Zapater, the principal of the Greater Egleston Community High School in Boston. I am grateful for the many insights they provided as I developed the case studies. The interviews took place in 1994 and the case studies in their entirety are included in a second edition of the original research (Nieto, 1996).

References

Akinyela, M. (1995) 'Rethinking Afrocentricity: the foundations of a theory of critical Afrocentricity', in Darder, A. (ed.) *Culture and Difference: Critical Perspectives on the Bicultural Experience in the United States*, Westport, CT: Bergin and Garvey, pp. 21–39.

Appiah, A. (1994) 'Identity, authenticity, survival: multicultural societies and social reproduction', in Gutmann, A. (ed.) *Multiculturalism*, Princeton, NJ: Princeton University Press, pp. 149–63.

Apple, M. (1992) 'The text and cultural politics', *Educational Researcher*, **21**, 7, pp. 4–11, 19.

Arias, M. and Casanova, U. (eds) (1993) *Bilingual Education: Politics, Practice, Research*, Chicago: University of Chicago Press.

Banks, J. (1993) 'The canon debate, knowledge construction, and multicultural education', *Educational Researcher*, **22**, 5, pp. 4–14.

—— (1995) 'The historical reconstruction of knowledge about race: implications for transformative teaching', *Educational Researcher*, **24**, 2, pp. 15–25.

Bartolomé, L. (1994) 'Beyond the methods fetish: toward a humanizing pedagogy', *Harvard Educational Review*, **64**, pp. 173–94.

Beane, J. (1991) 'Sorting out the self-esteem controversy', *Educational Leadership* (September), pp. 25–30.

Bempechat, J. (1992) *Fostering High Achievement in African American Children: Home, School, and Public Policy Influences*, New York: ERIC Clearinghouse on Urban Education, Institute for Urban and Minority Education, Teachers College, Columbia University.

Bennett, C. (1995) 'Research on racial issues in American higher education', in Banks, J. and Banks, C. (eds) *Handbook of Research on Multicultural Education*, New York: Macmillan, pp. 663–82.

Bigler, E. and Collins, J. (1995) *Dangerous Discourses: The Politics of Multicultural Literature in Community and Classroom*, Albany: National Research Center on Literature Teaching and Learning, University at Albany, Report Series 7.4.

Boateng, F. (1990) 'Combating deculturalization of the African-American child in the public school system: a multicultural approach', in Lomotey, K. (ed.) *Going to School: the African-American Experience*, Albany: State University of New York Press, pp. 73–84.

Corbett, D. and Wilson, B. (1995) 'Make a difference with, not for, students: a plea to researchers and reformers', *Educational Researcher*, **24**, 5, pp. 12–17.

Corson, D. (1993) *Language, Minority Education and Gender: Linking Social Justice and Power*, Clevedon, England: Multilingual Matters.

Cummins, J. (1994) 'From coercive to collaborative relations of power in the teaching of literacy', in Ferdman, B., Weber, R.-M. and Ramírez, A. (eds) *Literacy across Languages and Cultures*, Albany: State University of New York Press, pp. 295–331.

—— (1996) *Negotiating Identities: Education for Empowerment in a Diverse Society*, Ontario, CA: California Association for Bilingual Education.

Donaldson, K. (1996) *Through Students' Eyes*, New York: Bergin and Garvey.

Erickson, F. (1990) 'Culture, politics, and educational practice', *Educational Foundations*, **4**, 2, pp. 21–45.

Farrell, E., Peguero, G., Lindsey, R., and White, R. (1988) 'Giving voice to high school students: pressure and boredom, ya know what I'm sayin'?', *American Educational Research Journal*, **25**, pp. 489–502.

Fine, M. (1991) *Framing Dropouts: Notes on the Politics of an Urban High School*, Albany: State University of New York Press.

Ford, D. (1996) *Reversing Underachievement among Gifted Black Students: Promising Practices and Programs*, New York: Teachers College Press.

Fordham, S. and Ogbu, J. (1986) 'Black students' school success: coping with the 'burden of acting white', *Urban Review*, **18**, 3, pp. 176–206.

Frau-Ramos, M. and Nieto, S. (1993) ' "I was an outsider": Dropping out among Puerto Rican youths in Holyoke, Massachusetts', in Rivera, R. and Nieto, S. (eds) *The Education of Latino Students in Massachusetts: Issues, Research, and Policy Implications*, Boston: Gastón Institute for Latino Public Policy and Development, pp. 147–69.

Freire, P. (1970) *Pedagogy of the Oppressed*, New York: Seabury Press.

—— (1985) *The Politics of Education: Culture, Power, and Liberation*, New York: Bergin and Garvey.

Gándara, P. (1995) *Over the Ivy Walls: The Educational Mobility of Low-income Chicanos*, Albany: State University of New York Press.

García, E. (1994) *Understanding and Meeting the Challenge of Student Cultural Diversity*, Boston: Houghton Mifflin Company.

—— (1995) 'Educating Mexican American students: past treatment and recent developments in theory, research, policy, and practice', in Banks, J. and Banks, C. (eds) *Handbook of Research on Multicultural Education*, New York: Macmillan, pp. 372–87.

Gibson, M. (1995) 'Perspectives on acculturation and school performance', *Focus on Diversity*, **5**, 3, pp. 8–10.

Gillborn, D. (1995) *Racism and Antiracism in Real Schools*, Buckingham: Open University Press.

Goodlad, J. (1984) *A Place Called School*, New York: McGraw-Hill.

Greene, M. (1986) 'In search of a critical pedagogy', *Harvard Educational Review*, **56**, pp. 427–41.

Heath, S. (1983) *Ways with Words*, New York: Cambridge University Press.

Hidalgo, N. (1991) ' "Free time, school is like a free time": social relations in city high school classes', Unpublished doctoral dissertation, Harvard University.

hooks, b. (1994) *Teaching to Transgress: Education as the Practice of Freedom*, New York: Routledge.

Irvine, J. (1990) *Black Students and School Failure: Policies, Practices, and Prescriptions*, Westport, CT: Greenwood Press.

Irvine, J. and Foster, M. (eds) (1996) *Growing Up African American in Catholic Schools*, New York: Teachers College Press.

Jervis, K. (1996) ' "How come there are no brothers on that list?": hearing the hard questions all children ask', *Harvard Educational Review*, **66**, pp. 546–76.

Kahne, J. (1996) 'The politics of self-esteem', *American Educational Research Journal*, **33**, pp. 3–22.

Kalantzis, M. and Cope, B. (1999) 'Multicultural education: transforming the mainstream', in May, S. (ed.) *Critical Multiculturalism: Rethinking Multicultural and Antiracist Education*, London: Falmer Press, pp. 245–76.

Knapp, M., Shields, P., and Turnbull, B. (1995) 'Academic challenge in high-poverty classrooms', *Phi Delta Kappan*, **76**, pp. 770–6.

Kohl, H. (1993) 'The myth of "Rosa Parks, the tired" ', *Multicultural education*, **1**, 2, pp. 6–10.

—— (1994) *'I Won't Learn from You' and Other Thoughts on Creative Maladjustment*, New York: The New Press.

Kohn, A. (1994) 'The truth about self-esteem', *Phi Delta Kappan*, **76**, pp. 272–83.

Ladson-Billings, G. (1994) *The Dreamkeepers: Successful Teachers of African–American Children*, San Francisco, CA: Jossey-Bass.

Lee, V., Winfield, L., and Wilson, T. (1991) 'Academic behaviors among high-achieving African-American students', *Education and Urban Society*, **24**, pp. 65–86.

Lomotey, K. (1990) *Going to School: The African–American Experience*, Albany: State University of New York Press.

McLaren, P. (1995) 'White terror and oppositional agency: towards a critical multiculturalism', in Sleeter, C. and McLaren, P. (eds) *Multicultural Education, Critical Pedagogy, and the Politics of Difference*, Albany: State University of New York Press, pp. 33–70.

McLaren, P. and Torres, R. (1999) 'Racism and multicultural education: rethinking "race" and "whiteness" in late capitalism', in May, S. (ed.) *Critical Multiculturalism: Rethinking Multicultural and Antiracist Education*, London: Falmer Press, pp. 42–76.

May, S. (1999) 'Critical multiculturalism and cultural difference: avoiding essentialism', in May, S. (ed.) *Critical Multiculturalism: Rethinking Multicultural and Antiracist Education*, London: Falmer Press, pp. 11–41.

Moodley, K. (1999) 'Antiracist education through political literacy: the case of Canada', in May, S. (ed.) *Critical Multiculturalism: Rethinking Multicultural and Antiracist Education*, London: Falmer Press, pp. 138–52.

National Commission on Secondary Education for Hispanics (1984) *'Make Something Happen': Hispanics and Urban School Reform* (2 Vols), Washington, DC: Hispanic Policy Development Project.

New, C. (1996) 'Teacher thinking and perceptions of African-American male achievement in the classroom', in Ríos, F. (ed.) *Teaching Thinking in Cultural Contexts*, Albany: State University of New York Press, pp. 85–103.

Nieto, S. (1992) *Affirming Diversity: The Sociopolitical Context of Multicultural Education* White Plains, NY: Longman.

—— (1993) 'Creating possibilities: educating Latino students in Massachusetts', in Rivera, R. and Nieto, S. (eds) *The Education of Latino Students in Massachusetts: Issues, Research, and Policy Implications*, Boston: Gastón Institute for Latino Public Policy and Development, pp. 243–61.

—— (1994) 'Lessons from students on creating a chance to dream', *Harvard Educational Review*, **64**, pp. 392–426.

—— (1995) 'A history of the education of Puerto Rican students in US mainland schools: 'losers', 'outsiders', or 'leaders'?', in Banks, J. and Banks, C. (eds) *Handbook of Research on Multicultural Education*, New York: Macmillan, pp. 388–411.

—— (1996) *Affirming Diversity: The Sociopolitical Context of Multicultural Education* (2nd edn), White Plains, NY: Longman.

Ogbu, J. (1994) 'Racial stratification and education in the United States: why inequality persists', *Teachers College Record*, **96**, pp. 264–98.

Olsen, L. (1988) *Crossing the Schoolhouse Border: Immigrant Students and the California Public Schools*, San Francisco: California Tomorrow.

Pallas, A., Natriello, G., and McDill, E. (1989) 'The changing nature of the disadvantaged population: current dimensions and future trends', *Educational Researcher*, **18**, 5, 4, pp. 16–22.

Patchen, M. (1982) *Black-White Contact in Schools: Its Social and Academic Effects*, West Lafayette, IN: Purdue University Press.

Phelan, P., Davidson, A., and Cao, H. (1992) 'Speaking up: students' perspectives on school', *Phi Delta Kappan*, 73, pp. 695–704.

Pollard, D. (1989) 'A profile of underclass achievers', *Journal of Negro Education*, 58, pp. 297–308.

Poplin, M. and Weeres, J. (1992) *Voices from the Inside: A Report on Schooling from Inside the Classroom*, Claremont, CA: Claremont Graduate School, Institute for Education in Transformation.

Reyes, M. (1992) 'Challenging venerable assumptions: literacy instruction for linguistically different students', *Harvard Educational Review*, 62, pp. 427–46.

Rivera, R. and Nieto, S. (1993) *The Education of Latino Students in Massachusetts: Issues, Research, and Policy Implications*, Boston: Gastón Institute for Latino Community Development and Public Policy.

Sadker, M. and Sadker, D. (1994) *Failing at Fairness: How America's Schools Cheat Girls*, New York: Charles Scribner's Sons.

Shor, I. (1992) *Empowering Education: Critical Teaching for Social Change*, Chicago: University of Chicago Press.

Sleeter, C. (1994) 'White racism', *Multicultural Education*, 1, 4, pp. 5–8, 39.

Sleeter, C. and Grant, C. (1991) 'Mapping terrains of power: Student cultural knowledge vs. classroom knowledge', in Sleeter, C. (ed.) *Empowerment through Multicultural Education*, Albany: State University of New York Press, pp. 49–67.

Sleeter, C. and McLaren, P. (eds) (1995) *Multicultural Education, Critical Pedagogy, and the Politics of Difference*, Albany: State University of New York Press.

Smith, D., Gilmore, P., Goodman, S., and McDermott, R. (1993) 'Failure's failure', in Jacob, E. and Jordan, C. (eds) *Minority Education: Anthropological Perspectives*, Norwood, NJ: Ablex, pp. 209–31.

Soo Hoo, S. (1993) 'Students as partners in research and restructuring schools', *Educational Forum*, 57, pp. 386–93.

Steele, C. (1992) 'Race and the schooling of black Americans', *The Atlantic Monthly*, April, pp. 68–78.

Steinberg, L., Blinde, P., and Chan, K. (1984) 'Dropping out among language minority youth', *Review of Educational Research*, 54, pp. 113–32.

Tatum, B. (1992) 'Talking about race, learning about racism: the application of racial identity development theory in the classroom', *Harvard Educational Review*, 62, pp. 1–24.

Taylor, A. (1991) 'Social competence and the early school transition: risk and protective factors for African-American children', *Education and Urban Society*, 24, 1, pp. 15–26.

Treisman, U. (1992) 'Studying students studying calculus: a look at the lives of minority mathematics students in college', *The College Mathematics Journal*, 23, 5, pp. 362–72.

Upshur, C. and Darder, A. (1993) 'What do Latino children need to succeed in school? A study of four Boston public schools', in Rivera, R. and Nieto, S. (eds) *The Education of Latino Students in Massachusetts: Issues, Research, and Policy Implications*, Boston: Gastón Institute for Latino Public Policy and Development, pp. 127–46.

Valencia, R. (1991) 'The plight of Chicano students: an overview of schooling conditions and outcomes', in Valencia, R. (ed.) *Chicano School Failure and Success: Research and Policy Agendas for the 1990s*, London: Falmer Press, pp. 3–26.

Walsh, C. (1991) *Pedagogy and the Struggle for Voice: Issues of Language, Power, and Schooling for Puerto Ricans*, New York: Bergin and Garvey.

Weinberg, M. (1977) *A Chance to Learn: A History of Race and Education in the United States*, Cambridge: Cambridge University Press.

Zanger, V. (1993) 'Academic costs of social marginalization: an analysis of Latino students' perceptions at a Boston high school', in Rivera, R. and Nieto, S. (eds) *The Education of Latino Students in Massachusetts: Issues, Research, and Policy Implications*, Boston: Gastón Institute for Latino Public Policy and Development, pp. 170–90.

Zentella, A. (1992) 'Individual differences in growing up bilingual', in Saravia-Shore, M. and Arvizu, S. (eds) *Cross-cultural Literacy: Ethnographies of Communication in Multiethnic Classrooms*, New York: Garland, pp. 211–25.

CHAPTER 12

BLACK WOMEN IN EDUCATION
A collective movement for social change

Heidi Safia Mirza

In Heidi Safia Mirza (ed.) *Black British Feminism: A Reader*, London: Routledge, pp. 269–77, 1997

This chapter is concerned with the issue of how to theorize the paradox of inclusive acts by excluded groups. Research on young black (African-Caribbean) women's strategies to succeed at school and into further and higher education raises the question, 'How can such conservative and instrumental actions be deemed subversive?' On the surface, it appears that they are conforming, identifying with the ideology of meritocracy, climbing the conventional career ladder, wanting to succeed on society's terms – buying into the system. The problem is simply this, how can I claim (as I do) that black women's desire or motivation to succeed within the educational system is radical? How can what appears on the surface to be compliance and willingness to conform to systems and structures of educational meritocracy, be redefined as strategic or as evidence of a covert social movement for change?

What we need is a complex analysis of what is going on among the majority of black women who are not, as we have come to expect from the popular presumptions, 'failing'. We need to move towards a coherent understanding of black female educational orientation that begins to reveal the subversive and transformative possibilities of their actions. From school through to university and into the community black women access educational resources and subvert expected patterns of educational mobility. This active engagement challenges our expectations. Black women who have been, after all, theorized in our dominant academic discourse as 'the most oppressed', deemed the least 'visible', the least empowered, the most marginal of groups, do relatively well. They appear to strive for inclusivity.

However, no one wants to look at their success, their desire for inclusivity. They are out of place, disrupting, untidy. They do not fit. The notion of their agency and difference is problematic for the limited essentialist and mechanical social reproduction theories that dominate our explanations of black female inequality (Moore, 1996). Traditionally, and in common-sense accounts that rely on such theories, black women's contradictory actions are analysed in terms of subcultural resistance.

However, because young black women's subcultures of resistance are deemed conformist, the idea is cleverly reworked and presented instead as 'resistance through accommodation' (Mac an Ghaill, 1988). Black women, we are told, employ this particular strategy of resistance, because they are motivated by their identification with the role model of the 'strong black mother'. Such essentialist constructions presumes that the role model of the black mother provides young black women with special powers of endurance and transgenerational cultural understandings that especially equip them in their struggles against racism and sexism (Mirza, 1992).

But in this chapter, I want to suggest that black female educational urgency cannot be understood simply as 'resistance through accommodation'. Their desire for inclusion is strategic, subversive and ultimately far more transformative than what subcultural reproduction theory suggests. The irony is that black women are both succeeding and conforming in order to transform and change. By mapping black women's covert educational urgency, I hope to move towards a radical interpretation of black female educational motivation. Valorizing their agency as subversive and transformative rather than as a manifestation of resistance, it becomes clear that black women do not just resist racism, they live 'other' worlds.

Evidence of collective educational urgency

Black women do buy into the educational system. They do relatively well at school, relative that is to their male and female working-class peers as measured in terms of *average* exam performance at GCSE level. This phenomenon was first documented over ten years ago in 1985 in the Swann Report and confirmed by the ILEA in 1987 (Mirza, 1992). More recently the findings of the 1992 National Youth Cohort Study appear to confirm this (Drew *et al.*, 1992).

In my own research for *Young, Female and Black* (Mirza, 1992), which was a small local study of two inner city working-class schools, I also found black girls do as well as, if not better than, their peers in average exam performance. I found young black women collectively identified with the notion of credentialism. They subscribed to the meritocratic ideal, which within the parameters of their circumstances meant 'getting on'. In difficult and disruptive conditions the majority of young black women would sit in the back of the class getting on with their own work. However, whatever the young black women's achievements they were always within the constraints of the class conditions of inner city schooling.

What is clear from all the studies on race and education is that black girls have to stay on longer at school to achieve their long-term educational aspirations. In order to overcome obstacles of racism and sexism in school large numbers stay on in order to get the opportunities that enable them to take a 'backdoor' route into further and higher education. Young women do this by strategically rationalizing their educational opportunities. They opt for accessible careers (gendered and racialized jobs) which give them the opportunity to get onto a college course. Their career aspirations were tied to their educational motivation and by the prospect of upward mobility. A job was an expression of their desire to move ahead within the educational process. The young black women chose 'realistic careers' that they knew to be accessible and (historically) available to them. For example, social work and other caring jobs such as nursing or office work. The occupations they chose always required a course or several courses of rigorous professional training, and is why they choose them. Thus, while it may appear young black women are reproducing stereotypes of black women's work, they are in effect expressing their meritocratic values within the limits of opportunities allowed to them in a racially and sexually divisive educational and economic system. They are in effect subversively and collectively employing a 'backdoor' entry to further and higher education.

This picture of collective educational urgency among young black women to enter colleges of further and higher education is confirmed by national statistics. The 1993 Labour Force survey shows 61 per cent of all black women (aged 16–59) to have higher and other qualifications (*Employment Gazette*, 1993). Figures for 1995 show that 52 per cent of all black women (aged 16–24) are in full-time education, compared to 28 per cent of white women, 36 per cent of black men, and 31 per cent of white men (*Employment Gazette*, 1995). Similarly a recent study for the Policy Studies Institute shows that in relation to their respective population sizes, ethnic minority groups, overall, are over-represented in higher education (Modood and Shiner, 1994). This over-representation was especially apparent in the new universities. Here people of Caribbean origin were over-represented by 43 per cent, Asians by 162 per cent and Africans by 223 per cent! This compared to the white population which was under-represented by 7 per cent.

But educational urgency does not stop there. As mothers, black women strategically negotiate the educational advantage of their children within the constraints offered by the decaying urban education system and limited access to cultural capital (Reay, 1998). Black women are disproportionately involved in the setting up and running of black supplementary schools. They invest in the education of the next generation. In ongoing research on black supplementary schools, Diane Reay and myself have done a preliminary survey of black schools in London (Reay and Mirza, 1997). So far we found sixty officially documented black schools within four London boroughs, but we believe we only scratched the surface. Through networks and word of mouth we hear of more and more everyday. Sometimes there would be several on one council estate. They appear to spring up 'unofficially' in houses, community centres, and unused school rooms. Of those we found, 65 per cent were run by women; and of those run by men, women's involvement as teachers and mentors was the overwhelming majority input.

Is black female educational urgency a new social movement?

It could be argued, as indeed I wish to suggest here, that the extent, direction and intensity of the black female positive orientation to education is significant enough to qualify their collective action as a transformative social movement. However, Paul Gilroy does not think so. He describes the black struggles for educational opportunities as constituting 'fragile collectivities'. He argues such movements are symptoms of 'resistance to domination', defensive organizations, with their roots in a radical sense of powerlessness. As they cannot make the transition to 'stable forms of politics' they are not agents for social change (Gilroy, 1987, pp. 230–1).

However, I believe an analysis of female collective action offers a new direction in the investigation of black social movements. As Gilroy's argument demonstrates, black female agency has remained invisible in the masculinist discourse of 'race' and social change. There has clearly been a black and male monopoly of the 'black subject' (West, 1990). In the masculinist discourse on race and social change the assumption is that 'race' is contested and fought over in the masculine arena of the streets – among the (male) youth in the city (e.g. Solomos, 1988; Keith, 1993, 1995; Solomos and Back, 1995). Urban social movements, we are told, mobilize in protest, riots, local politics, and community organizations. We are told it is their action, and not the subversive and covert action of women that gives rise to so-called 'neo-populist liberatory authentic politics' (Gilroy, 1987, p. 245). This is the masculinist version of radical social change; visible, radical, confrontational, collective action, powerfully expressed in the politics of the inner city, where class consciousness evolves in response to urban struggle.

Thus notions of resistance which are employed in this male discourse of social change to signify and celebrate black struggle, remain entrenched in ideology that privileges dominance. The black feminist theorist Patricia Hill Collins tells us black women writers have rejected notions of power based on domination in favour of a notion of power based on a vision of self-actualization, self-definition and self-determination (Collins, 1991). However, the political language of 'community' around which black social movements are traditionally articulated in the masculinist discourse remains a relational idea. It suggests the notion of antagonism and oppositionality – of domination and subordination – between one community and another (Young, 1990). But what if, for black women, community identity is not relational and antagonistic but inclusive with regard to the mainstream? This could be a possibility; there must be another way of understanding our lives other than always in relation to the 'other'. There is after all more to life than opposition to racism (Mirza, 1995).

Black women's activism: strategies for transformation

Mapping the hidden histories, subjected knowledges, the counter memories of black women educators in black supplementary schools, reveals the possibilities for covert social movements to achieve social change. Black supplementary schools, as organic grassroots organizations, are not simply a response to mainstream educational exclusion and poor practice, as they are so often described. They are far more radical and subversive than their quiet conformist exterior suggests. It is little wonder they are viewed suspiciously by uninformed observers as 'black power places'!

Such schools provide an alternative world with different meanings and shared 'ways of knowing'. As one mother said, 'There is white bias everywhere except at Saturday school.' It is a place where whiteness is displaced and blackness becomes the unspoken norm. It is a place of refusal and difference; a place of belonging.

In the four supplementary schools in our research black children discovered 'really useful knowledge' (Johnson, 1988) which allowed them 'to step outside the white hermeneutic circle and into the black' (Gates, quoted in Casey, 1993, p. 110). Each of the four schools in our study was distinct, but they were underpinned by two main pedagogies. Some focused more on black images, black history and black role models. Others focused more on back to basics, the formal teaching of the three R's. Some did both.

In the same way as the schools were paradoxically radical and conservative in their aims, so too were the teachers both radical and conservative in their praxis. On the one hand, the women, who were for the most part voluntary unpaid teachers, talked of their 'joy' of what they do, the 'gift of giving back', of their work to 'raise the race'. Many had been giving up their weekends for twenty years. Others had become ill from overwork and dedication.

On the other hand, the same teachers saw themselves as complimenting mainstream education. They were concerned about 'fitting in', assisting parents with home–school relations and getting the children to do better. On the surface these schools appeared conformist and conservative, with their focus on formality and buying into the liberal democratic ideal of meritocracy.

But as Casey writes in her excellent book, *I Answer with My Life* (1993) in a racist society a black person is located very differently than a white person.

In a racist society for a black child to become educated is to contradict the whole system of racist signification . . . . to succeed in studying white knowledge is to undo the system itself . . . to refute its reproduction of black inferiority materially and symbolically.

(Casey, 1993, p. 123)

Thus it could be argued, as I am doing here, that in certain circumstances, *doing well can become a radical strategy*. An act of social transformation.

The black women educators did not accept the dominant discourse. In their space on the margin they have evolved a system of strategic rationalization of the dominant discourse. They operate within, between, under, and alongside the mainstream educational and labour market structures, subverting, renaming and reclaiming opportunities for their children through their transformative pedagogy of 'raising the race' – a radical pedagogy, that ironically appears conservative on the surface with its focus on inclusion and dialogue with the mainstream.

Patricia Hill Collins (1991) calls our attention to the dual nature of black women's activist traditions in their attempt to bring about social change. She suggests black women engage in activism that is both conservative and radical. Black women create culture and provide for their families. Fostering self-evaluation and self-reliance, patterns of consciousness and self-expression shape their cultures of difference. This struggle for group survival may appear conservative with its emphasis on preserving customs and cultural maintenance. Collins argues that this struggle for group survival is in contrast to the radical tradition of black women's engaged activism. Because black communities and families are so profoundly affected by the political, economic and social institutions they are situated in, black women also find themselves working for radical institutional transformation through legal and civil action in terms of the traditional and valorized (masculine) form of visible social action.

However, it is in the uncharted struggle for group survival that black women in supplementary schools are located. Rose, a mother in one of the schools, tells us:

We always have a session which is about giving children a voice. We teach them to speak, to develop a voice that can be heard. We tell them to be proud of what they are, to be strong about speaking out. I think perhaps that is the most important thing we do, helping them develop a voice that gets heard because it is easy for black children not to be listened to in school, to be thought of as a nuisance when they say something. I think in Saturday school it is quite clear that they are expected, entitled to speak out.

(Rose in Reay and Mirza, 1997)

Charity's narrative on how Colibri was started includes similar themes of activism, community and commitment that characterize the struggle for group survival and the desire for social change:

There was a group of about six parents who like myself, as a black teacher, were dissatisfied with what was happening to black pupils. They felt if they had been in the Caribbean their children would be much further on academically and they decided something had to be done, schools weren't doing anything, so it had to be them. I really wish someone had the time to chart the enormous amount of work they put in those first few years. It was immense. The school started off in someone's front room on Saturday mornings. The parents doing all the teaching themselves to start with and it was very much focused on what was their main concern; their children not being able to read and write properly. Then these parents found the group of children grew from 10 to 15 and soon it was 20 and at this point it was unmanageable running a Saturday school in someone's front room so they petitioned the council for accommodation and finally got one of the council's derelict properties. They spent their spare time shovelling rubbish out of the room, tramps had been living there. Also doing building, repair work, getting groups of parents together to decorate. They pulled together and did all this work themselves, used the expertise they had to get the school on its feet.

(Charity in Reay and Mirza, 1997)

What the black women appeared to have learnt is an awareness of the need for social support and collaborative action through their experience of marginality in a white racist society. From this awakening of consciousness and socio-analysis (Bourdieu, 1990, p. 116) the women created their own cultural capital. Their habitus embodied 'real intelligence' in their ways of knowing and understanding (Luttrell, 1992). As their words show, this ultimately led to collective action and social change.

Conclusion

In conclusion the question we must return to is this: is the coherent educational urgency uncovered among black women a radical social movement with transformative possibilities from the margin or, as some suggest, no more than a conservative act?

Research on black women in education shows there is much evidence to suggest black women do not accept the dominant discourse, nor do they construct their identities in opposition to the dominant discourse. They redefine the world, have their own values, codes and understandings, *refuse* (not resist) the gaze of the other. As Spivak says: 'Marginal groups do not wish to claim centrality but redefine the big word human in terms of the marginal' (Spivak quoted in hooks, 1991, p. 22). Black women live in counter-hegemonic marginal spaces where, as hooks describes: 'Radical black subjectivity is seen not overseen by any authoritative other claiming to know us better than we know ourselves' (hooks, 1991, p. 22).

For black women strategies for everyday survival consist of trying to create spheres of influence that are separate from but engaged with existing structures of oppression. Being successful and gaining authority and power within institutions that have traditionally not allowed black women formal authority or real power which enables them to indirectly subvert oppressive structures by changing them. By saying this, I do not wish to argue that black women are simply empowered through their educational achievement. Empowerment assumes a notion of power that is relational. It suggests the positive power of a collectivity or individual to challenge basic power relations in society (Yuval-Davis, 1994). The assumption here is that black women's actions empower them, but any gains are always oppositional and in relation to the hegemonic culture (Steady, 1993). What I have tried to show instead is that black women are not simply resisting, but have evolved a system of strategic rationalization which has its own logic, values and codes. Black women struggle for educational inclusion in order to transform their opportunities and so in the process subvert racist expectations and beliefs. By entering into dialogue with others they are not conservative or colluding with the mainstream. They are collectively opening up transformative possibilities for their community through their pragmatic recognition of the power of education to transform and change the hegemonic discourse (hooks, 1994; McLaren, 1994).

So, finally, can I claim black women's educational urgency and desire to do well within the system is radical and subversive? To answer the question I leave you with the words of a black woman university student:

> When not given success we need to be successful . . . that is the most radical thing you can do.
>
> (Alisha in Mirza 1994)

References

Bourdieu, P. (1990) *In Other Words: Essays Towards a Reflexive Sociology*, Cambridge, Polity Press.

Casey, K. (1993) *I Answer with My Life: Life Histories of Women Teachers Working for Social Change*, New York, Routledge.

Collins, P. H. (1991) *Black Feminist Thought: Knowledge Consciousness and the Politics of Empowerment*, London, Routledge.

Drew, D., Gray, J. and Sime, N. (1992) *Against the Odds: The Education and Labour Market Experiences of Young Black People*, Employment Department, Youth Cohort Series Report, no. 19, June, London, HMSO.

Employment Gazette (1993) 'Ethnic Origins and the Labour Market' Employment Department, February, London, HMSO.

—— (1995) 'Ethnic Minorities' Employment Department, June London, HMSO.

Gilroy, P. (1987) *There Ain't No Black in the Union Jack*, London, Hutchinson.

hooks, b. (1991) *Yearning: Race, Gender and Cultural Politics*, London, Turnaround.

—— (1994) *Teaching to Transgress: Education and the Practice of Freedom*, London, Routledge.

Johnson, R. (1988) 'Really Useful Knowledge 1790–1850: Memories for Education in the 1980s' in T. Lovett (ed.) *Radical Approaches to Education: A Reader*, New York, Routledge.

Keith, M. (1993) *Race, Riots and Policing: Lore and Disorder in a Multiracist Society*, London, UCL Press.

—— (1995) 'Shouts of the Street: Identity and Spaces of Authenticity', *Social Identities*, vol. 1, no. 2, August, pp. 297–315.

Luttrell, W. (1992) 'Working Class Women's Ways of Knowing: Effects of Gender, Race and Class' in J. Wrigley (ed.) *Education and Gender Equality*, London, Falmer Press.

Mac an Ghaill, M. (1988) *Young Gifted and Black: Student Teacher Relations in the Schooling of Black Youth*, Milton Keynes, Open University Press.

McLaren, P. (1994) 'Multiculturalism and the Postmodern Critique: Towards a Pedagogy of Resistance and Transformation' in H. Giroux and P. McLaren (eds) *Between the Borders: Pedagogy and the Politics of Cultural Change*, London, Routledge.

Mirza, H. S. (1992) *Young, Female and Black*, London, Routledge.

—— (1994) 'Making Sense of the Black Female Student Experience in Higher Education' paper given at the Society for Research in Higher Education (SRHE) Conference, The Student Experience, University of York, December.

—— (1995) 'Black Women in Higher Education: Defining a Space/Finding a Place' in L. Morley and V. Walsh (eds) *Feminist Academics: Creative Agents For Change*, London, Taylor and Francis.

Modood, T. and Shiner, M. (1994) *Ethnic Minorities and Higher Education: Why are there Differential Rates of Entry?* London, PSI Publishing.

Moore, R. (1996) 'Back to the Future: The Problem of Change and the Possibilities for Advance in the Sociology of Education', *British Journal of Sociology of Education*, vol. 17, no. 2, June, pp. 145–61.

Reay, D. (1998) *Class Work: Mothers' Involvement in their Children's Primary Schooling*, London, UCL Press.

Reay D. and Mirza, H. S. (1997) 'Uncovering Genealogies of the Margin: Black Supplementary Schooling', *British Journal of Sociology of Education*, vol. 18, pp. 477–99.

Solomos, J. (1988) *Black Youth, Racism and the State*, Cambridge, Cambridge University Press.

Solomos, J. and Back, L. (1995) *Race, Politics and Social Change*, London, Routledge.

Steady, F. C. (1993) 'Women and Collective Action: Female Models in Transition' in S. M. James and A. P. Busia (eds) *Theorizing Black Feminisms: The Visionary Pragmatism of Black Women*, London, Routledge.

West, C. (1990) 'The New Cultural Politics of Difference' in R. Ferguson, M. Gever, T. Minh-ha and C. West (eds) *Out There: Marginalisation and Contemporary Cultures*, New York, New Museum of Contemporary Art.

Young, I. M. (1990) 'The Ideal of Community and the Politics of Difference' in L. Nicholson (ed.) *Feminism/Postmodernism*, London, Routledge.

Yuval-Davis, N. (1994) 'Women, Ethnicity and Empowerment' in K. Bhavnani and A. Phoenix (eds) *Shifting Identities Shifting Racisms*, London, Sage.

PART IV

METHODS
Doing critical research

CHAPTER 13

BETWEEN NEO AND POST

Critique and transformation in critical educational studies

Michael W. Apple

In Carl A. Grant (ed.) *Multicultural Research: A Reflective Engagement with Race, Class, Gender and Sexual Orientation,* London: Falmer Press, pp. 54–67, 1999

I began writing this chapter after two recent books on which I had worked for a number of years were completed. One of the books, *Cultural Politics and Education* (Apple, 1996a), was the most recent of an entire series of books that sought to answer some "simple questions": Whose knowledge is taught? Why? Whose knowledge is not taught? Why? What is the relationship between culture and power in education? Who benefits from this relationship?[1] *Cultural Politics and Education* focused on what I think are the most powerful social movements redefining education today – what I call the conservative restoration. It employed the questions that I have noted here to critically interrogate conservative proposals for national curriculum, national testing, creating a closer connection between schooling and the economy, and "choice plans." It unpacked their economic, ideological, and political assumptions and argued that the ultimate results of such plans will be a society that is considerably more stratified, less equal, and less just.

The second book, *Democratic Schools* (Apple and Beane, 1995), was in many ways a companion volume to the other. Its basis is also in a few "simple questions": If the conservative restoration is having such a profound effect on what education is for and who it will benefit, what can educators do about it in schools? Are there more democratic possibilities in schools? What concrete practices are *now* going on that provide alternatives to the conservative policies and practices now gaining so much power? Thus, *Democratic Schools* tells the stories of four public, not private, schools that are both socially critical and educationally progressive.

These two books, then, form something of a package, complement each other, and in essence need to be read together. The first provides a critical analysis of the conservative alliance, of its economic and cultural agendas, and of what is at stake if it wins. The second turns its attention to critical practice. Each one gives meaning to the other. Both represent a continuation of my struggle – aided by, and in concert with, others – to comprehend and challenge the dominant ways education is carried on in our societies.

There were a number of tensions that stood behind these books. In this chapter, I want to employ these tensions to take a stand on some of the major conceptual and political commitments that I think are essential in critical educational studies.

I started both *Cultural Politics and Education* and *Democratic Schools* at a time when I had just returned from spending time in a Bosnian refugee camp populated by people (mostly women and children) who had somehow managed to flee the murderous situation there. What I saw in the camp and the stories the mostly Islamic Bosnian teachers told me, left me with a residue of anger that will never be erased. I was also left with a feeling of gratitude and awe as an educator. For in the midst of privations, fear, despair, and uncommon courage, one of the first acts of the people in that camp was to create a school for their children. It was a powerful reminder of how important education is to the maintenance of self and community and to what Raymond Williams so brilliantly called our journey of hope (Williams, 1983, pp. 243–69).

That journey of hope is not made any easier by the fact that these books were written at a time when the Right was (and is) resurgent, when it seems as if we basically have two right wing parties in the United States, and when education and so much else is talked about as if all that counted was either competition and profit or a thoroughly romanticized return to the "western tradition" (Apple, 1993). As I worked on the two books, rightist religious fundamentalism continued to grow and to have a greater influence on electoral politics, on social policy, and on what teachers will and will not teach in schools. The same was and is true about the growth of racist nativism. Such racist discourse is not limited to public debates about, say, immigration. The fact that the pseudo-science of Richard Herrnstein and Charles Murray in *The Bell Curve* (Herrnstein and Murray, 1994) is currently being treated to such sponsored mobility – even though it is utterly naive in its understanding of genetics and both overtly and covertly racist in its arguments – creates a horizon against which my own writing is constructed.[2] It is also a time when all too many of us seem to have become inured to human suffering nationally and internationally. This is a difficult period for anyone who is committed to progressive social and educational transformation.

This is a complicated and tense period intellectually as well. From the Right, the culture wars rage. Yet, equally importantly, these books were also produced when post-modern and post-structural theories are becoming more influential in cultural studies and in critical educational studies (a label I would prefer to use rather than the more limited one of critical theory or critical pedagogy). There are significant parts of what my friends call "postie" approaches that are very insightful and need to be paid very close attention to, especially their focus on identity politics, on multiple and contradictory relations of power, on non-reductive analysis, and on the local as an important site of struggle. The influences of some of this are readily visible in *Cultural Politics and Education*. I have no wish at all to widen a divide when alliances are crucial now. However, there are also significant parts of these approaches as they have been introduced into education that simply make me blanch because of their stylistic arrogance, their stereotyping of other approaches and their concomitant certainty that they've got "the" answer, their cynical lack of attachment to any action in real schools, their seeming equation of any serious focus on the economy as being somehow reductive, their conceptual confusions, and finally their trendy rhetoric that when unpacked often says some pretty commonsensical things that reflexive and activist educators have known and done for years. Let me hasten to add that this is true for only a portion of these approaches, but all of this gives me cause for concern.[3]

Thus, there is a fine line between necessary conceptual and political transformations and trendiness. Unfortunately, the latter sometimes appears in the relatively uncritical appropriation of post-modernism by some educational theorists and researchers. For example, there certainly are (too many) plans to turn schools over to market forces, to diversify types of schools and give "consumers" more choice. Some may argue that this is "the educational equivalent of . . . the rise of 'flexible specialization in place of the old assembly-line world of mass production', driven by the imperatives of differentiated consumption rather than mass production" (Whitty *et al.*, 1994, pp. 168–9). This certainly has a post-modern ring to it.

Yet, like many of the new reforms being proposed, there is less that is "post-modern" about them than meets the eye. Many have a "high-tech" image. They are usually guided by "an underlying faith in technical rationality as the basis for solving social, economic, and educational problems." Specialization is just as powerful, perhaps even more powerful, as any concern for diversity (Whitty *et al.*, 1994, pp. 173–4). Rather than an espousal of "heterogeneity, pluralism, and the local" – though these may be the rhetorical forms in which some of these reforms are couched – what we may also be witnessing is the revivification of more traditional class, gender, and especially race hierarchies. An unquestioning commitment to the notion that "we" are now fully involved in a post-modern world may make it easier to see surface transformations (some of which are undoubtedly occurring) and yet at the same time may make it that much more difficult to recognize that these also may be new ways of re-organizing and reproducing older hierarchies (Whitty *et al.*, 1994, pp. 180–1). The fact that parts of post-modernism as a theory and as a set of experiences may not be applicable to an extremely large part of the population of the world should make us be a bit more cautious as well.

In *Cultural Politics and Education*, it is clear that part, though certainly not all, of what I say there is based on a critical (and self-critical) structural understanding of education. While not economically reductive, it does require that we recognize that we live under capitalist relations. Milton Friedman and the entire gamut of privatizers and marketizers who have so much influence in the media and the corridors of power in corporate board rooms, foundations, and our government at nearly all levels spend considerable amounts of time praising these relations. If they can talk about them, why can't we? These relations *don't* determine everything. They are constituted out of, and reconstituted by, race, class, and gender relations, but it seems a bit naive to ignore them. There is a world of difference between taking economic power and structures seriously and reducing everything down to a pale reflection of them.

I am fully cognizant that there are many dangers with such an approach. It has as part of its history attempts to create a "grand narrative," a theory that explains everything based on a unitary cause. It can also tend to forget that not only are there multiple and contradictory relations of power in nearly every situation, but that the researchers themselves are participants in such relations (Roman and Apple, 1990). Finally, structural approaches at times can neglect the ways our discourses are constructed out of, and themselves help construct, what we do. These indeed are issues that need to be taken as seriously as they deserve. Post-structural and post-modern criticisms of structural analyses in education have been fruitful in this regard, especially when they have arisen from within the various feminist, anti-racist, and post-colonial communities (see, e.g. Luke and Gore, 1992; McCarthy and Crichlow, 1993), though it must be said that some of these criticisms have created wildly inaccurate caricatures of the neo-Marxist traditions.

Yet, even though the "linguistic turn," as it has been called in sociology and cultural studies, has been immensely productive, it is important to remember that the world of education and elsewhere is not only a text. There are gritty realities out there, realities whose power is often grounded in structural relations that are not simply social constructions created by the meanings given by an observer. Part of our task, it seems to me, is not to lose sight of these gritty realities in the economy and the state, at the same time as we recognize the dangers of essentializing and reductive analyses (Apple, 1992).

My point is not to deny that many elements of "post-modernity" exist, nor is it to deny the power of aspects of post-modern theory. Rather, it is to avoid over-statement, to avoid substituting one grand narrative for another (a grand narrative that actually never existed in the United States, since class and economy only recently surfaced in critical educational scholarship and were only rarely seen here in the form found in Europe where most post-modern and post-structural criticisms of these explanatory tools were developed. It would help if we remembered that the intellectual and political histories of the United States were very different than that castigated by some of the post-modern critics). Reductive analysis comes cheap and there is no guarantee that post-modern positions, as currently employed by some in education, are any more immune to this danger than any other position.

Thus, in much of my recent work, it will not be a surprise that side by side with post-structural and post-modern understandings are those based on structural theories. While they are not totally merged, each one serves as a corrective and complement to the other. This is a point I wish to emphasize. Rather than spending so much time treating each other so warily – and sometimes as enemies – the creative tension that exists is a good thing (see Apple and Oliver, 1996). We have a good deal to learn from each other in terms of a politics in and around education that makes a difference (no pun is intended here).

There are a number of other intellectual tensions that swirled around these books as well. As I reflected on the growth of certain styles of doing critical analysis in education, it was also clear that there had been a rapid growth of two other kinds of work – personal/literary/autobiographical and studies of popular culture. The former has often been stimulated by phenomenological, psychoanalytic, and feminist approaches. The latter has arisen from cultural studies. Let me say something about each of these.

Much of the impetus behind personal stories is moral. Education correctly is seen as an ethical enterprise. The personal is seen as a way to re-awaken ethical and aesthetic sensitivities that increasingly have been purged from the scientistic discourse of too many educators. Or it is seen as a way of giving a voice to the subjectivities of people who have been silenced. There is much to commend in this position. Indeed, any approach that, say, evacuates the aesthetic, the personal, and the ethical from our activities as educators is not about education at all. It is about training. As someone who spent years teaching in inner-city schools in a severely economically depressed community, I reject any approach that reduces education to mere training or is not grounded in the personal lives and "stories" of real teachers, students, and community members. Yet something remains a little too much in the background in many variants of the stories written by professional educators and academics – a biting sense of the political, of the social structures that condemn so many identifiable people to lives of economic and cultural (and bodily) struggle and, at times, despair. Making connections between what might be called the literary imagination and the concrete movements – both in education *and* the larger society – that seek to transform our institutions so that caring and social justice are not just slogans but realities, is essential here. Political arguments are not alternatives to moral and aesthetic concerns. Rather, they are these concerns taken seriously in their full implications (Eagleton, 1983). And this leads me to raise a caution about some of the hidden effects of our (generally commendable) urge to employ the personal and the autobiographical to illuminate our (admittedly differential) educational experiences.

For nearly twenty years, until the publication of another recent book of mine, *Official Knowledge* (Apple, 1993), I did not write about my experiences as a filmmaker with teachers and students, in part because I could not find an appropriate "voice." It would have required a fair dose of autobiography. I often find autobiographical accounts and narrative renderings compelling and insightful, and do not want in any way to dismiss their power in educational theory and practice. Yet – and let me be blunt here – just as often such writing runs the risk of lapsing into what has been called possessive individualism (Apple, 1990, 1993, 1995a). Even when authors do the "correct thing" and discuss their social location in a world dominated by oppressive conditions, such writing can serve the chilling function of simply saying "But enough about you, let me tell you about me" if we are not much more reflexive about this than has often been the case. I am still committed enough to raising questions about class and race dynamics to worry about perspectives that supposedly acknowledge the missing voices of many people in our thinking about education, but still wind up privileging the white, middle class woman's or man's need for *self display*.

Do not misconstrue what I am saying here. As so much feminist and postcolonial work has documented, the personal often is the absent presence behind even the most eviscerated writing and we do need to continue to explore ways of heightening the sense of the personal in our "stories" about education. But, at the same time, it is equally crucial that we interrogate our own "hidden" motives here. Is the insistence on the personal, an insistence that underpins much of our turn to literary and autobiographical forms, partly a class discourse as well? The "personal may be the political," but does the political end at the personal? Furthermore, why should we assume that the personal is any less difficult to understand than the "external" world? I cannot answer these questions for all situations; but I think that these questions must be asked by all of us who are committed to the multiple projects involved in struggling for a more emancipatory education. (And for this very reason, later on I shall end my contribution to this book with a personal story that is *consciously* connected to a clear sense of the realities of structurally generated inequalities that play such a large role in education.)

My intellectual/political tensions did not end here, however. "Boom times" in academic stocks and bonds come and go (McGuigan, 1992, p. 61). In some parts of the critical educational community, the study of popular culture – music, dance, films, language, dress, bodily transformations, the politics of consumption, and so on – is also big business. And in many ways it should be. After all, we should know by now that popular culture is partly a site of resistance and struggle (Willis *et al.*, 1990; Giroux, 1994; Koza, 1994), but also that for schooling to make a difference it must connect to popular understandings and cultural forms. Yet, our fascination with "the popular," our intoxication with all of these things, has sometimes had a paradoxical and unfortunate effect. It often has led us to ignore the actual knowledge that *is* taught in schools, the entire corpus and structure of the formal processes of curriculum, teaching, and evaluation that remain so powerful. In many ways, it constitutes a flight from education as a field. In my more cynical moments, I take this as a class discourse in which new elements within the academy in education fight for power not only over school folks but over positions within the academy itself.

In *Cultural Politics and Education*, I talk about the importance of popular culture and make a plea for its utter centrality both in understanding cultural politics and in struggling to institute more socially just models of curriculum and teaching. Yet, many members of the critical educational community have been a bit too trendy about this topic as well. They seem to have forgotten about schools, curricula, teachers, students, community activists, and so on. It's as if dealing with these issues is "polluting," as if they are afraid of getting their hands dirty with the daily realities of education. Or perhaps they feel that it's not theoretically elegant enough to deal with such "mundane" realities. While I fully understand the utter necessity of focusing on the popular, as a critical educator I am even more committed to taking the reality of school matters as seriously as they deserve.[4] For this very reason, *Cultural Politics and Education* devotes much of its attention to matters specifically related to the politics of curriculum and teaching, just as *Democratic Schools* is totally devoted to describing how we can make a real difference in the curriculum and teaching that now dominate too many schools.

I do not want to be overly negative here. Many of us have quite ambivalent feelings about the place called school. All of us who care deeply about what is and is not taught and about who is and is not empowered to answer these questions have a contradictory relationship to these institutions. We want to criticize them rigorously and yet in this very criticism lies a commitment, a hope, that they can be made more vital, more personally meaningful and socially critical. If ever there was a love/hate relationship, this is it.[5] This speaks directly to the situation many people in critical educational studies face today and underlies some of the emphases of both books.

The New Right is very powerful now. It has had the odd effect of simultaneously interrupting the progressive critique of schooling while at the same time leading many of us to defend an institution many of whose practices were and are open to severe criticism (Education Group, 1991, p. 33). As someone who has devoted years to analyzing and acting on the social and cultural means and ends of our curricula, teaching, and evaluation in schools, I am certainly not one who wants to act as an apologist for poor practices. Yet, during an era when – because of rightist attacks – we face the massive dismantling of the gains (limited as they were) that have been made in social welfare, in women's control of their bodies, in relations of race, class, gender, and sexuality, and in whose knowledge is taught in schools, it is equally important to make certain that these gains are defended.

Thus, there is another clear tension in these volumes. I wanted both to defend the idea of a public education and a number of the gains that do exist and to criticize many of its attributes at the same time. This dual focus may seem a bit odd at first, but it speaks to a crucial point I want to make about how we should think about the institutions of formal education in most of our nations.

Here I want to say something that may make a number of educators who are justifiably critical of existing power relations in education a bit uncomfortable. The problem I shall point to may at first seem minor, but its conceptual, political, and practical implications are not. I am referring to the discourse of *change*. It stands behind all of those claims about both the autobiographical and popular culture and behind the pressures to connect schools more closely to economic needs and goals. All too often we forget that in our attempts to alter and "reform" schooling there are elements that should not be changed but need to be kept and defended. Even with my criticisms of the unequal power relations surrounding education and the larger society, we need to remember that schooling was never simply an imposition on supposedly politically/culturally inept people. Rather, as

I have demonstrated elsewhere, educational policies and practices were and are the result of struggles and compromises over what would count as legitimate knowledge, pedagogy, goals, and criteria of determining effectiveness. In a more abstract way, we can say that education has been one of the major arenas in which the conflict between property rights and person rights has been fought (Apple, 1993, 1995a).

The results of these conflicts have not always been settled on the terms of dominant groups. Often, democratic tendencies have emerged and have been cemented into the daily practices of the institution. As William Reese (1986) shows in his history of populist reform in schools, many things that we take for granted were the direct results of populist movements that forced powerful groups to compromise, to even suffer outright losses. Thus, before we give a blanket condemnation to what schools do and turn to what we suppose is its alternative (say, popular culture), we need a much clearer and more historically informed appraisal of what elements of the practices and policies of these institutions are already progressive and should be maintained. Not to do so would be to assume that, say, radical teachers, people of color, women, working class groups, and physically challenged groups (these categories are obviously not mutually exclusive) have been puppets whose strings are pulled by the most conservative forces in this society and have not won any lasting victories in education. This is simply not the case. Not to defend some of the ideas behind person rights that are currently embodied in schools is to add more power to conservative attacks. There *have* been gains. The forces of the conservative restoration would not be so very angry at public schools – at the supposed "overemphasis" on "minority culture," on "feminism," on gay and lesbian rights – if educational and community activists hadn't had at least some success in transforming what was taken for granted in schools. These gains certainly aren't sufficient; but they *are* there.

I do not want to belabor this point, but it does make a major difference in how we approach education. At times, some critical educators have been so critical that we too often assume – consciously or unconsciously – that everything that exists within the educational system bears only the marks of, and is only, the result of domination. It's all capitalist; it's all racist; it's all patriarchal; it's all homophobic. As you would imagine given my own efforts over the past three decades, I do not want to dismiss the utter power of these and other forms of oppression in education or in anything else. Yet, in taking a stance that assumes – without detailed investigation – that all is somehow the result of relations of dominance, we also make it very difficult to make connections with progressive educators and community members who are currently struggling to build an education that is democratic in more than name only. (And there are many practicing educators who have been more than a little successful in such struggles.) It is all too easy for critical educators to fall into this position.

This assumption is problematic conceptually, historically, and politically. It rests on a theory of the role of state institutions that is too simplistic and on an ahistorical understanding of the power of democratically inclined groups (Carnoy and Levin, 1985; Jules and Apple, 1995). It also bears the marks of what seems like a form of self-hatred, as if the more we distance ourselves from the history and discourse of education – and turn to other, "more academically respectable," fields for all of our perspectives – the more academically legitimate we become. The ultimate effects of this are disabling for any of us who wish to continue the long and essential struggle to have our educational institutions respond to the needs not only of the powerful.

This is a difficult tightrope to walk for those of us involved in education. In a time of rightwing resurgence, how do we create the educational conditions in which our students can see (and teach us about as well) the very real and massive relations of inequality and the role of schooling in partly reproducing and contesting them and at the same time jointly create the conditions that assist all of us in empowering each other to act on these realities? Gramsci had a way of saying it: Pessimism of the intellect, optimism of the will. But my point goes well beyond this. Intellect, enlivened by passion and ethical/political sensitivities – and a fine sense of historical agency – will also see victories as well as losses, hope as well as despair. That it seems to me is our task.

Finally, and this is directly related to what I have just said, there has been one other tension behind these books. When I began writing *Cultural Politics and Education* not only did I want to both criticize and defend much that is happening in education, I also wanted to illuminate what it actually *is* that needs to be defended. What policies and practices now exist in schools and classrooms that are socially and educationally critical? Are there what I have elsewhere called crucial "non-reformist reforms" that need to be continued (Apple, 1995a)? This caused me no end of headaches. While throughout *Cultural Politics and Education* I refer to such policies and practices, for political and ethical reasons (and perhaps for reasons of sanity), I ultimately decided that extensive descriptions of such critical practice clearly deserved an entire book of their own. Furthermore, they should be written by the educator/activists who actually engage in them, in their own words. It is this very reason that at the same time that I was writing the first book, my colleague and friend, Jim Beane, and I produced *Democratic Schools*. As I noted, it details in much greater depth what is possible in public schools now. By focusing on the stories of a number of ongoing socially and educationally committed public schools run by educators who directly link their curricula and teaching to a clear sense of the economic, political, and cultural relations of power in the world, it gives what I believe is compelling evidence that the journey of hope in education continues in real schools with real teachers, students, and community members. Thus, if you read *Cultural Politics and Education*, and afterwards you still find yourself asking something like "Okay, Apple, now what? What concrete ideas do you have to practice what you preach? What alternatives would you propose, and what would you keep, to take your critical analysis seriously?" I can only reply that my answers to these questions are provided considerably more fully in *Democratic Schools*.

Memory and experience

The first section of this chapter laid out the "balancing act" that I've tried to engage in over the past years. This has involved me (and many others) in the following: criticizing dominant educational practices while defending gains; deepening and defending crucial aspects of structural analyses of education while recognizing a number of the insights in post-structural approaches and incorporating them into my work; engaging in detailed critical analyses of schools while trying to make public more democratic educational policies and practices; and wanting to stimulate a more personal and/or autobiographical appraisal of education but not at the expense of losing our sense of the ways education is currently structured around oppressive economic/political/cultural relations.

Of course, as I have shown throughout this chapter, this "balancing act" has roots in debates over concepts, methods, and politics in critical educational studies. Yet it roots go much deeper than that. As with most people, they grow out of one's biography in crucial ways. In my own case, they come from a personal history of poverty and from a family who because of this was deeply involved in political action. They come from the time I spent as an activist teacher in inner-city schools and as a president of a teachers union. They come from my early experiences in movements opposed to the racial structuring of this society and from the fact that I am the father of an African-American child, a fact that never lets me forget what race means in this society. And they come from my repeated and continuing experiences over the past three decades working with dissident groups, unions, critical educators, and others who are involved in struggling to create a more just and caring economy, polity, and culture. In essence, it is these early and ongoing activities that provide the impetus behind my work that constantly force me to confront the fact that education is intimately connected to relations of domination and subordination – and to struggles against them – whether we recognize this or not.[6]

Perhaps I can employ one personal story to illuminate why I think we must never forget such a structural sense of these relations and why the connections between education and the larger structures of inequality need to have a central place in our thought and action in education. In many ways, this story will crystallize and make explicit many of the points I have made here about the political, theoretical, and educational tensions that lie behind my work.

Education and cheap french fries

The sun glared off of the hood of the small car as we made our way along the two-lane road. The heat and humidity made me wonder if I'd have any liquid left in my body at the end of the trip and led me to appreciate Wisconsin winters a bit more than one might expect. The idea of winter seemed more than a little remote in this Asian country for which I have a good deal of fondness. But the topic at hand was not the weather; rather, it was the struggles of educators and social activists to build an education that was considerably more democratic than what was in place in that country now. This was a dangerous topic. Discussing it in philosophical and formalistically academic terms was tolerated there. Openly calling for it and situating it within a serious analysis of the economic, political, and military power structures that now exerted control over so much of this nation's daily life was another matter. And we were on our way to a meeting with a group of young teachers in a rural area who were involved in such struggles.[7]

As we traveled along that rural road in the midst of one of the best conversations I had engaged in about the possibilities of educational transformations and the realities of the oppressive conditions so many people were facing in that land, my gaze somehow was drawn to the side of the road. In one of those nearly accidental happenings that clarify and crystallize what reality is *really* like, my gaze fell upon a seemingly inconsequential object. At regular intervals, there were small signs planted in the dirt a few yards from where the road met the fields. The sign was more than a little familiar. It bore the insignia of one of the most famous fast food restaurants in the United States. We drove for miles past seemingly deserted fields along a flat hot plain, passing sign after sign, each a replica of the previous one, each less than a foot high. These were not billboards. Such things hardly existed in this poor rural region. Rather, they looked exactly – exactly – like the small signs one finds next to farms in the American midwest that signify the kinds of seed corn that each farmer had planted in her or his fields. This was a good guess it turned out.

I asked the driver – a close friend and former student of mine who had returned to this country to work for the social and educational reforms that were so necessary – what turned out to be a naive, but ultimately crucial, question in my own education. "Why are those signs for ✳✳✳✳✳ there? Is there a ✳✳✳✳✳ restaurant nearby?" My friend looked at me in amazement. "Michael, don't you know what these signs signify? There's no western restaurants within 50 miles of where we are. These signs represent exactly what is wrong with education in this nation. Listen to this." And I listened.

The story is one that has left an indelible mark on me, for it condenses in one powerful set of historical experiences the connections between our struggles as educators and activists in so many countries and the ways differential power works in ordinary life. I cannot match the tensions and passions in my friend's voice as this story was told; nor can I convey exactly the almost eerie feelings one gets when looking at that vast, sometimes beautiful, sometimes scarred, and increasingly depopulated plain.

Yet the story is crucial to hear. Listen to this.

The government of the nation has decided that the importation of foreign capital is critical to its own survival. Bringing in American, German, British, Japanese, and other investors and factories will ostensibly create jobs, will create capital for investment, and will enable the nation to speed into the twenty-first century. (This is, of course, elite group talk, but let us assume that all of this is indeed truly believed by dominant groups.) One of the ways the military dominated government has planned to do this is to focus part of its recruitment efforts on agri-business. In pursuit of this aim, it has offered vast tracts of land to international agri-business concerns at very low cost. Of particular importance to the plain we are driving through is the fact that much of this land has been given over to a large American fast food restaurant corporation for the growing of potatoes for the restaurant's french fries, one of the trademarks of its extensive success throughout the world.

The corporation was eager to jump at the opportunity to shift a good deal of its potato production from the United States to Asia. Since many of the farm workers in the United States were now unionized and were (correctly) asking for a liveable wage, and since the government of that Asian nation officially frowned on unions of any kind, the cost of growing potatoes would be lower. Further, the land on that plain was perfect for the use of newly developed technology to plant and harvest the crop with considerably fewer workers. Machines would replace living human beings. Finally, the government was much less concerned about environmental regulations. All in all, this was a fine bargain for capital.

Of course, people lived on some of this land and farmed it for their own food and to sell what might be left over after their own – relatively minimal – needs were met. This deterred neither agri-business nor the government. After all, people could be moved to make way for "progress." And after all, the villagers along that plain did not actually have deeds to the land. (They had lived there for perhaps hundreds of years, well before the invention of banks, and mortgages, and deeds – no paper, no ownership.) It would not be too hard to move off the people of the plain to other areas to "free" it for intensive potato production and to "create jobs" by taking away the livelihood of thousands upon thousands of small-scale farmers in the region.

I listened with rapt attention as the rest of the story unfolded and as we passed by the fields with their miniature corporate signs and the abandoned villages. The people whose land had been taken for so little moved, of course. As in so many other similar places throughout what dominant groups call the Third World, they trekked to the city. They took their meager possessions and moved into the ever-expanding slums within and surrounding the one place that held out some hope of finding enough paid work (if everyone – including children – labored) so that they could survive.

The government and major segments of the business elite officially discouraged this, sometimes by hiring thugs to burn the shanty towns, other times by keeping conditions so horrible that no one would "want" to live there. But still the dispossessed came, by the tens of thousands. Poor people are not irrational, after all. The loss of arable land had to be compensated for somehow and if it took cramming into places that were deadly at times, well what were the other choices? There *were* factories being built in and around the cities which paid incredibly low wages – sometimes less than enough money to buy sufficient food to replace the calories expended by workers in the production process – but at least there might be paid work if one was lucky. (Although, as in many instances of this type, it was women who were "preferred" for these low paid and exploitative factory jobs, since they supposedly were more dexterous, more docile, and were "willing" to work for less.)

So the giant machines harvested the potatoes and the people poured into the cities and international capital was happy. It's not a nice story, but what does it have to do with education? My friend continued my education.

The military-dominated government had given all of these large international businesses twenty years of tax breaks to sweeten the conditions for their coming to that country. Thus, there was now very little money to supply the health care facilities, housing, running water, electricity, sewage disposal, and schools for the thousands upon thousands of people who had sought their future in, or had literally been driven into, the city. The mechanism for *not* building these necessities was quite clever. Take the lack of any formal educational institutions as a case in point. In order for the government to build schools it had to be shown that there was a "legitimate" need for such expenditure. Statistics had to be produced in a form that was officially accepted. This could only be done through the official determination of numbers of registered births. Yet, the very process of official registration made it impossible for thousands of children to be recognized as actually existing.

In order to register for school, a parent had to register the birth of the child at the local hospital or government office – few of which existed in these slum areas. And even if you could somehow find such an office, the government officially discouraged people who had originally come from outside the region of the city from moving there. It often refused to recognize the legitimacy of the move as a way of keeping displaced farmers from coming into the urban areas and thereby increasing the population. Births from people who had no "legitimate" right to be there did not count as births at all. It is a brilliant strategy in which the state creates categories of legitimacy that define social problems in quite interesting ways (see Fraser, 1989; Curtis, 1992). Foucault would have been proud, I am certain.

Thus, there are no schools, no teachers, no hospitals, no infrastructure. The root causes of this situation rest not in the immediate situation. They can only be illuminated if we focus on the chain of capital formation internationally and nationally, on the contradictory needs of the state, on the class relations and the relations between country and city that organize and disorganize that country. And they can only be illuminated by recognizing the fact that under prevailing neo-colonial forms, the people of these slums become disposable and invisible – the "other" – given an international division of labor in which race plays such a large part. "We" eat; "they" remain unseen.

My friend and I had been driving for quite a while now. I had forgotten about the heat. The ending sentence of the story pulled no punches. It was said slowly and quietly, said in a way that made it even more compelling. "Michael, these fields are the reason there's no schools in my city. There's no schools because so many folks like cheap french fries."

I tell this story about the story told to me for a number of reasons. First, it is simply one of the most powerful ways I know of reminding myself and all of us of the utter importance of seeing schooling relationally, of seeing it as connected – fundamentally – to the relations of domination and exploitation (and to struggles against them) of the larger society. Second, and equally as importantly, I tell this story to make a crucial theoretical and political point. Relations of power are indeed complex and we do need to take very seriously the post-modern focus on the local and on the multiplicity of the forms of struggle that need to be engaged in. It is important as well to recognize the changes that are occurring in many societies and to see the complexity of the "power/knowledge" nexus. Yet in our attempts to avoid the dangers that accompanied some aspects of previous "grand narratives", let us not act as if capitalism has somehow disappeared. Let us not act as if class relations, nationally and internationally, don't count. Let us not act as if what are arrogantly called "center/periphery" relations that are often based on racial divisions of labor don't exist. Let us not act as if all of the things we learned about how the world might be understood politically have been somehow overthrown because our theories are now more complex. It is this that provides the center of gravity in my work.

The denial of basic human rights, the destruction of the environment, the deadly conditions under which people (barely) survive, the lack of a meaningful future for the thousands of children I noted in my story – all of this is not only or even primarily a "text" to be deciphered in our academic volumes as we pursue our post-modern themes. It is a reality that millions of people experience in their very bodies everyday. Educational work that is not connected deeply to a powerful understanding of these realities (and this understanding cannot evacuate a serious analysis of political economy and class, race, and gender relations without losing much of its power) is in danger of losing its soul. The lives of our children demand no less.

Postscript

I started out to do something that I thought was relatively "simple" in this chapter. My original intent was to put on paper some of the reasons why *Cultural Politics and Education* and *Democratic Schools* took the shape that they did. Yet this seemingly simple task soon got more complex. It caused me to go into more depth into a set of theoretical, political, and educational tensions and to be a bit more of a "story teller" than I had originally planned.

While a good deal of what I have said here is expanded in *Cultural Politics and Education*, I do want to add one other thing. I ended the "story" of my drive through that plain with a call for connecting our work as educators to a serious understanding of power, but one that doesn't get so complicated that it forgets that many times it really "ain't that hard" at times to recognize who benefits from the ways our societies are now organized. Yet, such recognition is not only a theoretic or academic task.[8] This recognition requires that we live our lives differently – for example, that we build alliances with, support, and learn from both the teacher and community activists represented in *Democratic Schools* and those young teachers I was driving to meet on that hot flat plain. No longer eating cheap french fries might help a little too.

Notes

Parts of this chapter appear in Apple, M. W. (1996a) *Cultural Politics and Education*, New York: Teachers College Press and London: Open University Press.

1   The following books made up the series and were written in the order of their listing: *Ideology and Curriculum* (1979; 2nd edn 1990), *Education and Power* (1982; revised ARK edn 1985; 2nd edn, 1995a), *Teachers and Texts* (1986), and *Official Knowledge* (1993).
2   For criticisms of the conceptual, empirical, and ideological agendas of *The Bell Curve*, see Kincheloe and Steinberg (1996). See also my own critical analysis of some of the reasons such arguments have an impact now in Apple (1996b).
3   See (Apple, 1994). I say *approaches* here because it is too easy to stereotype post-modern and post-structural theories. That would be unfortunate, since the political differences, for example, among and within the various tendencies associated with both are often substantial.
4   That one can deal with popular culture and school culture together in elegant ways is very nicely documented in Weinstein (1995).
5   Ian Hunter in fact argues that critical educational researchers are so wedded to schools that their criticisms function as part of the mobility strategies of an intellectual elite. This is provocative, but essentializing in the extreme. See Hunter (1994). See also my response to his book in Apple (1995b).
6   These more autobiographical details are laid out in more detail in an interview with me published as an appendix in Apple (1993).
7   I shall not name this country here, since to do so could put the teachers and my colleague at risk.
8   I do not want to dismiss the importance of theoretical or academic work, if such work is *overtly* connected to movements for social justice. For further discussion of this, see Apple (1996a and c).

References

Apple, M. W. (1986) *Teachers and Texts*, New York: Routledge.
—— (1990) *Ideology and Curriculum* (2nd edn), New York: Routledge.
—— (1992) "Education, culture, and class power," *Educational Theory*, 42, 127–45.
—— (1993) *Official Knowledge*, New York: Routledge.
—— (1994) "Cultural capital and official knowledge," in C. Nelson and M. Berube (eds) *Higher Education under Fire*, New York: Routledge.
—— (1995a) *Education and Power* (2nd edn), New York: Routledge.
—— (1995b) "Review of Ian Hunter: rethinking the school," *Australian Journal of Education*, 39, 95–6.
—— (1996a) *Cultural Politics and Education*, New York: Teachers College Press and London: Open University Press.
—— (1996b) "Dominance and dependency," in J. Kincheloe and S. Steinberg (eds) *Measured Lies*, New York: St Martin's Press.
—— (1996c) "Power, meaning, and identity," *British Journal of Sociology of Education*, 17, 125–44.
Apple, M. W. and Beane, J. A. (1995) *Democratic Schools*, Washington, DC: Association for Supervision and Curriculum Development.
Apple, M. W. and Oliver, A. (1996) "Becoming right: education and the formation of conservative movements," *Teachers College Record*, 97, pp. 419–45.
Carnoy, M. and Levin, C. (1985) *Schooling and Work in the Democratic State*, Stanford: Stanford University Press.
Curtis, B. (1992) *True Government by Choice Men?*, Toronto: University of Toronto Press.

Eagleton, T. (1983) *Literary Theory*, Minneapolis: University of Minnesota Press.

Education Group II (eds) (1991) *Education Limited*, London: Unwin Hyman.

Fraser, N. (1989) *Unruly Practices*, Minneapolis: University of Minnesota Press.

Giroux, H. (1994) "Doing cultural studies," *Harvard Educational Review*, 64, 278–308.

Herrnstein, R. and Murray, C. (1994) *The Bell Curve*, New York: The Free Press.

Hunter, I. (1994) *Rethinking the School*, St Leonards, Australia: Allen and Unwin.

Jules, D. and Apple, M. W. (1995) "The state and educational reform," in W. Pink and G. Noblit (eds) *Continuity and Contradiction: The Futures of the Sociology of Education*, Cresskill, NJ: Hampton Press.

Kincheloe, J. and Steinberg, S. (eds) (1996) *Measured Lies*, New York: St Martin's Press.

Koza, J. (1994) "Rap music," *The Review of Education/Pedagogy/Cultural Studies*, 16, 171–96.

Luke, C. and Gore, J. (eds) (1992) *Feminisms and Critical Pedagogy*, New York: Routledge.

McCarthy, C. and Crichlow, W. (eds) (1993) *Race, Identity, and Representation in Education*, New York: Routledge.

McGuigan, J. (1992) *Cultural Populism*, New York: Routledge.

Reese, W. (1986) *Power and the Promise of School Reform*, New York: Routledge.

Roman, L. and Apple, M. W. (1990) "Is naturalism a move beyond positivism?," in E. Eisner and A. Peshkin (eds) *Qualitative Inquiry in Education*, New York: Teachers College Press.

Weinstein, M. (1995) "Robot world: a study of science, reality, and the struggle for meaning," Unpublished PhD Dissertation, University of Wisconsin-Madison.

Whitty, G., Edwards, T., and Gewirtz, S. (1994) *Specialization and Choice in Urban Education*, New York: Routledge.

Williams, R. (1983) *The Year 2000*, New York: Pantheon.

Willis, P., Jones, S., Canaan, J., and Hurd, G. (1990) *Common Culture*, Boulder: Westview.

CHAPTER 14

THE SILENCED DIALOGUE
Power and pedagogy in educating other people's children

Lisa D. Delpit

Harvard Educational Review, 58, 280–98, 1988

A Black male graduate student who is also a special education teacher in a predominantly Black community is talking about his experiences in predominantly White university classes:

> There comes a moment in every class where we have to discuss "The Black Issue" and what's appropriate education for Black children. I tell you, I'm tired of arguing with those White people, because they won't listen. Well, I don't know if they really don't listen or if they just don't believe you. It seems like if you can't quote Vygotsky or something, then you don't have any validity to speak about your *own* kids. Anyway, I'm not bothering with it anymore, now I'm just in it for a grade.

A Black woman teacher in a multicultural urban elementary school is talking about her experiences in discussions with her predominantly White fellow teachers about how they should organize reading instruction to best serve students of color:

> When you're talking to White people they still want it to be their way. You can try to talk to them and give them examples, but they're so headstrong, they think they know what's best for *everybody*, for *everybody's* children. They won't listen, White folks are going to do what they want to do *anyway*.
>
> It's really hard. They just don't listen well. No, they listen, but they don't *hear* — you know how your mama used to say you listen to the radio, but you *hear* your mother? Well they don't *hear* me.
>
> So I just try to shut them out so I can hold my temper. You can only beat your head against a brick wall for so long before you draw blood. If I try to stop arguing with them I can't help myself from getting angry. Then I end up walking around praying all day "Please Lord, remove the bile I feel for these people so I can sleep tonight." It's funny, but it can become a cancer, a sore.
>
> So, I shut them out. I go back to my own little cubby, my classroom, and I try to teach the way I know will work, no matter what those folk say. And when I get Black kids, I just try to undo the damage they did.

> I'm not going to let any man, woman, or child drive me crazy – White folks
> will try to do that to you if you let them. You just have to stop talking to them,
> that's what I do. I just keep smiling, but I won't talk to them.

A soft-spoken Native Alaskan woman in her forties is a student in the
Education Department of the University of Alaska. One day she storms into a
Black professor's office and very uncharacteristically slams the door. She plops
down in a chair and, still fuming, says, "Please tell those people, just don't help us
anymore! I give up. I won't talk to them again!"

And finally, a Black woman principal who is also a doctoral student at a well-
known university on the West Coast is talking about her university experiences,
particularly about when a professor lectures on issues concerning educating Black
children:

> If you try to suggest that that's not quite the way it is, they get defensive, then
> you get defensive, then they'll start reciting research.
>
> I try to give them my experiences, to explain. They just look and nod. The
> more I try to explain, they just look and nod, just keep looking and nodding.
> They don't really hear me.
>
> Then, when it's time for class to be over, the professor tells me to come to
> his office to talk more. So I go. He asks for more examples of what I'm talking
> about, and he looks and nods while I give them. Then he says that that's just
> my experiences. It doesn't really apply to most Black people.
>
> It becomes futile because they think they know everything about everybody.
> What you have to say about your life, your children, doesn't mean anything.
> They don't really want to hear what you have to say. They wear blinders and
> earplugs. They only want to go on research they've read that other White
> people have written.
>
> It just doesn't make any sense to keep talking to them.

Thus was the first half of the title of this text born – "The silenced dialogue."
One of the tragedies in the field of education is that scenarios such as these are
enacted daily around the country. The saddest element is that the individuals about
whom the Black and Native American educators speak of in these statements are
seldom aware that the dialogue *has* been silenced. Most likely the White educators
believe that their colleagues of color did, in the end, agree with their logic. After
all, they stopped disagreeing, didn't they?

I have collected these statements since completing a recently published article
(Delpit, 1986). In this somewhat autobiographical account, entitled "Skills and
Other Dilemmas of a Progressive Black Educator," I discussed my perspective as
a product of a skills-oriented approach to writing and as a teacher of process-
oriented approaches. I described the estrangement that I and many teachers of
color feel from the progressive movement when writing-process advocates dismiss
us as too "skills oriented." I ended the article suggesting that it was incumbent
upon writing-process advocates – or indeed, advocates of any progressive movement – to enter into dialogue with teachers of color, who may not share their
enthusiasm about so-called new, liberal, or progressive ideas.

In response to this article, which presented no research data and did not even cite
a reference, I received numerous calls and letters from teachers, professors, and even
state school personnel from around the country, both Black and White. All of the
White respondents, except one, have wished to talk more about the question of skills
versus process approaches – to support or reject what they perceive to be my position.

On the other hand, *all* of the non-White respondents have spoken passionately on being left out of the dialogue about how best to educate children of color.

How can such complete communication blocks exist when both parties truly believe they have the same aims? How can the bitterness and resentment expressed by the educators of color be drained so that the sores can heal? What can be done?

I believe the answer to these questions lies in ethnographic analysis, that is, in identifying and giving voice to alternative worldviews. Thus, I will attempt to address the concerns raised by White and Black respondents to my article "Skills and Other Dilemmas" (Delpit, 1986). My charge here is not to determine the best instructional methodology; I believe that the actual practice of good teachers of all colors typically incorporates a range of pedagogical orientations. Rather, I suggest that the differing perspectives on the debate over "skills" versus "process" approaches can lead to an understanding of the alienation and miscommunication, and thereby to an understanding of the "silenced dialogue."

In thinking through these issues, I have found what I believe to be a connecting and complex theme: what I have come to call "the culture of power." There are five aspects of power I would like to propose as given for this presentation:

1 Issues of power are enacted in classrooms.
2 There are codes or rules for participating in power; that is, there is a "culture of power."
3 The rules of the culture of power are a reflection of the rules of the culture of those who have power.
4 If you are not already a participant in the culture of power, being told explicitly the rules of that culture makes acquiring power easier.
5 Those with power are frequently least aware of – or least willing to acknowledge – its existence. Those with less power are often most aware of its existence.

The first three are by now basic tenets in the literature of the sociology of education, but the last two have seldom been addressed. The following discussion will explicate these aspects of power and their relevance to the schism between liberal educational movements and that of non-White, non-middle-class teachers and communities.[1]

1 *Issues of power are enacted in classrooms.*
These issues include the power of the teacher over the students; the power of the publishers of textbooks and of the developers of the curriculum to determine the view of the world presented; the power of the state in enforcing compulsory schooling; and the power of an individual or group to determine another's intelligence or "normalcy." Finally, if schooling prepares people for jobs, and the kind of job a person has determines her or his economic status and, therefore, power, then schooling is intimately related to that power.

2 *There are codes or rules for participating in power; that is, there is a "culture of power."*
The codes or rules I'm speaking of relate to linguistic forms, communicative strategies, and presentation of self; that is, ways of talking, ways of writing, ways of dressing, and ways of interacting.

3 *The rules of the culture of power are a reflection of the rules of the culture of those who have power.*
This means that success in institutions – schools, workplaces, and so on – is predicated upon acquisition of the culture of those who are in power. Children from

middle-class homes tend to do better in school than those from non-middle-class homes because the culture of the school is based on the culture of the upper and middle classes – of those in power. The upper and middle classes send their children to school with all the accoutrements of the culture of power; children from other kinds of families operate within perfectly wonderful and viable cultures but not cultures that carry the codes or rules of power.

4   *If you are not already a participant in the culture of power, being told explicitly the rules of that culture makes acquiring power easier.*

In my work within and between diverse cultures, I have come to conclude that members of any culture transmit information implicitly to co-members. However, when implicit codes are attempted across cultures, communication frequently breaks down. Each cultural group is left saying, "Why don't those people say what they mean?" as well as, "What's wrong with them, why don't they understand?"

Anyone who has had to enter new cultures, especially to accomplish a specific task, will know of what I speak. When I lived in several villages of Papua New Guinea for extended periods to collect data, and when I went to Alaskan villages for work with Alaskan Native communities, I found it unquestionably easier – psychologically and pragmatically – when some kind soul directly informed me about such matters as appropriate dress, interactional styles, embedded meanings, and taboo words or actions. I contend that it is much the same for anyone seeking to learn the rules of the culture of power. Unless one has the leisure of a lifetime of "immersion" to learn them, explicit presentation makes learning immeasurably easier.

And now, to the fifth and last premise:

5   *Those with power are frequently least aware of – or least willing to acknowledge – its existence. Those with less power are often most aware of its existence.*

For many who consider themselves members of liberal or radical camps, acknowledging personal power and admitting participation in the culture of power is distinctly uncomfortable. On the other hand, those who are less powerful in any situation are most likely to recognize the power variable most acutely. My guess is that the White colleagues and instructors of those previously quoted did not perceive themselves to have power over the non-White speakers. However, either by virtue of their position, their numbers, or their access to that particular code of power of calling upon research to validate one's position, the White educators had the authority to establish what was to be considered "truth" regardless of the opinions of the people of color, and the latter were well aware of that fact.

A related phenomenon is that liberals (and here I am using the term "liberal" to refer to those whose beliefs include striving for a society based upon maximum individual freedom and autonomy) seem to act under the assumption that to make any rules or expectations explicit is to act against liberal principles, to limit the freedom and autonomy of those subjected to the explicitness.

I thank Fred Erickson for a comment that led me to look again at a tape by John Gumperz[2] on cultural dissonance in cross-cultural interactions. One of the episodes showed an East Indian interviewing for a job with an all-White committee. The interview was a complete failure, even though several of the interviewers appeared to really want to help the applicant. As the interview rolled steadily downhill, these "helpers" became more and more indirect in their questioning, which exacerbated the problems the applicant had in performing appropriately. Operating from a different cultural perspective, he got fewer and fewer clear clues as to what was expected of him, which ultimately resulted in his failure to secure the position.

I contend that as the applicant showed less and less aptitude for handling the interview, the power differential became even more evident to the interviewers. The "helpful" interviewers, unwilling to acknowledge themselves as having power over the applicant, became more and more uncomfortable. Their indirectness was an attempt to lessen the power differential and their discomfort by lessening the power-revealing explicitness of their questions and comments.

When acknowledging and expressing power, one tends towards explicitness (as in yelling to your 10-year-old, "Turn that radio down!"). When de-emphasizing power, there is a move toward indirect communication. Therefore, in the interview setting, those who sought to help, to express their egalitarianism with the East Indian applicant, became more and more indirect – and less and less helpful – in their questions and comments.

In literacy instruction, explicitness might be equated with direct instruction. Perhaps the ultimate expression of explicitness and direct instruction in the primary classroom is Distar. This reading program is based on a behaviorist model in which reading is taught through the direct instruction of phonics generalizations and blending. The teacher's role is to maintain the full attention of the group by continuous questioning, eye contact, finger snaps, hand claps, and other gestures, and by eliciting choral responses and initiating some sort of award system.

When the program was introduced, it arrived with a flurry of research data that "proved" that all children – even those who were "culturally deprived" – could learn to read using this method. Soon there was a strong response, first from academics and later from many classroom teachers, stating that the program was terrible. What I find particularly interesting, however, is that the primary issue of the conflict over Distar has not been over its instructional efficacy – usually the students did learn to read – but the expression of explicit power in the classroom. The liberal educators opposed the methods – the direct instruction, the explicit control exhibited by the teacher. As a matter of fact, it was not unusual (even now) to hear of the program spoken of as "fascist."

I am not an advocate of Distar, but I will return to some of the issues that the program – and direct instruction in general – raises in understanding the differences between progressive White educators and educators of color.

To explore those differences, I would like to present several statements typical of those made with the best of intentions by middle-class liberal educators. To the surprise of the speakers, it is not unusual for such content to be met by vocal opposition or stony silence from people of color. My attempt here is to examine the underlying assumptions of both camps.

"I want the same thing for everyone else's children as I want for mine."

To provide schooling for everyone's children that reflects liberal, middle-class values and aspirations is to ensure the maintenance of the status quo, to ensure that power, the culture of power, remains in the hands of those who already have it. Some children come to school with more accoutrements of the culture of power already in place – "cultural capital," as some critical theorists refer to it (e.g. Apple, 1979) – some with less. Many liberal educators hold that the primary goal for education is for children to become autonomous, to develop fully who they are in the classroom setting without having arbitrary, outside standards forced upon them. This is a very reasonable goal for people whose children are already participants in the culture of power and who have already internalized its codes.

But parents who don't function within that culture often want something else. It's not that they disagree with the former aim, it's just that they want something more. They want to ensure that the school provides their children with discourse patterns, interactional styles, and spoken and written language codes that will allow them success in the larger society.

It was the lack of attention to this concern that created such a negative outcry in the Black community when well-intentioned White liberal educators introduced "dialect readers." These were seen as a plot to prevent the schools from teaching the linguistic aspects of the culture of power, thus dooming Black children to a permanent outsider caste. As one parent demanded, "My kids know how to be Black – you all teach them how to be successful in the White man's world."

Several Black teachers have said to me recently that as much as they'd like to believe otherwise, they cannot help but conclude that many of the "progressive" educational strategies imposed by liberals upon Black and poor children could only be based on a desire to ensure that the liberals' children get sole access to the dwindling pool of American jobs. Some have added that the liberal educators believe themselves to be operating with good intentions, but that these good intentions are only conscious delusions about their unconscious true motives. One of Black anthropologist John Gwaltney's (1980) informants reflects this perspective with her tongue-in-cheek observation that the biggest difference between Black folks and White folks is that Black folks *know* when they're lying!

Let me try to clarify how this might work in literacy instruction. A few years ago, I worked on an analysis of two popular reading programs, Distar and a progressive program that focused on higher-level critical thinking skills. In one of the first lessons of the progressive program, the children are introduced to the names of the letter *m* and *e*. In the same lesson they are then taught the sound made by each of the letters, how to write each of the letters, and that when the two are blended together they produce the word *me*.

As an experienced first-grade teacher, I am convinced that a child needs to be familiar with a significant number of these concepts to be able to assimilate so much new knowledge in one sitting. By contrast, Distar presents the same information in about forty lessons.

I would not argue for the pace of the Distar lessons; such a slow pace would only bore most kids – but what happened in the other lesson is that it merely provided an opportunity for those who already knew the content to exhibit that they knew it, or at most perhaps to build one new concept onto what was already known. This meant that the child who did not come to school already primed with what was to be presented would be labeled as needing "remedial" instruction from day one; indeed, this determination would be made before he or she was ever taught. In fact, Distar was "successful" because it actually *taught* new information to children who had not already acquired it at home. Although the more progressive system was ideal for some children, for others it was a disaster.

I do not advocate a simplistic "basic skills" approach for children outside of the culture of power. It would be (and has been) tragic to operate as if these children were incapable of critical and higher-order thinking and reasoning. Rather, I suggest that schools must provide these children the content that other families from a different cultural orientation provide at home. This does not mean separating children according to family background, but instead, ensuring that each classroom incorporate strategies appropriate for all the children in its confines.

And I do not advocate that it is the school's job to attempt to change the homes of poor and non-White children to match the homes of those in the culture of power. That may indeed be a form of cultural genocide. I have frequently heard schools call poor parents "uncaring" when parents respond to the school's urging, that they change their home life in order to facilitate their children's learning, by saying, "But that's the school's job." What the school personnel fail to understand is that if the parents were members of the culture of power and lived by its rules and codes, then they would transmit those codes to their children. In fact, they transmit another culture that children must learn at home in order to survive in their communities.

> *"Child-centered, whole language, and process approaches are needed in order to allow a democratic state of free, autonomous, empowered adults, and because research has shown that children learn best through these methods."*

People of color are, in general, skeptical of research as a determiner of our fates. Academic research has, after all, found us genetically inferior, culturally deprived, and verbally deficient. But beyond that general caveat, and despite my or others' personal preferences, there is little research data supporting the major tenets of process approaches over other forms of literacy instruction, and virtually no evidence that such approaches are more efficacious for children of color (Siddle, 1986).

Although the problem is not necessarily inherent in the method, in some instances adherents of process approaches to writing create situations in which students ultimately find themselves held accountable for knowing a set of rules about which no one has ever directly informed them. Teachers do students no service to suggest, even implicitly, that "product" is not important. In this country, students will be judged on their product regardless of the process they utilized to achieve it. And that product, based as it is on the specific codes of a particular culture, is more readily produced when the directives of how to produce it are made explicit.

If such explicitness is not provided to students, what it feels like to people who are old enough to judge is that there are secrets being kept, that time is being wasted, that the teacher is abdicating his or her duty to teach. A doctoral student in my acquaintance was assigned to a writing class to hone his writing skills. The student was placed in the section led by a White professor who utilized a process approach, consisting primarily of having the students write essays and then assemble into groups to edit each others' papers. That procedure infuriated this particular student. He had many angry encounters with the teacher about what she was doing. In his words:

> I didn't feel she was teaching us anything. She wanted us to correct each others' papers and we were there to learn from her. She didn't teach anything, absolutely nothing.
>
> Maybe they're trying to learn what Black folks knew all the time. We understand how to improvise, how to express ourselves creatively. When I'm in a classroom, I'm not looking for that, I'm looking for structure, the more formal language.

> Now my buddy was in [a] Black teacher's class. And that lady was very good. She went through and explained and defined each part of the structure. This [White] teacher didn't get along with that Black teacher. She said that she didn't agree with her methods. But *I* don't think that White teacher *had* any methods.

When I told this gentleman that what the teacher was doing was called a process method of teaching writing, his response was, "Well, at least now I know that she *thought* she was doing *something*. I thought she was just a fool who couldn't teach and didn't want to try."

This sense of being cheated can be so strong that the student may be completely turned off to the educational system. Amanda Branscombe, an accomplished White teacher, recently wrote a letter discussing her work with working-class Black and White students at a community college in Alabama. She had given these students my "Skills and Other Dilemmas" article (Delpit, 1986) to read and discuss, and wrote that her students really understood and identified with what I was saying. To quote her letter:

> One young man said that he had dropped out of high school because he failed the exit exam. He noted that he had then passed the GED without a problem after three weeks of prep. He said that his high school English teacher claimed to use a process approach, but what she really did was hide behind fancy words to give herself permission to do nothing in the classroom.

The students I have spoken of seem to be saying that the teacher has denied them access to herself as the source of knowledge necessary to learn the forms they need to succeed. Again, I tentatively attribute the problem to teachers' resistance to exhibiting power in the classroom. Somehow, to exhibit one's personal power as expert source is viewed as disempowering one's students.

Two qualifiers are necessary, however. The teacher cannot be the only expert in the classroom. To deny students their own expert knowledge *is* to disempower them. Amanda Branscombe, when she was working with Black high school students classified as "slow learners," had the students analyze RAP songs to discover their underlying patterns. The students became the experts in explaining to the teacher the rules for creating a new RAP song. The teacher then used the patterns the students identified as a base to begin an explanation of the structure of grammar, and then of Shakespeare's plays. Both student and teacher are experts at what they know best.

The second qualifier is that merely adopting direct instruction is not the answer. Actual writing for real audiences and real purposes is a vital element in helping students to understand that they have an important voice in their own learning processes. Siddle (1988) examines the results of various kinds of interventions in a primarily process-oriented writing class for Black students. Based on readers' blind assessments, she found that the intervention that produced the most positive changes in the students' writing was a "mini-lesson" consisting of direct instruction about some standard writing convention. But what produced the *second* highest number of positive changes was a subsequent student-centered conference with the teacher. (Peer conferencing in this group of Black students who were not members of the culture of power produced the least number of changes in students' writing. However, the classroom teacher maintained – and I concur – such activities are necessary to introduce the elements of "real audience" into the task, along with more teacher-directed strategies.)

"It's really a shame but she (that Black teacher upstairs) seems to be so authoritarian, so focused on skills and so teacher directed. Those poor kids never seem to be allowed to really express their creativity. (And she even yells at them.)"

This statement directly concerns the display of power and authority in the classroom. One way to understand the difference in perspective between Black teachers and their progressive colleagues on this issue is to explore culturally influenced oral interactions.

In *Ways With Words*, Shirley Brice Heath (1983) quotes the verbal directives given by the middle-class "townspeople" teachers (p. 280):

– "Is this where the scissors belong?"
– "You want to do your best work today."

By contrast, many Black teachers are more likely to say:

– "Put those scissors on that shelf."
– "Put your name on the papers and make sure to get the right answer for each question."

Is one oral style more authoritarian than another?

Other researchers have identified differences in middle-class and working-class speech to children. Snow *et al.* (1976), for example, report that working-class mothers use more directives to their children than do middle- and upper-class parents. Middle-class parents are likely to give the directive to a child to take his bath as, "Isn't it time for your bath?" Even though the utterance is couched as a question, both child and adult understand it as a directive. The child may respond with "Aw Mom, can't I wait until . . ." but whether or not negotiation is attempted, both conversants understand the intent of the utterance.

By contrast, a Black mother, in whose house I was recently a guest, said to her 8-year-old son, "Boy, get your rusty behind in that bathtub." Now I happen to know that this woman loves her son as much as any mother, but she would never have posed the directive to her son to take a bath in the form of a question. Were she to ask, "Would you like to take your bath now?" she would not have been issuing a directive but offering a true alternative. Consequently, as Heath suggests, upon entering school the child from such a family may not understand the indirect statement of the teacher as a direct command. Both White and Black working-class children in the communities Heath studied "had difficulty interpreting these indirect requests for adherence to an unstated set of rules" (p. 280).

But those veiled commands are commands nonetheless, representing true power, and with true consequences for disobedience. If veiled commands are ignored, the child will be labeled a behavior problem and possibly officially classified as behavior disordered. In other words, the attempt by the teacher to reduce an exhibition of power by expressing herself in indirect terms may remove the very explicitness that the child needs to understand the rules of the new classroom culture.

A Black elementary school principal in Fairbanks, Alaska, reported to me that she has a lot of difficulty with Black children who are placed in some White teachers' classrooms. The teachers often send the children to the office for disobeying teacher directives. Their parents are frequently called in for conferences. The parents' response to the teacher is usually the same: "They do what I say; if you just *tell* them what to do, they'll do it. I tell them at home that they have to listen to what you say." And so, does not the power still exist? Its veiled nature only makes it more difficult for some children to respond appropriately, but that in no way mitigates its existence.

I don't mean to imply, however, that the only time the Black child disobeys the teacher is when he or she misunderstands the request for certain behavior. There are other factors that may produce such behavior. Black children expect an authority figure to act with authority. When the teacher instead acts as a "chum," the message sent is that this adult has no authority, and the children react accordingly. One reason this is so is that Black people often view issues of power and authority differently than people from mainstream middle-class backgrounds.[3] Many people of color expect authority to be earned by personal efforts and exhibited by personal characteristics. In other words, "the authoritative person gets to be a teacher because she is authoritative." Some members of middle-class cultures, by contrast, expect one to achieve authority by the acquisition of an authoritative role. That is, "the teacher is the authority because she is the teacher."

In the first instance, because authority is earned, the teacher must consistently prove the characteristics that give her authority. These characteristics may vary across cultures, but in the Black community they tend to cluster around several abilities. The authoritative teacher can control the class through exhibition of personal power; establishes meaningful interpersonal relationships that garner student respect; exhibits a strong belief that all students can learn; establishes a standard of achievement and "pushes" the students to achieve that standard; and holds the attention of the students by incorporating interactional features of Black communicative style in his or her teaching.

By contrast, the teacher whose authority is vested in the role has many more options of behavior at her disposal. For instance, she does not need to express any sense of personal power because her authority does not come from anything she herself does or says. Hence, the power she actually holds may be veiled in such questions/commands as "Would you like to sit down now?" If the children in her class understand authority as she does, it is mutually agreed upon that they are to obey her no matter how indirect, soft-spoken, or unassuming she may be. Her indirectness and soft-spokenness may indeed be, as I suggested earlier, an attempt to reduce the implication of overt power in order to establish a more egalitarian and non-authoritarian classroom atmosphere.

If the children operate under another notion of authority, however, then there is trouble. The Black child may perceive the middle-class teacher as weak, ineffectual, and incapable of taking on the role of being the teacher; therefore, there is no need to follow her directives. In her dissertation, Michelle Foster (1987) quotes one young Black man describing such a teacher:

> She is boring, bo::ing.[4] She could do something creative. Instead she just stands there. She can't control the class, doesn't know how to control the class. She asked me what she was doing wrong. I told her she just stands there like she's meditating. I told her she could be meditating for all I know. She says that we're supposed to know what to do. I told her I don't know nothin' unless she tells me. She just can't control the class. I hope we don't have her next semester.
> (pp. 67–68)

But of course the teacher may not view the problem as residing in herself but in the student, and the child may once again become the behavior-disordered Black boy in special education.

What characteristics do Black students attribute to the good teacher? Again, Foster's dissertation provides a quotation that supports my experience with Black students. A young Black man is discussing a former teacher with a group of friends:

> We had fu::n in her class, but she was mean. I can remember she used to say, "Tell me what's in the story, Wayne." She pushed, she used to get on me and push me to know. She made us learn. We had to get in the books. There was this tall guy and he tried to take her on, but she was in charge of that class and she didn't let anyone run her. I still have this book we used in her class. It's a bunch of stories in it. I just read one on Coca-Cola again the other day.
>
> (p. 68)

To clarify, this student was *proud* of the teacher's "meanness," an attribute he seemed to describe as the ability to run the class and pushing and expecting students to learn. Now, does the liberal perspective of the negatively authoritarian Black teacher really hold up? I suggest that although all "explicit" Black teachers are not also good teachers, there are different attitudes in different cultural groups about which characteristics make for a good teacher. Thus, it is impossible to create a model for the good teacher without taking issues of culture and community context into account.

And now to the final comment I present for examination:

> "*Children have the right to their own language, their own culture. We must fight cultural hegemony and fight the system by insisting that children be allowed to express themselves in their own language style. It is not they, the children, who must change, but the schools. To push children to do anything else is repressive and reactionary.*"

A statement such as this originally inspired me to write the "Skills and Other Dilemmas" article. It was first written as a letter to a colleague in response to a situation that had developed in our department. I was teaching a senior-level teacher education course. Students were asked to prepare a written autobiographical document for the class that would also be shared with their placement school prior to their student teaching.

One student, a talented young Native American woman, submitted a paper in which the ideas were lost because of technical problems – from spelling to sentence structure to paragraph structure. Removing her name, I duplicated the paper for a discussion with some faculty members. I had hoped to initiate a discussion about what we could do to ensure that our students did not reach the senior level without getting assistance in technical writing skills when they needed them.

I was amazed at the response. Some faculty implied that the student should never have been allowed into the teacher education program. Others, some of the more progressive minded, suggested that I was attempting to function as gatekeeper by raising the issue and had internalized repressive and disempowering forces of the power elite to suggest that something was wrong with a Native American student just because she had another style of writing. With few exceptions, I found myself alone in arguing against both camps.

No, this student should not have been denied entry to the program. To deny her entry under the notion of upholding standards is to blame the victim for the crime. We cannot justifiably enlist exclusionary standards when the reason this student lacked the skills demanded was poor teaching at best and institutionalized racism at worst.

However, to bring this student into the program and pass her through without attending to obvious deficits in the codes needed for her to function effectively as a teacher is equally criminal – for though we may assuage our own consciences for not participating in victim blaming, she will surely be accused and convicted as soon as she leaves the university. As Native Alaskans were quick to tell me, and as I understood through my own experience in the Black community, not only would she not be hired as a teacher, but those who did not hire her would make the (false) assumption that the university was putting out only incompetent Natives and that they should stop looking seriously at any Native applicants. A White applicant who exhibits problems is an individual with problems. A person of color who exhibits problems immediately becomes a representative of her cultural group.

No, either stance is criminal. The answer is to *accept* students but also to take responsibility to *teach* them. I decided to talk to the student and found out she had recognized that she needed some assistance in the technical aspects of writing soon after she entered the university as a freshman. She had gone to various members of the education faculty and received the same two kinds of responses I met with four years later: faculty members told her either that she should not even attempt to be a teacher, or that it didn't matter and that she shouldn't worry about such trivial issues. In her desperation, she had found a helpful professor in the English Department, but he left the university when she was in her sophomore year.

We sat down together, worked out a plan for attending to specific areas of writing competence, and set up regular meetings. I stressed to her the need to use her own learning process as insight into how best to teach her future students those "skills" that her own schooling had failed to teach her. I gave her some explicit rules to follow in some areas; for others, we devised various kinds of journals that, along with readings about the structure of the language, allowed her to find her own insights into how the language worked. All that happened two years ago, and the young woman is now successfully teaching. What the experience led me to understand is that pretending that gatekeeping points don't exist is to ensure that many students will not pass through them.

Now you may have inferred that I believe that because there is a culture of power, everyone should learn the codes to participate in it, and that is how the world should be. Actually, nothing could be further from the truth. I believe in a diversity of style, and I believe the world will be diminished if cultural diversity is ever obliterated. Further, I believe strongly, as do my liberal colleagues, that each cultural group should have the right to maintain its own language style. When I speak, therefore, of the culture of power, I don't speak of how I wish things to be but of how they are.

I further believe that to act as if power does not exist is to ensure that the power status quo remains the same. To imply to children or adults (but of course the adults won't believe you anyway) that it doesn't matter how you talk or how you write is to ensure their ultimate failure. I prefer to be honest with my students. Tell them that their language and cultural style is unique and wonderful but that there is a political power game that is also being played, and if they want to be in on that game there are certain games that they too must play.

But don't think that I let the onus of change rest entirely with the students. I am also involved in political work both inside and outside of the educational system, and that political work demands that I place myself to influence as many gate-keeping points as possible. And it is there that I agitate for change – pushing gatekeepers to open their doors to a variety of styles and codes. What I'm saying, however, is that I do not believe that political change toward diversity can be effected from the bottom up, as do some of my colleagues. They seem to believe that if we accept and encourage diversity within classrooms of children, then diversity will automatically be accepted at gatekeeping points.

I believe that will never happen. What will happen is that the students who reach the gatekeeping points – like Amanda Branscombe's student who dropped out of high school because he failed his exit exam – will understand that they have been lied to and will react accordingly. No, I am certain that if we are truly to effect societal change, we cannot do so from the bottom up, but we must push and agitate from the top down. And in the meantime, we must take the responsibility to *teach*, to provide for students who do not already possess them, the additional codes of power.[5]

But I also do not believe that we should teach students to passively adopt an alternate code. They must be encouraged to understand the value of the code they already possess as well as to understand the power realities in this country. Otherwise they will be unable to work to change these realities. And how does one do that?

Martha Demientieff, a masterly Native Alaskan teacher of Athabaskan Indian students, tells me that her students, who live in a small, isolated, rural village of less than two hundred people, are not aware that there are different codes of English. She takes their writing and analyzes it for features of what has been referred to by Alaskan linguists as "Village English," and then covers half a bulletin board with words or phrases from the students' writing, which she labels "Our Heritage Language." On the other half of the bulletin board she puts the equivalent statements in "standard English," which she labels "Formal English."

She and the students spend a long time on the "Heritage English" section, savoring the words, discussing the nuances. She tells the students, "That's the way we say things. Doesn't it feel good? Isn't it the absolute best way of getting that idea across?" Then she turns to the other side of the board. She tells the students that there are people, not like those in their village, who judge others by the way they talk or write.

> We listen to the way people talk, not to judge them, but to tell what part of the river they come from. These other people are not like that. They think everybody needs to talk like them. Unlike us, they have a hard time hearing what people say if they don't talk exactly like them. Their way of talking and writing is called "Formal English."
>
> We have to feel a little sorry for them because they have only one way to talk. We're going to learn two ways to say things. Isn't that better? One way will be our Heritage way. The other will be Formal English. Then, when we go to get jobs, we'll be able to talk like those people who only know and can only really listen to one way. Maybe after we get the jobs we can help them to learn how it feels to have another language, like ours, that feels so good. We'll talk like them when we have to, but we'll always know our way is best.

Martha then does all sorts of activities with the notions of Formal and Heritage or informal English. She tells the students,

> In the village, everyone speaks informally most of the time unless there's a potlatch or something. You don't think about it, you don't worry about

following any rules – it's sort of like how you eat food at a picnic – nobody pays attention to whether you use your fingers or a fork, and it feels *so* good. Now, Formal English is more like a formal dinner. There are rules to follow about where the knife and fork belong, about where people sit, about how you eat. That can be really nice, too, because it's nice to dress up sometimes.

The students then prepare a formal dinner in the class, for which they dress up and set a big table with fancy tablecloths, china, and silverware. They speak only Formal English at this meal. Then they prepare a picnic where only informal English is allowed.

She also contrasts the "wordy" academic way of saying things with the metaphoric style of Athabaskan. The students discuss how book language always uses more words, but in Heritage language, the shorter way of saying something is always better. Students then write papers in the academic way, discussing with Martha and with each other whether they believe they've said enough to sound like a book. Next, they take those papers and try to reduce the meaning to a few sentences. Finally, students further reduce the message to a "saying" brief enough to go on the front of a T-shirt, and the sayings are put on little paper T-shirts that the students cut out and hang throughout the room. Sometimes the students reduce other authors' wordy texts to their essential meanings as well.

The following transcript provides another example. It is from a conversation between a Black teacher and a Southern Black high school student named Joey, who is a speaker of Black English. The teacher believes it very important to discuss openly and honestly the issues of language diversity and power. She has begun the discussion by giving the student a children's book written in Black English to read.

Teacher: What do you think about that book?

Joey: I think it's nice.

Teacher: Why?

Joey: I don't know. It just told about a Black family, that's all.

Teacher: Was it difficult to read?

Joey: No.

Teacher: Was the text different from what you have seen in other books?

Joey: Yeah. The writing was.

Teacher: How?

Joey: It use more of a southern-like accent in this book.

Teacher: Uhm-hmm. Do you think that's good or bad?

Joey: Well, uh, I don't think it's good for people down this a way, cause that's the way they grow up talking anyway. They ought to get the right way to talk.

Teacher: Oh. So you think it's wrong to talk like that?

Joey: Well . . . [*Laughs*]

Teacher: Hard question, huh?

Joey: Uhm-hmm, that's a hard question. But I think they shouldn't make books like that.

Teacher: Why?

Joey: Because they not using the right way to talk and in school they take off for that and li'l chirren grow up talking like that and reading like that so they might think that's right and all the time they getting bad grades in school, talking like that and writing like that.

Teacher: Do you think they should be getting bad grades for talking like that?

Joey:	[*Pauses, answers very slowly*] No . . . No.
Teacher:	So you don't think that it matters whether you talk one way or another?
Joey:	No, not long as you understood.
Teacher:	Uhm-hmm. Well, that's a hard question for me to answer, too. It's, ah, that's a question that's come up in a lot of schools now as to whether they should correct children who speak the way we speak all the time. Cause when we're talking to each other we talk like that even though we might not talk like that when we get into other situations, and who's to say whether it's –
Joey:	[*Interrupting*] Right or wrong.
Teacher:	Yeah.
Joey:	Maybe they ought to come up with another kind of . . . maybe Black English or something. A course in Black English. Maybe Black folks would be good in that cause people talk, I mean Black people talk like that, so . . . but I guess there's a right way and wrong way to talk, you know, not regarding what race. I don't know.
Teacher:	But who decided what's right or wrong?
Joey:	Well that's true . . . I guess White people did.
[*Laughter. End of tape.*]	

Notice how throughout the conversation Joey's consciousness has been raised by thinking about codes of language. This teacher further advocates having students interview various personnel officers in actual workplaces about their attitudes toward divergent styles in oral and written language. Students begin to understand how arbitrary language standards are, but also how politically charged they are. They compare various pieces written in different styles, discuss the impact of different styles on the message by making translations and back translations across styles, and discuss the history, apparent purpose, and contextual appropriateness of each of the technical writing rules presented by their teacher. *And* they practice writing different forms to different audiences based on rules appropriate for each audience. Such a program not only "teaches" standard linguistic forms, but also explores aspects of power as exhibited through linguistic forms.

Tony Burgess, in a study of secondary writing in England by Britton *et al.*, (1975/1977), suggests that we should not teach "iron conventions . . . imposed without rationale or grounding in communicative intent," . . . but "critical and ultimately cultural awarenesses" (p. 54). Courtney Cazden (1987) calls for a two-pronged approach:

1 Continuous opportunities for writers to participate in some authentic bit of the unending conversation . . . thereby becoming part of a vital community of talkers and writers in a particular domain, and

2 Periodic, temporary focus on conventions of form, taught as cultural conventions expected in a particular community.

(p. 20)

Just so that there is no confusion about what Cazden means by a focus on conventions of form, or about what I mean by "skills," let me stress that neither of us is speaking of page after page of "skill sheets" creating compound words or identifying nouns and adverbs, but rather about helping students gain a useful knowledge of the conventions of print while engaging in real and useful communicative activities. Kay Rowe Grubis, a junior high school teacher in a multicultural school, makes lists of certain technical rules for her eighth graders' review and then gives them papers from a third grade to "correct." The students not only have to correct other students' work, but also tell them why they have changed or questioned aspects of the writing.

A village teacher, Howard Cloud, teaches his high school students the conventions of formal letter writing and the formulation of careful questions in the context of issues surrounding the amendment of the Alaska Land Claims Settlement Act. Native Alaskan leaders hold differing views on this issue, critical to the future of local sovereignty and land rights. The students compose letters to leaders who reside in different areas of the state seeking their perspectives, set up audioconference calls for interview/debate sessions, and, finally, develop a videotape to present the differing views.

To summarize, I suggest that students must be *taught* the codes needed to participate fully in the mainstream of American life, not by being forced to attend to hollow, inane, decontextualized subskills, but rather within the context of meaningful communicative endeavors; that they must be allowed the resource of the teacher's expert knowledge, while being helped to acknowledge their own "expertness" as well; and that even while students are assisted in learning the culture of power, they must also be helped to learn about the arbitrariness of those codes and about the power relationships they represent.

I am also suggesting that appropriate education for poor children and children of color can only be devised in consultation with adults who share their culture. Black parents, teachers of color, and members of poor communities must be allowed to participate fully in the discussion of what kind of instruction is in their children's best interest. Good liberal intentions are not enough. In an insightful study entitled "Racism without Racists: Institutional Racism in Urban Schools," Massey, Scott, and Dornbusch (1975) found that under the pressures of teaching, and with all intentions of "being nice," teachers had essentially stopped attempting to teach Black children. In their words: "We have shown that oppression can arise out of warmth, friendliness, and concern. Paternalism and a lack of challenging standards are creating a distorted system of evaluation in the schools" (p. 10). Educators must open themselves to, and allow themselves to be affected by, these alternative voices.

In conclusion, I am proposing a resolution for the skills/process debate. In short, the debate is fallacious; the dichotomy is false. The issue is really an illusion created initially not by teachers but by academics whose worldview demands the creation of categorical division – not for the purpose of better teaching, but for the goal of easier analysis. As I have been reminded by many teachers since the publication of my article, those who are most skillful at educating Black and poor children do not allow themselves to be placed in "skills" or "process" boxes. They understand the need for both approaches, the need to help students to establish their own voices, but to coach those voices to produce notes that will be heard clearly in the larger society.

The dilemma is not really in the debate over instructional methodology, but rather in communicating across cultures and in addressing the more fundamental issue of power, of whose voice gets to be heard in determining what is best for poor children and children of color. Will Black teachers and parents continue to be silenced by the very forces that claim to "give voice" to our children? Such an outcome would be tragic, for both groups truly have something to say to one another. As a result of careful listening to alternative points of view, I have myself come to a viable synthesis of perspectives. But both sides do need to be able to listen, and I contend that it is those with the most power, those in the majority, who must take the greater responsibility for initiating the process.

To do so takes a very special kind of listening, listening that requires not only open eyes and ears, but open hearts and minds. We do not really see through our eyes or hear through our ears, but through our beliefs. To put our beliefs on hold is to cease to exist as ourselves for a moment – and that is not easy. It is painful as well, because it means turning yourself inside out, giving up your own sense of who you are, and being willing to see yourself in the unflattering light of another's angry gaze. It is not easy, but it is the only way to learn what it might feel like to be someone else and the only way to start the dialogue.

There are several guidelines. We must keep the perspective that people are experts on their own lives. There are certainly aspects of the outside world of which they may not be aware, but they can be the only authentic chroniclers of their own experience. We must not be too quick to deny their interpretations, or accuse them of "false consciousness." We must believe that people are rational beings, and therefore always act rationally. We may not understand their rationales, but that in no way militates against the existence of these rationales or reduces our responsibility to attempt to apprehend them. And finally, we must learn to be vulnerable enough to allow our world to turn upside down in order to allow the realities of others to edge themselves into our consciousness. In other words, we must become ethnographers in the true sense.

Teachers are in an ideal position to play this role, to attempt to get all of the issues on the table in order to initiate true dialogue. This can only be done, however, by seeking out those whose perspectives may differ most, by learning to give their words complete attention, by understanding one's own power, even if that power stems merely from being in the majority, by being unafraid to raise questions about discrimination and voicelessness with people of color, and to listen, no, to *hear* what they say. I suggest that the results of such interactions may be the most powerful and empowering coalescence yet seen in the educational realm – for *all* teachers and for *all* the students they teach.

Acknowledgments

I take full responsibility for all that appears herein; however, aside from those mentioned by name in this text, I would like to thank all of the educators and students around the country who have been so willing to contribute their perspectives to the formulation of these ideas, especially Susan Jones, Catherine Blunt, Dee Stickman, Sandra Gamble, Willard Taylor, Mickey Monteiro, Denise Burden, Evelyn Higbee, Joseph Delpit, Jr., Valerie Montoya, Richard Cohen, and Mary Denise Thompson.

Notes

1   Such a discussion, limited as it is by space constraints, must treat the intersection of class and race somewhat simplistically. For the sake of clarity, however, let me define a few terms: "Black" is used herein to refer to those who share some or all aspects of "core black culture" (Gwaltney, 1980, p. xxiii), that is, the mainstream of Black America – neither those who have entered the ranks of the bourgeoisie nor those who are participants in the disenfranchised underworld. "Middle-class" is used broadly to refer to the predominantly White American "mainstream." There are, of course, non-White people who also fit into this

category; at issue is their cultural identification, not necessarily the color of their skin. (I must add that there are other non-White people, as well as poor White people, who have indicated to me that their perspectives are similar to those attributed herein to Black people.)

2   *Multicultural Britain: "Crosstalk,"* National Centre of Industrial Language Training, Commission for Racial Equality, London, England, John Twitchin, Producer.

3   I would like to thank Michelle Foster, who is presently planning a more in-depth treatment of the subject, for her astute clarification of the idea.

4   *Editor's note*: The colons [::] refer to elongated vowels.

5   Bernstein (1975) makes a similar point when he proposes that different educational frames cannot be successfully institutionalized in the lower levels of education until there are fundamental changes at the post-secondary levels.

References

Apple, M. W. (1979). *Ideology and Curriculum*. Boston: Routledge and Kegan Paul.

Bernstein, B. (1975). Class and pedagogies: visible and invisible. In B. Bernstein (ed.) *Class, Codes, and Control* (vol. 3). Boston: Routledge and Kegan Paul.

Britton, J., Burgess, T., Martin, N., McLeod, A., and Rosen, H. (1975/1977). *The Development of Writing Abilities*. London: Macmillan Education for the Schools Council, and Urbana, IL: National Council of Teachers of English.

Cazden, C. (1987). *The Myth of Autonomous Text*. Paper presented at the Third International Conference on Thinking, Hawaii, January.

Delpit, L. D. (1986). Skills and other dilemmas of a progressive Black educator. *Harvard Educational Review*, 56(4), 379–85.

Foster, M. (1987). *"It's cookin' now": an Ethnographic Study of the Teaching Style of a Successful Black Teacher in an Urban Community College*. Unpublished doctoral dissertation, Harvard University.

Gwaltney, J. (1980). *Drylongso*. New York: Vintage Books.

Heath, S. B. (1983). *Ways with Words*. Cambridge: Cambridge University Press.

Massey, G. C., Scott, M. V., and Dornbusch, S. M. (1975). Racism without racists: institutional racism in urban schools. *The Black Scholar*, 7(3), 2–11.

Siddle, E. V. (1986). *A Critical Assessment of the Natural Process Approach to Teaching Writing*. Unpublished qualifying paper, Harvard University.

—— (1988). *The Effect of Intervention Strategies on the Revisions Ninth Graders make in a Narrative Essay*. Unpublished doctoral dissertation, Harvard University.

Snow, C. E., Arlman-Rup, A., Hassing, Y., Josbe, J., Joosten, J., and Vorster, J. (1976). Mother's speech in three social classes. *Journal of Psycholinguistic Research*, 5, 1–20.

CHAPTER 15

THE MYTH OF NEUTRALITY IN EDUCATIONAL RESEARCH

Maud Blair

In P. Conolly and B. Troyna (eds) *Researching Racism in Education,* Buckingham: Open University Press, pp. 12–20, 1998

Privilege keeps the terms of your privilege invisible.

Michael Kimmel

Introduction

During a symposium on gender held at a conference of the American Educational Research Association in New York in April 1996, the participants (predominantly women), were asked to go into groups to talk about how they might become more supportive of each other in the academy. The group I attended went into a long discussion about how women from minority ethnic groups felt let down in different ways and sometimes betrayed by their white women colleagues. Examples were given of racist assumptions held by white colleagues, of white women colluding either actively or passively with racially discriminatory decisions, not registering their objections to racial slurs, and so on. The 'scribe' (a white woman) took notes and also wrote up, for a report back to the plenary, 'ways forward' for all women. These 'ways forward' included the need to question assumptions about 'others', for white women to recognize that they had more power than minority women in predominantly white institutions, and the need to use such (albeit limited) power to advance the interests of women generally.

After the discussion had gone on in this vein for some time, the question was posed as to why after all these years of feminism and of debates about racism within feminism, the same assumptions about 'others' still existed, the same practices were prevalent and the same discussions were still taking place. It was suggested that perhaps it was time we stopped looking only at *what* happened and *how* these negative relations happened, and began to examine *why* they were continuously being reproduced. The speaker continued with the suggestion that perhaps a focus on how social identities, and in particular how white identities were produced and reproduced, might help to shed light on some of the factors which created boundaries between women and mitigated against an inclusive sense of sisterhood. Examples were given of studies which had begun to look beyond merely how men behaved, to studies of masculinity which sought to understand the discourses which produced 'men' and 'women' and helped to sustain gender inequalities. It was suggested that in addition to the recommendations already agreed, a further recommendation that we examine the notion of white identity be put forward. At this point the conversation ground to a halt, the 'scribe' handed her notes to the Chair of the group declaring that she did not know what to write and did not therefore know what to report back to the plenary. The other groups reported back their discussions and resolutions, which were all couched within the same somewhat soporific 'good intentions' framework, and our group did not report.

What does this story have to do with research theories? To begin with, it is important to make the distinction between *striving* for neutrality and *guaranteeing* neutrality. What the above story seems to me to illustrate is that no matter what our good intentions, we cannot guarantee neutrality in our interpretations and analyses. This is because our histories and memories are shot through with gendered, classed, racialized and other 'excluding' understandings which give us our particular perspectives on the world. Most of the participants at the conference, and certainly all those in the group described above, were academics or students and either had been or were currently engaged in research. There is no reason to suppose that they conducted their research with anything other than integrity, honesty and rigour. It is necessary, nevertheless, to ask to what extent researchers' definitions and interpretations can be neutral given the 'blindspots' that seem to arise when the 'gaze' is transferred from the 'other' to one's subjective self and the group with which one identifies? How easy is it for members of powerful groups to 'decentre' and make, not only the powerful group, but one's own personal investment in belonging to that group the object of inquiry in order to assess the extent to which this influences and affects the knowledge one produces? Laura E. Perez (1993, p. 270) states that constructions of identity are not only different but 'heavily invested in a *difference of interests* [her emphasis]'.

It is of course not only in relation to 'race' and ethnicity that blindspots of this kind can occur. According to hooks: 'Often brilliant political thinkers have had such blindspots. Men like Fanon, Albert Mennin, Paulo Freire and Aimé Césaire whose works teach us much about the nature of colonization, racism, classism, and revolutionary struggle often ignore issues of sexist oppression in their own writing' (hooks, 1984, p. 39). Such blindspots occur when researchers conduct their research without also acquainting themselves with the broader historical, political and social context within which the research is conducted. Researchers might be concerned about critical reflexivity, but what exactly does this mean? What is the content of such critical reflection? Does it include reflection on one's own 'whiteness' (or heterosexuality, or maleness, or class position or absence of impairment)? Does it include reflection on whether and how these subjective identities might be significant to the way in which researchers interpret the lives of those they study?

The argument that those who conduct partisan research are more likely to be biased (see Hammersley, 1998), is, in my view mistaken. Making one's politics explicit is no more likely to introduce bias into one's analysis than declaring that one does *not* have a value position. What the latter position does is to mask the fact that research interpretations are arrived at via styles of reasoning and deduction which fit particular theories and particular world views. These in turn derive from one's life history or cultural experience as a member of an ethnic group: female or male; middle-class or heterosexual; non-disabled; or a combination of some or all of these.

What do we mean by neutrality?

The most relevant definitions of the term for our purposes are the following: *impartial; taking the middle position; not helping or supporting either of two opposing sides* (see Concise Oxford Dictionary; Chambers Dictionary; Universal Dictionary respectively).

The debate about values, and about researchers not being blank pages waiting for research 'findings' to fill the blanks, has been well rehearsed over the years. It is accepted that researchers bring their 'baggage' with them into the research process, but that every attempt is made, in Margaret Mead's words, 'to sweep one's mind clear of every presupposition' (cited in Walker, 1986). Instead, the researcher's definitions and understandings should be guided by and adjusted in relation to the data collected. Through the research, one might learn new ways of 'seeing'. However, research does not necessarily alter previous theories, but can and often does reinforce what previous studies have found.

If we assume that most researchers have integrity and are concerned primarily with trying to uncover and to understand 'the problem', and will therefore conduct their study with the rigour that a self-respecting research community expects, then the question of neutrality must impinge most strongly at the point of analysis of the data. Presumably, according to proponents of objectivity and neutrality, one stands back from the data and employs methods of interpretation which do not 'help or support either of two opposing sides' (see Foster *et al.*, 1996). The assumption here is that analysing research data is like umpiring a game of cricket – anyone looking at that same data would reach the same conclusions because 'the facts' are there to be seen and judged by a set of rules which apply to all players at all times, regardless of which side the umpires would in their heart of hearts like to see win the game. This is, in my view, an untenable position. It is untenable not only because research is, as already indicated, a political activity in which the researcher is heavily implicated, but also because it creates a hegemonic research community. Through this hegemony, not only are the rules of the game decided by an established elite, but alternative voices are likely to be excluded if they do not fit within predetermined criteria for what is deemed to be valid research. Those who consider that research should be no more than an exercise in 'naval-gazing' are likely to dismiss or find unconvincing the 'findings' of those who consider research which is done for the sole benefit of the researcher to be unethical. Such research takes information from or about already oppressed groups, and gives nothing back, a model which Lather (1986) refers to as the 'rape' model. The 'umpire' model of analysis discussed earlier thus creates an obvious difficulty for researchers who believe in using their research for social change. Unlike cricket, research into social inequalities is by its very nature about umpiring a game that is played on different and unequal levels. Whilst the (declared) partisan researcher would consider it necessary to take this inequality into account by examining the power relations that exist and exploring the effects of these differential power relations, the non-partisan researcher might choose to ignore this inequality and the inherent power relations and focus only on the rules (Connolly, 1992). What this illustrates is not only that research is contested terrain, but also that neither position is or can be neutral.

It is, moreover, an error on the part of those who conclude that bias is an inevitable consequence of political commitment, to assume that partisan researchers have no interest in probing 'the truth', however unpleasant that may be. Indeed, social justice demands absolute integrity and a rigorous attitude and approach to one's research. How, otherwise, could one hope to understand 'the problem' and contribute to change? This does not, of course, mean that the dangers of bias are absent. But this is not the argument here. What is argued is that commitment to social justice does not make the research and the analysis any more biased than absence of commitment. It must be the dream of every black or minority parent living in the West to reach a stage when extensive research can reveal that there is no more racism in schools. Without racism as a complicating factor, it might make finding solutions to the problems faced by black children in schools that much easier. Mead comments that: 'The point of going into the field at all is to extend further what is already known, and so there is little value merely in identifying new versions of the familiar when we might instead, find something wholly new' (cited in Walker, 1986, p. 208).

Racism: what is it and who decides?

It is important to ask whether 'what is already known' is accepted within the research and academic community as a valid position from which to start. Can one, for example, begin on the assumption that 'race' is a social construction and not a scientific or biological fact, or does one have to go back and establish this in every project, and how and where does one do this? More importantly, do the research and academic community accept work that has been internationally acknowledged and accepted as 'what is already known' and hence a valid position to start from? And if they do not, then on what basis do they reject that work?

Presumably the answer to the first question is 'yes'; one can begin on the basis that social groups are 'produced' in discourse as 'races' and that in societies where 'race' is an important axis of differential power, this will affect the life chances and opportunities of the less powerful 'races'. If this is indeed accepted, how is racism in its different forms *and as experienced by black people*, to be defined and who does the defining? This, then leads onto the second question raised earlier where we find that there is much less consensus of opinion. For instance, is the experience as defined by black people and taken on by antiracists more biased than the definition imposed by those who have never and never could have such an experience? Who decides this and by what right or authority? Was the decision by Peter Foster (1990) (a major proponent of neutrality in research) to ignore the experience of racism as defined by black students in his study a neutral decision and if so, why? To what extent might his own identity as a white researcher, together with his rejection of how black students felt that racism affected them, have introduced bias into his findings? Furthermore, if white researchers do not accept the numerous findings of black and antiracist researchers, findings which resonate so powerfully with the experiences of black people, then from where do they derive their claims to neutrality?

Understanding ethnocentrism

I have at times been surprised and frustrated by responses to my own work. For example, in my research into the over-representation of black pupils (not including pupils of South Asian descent) in exclusions from schools, one of my earliest observations was that black pupils in Britain are a diverse group coming as they do from a range of different cultural, linguistic, social class and family backgrounds, including differences in gender. It was also clear from my observations and from interviews with teachers, parents and pupils, that black pupils presented diverse responses to particular phenomena, including schooling, and that there were similarities and overlaps in their behaviours and responses with their white and Asian counterparts of similar backgrounds, as indicated by interviews and teacher referral records. I had also deliberately chosen three schools that differed in their social and material circumstances, their social class intake, their location and the percentage of black students within them. Controlling therefore for these various factors of class, ethnicity, gender, location, numbers etc. (and bearing in mind that official government statistics had found this over-representation to be a national pattern (DFE, 1992) and therefore not confined to the schools in my study) I concluded that the over-representation of black males as a group in exclusions from these schools must relate to factors outside this group and not inherent to it. This did not mean that there would be no exclusions but that there would be a random distribution of black pupils among those excluded, proportionate to their numbers in a particular school, as there were for pupils from white and Asian ethnic groups. In other words, it was unlikely that black pupils as a group would exhibit behaviour patterns and responses which were different from their white (working class) counterparts when responding to the ordinary everyday phenomena of schooling common to all pupils regardless of background. If any difference did emerge in the behaviour of black pupils as a group, compared to their white peers, then this can only be explained in relation to their differential treatment *as a group* by the school.

What then were these patterns? Interviews with over a 100 black pupils aged between 14 and 18 produced one clear pattern of response – that black (male) pupils received an unfair share of negative comments and reprimands from teachers, that white and Asian pupils received more help and encouragement, that black pupils were picked out for reprimand even when other ethnic groups were involved, and that they were given harsher punishment than their white and Asian peers for the same offences in these schools. This was confirmed by a study of referral forms for one year in one of the schools. The forms outlined the nature of the offence committed by students and the length of exclusion given. These forms revealed clear discrepancies between the length of exclusion given to some black students for the same – and sometimes *lesser* – offences than their white and Asian peers. They also experienced blatant racism from teachers in the form of racist comments and 'jokes'. These findings confirmed what many others before me had found in relation to the experiences of black pupils. This includes the findings of large-scale studies conducted in primary schools (Tizard *et al.*, 1988) and in junior schools (Mortimore *et al.*, 1988) where it was found that black pupils received more criticism and negative feedback than other groups. Such overwhelming evidence, suggested that black pupils were perceived in schools as one homogenous and undifferentiated group and that this was resulting in their being treated, *as a group*, differently from their white and Asian peers.

I was therefore interested in the ways in which black pupils were not only constructed, but 'produced' as a homogenous group in schools and how this impacted on their school experiences, in particular their experiences of exclusion. In drawing out the themes that emerged from my interviews, I divided teacher responses into three groups: those who saw black pupils as the problem; those who saw it as a combined problem of racism and pupil behaviour; and those who saw racism in the education system as the problem. My technique was to deconstruct teachers' discourses in order to understand the frameworks used by teachers for understanding pupil behaviour. It emerged that the teachers who saw the problem as mainly one of discrimination against black students were more likely to talk about black students as individuals and less likely to use stereotypes in their explanations of pupil behaviour. On the other hand, teachers who saw black students as being responsible for their over-representation in exclusions tended to talk about them as members of a racial group, and not as individual personalities. I thus concluded that stereotyping was indeed one way in which teachers made sense of the behaviours of black pupils. I decided to analyse closely these stereotypes in order to show how they might contribute to the problem of over-representation of black pupils in exclusions. One colleague's observation was that I had been unfair to subject some teachers' discourses to closer scrutiny than others. This means, presumably, that I had not been neutral in my approach. It is difficult to see, under the circumstances, what kind of neutrality was required. The problem that I thought necessary to investigate was one of stereotypes. The focus therefore was not on teachers who did not stereotype, but on those who did – regardless of the ethnicity of the teacher.

A useful outcome of this critique of my paper was that it reinforced the importance of being explicit and not leaving meanings embedded in the text, especially in as 'sensitive' an area as 'race'. However, another colleague suggested that I was focusing too much on teachers and not enough on the behaviour of pupils and that I should turn my attention to the possibility that black pupils *qua* black pupils do behave worse than their white and/or Asian peers. Given the diversity of black students, the implication therefore was that there must be something racial, or biological which makes black pupils, as a group, more prone to bad behaviour and therefore more deserving of exclusion. Indeed, this is precisely the underlying assumptions in the work of Peter Foster (1990) discussed earlier, who suggested that black pupils, by virtue of their worse behaviour, were less deserving of places in the academic streams in the school in which he worked (see also Gillborn, 1998). We were, however, given no information as to why skin colour should be the criteria that marked these students out from their peers. There was no discussion of the cultures of these students, so it was impossible to tell from where this behaviour was coming. In my opinion, this was in part a product of Foster's superficial understanding of the history and politics of 'race', I would argue also that his whole theoretical orientation is rooted firmly in what Stanfield refers to as, 'folk notions' of racial differences (Stanfield, 1993, p. 4). I would go further to suggest that it was also due to a failure on Foster's part to reflect back in on himself and interrogate the possible role that his world view as a white person might play in his interpretation and analysis of 'race' (Connolly, 1992; Gillborn, 1995). Despite his numerous criticisms and dismissals of the work of antiracist researchers, the conclusions he drew in his own work, bearing in mind his rejection of the views of black pupils, could hardly be said to be based on a neutral analysis in the context of race relations in Britain (Connolly, 1992).

Neutrality or white defensiveness?

As my story at the beginning of this chapter shows, self-reflection when one is in a position of (relative) power is by no means an easy thing to do, especially when one's actions are not necessarily motivated by racial prejudice. Christine Sleeter (a white professor of teacher education at the University of Wisconsin), writing about a two-year staff development programme on 'race' which she conducted for teachers, describes how, over that period, she 'saw them [white teachers] select information and teaching strategies to add to a framework for understanding race that they took for granted, which they had constructed over their lifetimes from their position as white people in a racist society' (Sleeter, 1993, p. 168). She also comments that 'Whites so internalize their own power and taken-for-granted superiority that they resist self-questioning' (167). (See also hooks, 1984; Roman, 1993.)

I would agree with McCarthy and Crichlow that we need a more complex understanding of the contradictory interests and needs as well as the educational and political behaviour of minority groups, but also that 'much work needs to be done to understand and intervene in the ways in which whites are positioned and produced as "white," in the language, symbolic and material structures that dominate culture in the West' (McCarthy and Crichlow, 1993, p. xix).

Black and antiracist researchers do, nevertheless, need to pay attention to the criticisms that are levelled against us if we are to produce sharper and more refined analyses. However, there is a sense of frustration on the part of black researchers when we can see that our work on 'race' is assessed from within frameworks which are ethnocentric in that they assume one 'correct' view of the world, and are blind to the subtle nuances of racism (Essed, 1991). The expectation that experiences of racism must be observable (by anybody), measurable, and show intention if they are to qualify as racism only confirms the hegemonic nature of these requirements (see, e.g. Hurrell, 1995). This perspective ignores the complex nature of racism. As Kovel (1988, p. 54) states: 'No one behaves simply; he [*sic!*] is the amalgamated product of a host of historical, cultural and personal influences'.

An example of the different frameworks through which 'race' and racism are seen by white colleagues who have not acquired the necessary theoretical framework for understanding the different ways in which racism operates is recounted by Britzman *et al.* (1993, p. 191). They cite Patricia Williams, an African American legal scholar who wrote a critique of a law exam in which students had to argue a case based upon 'a decontextualized version of Shakespeare's *Othello*, in which Othello is described as a "Black militaristic African leader" who marries the "young white Desdemona" whom he then kills "in a fit of sexual rage" '. William's critique was that:

> The problem presents a defendant who is black, militaristic, unsophisticated, insecure, jealous, and sexually enraged. It reduces the facts to the very same racist generalizations and stereotypes this nation has used to subjugate black people since the first slave was brought from Africa. Moreover, it places an enormous burden on black students in particular who must assume, for the sake of answering this question, these things about themselves – that is the trauma of gratuitous generalization. The frame places blacks in the position of speaking against ourselves. It forces us to accept as 'truth' constructions that go to the heart of who we are.
>
> (Williams, 1991, p. 82)

Williams' colleagues responded by asking why she couldn't be 'objective', and why she imposed her own personal agenda on something as 'innocent' as an exam. The student who complained about the question was labelled 'an activist'.

When our contributions are thus judged and dismissed from within an ethnocentric framework, it presents us with a real dilemma. On the one hand, we consider our work important and wish to disseminate it widely, and on the other we are conscious that in order to do so we have to work within disciplinary conventions in which the rules which govern procedure and validity are themselves non-representative and exclusionary. This is not to suggest that work on 'race' or other areas that deal with social justice issues should operate entirely by different sets of rules. We all need to be critical of, and reflect on the knowledge and information we produce and the methods by which we produce such knowledge. Feminists, for example, are more critical of or reject outright the supposed dichotomy between quantitative and qualitative studies (Siraj-Blatchford, 1994; Jayaratne and Stewart, 1995). My argument here is that we need to question whether decisions to accept or not accept the work of black and antiracist researchers are indeed based on neutral criteria, or are 'a defense mechanism exhibited by those who wish to not acknowledge the importance of the empirical findings or claims of these researchers' (Stanfield, 1993, p. 29).

Conclusion

My concern in this chapter has been to question the notion of neutrality in research analyses, and to suggest that what often passes for neutrality in social research is no more than a mask which hides taken for granted partisan notions of what constitutes 'good' research. It is partisan because it ignores the possibility of diverse systems of knowledge production and multiple interpretations of social phenomena. This diversity does not exclude the importance of agreeing that every researcher needs to be guided by ethical codes of conduct. I argued that our interpretations are underpinned by our life histories and our investment (whether or not acknowledged) in our personal and group identities. Neutrality in social justice research is therefore a myth, whether or not one declares one's value system. I would argue further that the myth of neutrality may well serve to hide processes which exclude from publication the work of black and antiracist researchers who write about sensitive (and emotive) issues around 'race' and ethnicity. As most gatekeepers in the West are white, it is necessary that we look at how 'whiteness' and 'blackness' are socially constructed and differentially positioned in discourses of 'race', in order to better understand the processes which exclude. At issue, as Arorrowitz and Giroux contend, 'is the quest of diversity in ways of producing knowledge, and, more broadly, the validity of the distinction between legitimate intellectual knowledge and other kinds of knowledge' (Aronowitz and Giroux, 1991, p. 17).

It is not enough, however, to *understand* the role of subjective identities in the production of knowledge, but for marginalized and subordinate groups to actively *assert* our place in this process and challenge the canon of received notions of what constitutes legitimacy in academic work. Feminists have largely succeeded in carving out a space in which their voices are heard and taken seriously, and this has reaped some rewards in relation to the contribution of feminist research in the education of girls. Research on 'race' and education cannot claim similar success; the level of awareness raised and the changes in practice implemented as a result have been more than an uphill struggle. It is as necessary as it has ever been that in researching 'race' and education, we keep the focus firmly on commitment to social justice.

References

Aronowitz, S. and Giroux, H. A. (1991) *Postmodern Education: Politics, Culture and Social Criticism.* Oxford: University of Minnesota Press.

Britzman, D., Santiago-Valles, K., Jimenez-Munoz, G. and Lamash, M. (1993) Slips that show and tell: fashioning multiculture as a problem of representation, in C. McCarthy and W. Crichlow (eds) *Race, Identity and Representation in Education.* London: Routledge.

Connolly, P. (1992) Playing it by the rules: the politics of research in 'race' and education. *British Educational Research Journal,* 18 (2): 133–48.

Department for Education and Employment (1992) *Exclusions: A Discussion Document.* London: DFE.

Essed, P. (1991) *Understanding Everyday Racism*. London: Sage.
Foster, P. (1990) *Policy and Practice in Multicultural and Anti-Racist Education*. London: Routledge.
Foster, P., Gomm, R. and Hammersley, M. (1996) *Constructing Educational Inequality: An Assessment of Research on School Processes*. London: Falmer.
Gillborn, D. (1995) *Racism and Antiracism in Real Schools: Theory. Policy. Practice*. Buckingham: Open University Press.
—— (1998) Racism and the politics of qualitative research: learning from controversy and critique, in P. Connolly and B. Troyna (eds) *Researching Racism in Education: Politics, Theory and Practice*, pp. 34–54. Buckingham: Open University Press.
Hammersley, M. (1998) Partisanship and credibility: the case of antiracist educational research, in P. Connolly and B. Troyna (eds) *Researching Racism in Education: Politics, Theory and Practice*, pp. 21–33. Buckingham: Open University Press.
hooks, b. (1984) *Feminist Theory: From Margin to Center*. Boston, MA: South End Press.
Hurrell, P. (1995) Do teachers discriminate? Reactions to pupil behaviour in four comprehensive schools. *Sociology*, 29 (1): 59–72.
Jayaratne, J. and Stewart, A. (1995) Quantitative and qualitative methods in the social sciences: feminist issues and practical strategies, in J. Holland, M. Blair and S. Sheldon (eds) *Debates and Issues in Feminist Research and Pedagogy*. Clevedon: Multilingual Matters.
Kovel, J. (1988) *White Racism, a Psychohistory*. London: Free Association Books.
Lather, P. (1986) Research as praxis. *Harvard Educational Review*, 56 (3): 257–77.
McCarthy, C. and Crichlow, W. (1993) *Race, Identity and Representation in Education*. London: Routledge.
Mortimore, P., Sammons, P., Stoll, L., Lewis, D. and Ecob, R. (1988) *School Matters: The Junior Years*. Wells: Open Books.
Perez, L. E. (1993) Opposition and the education of Chicana/os, in C. McCarthy and W. Crichlow (eds) *Race, Identity and Representation in Education*. London: Routledge.
Roman, L. G. (1993) White is a color! White defensiveness, postmodernism and antiracist pedagogy, in C. McCarthy and W. Critchlow (eds) *Race, Identity and Representation in Education*. New York: Routledge.
Siraj-Blatchford, I. (1994) *Praxis Makes Perfect: Critical Educational Research for Social Justice*. Derbyshire: Education Now Books.
Sleeter, C. (1993) How white teachers construct race, in C. McCarthy and W. Crichlow (eds) *Race, Identity and Representation in Education*. London: Routledge.
Stanfield, J. H. (1993) Epistemological considerations, in J. H. Stanfield and R. M. Dennis (eds) *Race and Ethnicity in Research Methods*. London: Sage.
Tizard, B., Blatchford, P., Burke, J., Sarquhan, C. and Plewis, I. (1988) *Young Children in the Inner City*. Hove: Lawrence Earlbaum Associates.
Walker, R. (1986) The conduct of educational case studies: ethics, theory and procedures, in M. Hammersley (ed.) *Controversies in Classroom Research*. Milton Keynes: Open University Press.
Williams, P. (1991) *The Alchemy of Race and Rights*. Harvard, MA: Harvard University Press.

CHAPTER 16

THE POWER TO KNOW ONE THING IS NEVER THE POWER TO KNOW ALL THINGS

Methodological notes on two studies of Black American teachers

Michèle Foster

In A. Gitlin (ed.) *Power and Method: Political Activism and Educational Research*, New York: Routledge, pp. 129–146, 1994

In a 1988 novel by Gloria Naylor, a well-educated young man known only as "Reema's boy" returns home from across the river where he had gone to be educated to conduct research among his own people on Willow Springs, a coastal sea island that, according to Naylor, belonged neither to Georgia nor South Carolina. Armed with notebooks and a tape recorder, the indispensable instruments of an anthropologist, Reema's boy begins questioning relatives and neighbors about a commonly used phrase.

> And when he went around asking about 18 & 23, there weren't nothing to do but take pity on him as he rattled on about "ethnography," "unique speech patterns," "cultural preservation," and whatever else he seemed to be getting so much pleasure out of while talking into his little gray machine. He was all over the place – What 18 & 23 mean? What 18 & 23 mean? And we told him the God-honest truth: it was just our way of saying something. Winky was awful, though, he even spit tobacco juice for him. Sat on his porch all day, chewing up the boy's Red Devil premium and spitting so the machine could pick it up. There was enough fun in that to take us through the fall and winter when he had hauled himself back over The Sound to wherever he was getting what was supposed to be passing for an education. And he sent everybody he'd talked to copies of the book he wrote, bound all nice with our name and his signed on the first page. We couldn't hold Reema down, she was so proud. It's a good thing she didn't read it. None of us made it much through the introduction, but that said it all: you see, he had come to the conclusion after "extensive field work" (ain't never picked a boll of cotton or head of lettuce in his life – Reema spoiled him silly), but he done still made it to the conclusion that 18 & 23 wasn't 18 & 23 at all – was really 81 and 32, which just so happened to be the lines of longitude and latitude marking off where Willow Springs sits on the map. And we were just so damned dumb that we turned the whole thing around.

Not that he called it being dumb, mind you, called it "asserting our cultural identity," "inverting hostile social and political parameters." 'Cause,
see, being we was brought here as slaves, we had no choice but to look at
everything upside-down. And then being that we was isolated off here on this
island, everybody else in the country went on learning good English and calling things what they really was – in the dictionary and all that – while we kept
on calling things ass-backwards. And he thought that was just so wonderful
and marvelous, et cetera, et cetera . . . Well, after that crate of books came
here, if anybody had any doubts about what them developers were up to, if
there was just a tinge of seriousness behind them jokes about the motorboats
and swimming pools that could be gotten from selling a piece of land them
books squashed it. The people who ran the type of schools that could turn our
children into raving lunatics – and then put his picture on the back of the book
so we couldn't even deny it was him – didn't mean us a speck of good.

(Naylor, 1988, pp. 7–8)

For those of us doing research in our own communities, this excerpt from
Naylor's novel should serve as a cautionary tale. Increasingly, those undertaking
fieldwork and conducting life-history research are insiders, members of the subordinate groups they have chosen to study. Social science reveals a growing trend
toward "native anthropology" and other insider research, studies by ethnic
minorities of our own communities.

Despite this trend and a large literature on ethnographic and anthropological
method that treats the involvement, role, and stance that researchers adopt
vis-à-vis the communities they are studying, most of these references – contemporary work as well as that from earlier periods – deal with research conducted
among others whether the others are the "natives" in "exotic" communities in
United States society or abroad. This is not surprising. Traditionally, anthropologists have studied "the other." Thus, anthropology, even as it has promoted cultural relativity, was conceived and nurtured in a colonial world of haves and
have-nots, powerful and powerless, self and other. As the ethnographic method
became more commonplace and studies grew to include more complex industrial
and postindustrial societies like the United States, the power relationship between
researcher and researched remained unaltered. For the most part, this research
has also been dichotomized, with the self studying the other, the powerful the
powerless, the haves the have-nots. However, a distinctive hallmark of the newer
literature in ethnographic theory and method, including recent work in education,
is its self-conscious examination of the subjective nature of the research endeavor.

Presently it is widely acknowledged that all researchers are influenced by their
particular perspectives. But what about the perspectives of ethnic minorities? In
what ways do our experiences inform our research endeavors? Many of us are first
socialized into the values, norms, and communication standards of our home
communities and later, after many years of education, into those of the mainstream
culture. Moreover, the subordinate position assigned to our communities in the
American social order forces us to see ourselves through others' eyes. This means
that we are more likely to understand, if only through our own lived experiences,
what it means to be marginalized.

Crossing the cultural borders into the mainstream is often fraught with contradictions. In matriculating into the dominant culture, we are instructed in different
paradigms, tutored in new world views, and trained in correct "ways of knowing."
Years of schooling teach us to rename, recategorize, reclassify, and reconceptualize

our experiences. Like the transition to English, the transition to dominant ways of thinking, valuing, and behaving is often complete and one-way. New values implanted, new voices acquired like the fictional character in Naylor's account; or, like the unfictitious Richard Rodriguez (1982), we may have forfeited the ability to communicate appropriately, may have renounced community belief systems, or embraced an ideology no longer in accord with that of our communities.

But these experiences also contain the potential for developing multiple perspectives that can be brought to bear on our research endeavors. Noted Black feminist bell hooks (1984) maintains that including the experiences of those who have lived on margin and in the center not only can enrich contemporary paradigms but can also invigorate progressive movements as well.

This chapter is concerned with the problems and the possibilities that obtain when researcher and researched are members of the same cultural and speech community. It is written from the vantage of a Black woman with eight years' experience conducting ethnographic and life-history research in the Black community. Drawing on my personal autobiography as well as on firsthand experiences accumulated in two separate studies as a researcher studying the lives and practices of Black teachers, this chapter examines some of the political conflicts in which I have become entangled, the methodological dilemmas and ethical issues I have grappled with, and the multiple and often conflicting roles I have had to adopt in order to accomplish my research. The goal of this essay is twofold: first, to compare the competing mainstream and Black value systems at work in my own background and which frequently marked the research settings and resulted in political struggles; and second, to demonstrate the positive effect that a shared identity can have on establishing rapport and recovering authentic accounts, but also to illustrate that even members of the same speech and cultural community are differentiated by other equally important characteristics that make the researcher both an insider as well as an outsider.

Problem, theory, and method

A review of the sociological, anthropological, and first-person literature on teachers convinced me that African-American teachers had largely been ignored by the literature; where they had been portrayed, except in a few instances, it had generally been in a negative not a positive light. Most of the negative portrayals of African Americans were written by outsiders and at a time when the rhetoric of equal opportunity made attacks on segregated schools with all their attendant shortcomings, including Black teachers as legitimate targets. These findings seemed to endorse DuBois's comment (1945) that because the fates of Black teachers have been so entangled with the maintenance of segregated schools for Black pupils, it has been difficult to attack segregated schools and at the same time to commend and respect Black teachers.

To my surprise, when Blacks wrote about Black teachers, their descriptions were considerably more flattering and well balanced than those penned by Whites. Finally, though I found several historical accounts that chronicled the fight undertaken by the Black community to secure Black teachers for its children, accounts written by Black teachers themselves, either historic or contemporary, are relatively rare.

The preponderance of negative portrayals of Black teachers written by outsiders, the contrasting more flattering and well-balanced insider descriptions, and the paucity of Black teachers telling their own stories convinced me of the need to augment the literature of Black teachers speaking in their own voices. Voice is a multifaceted concept. On one hand, it may be understood simply as words; on the other the concept of voice can extend beyond mere words to include perspectives and particular orientations. Consequently in developing my research strategy, I had to deal with several other issues – the choice of subjects, the definition of the problem, the source of the analytic categories employed, and the appropriateness of theories applied to interpreting the words – all essential to the concept of voice.

My first consideration was developing a process that would enable me to study those Black teachers whose practice could typify what the Black community thought best about its teachers. To this end, I developed "community nomination," a term and method of selecting the teachers designed specifically for this study. Community nomination builds on the concept of "native anthropology" developed by Jones (1970) and Gwaltney (1980, 1981) in order to gain what anthropologists call an "emic" perspective, an insider's view – in this case the Black community's perspective of a good teacher. Teachers selected by this method were chosen though direct contact with Black communities. African-American periodicals, organizations, institutions, and individuals provided the names of the teachers.

Another consideration was deciding among the various theoretical orientations. My graduate training had been in the traditions of phenomenology, African-American anthropology and sociolinguistics, and the related field (ethnography) of speaking. Each of these perspectives and a more recent interest in critical theory influenced my understanding and approach to the topic. At the same time, I was mindful of hooks's (1984) caution that just because individuals are unable to articulate a particular position is not evidence per se of their never having embraced it. Her admonition, coupled with my own desire to preserve the authenticity and integrity of the teachers' experience, inclined me to search for explanations that would enable me to meld their interpretations with the theories that guided my work.

Researcher as subject

The process of the research as well as the subjective experiences of the researcher are currently the subject of intense debate (Peshkin, 1988; Lather, 1991). In my case, these are important considerations. In a number of respects, my experiences are not unlike those of the teachers whose lives and practices form the basis of my inquiries. Like them I have been a teacher for most of my professional life. And though younger than some, what we all have in common is having belonged to the generations that came of age during the period when separate but equal was a controlling principle of American society.

It was within my family and local community that I learned my first lessons about simultaneously being an insider and an outsider. My family also made sure that I understood the need for individual and collective struggle against the structures of racism. Being both an insider and outsider in the small, predominantly White, New England community where my family had lived since 1857 necessitated not only that I understand mainstream Anglo values but also become proficient in its norms and behavior. It was not only household and community circumstances that dictated these lessons but also my family's expressed desire for me to prepare myself to take advantage of the improved opportunities for Blacks they believed were on the horizon. At the same time, however, my family wanted me to have a strong racial identity, to feel at ease and be a part of the Black community in which we spent the most significant portion of our social lives. Consequently, they expected me to recognize when the values of the separate but overlapping community were at odds and, depending on the context, to demonstrate appropriate behavior. Whether taught explicitly by pointing out where specific transgressions had occurred or more indirectly through family stories, the training was unambiguous and the lessons to be learned unequivocal. For instance, because of my early school success and the prospect of a favorable future in academic pursuits, my mother made sure I internalized the lesson that, while scholarly pursuits were important, they were not more important nor were they to override competence in social interaction. One could never retreat to solitary activities if others desired social interaction; to do so was considered rude and self-centered. Another lesson drilled into me was the community prohibition against self-aggrandizement, a behavior commonly associated with the White community, which my family scorned. It was not uncommon to hear the sarcastic retort "That's damn White of you" addressed to someone for calling attention to some act that was generally expected of them. Correspondingly, it was not unusual for a person who had been complimented for some personal achievement to minimize its importance by responding that "White folks raised me."

In order to establish the fact that our family was both insider and outsider, and to reinforce a responsibility to fight any injustice, my grandmother told many stories. One of her favorites described an incident that occurred when my uncle was a teenager. While walking with friends on the way home from school one day, he was verbally attacked by a group of out of towners, who were in town to work on a construction project. A person who rarely tolerated insults of any kind, my grandmother insisted that the town fathers take action. The mayor, along with other city officials, responded by demanding that the crew leave town "by sundown." Outsiders, they insisted, could not harass any of the townspeople.

While this story can be read as an acknowledgement of my family's insider status, my grandmother told others that it highlighted the family's standing as outsiders. In one story, my grandmother recalled the fierce battle she had undertaken to ensure that my mother and uncle were placed in the high school's college preparatory program instead of the vocational track deemed more suitable to the employment prospects for Negroes. Accompanying my grandmother's stories were my grandfather's anecdotes of his early involvement in founding the Brotherhood of Sleeping Car Porters, one of the first unions to wage a collective struggle for fair treatment of Black workers.

While the perception of limited opportunity can result in developing an oppositional frame of reference with respect to academic achievement (Ogbu, 1988, 1989, 1991) or in developing a raceless persona in order to achieve academically (Fordham, 1988), my family's response to limited opportunity was to excel in spite of the limitations and to maintain strong cultural and political affiliations and ties to the Black community in the process. In other words, my family strove to make sure that I would develop what DuBois (1903) referred to as a double consciousness, an awareness of who I was and what I was capable of achieving regardless of the prevailing beliefs of society.

Unwittingly, with its explicit teaching and unambiguous expectations, my Catholic schooling bolstered my family's teaching. Not until college – the locus of my initial socialization into the bourgeois tradition of academia and the culture of the academy, a process that continued in graduate school – did the ambiguities become prominent. Attending a college with fewer than thirty Black students and living away from the confines of family and community obscured the separation between the two worlds. Concomitantly, the coaching that had previously been available about how to negotiate both worlds became more sporadic and less explicit.

After completing college and relocating to Roxbury, Boston's Black community, I began a twenty-year career as a professional educator. Several years as a substitute teacher in the Boston public schools (where, prior to desegregation Black teachers were unilaterally assigned to de facto segregated schools) and a subsequent position as a director of METCO (a voluntary urban–suburban desegregation program that bused Black students to predominantly White suburban school districts) cast me into the role of outsider once more. Most of the substitutes assigned to all-Black schools found it difficult if not impossible to teach in them. Like the students they served, these schools were considered undesirable. Consequently, the students in the schools to which I was assigned typically saw a procession of substitutes, many who endured only one day, others who vanished by recess. Unlike these substitutes, by revisiting and recovering the belief systems, values, and behaviors learned in my childhood, I not only survived but thrived in these schools.

One of my major responsibilities as a METCO director was serving as a cultural broker, which primarily entailed simultaneously interpreting between White suburban teachers and urban Black students. One task was helping White teachers, many of whom were considered effective with White students and appeared to encounter few serious difficulties teaching them, learn how to interact successfully with Black students participating in the METCO program. This task was matched only by the equally difficult one of trying to convince the Black students that they should cooperate with their teachers. My efforts at cultural brokering were only partially successful. Although teachers and students gradually expanded the meanings they attached to specific behaviors, rarely did these expanded interpretations produce any adjustments in their behavior.

Returning to graduate school, I resumed my struggle with the culture of the academy. One of my principal frustrations was the lack of fit between my experiences and the germinal theories being taught in graduate school. African-American conceptions, values, or belief systems rarely figured into analyses or solutions. My insights into characteristics that differentiated the Black and White communities had no forum in the graduate school classroom, nor did the considerable personal information I had accumulated about how to teach Black students. Consequently, I was left alone to try to reconcile what I was learning in graduate school with my own lived experiences. In her forthright discussion about the formulation and distribution of a particular perspective as if it were universal, Smith (1987) writes:

> The forms of thought we make use of to think about ourselves and our society are part of the relations of ruling and hence originate in positions of power. These positions are occupied by men almost exclusively, which means that our forms of thought put together a view of the world from a place women do not occupy. The means that women have had available to them to think, imagine and make actionable their experience have been made for us and not by us. It means that our experience has not been represented in the making of our culture. There is a gap between where we are and the means we have to express and act. It means that our concerns, interests and experiences forming "our" culture are those of men in positions of dominance whose perspectives are built on the silence of women (and of others). As a result the perspectives, concerns, interests of only one sex and one class are directly and actively involved in producing, debating, and developing its ideas, in creating its art, in forming its medical and psychological conceptions, in framing its laws, its political principles, its educational values and objectives.

(19–20)

Though in this passage Smith is referring to the absence of women in the construction of the culture, her words apply to the experiences of other subordinate groups as well. Her words represent the voicelessness I felt in graduate school, where faculty strove to ground me in the particular understandings and knowledge that they assumed were generalizable to everyone, a phenomenon that others have described (Murrell, 1991). Despite my determination to maintain my racial identity and cultural behaviors, the faculty also undertook with the assistance of my peers to indoctrinate me into a distinctive mind set and, by altering my manner and deportment, to align my behavior more closely with that expected of academics. As typifies the middle class, the power exerted in the academy was hidden, concealed from view (Delpit, 1988).

Regardless of academic potential, failure to conform to middle-class norms exacts severe penalties, including exclusion from the "star system," a process whereby early in their graduate education particular individuals are marked for distinguished achievements. Admission into the star system depends principally on the level of comfort and familiarity potential stars communicate to their sponsors, and only secondarily on talent and persistence (Carter, 1991). Denied admission to the star system cast me once again into the role of outsider.

The studies

As mentioned earlier, this chapter draws on my own experiences conducting research in two separate studies on the lives and practices of Black teachers. While both studies are similar with respect to subject matter, there were important differences pertaining to methodology and context. In the first one, I undertook a study of the practice of one Black teacher, whom students had consistently rated as an "ideal type." The dominant approach to gathering data was ethnography – principally sociolinguistic behavior – with only a secondary focus on life history. As I reviewed the notes from informal conversations and the transcripts of the more formal interviews undertaken with this teacher, it became increasingly apparent the extent to which the teacher's philosophy of teaching and her pedagogy had been influenced by and was grounded in her social and cultural experiences in the Black community. Interested in comparing this teacher to others, I expanded my research to include a larger, more geographically diverse and age-stratified group. In this way, the second research project, a life-history study of Black teachers, grew out of the first. While this decision moved me beyond the idiosyncratic nature of a single case study, it shifted the primary focus of investigation from behavioral and sociolinguistic data to information collected in face-to-face interviews. Thus while the subject matter in both studies was similar, the primary method of data collection in the first study emphasized observation over interviews and the second study emphasized interviews, with observations playing only a secondary role. Using Goodson's (1988) analysis of studies of teachers, it is possible to characterize my two studies as emphasizing varying degrees of focus on the "song" or the "singer." Since the research context was a critical variable that both influenced the course of my research and shaped my relationships with the teachers, the next section characterizes the settings.

Setting I: Regents Community College

I undertook the first study at Regents Community College in Massachusetts, a predominantly Black community college in the Northeast, where I had once been on the faculty. It is beyond the scope of this chapter to describe in great detail its demographics and setting. A task that is undertaken elsewhere (Foster 1987, 1989). What is important to advancing this chapter is addressing the political situation at the college and providing a brief explanation of the two competing value systems that were at work there.

Founded in 1973 during a period of considerable community activism, the College was the fifteenth community college to be charted by the State Board of Regents. Its founders envisioned it as a Black college with a unique mission: to serve the underprepared students from the local Black community, a task which the other community colleges had neglected. From its inception, Regents was plagued by a series of problems, a succession of presidents and administrators, three temporary sites, high turnover rates among faculty, and, most important, a marked tension between Black and White faculty over the best way to educate its students.

Most often these conflicts arose because Black and White faculty held different ideas about what were appropriate goals for students. In an example from the college's early history, a group of Black faculty, seeking to establish a comprehensive writing program, forced the English department chair, a White woman, to resign for her comment that "their [Black students] was quaint and shouldn't be changed." Although some Black faculty conceded that the chair's comments could have indicated an acceptance and valuing of Black students' language, they were outraged by her suggestion that the Black students did not need to command standard American written English. In a controversial essay, Delpit (1988) provides a detailed analysis and clarification of both points of this controversy.

At the time of my study, an external grant whose overarching goal was to improve teaching and learning, but which was specifically designed "to train teachers to understand students' use of language and other culturally learned behaviors," was underway at Regents. Through a set of training sessions, workshops, and discussions led by experts, the project aimed to introduce the participants to anthropological research techniques through which they might learn how their students as well as they themselves behaved and used language in and outside the classroom. Because I was Black and knowledgeable about the issues the project sought to address, its director, a White woman, had enlisted my support. And although an outsider at the time, the director was aware many faculty still perceived me as an insider.

During the year that the project was begun the tensions between Black and White faculty reached a boiling point. Many Black faculty members were irritated because they believed White faculty were gaining too much power in the college. Two factors – subtle changes taking place in faculty composition and changes in the faculty leadership – lent support to their perception. Though the absolute number of Black faculty had remained constant, over the two preceding years the percentage of Black faculty had dropped from thirty-eight to thirty-three. The fact that the faculties at the other community colleges in the state were overwhelmingly White made the increasing numbers of White faculty at Regents an especially sore point among Black faculty. At the same time two organizations – the Faculty Union and the Faculty Assembly, part of the college's governance structure – were scheduled to merge. Historically there has been a division of power based on race with respect to faculty leadership. Almost without exception, the Faculty Union leadership had been White and the Faculty Assembly leadership Black. Prior to the merger, the faculty had participated sporadically and rather unsuccessfully in both organizations. For some, then, merging the two organizations seemed a logical solution in a college where faculty were already overburdened. For others, however, the merger represented another attempt by White faculty to dominate the college. All of these factors coupled with the fact that all except one of the project trainers was White fueled the discontent of the Black faculty. Taken together, these facts suggested, if not a diminishing role for Blacks, an increasing one for Whites. The result was that the project became the flashpoint for increased hostilities between White and Black faculty.

From the beginning, the project was embroiled in controversy, the faculty divided over its merits. Faculty, both Black and White, gave similar reasons for refusing to participate. The reasons ranged from the irrelevancy of anthropology over politics in determining power relations and thus education, to the belief that class content – the subject matter taught – was more critical than the process used to teach it. But, for Black faculty especially, the project became entangled in the larger political issues that gripped the campus.

In order to accomplish the project, a series of workshops and seminars was undertaken with the expectation that the faculty would modify their classroom practices. Although fifty faculty, staff, and administrators participated in at least one of the activities, and while a fourth of these participants were African American, the large majority of those who actively participated and all of those that undertook major curricular changes were White.

Consequently, despite the fact that the project's stated goal was improving the education students received and involving faculty in curricular reform by providing release time – goals that the majority of Black faculty deemed inherently worthwhile – many were overtly hostile to the project and its director.

From the beginning the director was on the defensive. One of the first people to challenge the project was Ms Morris, the teacher I was studying, who demanded that the director explain how "the study of primitive people" – the definition of ethnography she had read in the dictionary – had anything to with teaching Black students. Other Black faculty questioned what Whites could tell them about their own language and culture, which they believed they shared with the students.

Initially I tried to encourage Black faculty participation. Trying to persuade some Black faculty who were not involved in the project to reap some of its benefits became a personal goal. But despite my efforts, Black faculty remained distant. Part of the problem stemmed from the different value systems that were manifest in different styles of communication, which could be detected in the different patterns of interaction and which reflected the typical patterns for Black and White faculty. One of the major differences was Ms Morris's use of more official channels as contrasted with my dependence on the more informal networks at the college. Although specific rules controlled routine tasks like photocopying, securing library materials, and other bureaucratic matters, following the guidelines did not guarantee that tasks would be completed. The prevailing but unofficial culture of the school dictated using informal channels to get the tasks accomplished. Related to this was the director's tendency to avoid confrontation, which she did by conducting most of her communication, whether official or personal, by written channels. In contrast, the preferred style of African-American faculty, also my own, was to confront problems as they arose using written correspondence only to arrange face-to-face meetings. Despite the frustration, inconvenience, and roadblocks they faced in getting tasks accomplished and engaging in fruitful interactions, for the most part White faculty declined to take up unfamiliar ways of behaving. Ultimately, the escalating conflict within the project, a microcosm of that extant in the larger college, threatened to jeopardize my relationships with Black faculty and to derail and compromise my study, so I severed my affiliation with the project.

The irony of this project was that while faculty were attempting to understand the community-oriented participation of Regents's Black students, they were unable or perhaps unwilling to recognize the community norms and preferences of Black faculty colleagues. To be sure, the faculty and the researchers associated with the project wanted to understand the effect of cultural diversity on teaching and learning. Unwilling to engage in critical dialogue with Black and other faculty of color, however, they incorrectly assumed they could gain access to this cultural knowledge without seeking authentic renditions of that knowledge.

Setting II: the construction of Black teachers' life histories

In February of 1988, the active phase of my second research project, a life-history study of Black teachers, began with the interview of my first informant. Unlike the study at Regents, the teachers who participated in this second study resided in many regions of the country. Although all of the teachers I contacted agreed to an interview, there were long periods between initial written contact, subsequent phone conversations, and visits to interview the informants. One of my greatest fears was that when I arrived in an unfamiliar city, the teacher would not be there.

Eager to secure cooperation, but realizing that my informants were being confronted with a complete stranger, I claimed insider status, making sure from the outset to emphasize our shared characteristics in my initial letter and subsequent phone conversations. Whether claiming insider status minimized the social distance and ultimately influenced the informants' decision to participate is unclear. Most were flattered to have been selected to be interviewed; only once was an interview refused and then because of illness. John Gwaltney (1980), an African-American anthropologist who conducted a major life-history study of African Americans, discussed the willingness of his narrators who knew he was a "native" to assist him with his life-history project. My own experiences paralleled those reported by Gwaltney. Without exception, all of the teachers I sought to interview cooperated with my efforts. This generosity was exceptional since all of the arrangements for interviews had been made by letter and telephone.

Arranging and negotiating the details of my interview and visit provided me with some insights regarding the extent to which the teachers accepted my claims of insider status. Two-thirds of the teachers invited me into their homes to conduct interviews, a fact that seemed to acknowledge my claims of insider status. A few picked me up at my hotel, some had their friends drive me to the airport, and at least one insisted that I sleep in a spare bedroom rather than waste money on a hotel. In these informal settings, I interacted with the participants and their families, frequently accompanying and participating with them in activities within their communities. It is possible to interpret these courtesies as mere instances of hospitality; however, in retrospect I believe that they probably served a dual purpose. Watching me interact with family, friends, and other community members allowed them to observe my behavior and assess for themselves whether my claims of insider status were warranted.

My experiences during my first visit with Miss Ruthie illustrate this dual purpose of hospitality and testing that I was subjected to. When I arrived on Pawley's Island, a small community not far from Charleston, South Carolina, I called Miss Ruthie to find out how far my motel was from her house. "Just up the road," she assured me.

"About a mile?" I asked.
"About a mile," she replied.

Not wanting to be late, I set out at 7:30 the next morning to reach her house in time for our 9 o'clock appointment. The walk along the highway toward her house seemed interminable. Only when I arrived and was greeted by the teacher and two of her friends, who laughingly told me that they "didn't expect a city slicker to be able to make it," did I discover that the distance I had walked was over three miles. Once I had passed this initial test, Miss Ruthie and other members of the community were extremely hospitable, though I was mindful of their continuing scrutiny of my behavior. What I have concluded from this and other encounters is that invitations into their family and community worlds represented an attempt to tip the power balance in their favor.

A third of the participants suggested a more neutral location for the interviews, usually their school, but in some cases my hotel room. Often, but not always, after the initial interviews were over the teachers suggested that the next interview be held at their homes. This happened frequently enough to suggest that these teachers had felt at ease during our first meeting. Whether the interviews took place in homes or a classroom, a meal eaten at home or in a restaurant often preceded the interview.

My claims of insider status notwithstanding, a number of my interviewees were surprised to discover I was Black, claiming that I didn't sound Black over the telephone. Sometimes merely discovering that I was Black modified their expectations of the interview that was to take place. In other cases, teachers seemed genuinely pleased when they saw I was Black. But they gave no overt indication that they expected that our shared background might shape or influence the interview. Ella Jane was one teacher whose expectations were immediately altered when we met. Like all of the other narrators, she had never seen me before we met at her East Texas elementary school at the close of the school day. As soon as she saw I was Black, she excused herself to telephone her husband. When she returned, she explained she had telephoned to tell him she would be later than expected. "As I saw you were Black, I knew the interview was going to be a lot longer than I thought. White folks want to interview you, but they really don't want to hear all that you have to say."

Miss Ruthie, an eighty-year-old woman who had taught over fifty years in a one-room schoolhouse, had previously spoken with a number of other interviewers. Nonetheless, she was delighted to discover I was Black because as she said, "I've been waiting a long time for somebody Black to come and hear my story."

From my perspective these initial, overt markers of acceptance were insufficient evidence that the conversations were authentic candid versions of my narrators' lives. Therefore, I paid close attention to the ways in which the teachers used language throughout the interviews. Though I did not transcribe the tapes myself, I spent many hours reviewing them because my training in sociolinguistics had taught me that in order to understand completely what was being conveyed I needed to attend to not only what was being said but also the manner in which it was said. Listening to the tapes revealed a consistent pattern. Early in the interviews, the discourse patterns were those of standard English. As the interviews progressed, the language shifted from standard English to include more markers of Black English. There were many morphological, intonational, and discourse features of Black English later in the interviews, suggesting that my insider status was being negotiated throughout the course of the interviews.

There were other characteristics that separated me from individual narrators, making me an insider and outsider in ways that were intricate and intertwined. I was a northerner when I interviewed southerners, an urban resident when

I talked with rural residents, a younger person when I conversed with older teachers, a woman when I interviewed men. Often I was positioned as an outsider on several dimensions simultaneously. These characteristics shaped the interviews in some immediately obvious and less obvious ways. Consider the dimension of generation. Because I had lived through the turbulent time of the 1960s, it was easier for me to identify emotionally with the racial struggles of the teachers who came of age during the same period. Conversely, although I had read a lot about the struggles of Blacks during the 1920s, 1930s, 1940s, and 1950s, and heard about them from my grandparents who experienced them firsthand, my emotional responses were muted compared to those I'd experienced when interviewing my age mates. This generational disjunction affected my interview with Miss Ruthie, a teacher born at the turn of the century. Throughout her interview she repeated her assertion that during the first and second decades of the twentieth-century when she had attended Avery Institute, a private normal school founded by the American Missionary Association, the students regularly put on Shakespeare plays. At first, I missed the significance of her statement. It was only after reviewing the tape several times and hearing her repeat the claim in marked intonation that I understood its importance in her own mind. Not until I had read several books on the education of Blacks in the South, however, did I understand the historical significance of her assertion. What I discovered as I read these accounts was her attempt to convey that she considered the classical and liberal arts education received at Avery Institute to have been a challenge to the social order of the time, schooling that typically consisted of vocational training advocated by Washington and supported by the larger White educational establishment of the time (Anderson, 1988). What this experience taught me was that my own outsider status, the result of generational differences, made it difficult for me to perceive easily or appreciate fully the significance of the racial struggles waged by some of the older teachers whose eras I had not experienced.

A comparison of the interviews of men with those of women also provided evidence that the connections that emerged from race were easily overshadowed by those of gender. The interviews with men showed sharply divergent turn-taking patterns compared to those conducted with the women. When I spoke with women, the talk was more conversational. Turn-taking exchanges were more balanced and there were many more instances of overlapping speech to mark comembership. In contrast, in the interviews with men there were considerably fewer occurrences of overlapping speech, and the turn-taking patterns were more asymmetrical, with men speaking for much longer stretches at a time.

The power to know

I undertook this research in order to recover part of the cultural knowledge and history of the Black community. By using the personal histories and personal experiences of members of the Black community and framing them in theoretical and conceptual perspectives that gave voice to their realities, it was my hope to contribute to a more complete understanding and empowerment of Black communities and that the work would become part of the collective memory of the Black community as well as part of the scholarship studied within the academy.

Even though there is a substantial and steadily accumulating body of research written by African-American scholars from an African-American perspective, it is too often the case that this work is marginalized from mainstream academic discourse. Let me cite a personal example. My early work on the performative aspects of "sharing time" (Foster, 1982) and my subsequent work on the Black tradition of performance that undergirded the study of a successful Black teacher at Regents (Foster, 1986, 1987, 1989) (reported earlier in this chapter) remain largely overlooked in scholarly considerations in favor of alternate, more mainstream, and Eurocentric explanations, despite the fact that West (1985) has identified the Black tradition of performance as one of the organic intellectual traditions in African-American life. It was only when the teacher in the Regents study authenticated her reliance on the Black traditions of preaching and performance and the students confirmed its significance that I felt that I had adequately captured her perspective and consequently that this theoretical perspective had merit as an analytic construct able to represent the organic intellectual tradition of contemporary African-American life.

I am convinced that the teachers' acceptance of me as an insider influenced their willingness to participate and shaped their expectations and responses. At the same time, I know that my claims to insider status were continuously tested and renegotiated, and that differences of gender, generation, and geography produced varying degrees of solidarity. Consequently, I make no claim that the information acquired through interviews and observations is absolute. Nor do I claim that the interpretations I have brought to bear on them are the only ones possible.

Research conducted by insiders cannot capture the total experience of an entire community. But neither can research conducted by outsiders. We must be mindful of this fact for, as the title of this chapter attests, no one commands the power to know all things.

There were many times when I interacted with my subjects that I heard my own voice in theirs, voices that had waged a continuing struggle against an analysis of their lives imposed by outsiders; voices that had struggled to be heard among the echoes of dissonant interpretive frames seeking to reorder their realities to conform to an external agenda; voices that reflected the complexities of their lives unacknowledged by liberals, conservatives, or progressives speaking from their various camps, but seeking to appropriate them nonetheless. Research undertaken by scholars of color can be revisionist: it can offer new if disturbing insights, alternative and disquieting ways of thinking, can be a means of creating new paradigms and expanding existing ones, and can result in a much needed dialogue between scholars of color and their White peers. Regrettably, it is still the rule rather than the exception to distort and to exclude the realities and to subjugate the voices of people of color to further prevailing paradigms so as to fit the requirements of a caste society.

References

Anderson, J. (1988). *The Education of Blacks in the South, 1860–1935*. Chapel Hill: University of North Carolina Press.

Carter, S. (1991). *Reflections of an Affirmative Action Baby*. New York: Basic Books.

Delpit, L. (1988). The silenced dialogue: power and pedagogy in educating other people's children. *Harvard Educational Review* 58 (3): 280–98.

DuBois, W. E. B. (1903). *The Souls of Black Folk*. Greenwich, CT: Fawcett.

—— (1945). *The Winds of Time. Chicago Defender* (13 October), 13.

Fordham, S. (1988). Racelessness as a factor in Black students' success: pragmatic strategy or Pyrrhic victory? *Harvard Educational Review* 58 (1): 29–84.

Foster, M. (1982). Sharing time: A student-run speech event, ERIC Document Reproduction Service No. ED 234 906.

—— (1986). Folklore and performance theories: models for analyzing classrooms. Special qualifying paper. Cambridge, MA: Harvard Graduate School of Education.

—— (1987). It's cookin' now: an ethnographic study of the teaching style of a Black teacher in an urban community college. PhD dissertation, Harvard University.

—— (1989). It's cookin' now: a performance analysis of the speech events of a Black teacher in an urban community college. *Language in Society* 18 (1): 1–29.

Goodson, I. (1988). Teachers' lives. *Qualitative Research in Education: Teaching and Learning Qualitative Traditions*. Proceedings from the second annual conference of the Qualitative Interest Group. University of Georgia, Athens, GA.

Gwaltney, J. (1980). *Drylongso: A Self-portrait of Black America*. New York: Random House.

—— (1981). Common sense and science: urban core Black observations. In D. Messerschmidt, ed., *Anthropologists at Home in North America: Methods and Issues in the Study of One's Own Society*, 46–61. New York: Cambridge University Press.

hooks, b. (1984). *Feminist theory: from Margin to Center*. Boston: South End.

Jones, D. (1970). Toward a native anthropology. *Human Organization* 29 (4) (Winter): 251–9.

Lather, P. (1991). *Getting Smart: Feminist Research and Pedagogy within the Postmodern*. New York: Routledge.

Murrell, P. (1991). Cultural politics in teacher education: what is missing in the preparation of minority teachers? In M. Foster, ed., *Reading on Equal Education, Volume 11: Qualitative investigations into schools and schooling*, 205–25, New York: AMS.

Naylor, G. (1988). *Mama Day*. New York: Vintage.

Ogbu, J. (1988). Diversity in public education: community forces and minority school adjustment and performance. In R. Haskins and D. Macrae, eds, *Policies for America's Public Schools: Teachers, Equity and Indicators*, 127–70. Norwood, NJ: Ablex.

—— (1989). The individual in collective adaptation: a framework for focusing on academic underperformance and dropping out among involuntary minorities. In L. Weiss, E. Farrar, and H. Petrie, eds, *Dropouts from schools: Issues, Dilemmas and Solutions*, 181–204. Albany, NY: State University of New York Press.

—— (1991). Low school performance as an adaptation: the case of Blacks in Stockton, California. In M. A. Gibson and J. U. Ogbu, eds, *Minority Status and Schooling: A Comparative Study of Immigrants and Involuntary Immigrants*, 249–85. New York: Garland.

Peshkin, A. (1988). In search of subjectivity – One's own. *Educational Researcher* (October): 17–21.

Rodriguez, R. (1982). *Hunger of Memory: The Education of Richard Rodriguez: An autobiography*. New York: Godine.

Smith, D. (1987). *The Everyday World as Problematic: A Feminist Sociology*. Boston: Northeastern University Press.

West, C. (1985). The dilemma of the Black intellectual. *Cultural Critique* 1: 109–24.

Race Ethnicity and Education

EDITOR
David Gillborn, *Institute of Education, University of London, UK*

ASSOCIATE EDITOR
Annette Henry, *University of Illinois at Chicago, USA*

Supported by an International Editorial Board

Race Ethnicity and Education is an interdisciplinary journal which provides a focal point for international scholarship, research and debate. It publishes original and challenging research which explores the dynamics of race, racism and ethnicity in education policy, theory and practice. The journal has quickly established itself as essential reading for those working in this field and especially welcomes writing which addresses the inter-connections between race, ethnicity and multiple forms of oppression including class, gender, sexuality and disability. All articles are independently refereed and the journal is supported by a distinguished international editorial panel.

This journal is also available online. Please connect to www.tandf.co.uk/online.html for further information.

To request a sample copy please visit: **www.tandf.co.uk/journals**

SUBSCRIPTION RATES
2004 – Volume 7 (4 issues)
Print ISSN 1361-3324
Online ISSN 1470-109X
Institutional rate: US$457; £279
(includes free online access)
Personal rate: US$132; £82 (print only)

Carfax Publishing
Taylor & Francis Group

Please contact Customer Services at either:

Taylor & Francis Ltd, Rankine Road, Basingstoke, Hants RG24 8PR, UK
Tel: +44 (0)1256 813002 **Fax:** +44 (0)1256 330245 **Email:** enquiry@tandf.co.uk
Website: www.tandf.co.uk

Taylor & Francis Inc, 325 Chestnut Street, 8th Floor, Philadelphia, PA 19106, USA
Tel: +1 215 6258900 **Fax:** +1 215 6258914 **Email:** info@taylorandfrancis.com
Website: www.taylorandfrancis.com

cree